The Harriman House

Book of

Investing Rules

edited by

Philip Jenks and Stephen Eckett

HARRIMAN HOUSE LTD

43 Chapel Street
Petersfield
Hampshire
GU32 3DY
GREAT BRITAIN

Tel: +44 (0)1730 233870
Fax: +44 (0)1730 233880
email: enquiries@harriman-house.com
web site: www.harriman-house.com

First published in Great Britain in 2001
Reprinted 2006
Copyright Harriman House Ltd

The right of the contributors to be identified as authors has been asserted by
them in accordance with the Copyright, Design and Patents Act 1988.

ISBN 1-905641-22-2
978-1-905641-22-2

British Library Cataloguing in Publication Data
A CIP catalogue record for this book can be obtained from the British Library.

Printed and bound in Great Britain by Biddles Ltd, Kings Lynn, Norfolk

Contents

Acknowledgements

The people we invited to contribute to this book are, without exception, busy professionals whose expertise is in strong demand. When asked to give up their time for no compensation, they might easily have declined for any number of reasons. They didn't. Instead, they contributed freely and enthusiastically. We are grateful to them, and hope that they think the effort was worthwhile.

We also thank them for producing such thought-provoking rules. One of our worries when we started was that the book would end up with 150 versions of 'Cut losses and run profits'! As it turned out, the material was far more interesting and diverse than that. In all cases the personality of the contributor comes through strongly, confirming that investing is more than the dry science it is sometimes assumed to be.

Thank you, too, to everybody at Harriman House who helped on the book, especially to Myles Hunt and Claire Wright, and to the other individuals who covered for us while we buried ourselves in the project - in particular Suzanne Anderson, Ansobe Smal, and Alec Harkness.

Philip Jenks, Stephen Eckett

Introduction

Investors who want to improve their understanding of financial markets do not have to look far for advice. The financial jungle is richly stocked with books on market lore and tactics, each confidently promising a fast track to profits.

The problem for investors is not one of scarcity but of selection. Like Buridan's Ass, which starved to death because it was unable to choose between two plump bales of hay, it is easy to be overwhelmed by choice.

- *How do you choose between hundreds of different books on stock picking?*
- *If you only need a grounding in technical analysis, do you have to read a 700-page tome on the subject?*
- *Does it matter if an investing book is more than three years old?*

And so on.

This book is an antidote to oversupply. It compacts 150 investing themes into one book, and the latest knowledge on those themes into 10 'rules'. In one go, you can learn what the leading experts in each field consider to be the key determinants of success.

As far as we know, this format is unique. Certainly no other book has put together a roster of such high calibre contributors. If our instincts are right, it will appeal strongly to investors. Nevertheless, we should point out that:

1. The book does not aim to be the ultimate word on the subjects it addresses. For that you'll need to read the contributors' own books, or visit their web sites – details of which are included in the text.

2. It is a reference book to be dipped into, not a narrative to be read from cover to cover. You don't have to start at 'A'.

3. It does not try to be all things to all people. If you find 30% of the rules useful, you should be pleased. It probably means you've sharpened your technique. If you find 100% of them useful, you should worry. It probably means your technique is muddled.

4. It aims to illustrate the diversity and conflicting nature of investing, not to proselytize a faith. Many of the rules conflict with each other. That's the point.

5. It will not make you a millionaire overnight! It will however provide you with the foundations for accumulating wealth and protecting it.

6. It is a work in progress, not a finished product. New rules are added regularly on the book's web site at **www.global-investor.com/rules.**

The main aim of the book is to enable you to identify the rules which suit *you,* and which will improve *your* investment performance. For each reader, these will be different. You should also gain an understanding of the 'big questions' of investing:

- *Do stocks go up in the long term?*
- *Should you diversify your stock portfolio?*
- *How should you measure risk?*
- *Is investing long-term really better than trading short-term?*
- *Should you invest internationally?*

Many of the rules in this book touch on these questions, and the answers are not always obvious. If you think you already know them, read what our contributors have to say - you may be surprised!

A practical point:

- The book is organised alphabetically by contributor name, but there is also a detailed subject index at the back that may provide quicker access to specific information for some readers.

We hope you enjoy reading The Book of Investing Rules as much as we enjoyed compiling it.

Philip Jenks, Stephen Eckett

Robert Z. Aliber

Robert Z. Aliber is Professor of International Economics and Finance at the Graduate School of Business, University of Chicago.

His research activities include: the international financial system; exchange rate issues; international money, capital markets and capital flows; the multinational firm; international banking; public policy issues.

Books
The New International Money Game, Palgrave, 2001
The International Money Game, Palgrave, 1988
The Selected Essays of Robert Aliber (Economists of the Twentieth Century.) Edward Elgar, 2004
The Multinational Paradigm, The MIT Press, 2003
Manias, Panics and Crashes: A History of Financial Crises (Charles P. Kindleberger), Palgrave Macmillan, 2005

International markets and capital flows

1. All propositions about rates of return in financial markets are clichés.

Market literature is full of rules about achieving above average returns. These rules are clichés rather than eternal truths. No scientific proposition about beating the market beats the market for an extended period.

2. Financial markets are mean-reverting.

Prices in financial markets always tend to move back toward equilibrium values when they are not moving away from these equilibrium values.

3. Currency markets overshoot and undershoot and equity markets overshoot and undershoot.

There are observable trend values in both the currency markets and the stock markets. The variations around these trends (overshooting and undershooting) reflect the variability of cross border flows of capital in the foreign exchange markets and changes in investor optimism and pessimism in the stock markets.

4. Buy and hold strategies generally are less rewarding than trading strategies.

The cliché that "markets can't be timed" may be right for some investors all of the time, and for all investors some of the time, but there are times when market prices are far above or far below their long run equilibrium prices.

5. Watch the capital flows in and out of countries.

An increase in the inflow of capital to a country is likely to be associated with an increase in the foreign exchange value of its currency and an increase in prices of stocks of firms headquartered in the country.

6. An increase in the inflation rate in a country is likely to be associated with a depreciation of its currency.

It is also likely to lead to a decrease in prices of stocks of domestic firms.

7. The smaller the country, the larger the impact of capital flows on currency values and stock prices.

Because of the positive correlation between changes in currency values and changes in stock prices, global investing is much more opportunistic than domestic investing.

8. Many firms have 'fifteen minutes of fame'.

Few of the 'Nifty Fifty' firms that that were the market favorites in the 1960s are market leaders today.

9. The national location of the low cost center of production of particular products shifts among countries.

So does the national identity of the most profitable firms in an industry when viewed in a global context.

10. The size of the investor's domestic market matters.

The strength of the case for global investing by the residents of each country is inversely related to the size of the domestic market and the growth rate for new companies. Investors resident in relatively small countries have a much stronger need to diversify internationally than investors resident in larger countries.

11. U.S. investors may not need to invest internationally as much as investors from other countries.

The share of rapid growth companies headquartered in the United States is disproportionately large relative to the U.S. share of global GDP.

12. Currency hedging is not useful for all.

The cost of hedging the foreign exchange exposure is likely to be positive for currencies with a tendency to depreciate and negative for currencies with a tendency to appreciate.

---

www.gsb.uchicago.edu

'Stocks are unquestionably riskier than bonds in the short run, but for longer periods of time, their risk falls below that on bonds. For 20 year holding periods, they have never fallen behind inflation, while bonds and bills have fallen 3 per cent per year behind inflation over the same time period. So although it might appear to be riskier to hold stocks than bonds, precisely the opposite is true if you take a long-term view.'

Jeremy Siegel

David Andrea

David Andrea is Director of the Forecasting Group at the Center for Automotive Research within the Environment Research Institute of Michigan, Ann Arbor, Michigan. His group focuses on forecasting the business operating environment (market demand, regulatory requirements, product technology) and associated risks to existing business models, invested capital base, and company technology portfolios.

The auto sector

1. Invest with the leading economic indicators.

Industry profitability and cash flow all begin and end with vehicle sales. These sales are inversely correlated with unemployment and consumer lending rates, and are directly correlated with income levels and stock market performance. As sales slow, inventories build and manufacturers are attracted to margin (and brand) destroying incentives to push vehicles off the lots and maintain production schedules. Margin reductions lead to delayed new vehicle programmes and component price reduction programmes to suppliers.

2. Invest as a utility model.

Before deregulation, utilities were judged by their cash flows and dividend streams. Autos are still heavily regulated and, like utilities, have few substitutions. The manufacturers and the largest mechanical component suppliers offer significant dividend yield opportunities. Granted, the dividend streams are always at risk to the production cycle - however, 4% to 6% yields offered by these companies position them well for an income instrument in diversified portfolios. But you should continually question the quality of earnings supporting the dividend stream - as one seasoned analyst taught me: "buy on the dividend increases, sell on the dividend cuts".

3. Invest in value stories.

It is not uncommon to see quality balance sheets and management teams selling at a 60% to 80% discount (P/E basis) to the overall market. However, these are not 'dresser drawer' stocks. Look to buy when the discount is high, and target an exit when the discount has fallen into the 20% to 40% range.

Based on perceived business cycle risk, it is the rare auto stock that trades consistently with the overall market.

4. Invest in growth stories.

The industry offers opportunities to invest in stories of growth via increased content per vehicle produced. Look for electronics (which may or may not be automotive pure-plays) and new technologies (providing solutions to emissions, safety, and fuel economy concerns as well as improved consumer value). Combined with an overall improvement in the margins of booked business, increasing content per vehicle provides a growth opportunity in a mature industry.

5. Invest in forward product.

A hot coupe's half-life is approximately 12 to 16 months. A supplier's profitability is easily tied into a single hot vehicle segment. One informational advantage of the auto industry is that product development cycles are 2 to 4 years in length. This gives investors the ability to analyse manufacturer strategies and suppliers' forward book of business.

Look for manufacturers exploiting hot segments with new models and defending current market share with fresh styling, innovation, and value pricing. For suppliers, invest in a book of business that is migrating towards high vehicle content growth (electronics), and value-added (complete systems or modules).

6. Invest in cash flow.

While the production cycles may have become less cyclical, the financial fortunes of vehicle manufacturers and suppliers swing dramatically once capacity utilizations fall below 85%. That's 85% utilization of an assembly plant or component facility. This is particularly true for capital-intensive suppliers such as forgers and casters whose cash flows move radically around production schedules.

7. Invest in experience.

Corporate performance from core competencies comes only through deep experience. It takes a special understanding of the complexities of engineering and assembly plant launches to successfully run a vehicle manufacturer. Suppliers typically are best in serving the original equipment market *or* the aftermarket - not both at the same time. And always be sceptical of any manufacturer strategy that involves moving into retail. Manufacturing and retailing (at least in the auto sector) require two different mindsets.

8. Invest in the best cost structure

Due to the cyclicality of auto production, invest in the vehicle manufacturers with the best cost structure. Higher margins going into downturns provide flexibility in pricing and capital spending that will maintain a manufacturer's long-term competitiveness. Vehicle manufacturers will always keep three or four suppliers competing for the business to maintain price discipline. Therefore, the supplier with a track record of improving its cost structure will typically offer a longer-term advantage.

9. Invest in established trends.

Year-over-year and quarter-over-quarter comparisons are difficult due to the cyclicality of sales, the seasonality of sales within a year, and the common occurrence of extraordinary events (delayed product launches, labor disputes, and weather disruptions). Therefore, always question the base date when you see significant increases or decreases in operating performance ratios.

10. Invest in liquidity and visibility.

Because of the industry's volume, 'small' suppliers can still have revenue levels of $300 to $500 million. However, many of these companies have limited float and few research analysts following the story. Always take into consideration family and management-owned shares that are unlikely to trade. It is unlikely that institutional investors are drawn to these limited float companies and typically it is the institutional money that pushes demand and share price increases.

'Market sectors vary in how quickly they respond to information. Large cap U.S. stocks, for example, are followed by so many analysts and reflect company fundamentals so quickly, that it is nearly impossible to add value through active strategies. I recommend indexing such sectors.'

Ben Warwick

Nick Antill

Nick Antill is a Director of EconoMatters, an energy consultancy offering an extensive range of skills to clients involved with gas markets worldwide. He is also an associate of BG Training, a City financial training company, specialising in equity valuation. Prior to this, Nick spent 16 years as a financial analyst covering the oil and gas sector and was responsible for Morgan Stanley's European team.

Books

Company Valuation Under IFRS: Interpreting and Forecasting Accounts Using International Financial Reporting Standards, Harriman House Publishing, 2005
Oil Company Crisis: Managing Structure,Profitability,and Growth, Oxford Institute for Energy Studies, 2002
Valuing Oil and Gas Companies: A Guide to the Assessment and Evaluation of Assets, Performance and Prospects (Robert Arnott), 2000

Company valuation

---

1. The most often-repeated mistake in finance is "It doesn't matter - it's only a non-cash item".

While it is true that the value of a company is the discounted value of its future free cash flows, it does not follow that non-cash items do not matter. There is a clear difference between provisions for deferred taxation that are unlikely ever to be paid, and provisions for decommissioning a nuclear power station - a large future cost that will certainly be incurred.

2. It is easy to get to a high value for a company - just underestimate the capital investments that it will need to make.

There are three components to a cash flow forecast: profit, which is often analysed quite carefully; depreciation and other non-cash items, which are usually analysed adequately; and capital expenditure, which is often a banged-in number that is quite inconsistent with the other two, and generally much too low.

3. Valuations must be based on realistic long term assumptions - at best GDP growth rates and barely adequate returns.

It is tempting, when valuing fast growing companies with strong technical advantages over their rivals, to assume that these conditions will continue forever. They will not. As the saying goes, 'In the end, everything is a toaster'. If this means that the forecast needs to be a very long one, so be it - it will be less inaccurate than running a valuation off an accurate five year forecast, and then extrapolating this to infinity.

4. Don't spend too much time worrying about financial efficiency.

Playing mathematical games with the weighted average cost of capital is tempting and fun, but generally has a disappointingly small effect on valuation. Substituting debt for equity shifts value from the government to the providers of capital because the company pays less tax. That is it. And even then there is an offsetting factor - it is more likely to incur everyone the inconvenience of going bankrupt.

5. Remember the 'Polly Peck phenomenon', especially in countries with high inflation.

If a company operates in a weak currency with high inflation, its revenues, costs and profits will probably grow quickly. If it funds itself by borrowing in a strong currency, with low interest rates, it will pay little interest, but will tend to make large unrealised currency losses on its debt. It may still be looking very profitable on the day that it is declared insolvent.

6. Unfunded pension schemes should be treated as debt.

Many companies fund their employees' pensions by paying into schemes operated by independent fund managers. These schemes are off their balance sheets. Some companies operate a 'pay-as-you-go' system. They will show a provision for pension liabilities on their balance sheets, generally offset by a pile of cash among their assets. These companies are effectively borrowing from their employees - the provision should be treated as debt.

7. Remember to ask: 'Who's cash flow is it anyway?'

Companies consolidate 100% of the accounts of their subsidiaries, even if they only own 51% of the shares in the subsidiary. In the profit and loss account the profit that is not attributable to their shareholders is deducted and shown as being attributable to third parties. Unless it is paid out in dividend, however, the cash remains inside the company. This means that the popular 'cash flow per share' measure implies that the shares should be valued by including something that does not belong to them - they should not.

8. Accounting depreciation is a poor measure of impairment of value.

If an asset is bought for £100 and has a five year life then it will be depreciated at a rate of £20 a year. This is not the same as saying that its value falls at a rate of £20 a year. The result is that the profitability of the asset is generally understated early in its life and overstated later in its life. This means that companies' profitability tends to be understated when they grow, and overstated when they stop growing.

9. You can't judge an acquisition by whether it adds to earnings.

Acquisitions are just very big, very long term, investments. So they are extreme examples of the rule mentioned above that new investments tend to look unprofitable in the early years. This does not mean that they are bad investments. Company managers have preferred not to explain this awkward fact, but to evade it by using accounting tricks to avoid creating and amortising goodwill. New accounting rules are increasingly making this more difficult. It should not matter, but managers still believe that it does.

10. Operating leases are debt - they just don't look like it.

Companies often lease assets - aeroplanes, ships or hotels, for example. If the lease effectively transfers the asset, it is a finance lease, and looks like debt in the accounts. If it doesn't then the lease just appears as rental payments in the operating costs. But it is still debt, and the shares will still reflect that fact, being much more volatile than it looks as if they 'ought' to be.

www.economatters.com

'The backlash against analysts is in full swing. Don't be diverted by the spectacle, however enjoyable it might appear. Use the research available dispassionately. As in all human life, you'll find there's good and bad there. Just be sure, once you've digested, to formulate your own conclusions.'

Edmond Warner

Martin Barnes

Martin Barnes is Managing Editor of *The Bank Credit Analyst*. He has almost 30 years of experience in analyzing and writing about global economic and financial market developments. In recent years, he has written extensively about new technologies and long-wave cycles, the financial market implications of low inflation and trends in corporate profitability.

General principles and the role of liquidity

1. Know when to be a contrarian.

The crowd is often correct for long periods of time, so it does not always pay to be a contrarian. The time to bet against the crowd is when market prices deviate significantly from underlying fundamentals. For example, gold has been in a bear market for years and it has been correct to stay negative toward the market given the falling trend of inflation. Contrarian strategies have not worked. On the other hand, the surge in technology stocks in 1999/2000 in the face of suspect earnings trends clearly provided an excellent opportunity to take a contrarian stance and this paid huge dividends when the bubble inevitably burst.

2. Don't use yesterday's news to forecast tomorrow's markets.

Many people make the mistake of forecasting the stock market on the basis of current economic data (which usually relate to developments of at least a month ago). This is a mistake because the stock market leads rather than follows the economy. It makes more sense to use the stock market as an indication of what the economy is likely to do in the future. By the time that the economic data has confirmed a trend, the market is often discounting the next phase of the cycle. The market is forward looking while economic data are backward looking.

3. Liquidity is key.

All great bull markets are rooted in easy money. Stimulative monetary conditions mean low interest rates that, in turn, encourage investors to take on more risk. Buoyant liquidity will always find its way into asset markets, pushing prices higher. The corollary is that a bull market cannot persist in the face of tightening liquidity. Thus, investors must pay close attention to the factors that drive monetary policy.

4. Understanding the inflation trend is critical to success.

Following on from the previous rule, inflation is the single most important economic variable when it comes to predicting the trends in financial markets. Rising inflation is toxic for both bonds and stocks because it points to tighter monetary policy and rising interest rates. On the other hand, falling inflation is extremely bullish for the opposite reasons. Most bear markets have occurred in response to rising inflation pressures. Correspondingly, falling inflation was the single most important force behind the powerful bull markets in bonds and stocks during the 1980s and 1990s.

5. Take a long-run view.

An increased focus on the short run has become one of the scourges of modern life. Companies are often more obsessed with propping up near-term earnings than with taking long-term strategic decisions, while investors are often looking for quick gratification when they buy stocks. The day-trading mania was the most extreme manifestation of this. Patience is a virtue when investing because even the best ideas sometimes take a while to play out. By all means abandon ship when fundamental conditions deteriorate. However, if you are confident that you have a purchased a good company, then don't despair just because the price does not rise right away – as long as the fundamentals remain positive.

6. Allocate a small part of your portfolio to 'play' with.

It is okay to take speculative risks with some of your investments. However, don't bet the ranch on a long shot. A good strategy is to have the vast bulk of your portfolio in a diversified group of blue-chip investments, and to leave a small amount for higher-risk opportunities. That way, you get the best of both worlds. The bulk of your assets is relatively protected, but you can still have some 'fun' chasing some hot ideas.

7. The stock market rises most of the time.

Bear markets are the exception rather than the rule. The market rises about two-thirds of the time. This means you should avoid being trapped in a bear market psychology for long periods of time. There are always reasons to be gloomy about the outlook, whether it relates to valuations, economic conditions or structural concerns such as debt levels. The U.S. economy is extremely resilient and it has generally paid to err on the side of bullishness. There have been long bear markets in the past, but these have usually occurred in the context of disastrous economic environments such as deflation (the 1930s) or high inflation (the 1970s). Neither environment is likely for the foreseeable future.

8. Know when you are speculating.

You invest in a company when you are buying shares in order to participate in its long-run growth. You are speculating when you are buying shares only because you expect to sell them at a higher price to someone else, and you are not even looking at the company's fundamentals. It is okay to do both, but you must understand the difference. For example, the internet mania was all speculation because few companies were making profits and few investors were holding the shares for long enough to benefit from the discovery of the next Microsoft. When you know that you are speculating, then you will be more ready to bail out quickly when market conditions turn sour.

9. Have realistic expectations.

Between 1982 and 2000, Wall Street enjoyed its most powerful bull market of all time with average annual returns of about 15% a year after inflation. This was close to twice its historical average. The exceptional returns reflected falling inflation, a revival in corporate profitability and a revaluation of the market from cheap to expensive. Those forces have now been fully exploited and long-run returns are likely to average less than 6% a year after inflation in the next decade. Investor expectations are for much higher returns according to various surveys, and that can only lead to disappointment and increased risk taking.

---

www.bcaresearch.com

'Research suggests we tend to become more confident and less accurate as we process increasing amounts of information. As most people can handle no more than seven pieces of information at once, it is wise to employ no more than seven criteria for choosing each stock.'

Paul Melton

Richard J. Bauer Jr.

Dr Richard J. Bauer, Jr., is Professor of Finance at St. Mary's University in San Antonio, Texas. His research has appeared in many journals including *Financial Analysts Journal*, *Journal of Business Research*, and *Managerial Finance*.

He is co-founder and co-owner of ANSR Company LLC, which develops investment software based on evolutionary computation techniques.

Books

Genetic Algorithms and Investment Strategies, John Wiley, 1994
Technical Market Indicators, John Wiley, 1998
Technical Market Indicators: Analysis and Performance, Wiley Trading Advantage Series, 1999

Building trading systems using genetic algorithms

1. Begin by thinking about 'proof'.

A good starting point is to ask yourself the following question: if someone brought you evidence that a given investment strategy had merit, what would constitute enough proof that you would be willing to follow the strategy?

The reason this question is important is that evolutionary computation techniques, such as genetic algorithms and genetic programming, are optimization procedures. They search for optimal or near-optimal solutions to complex problems. Using these techniques to search for attractive trading rules requires that you first define the parameters of the search and a 'fitness' function.

The fitness function could be something simple (see rule 3) like highest compound return over some time period. If you would be willing to employ a trading rule because it had the highest compound return of a general class of rules, then that is all you require as proof. That would form the basis of your system. In practice, you probably require more than that.

2. Think carefully about your constraints.

Suppose you are building a system to optimize stock selection criteria based on fundamental variables. Further suppose that you use a genetic algorithm procedure to identify the optimal stock selection variables. When you evaluate the results, you realize that the selection criteria leads to just one stock every year. Are you really willing to put all your eggs in one basket? Or, do you require the criteria to be general enough to identify at least 20 stocks each year? If the latter, you will need to build this constraint (and others) into your search procedure or fitness function.

3. Obvious fitness choices probably won't work.

Good trading rules are the ones that make the most money, right? Yes and no. While this is the ultimate goal, rules built to simply maximize return over some historical test period without any other constraints will probably be useless going forward. Good fitness functions require lots of work.

4. Beware of overfitting.

If you don't build in some good constraints, you are likely to end up with a rule that fits the historical test period nicely but has little value. Genetic algorithms, for example, can find some really bizarre rules that overfit the test period.

5. Put lots of thought into your database design.

Your first attempts will probably be modified or expanded in some way. Much of the programming effort concerns data management and data interface issues. Try to think ahead when you design your database.

6. Check results from a theory standpoint.

A rule that at first looks strange may be just that. You may have overfitted and found a useless rule. Or, there may be a good rationale as to why this rule has worked and will continue to work. Think critically about your results.

7. Beware of data mining.

Today's computer horsepower allows us to explore enormous numbers of potential trading rules. If you look long enough, you will no doubt find rules that work great over the test period, but are not necessarily so good for other periods.

8. There is a tradeoff between quantity and quality.

Suppose you are developing trading rules based on technical analysis. Rule A says to buy when pattern X occurs. Rule B says to buy when pattern Y occurs. Will combining A and B lead to a really great trading rule? Perhaps. However, the combination rule may occur so infrequently that it is not as good as simply buying whenever either A or B is applicable.

9. Consider using a portfolio of rules.

Another way to diversify is to use a portfolio of rules rather than a single rule.

10. Decide in advance when to bail out.

In a way, the question here is similar to that raised in rule 1. What will you consider proof that your rule is *not* working?

---

www.stmarytx.edu/business/?go=fac&page=bauer

'Since 1950 an excellent strategy has been to invest in the market between November 1st and April 30th each year, and then to switch into fixed income securities for the other six months of the year.'

Yale Hirsch

Gary Belsky

Gary Belsky was a writer at *Money* magazine from 1991 to 1998. From 1994 to 1998 he was a regular weekly commentator on CNN's *Your Money* and a frequent contributor to *Good Morning America, CBS This Morning, Crossfire* and *Oprah*. He is currently a deputy editor at *ESPN The Magazine*.

In 1990, Belsky won the Gerald Loeb Award for Distinguished Business and Financial Journalism, administered by The Anderson School at UCLA. He lives in New York.

Books

Why Smart People Make Big Money Mistakes and How They Correct Them, (co-authored with Thomas Gilovich), Fireside, 2000
ESPN the Magazine Presents: Answer Guy: Extinguishing the Burning Questions of Sports with the Water Bucket of Truth, (Brendan O'Connor, Neil Fine), Hyperion Books, 2002
23 Ways to Get to First Base: The ESPN Sports Uncyclopedia, ESPN Books, 2006

Behavioral finance

1. Every dollar spends the same.

People tend to treat money differently depending on where it's come from. They spend money received as a gift, bonus or tax refund freely and easily, while spending other money - money they've earned - more carefully. Try not to compartmentalise your money in this way. Treat it all the same. One way to do this is to park 'found' money in a savings account before you decide what to do with it. The more time you have to think of money as savings - hard-earned or otherwise - the less likely you'll be to spend it recklessly.

2. Control your fear of losses.

A bedrock principle of behavioral economics is that the pain people feel from losing $100 is much greater than the pleasure they get from winning $100. Be careful that this does not lead you to cling on to losing investments in the hope that they'll return to profit, or to sell good investments during periods of market turmoil when holding them would be better in the long term.

3. Look at decisions from all points of view.

Too many choices make choosing harder. If you suffer from 'decision paralysis' try looking at the options from a different perspective. For instance, if you are trying to decide between different stocks or funds, imagine that you already own them all. Your decision then becomes one of rejection ("which one am I least comfortable owning?") rather than of selection, and you may find this helps.

4. All numbers count, even if you don't like to count them.

The tendency to dismiss or discount small numbers as insignificant - the 'bigness bias' - can lead you to pay more than you need to for brokerage commissions and fund charges. Over time, this can have a surprisingly deleterious effect on your investment returns. Avoid this 'bigness bias'. Count all the numbers.

5. Acknowledge the role of chance.

A failure to fully grasp the role that chance plays in life leads many investors to be overly-impressed with short-term success and other random or unusual occurrences. Thus, many investors pour money into mutual funds that have performed well in recent years under the mistaken belief that the funds' success is the result of something other than dumb luck.

6. Your confidence is often misplaced.

Nearly everyone falls prey, at some time or another, to an overestimation of their knowledge and abilities. Most dangerous for investors is the delusion that, with a little knowledge or homework, you can pick investments with better-than-average success. In reality, there is little reason for even the most sophisticated investor to believe that she can pick stocks - or mutual funds - better than the average man or woman on the street.

7. It's hard to admit mistakes.

This sounds basic, but we're not talking about pride so much as the subconscious inclination people have to confirm what they already know or want to believe. Because of this 'confirmation bias' it's important to share your financial decisions with others - seeking not only specific advice, but also critiques of your decision-making process.

8. The trend may not be your friend.

In the long term, conventional wisdom is often on target - as it has been over the past 25 years in the trend away from fixed income investments towards stocks. In the short run, however, the vagaries of crowd behavior - particularly 'information cascades' that result in dramatic shifts in tastes and actions - frequently lead to costly overreactions and missed opportunities. Treat trends and fads with skepticism and caution.

9. You can know too much.

Knowledge is power, but too much 'illusory' information can be destructive. Studies have shown that investors who tune out the majority of financial news fare better than those who subject themselves to an endless stream of information, much of it meaningless.

10. Don't check your investments too regularly.

The less frequently you check on your investments, the less likely you'll be to react emotionally to the natural ups and downs of the securities markets. For most investors, a yearly review of their portfolios is frequent enough.

gary.beslky@espn.com

'There is no such thing as a 'hold' decision. If you wouldn't buy the stock again today, assuming you had additional money, you should either sell, or admit that you are confused.'

Robert V. Green

Bruce Berman

Bruce Berman is president and principal owner of Brody Berman Associates, Inc., a consulting firm for positioning intellectual property owners, advisors and investors.

Over the past 15 years Mr. Berman has acted for technology-based companies, m&a candidates, licensing departments and consultants, investment bankers, investment partnerships, owners of branded products, and law firms. Mr. Berman has taught at CCNY, Columbia University and Sir George Williams University, and is a member of the financial markets committee of the Licensing Executives Society (L.E.S.).

Books

Hidden Value: Profiting from The Intellectual Property Economy
Euromoney Institutional Investor, 1999
Making Innovation Pay: People Who Turn IP Into Shareholder Value, John Wiley & Sons Inc, 2006

Understanding the value of patents

Introduction

Patents are rights granted to inventors by governments. Owners of patents, or their assignees, are awarded a period of exclusivity in exchange for giving whoever wants to look a glimpse of how their invention works.

While frustrating to some, these restrictions stimulate innovation. Without patents, competitors would simply copy innovations made by others, thus destroying the advantage of doing R&D. This is called the 'free-rider' problem. Free-riders reduce the level of R&D, a socially unacceptable and potentially dangerous outcome. Patent protection gives companies the confidence to spend R&D dollars on innovations which could otherwise be easily copied.

Intellectual property (IP) investors include a diverse range of stakeholders: senior management, money managers, investment bankers, universities and individuals. IP rights, business performance and market value are inextricably bound. Smart companies innovate. Really smart companies innovate, protect and leverage IP assets for performance, profit and shareholder value.

1. Not all patents are assets.

A patent is merely a right to defend an invention, even if it has no value. Many companies are using techniques for increasing R&D efficiency and patenting strategy, and aligning them with business objectives. While it is good to have many patents (IBM secured more than 2,800 U.S. patents in 2000), it is far better to have the *right* patents. Seven of the top ten recipients of U.S. patents are companies based outside of the U.S.

2. It is relatively easy to secure a patent - but difficult to predict its future value.

Most patent agents can get a patent to issue on almost any invention. Even a 'hairy fuzz ball' is patentable if the claims are adjusted to comply with patent office requirements that the invention covered be non-obvious and novel.

However, this does not mean the patent is or will be worth anything, or that it will survive costly legal challenges. Good legal advisors can determine the likely strength of a patent, even if it is difficult to predict its future value.

3. One patent strategy does not fit every business.

Approaches to attaining strong patent position tend to differ by industry. Pharmaceutical companies, for example, spend a lot of money securing relatively few expensive patents. Pharma company patents tend to be associated with product 'home runs' (ViagraTM, ProzacTM, ClaritinTM, etc).

Conversely, groups of overlapping patents that cover a product or products and establish patent 'fences' are common in the semiconductor industry.

4. Licensing royalties help some companies to compete.

Companies can generate high-margin income by licensing their technology or inventions to non-competitors and, in some instances, even competitors.

Income from technology licenses can be extremely rewarding. Qualcomm, for example, which has decided to manufacture less and license more, may be a model for technology companies that want to cash in quickly on key technologies (like CDMA wireless) which may have a short shelf life.

5. Under or mis-exploited patents can reduce profit and depress shareholder value.

Because patents and the innovation they protect are abstract, most companies are only partially aware of the potential of their patent portfolio and how to best exploit it. Many firms separate R&D, legal and the line engineering to such a degree that valuable patents 'get lost in the shuffle.'

6. Communicating patent performance to the right audiences can enhance value.

Companies that are candid about their IP strengths and articulate about their performance may be able to positively impact profitability and shareholder value. Companies with a strategic patent position (a carefully constructed 'portfolio' that focuses on business objectives) are often worth more than those with ad hoc inventions.

7. People who should know something about patents often do not.

Until recently, showing a patent to an investment banker might result in a new company. Today, bankers know to ask about specific 'claims' made in the patent and how they match up against competitors'. Be wary of VCs, stock analysts and other financial types involved in technology who minimize the importance of IP or who lack basic knowledge of patents.

8. Never invest in a company on the basis of a single patent.

Too many factors influence successful inventions, including management, competitive position, financing, the ability to commercialize inventions in a timely manner, as well as challenges to the validity of patent rights. In few industries can a single patent transform a company. It is more likely that a group of patents in a related art will make a greater if less dramatic impact.

9. Successfully enforcing patent rights sends a message.

Companies that enforce their patents by securing licenses from potential infringers and, when necessary, bringing and winning law suits, can win big. Enforcing rights in innovation sends a message. Patent litigation, while expensive, not only helps to generate income, it creates shareholder value.

10. Accidents can be rewarding.

Smart companies know how to apply technologies to business needs - others if not their own. Many successful patented products initially 'failed' as an intended application. The technology underlying IBM's excimer laser was originally intended as a stylus for reading optical media. SeldaneTM, one of the most successful prescription drugs ever, started life as a blood pressure medication.

11. Business inventors come in different shapes and sizes.

Not all inventors are scientists or technologists, or all innovation incubators dominated by engineers. Successful inventors include teachers, builders, musicians and Wall Street bankers. The future of innovation is about business strategy and inventing teams. Lawyers with business experience and executives with legal knowledge make for formidable alliances.

12. Some patents have a second life.

Most patents issued are worth little, if anything. However, in the right hands value can be distilled from the slagheap of unused, unwanted or otherwise discarded patents. A combination of market knowledge, good timing, legal skill and motivation can imbue some patents with new or additional value.

www.brodyberman.com

William Bernstein

William Bernstein is a principal in Efficient Frontier Advisors, a Connecticut investment management firm. He also operates a nonprofit online journal of asset allocation and portfolio theory - www.efficientfrontier.com.

Bernstein has developed basic portfolio management principles for individual investors, contributed online pieces for *Money* and Morningstar.com, and is frequently quoted in *The Wall Street Journal* and other publications.

Books

The Four Pillars of Investment Success, McGraw-Hill, 2002
The Intelligent Asset Allocator, McGraw-Hill, 2000
The Birth of Plenty: How the Prosperity of the Modern World Was Created, McGraw-Hill Education, 2004

Intelligent asset allocation

1. The portfolio's the thing.

Get used to the fact that, at any one time, a few parts of your portfolio will be doing terribly. Over a long enough time period, each and every component will have had a bad year or two. This is normal asset-class behavior and cannot be avoided. Focus on the performance of the portfolio as a whole, not the individual parts.

2. In asset allocation, job one is to pick an appropriate stock/bond mix.

This is determined primarily by your risk tolerance. Do not bite off more risk than you can chew - a classic beginner's mistake. Calmly and coolly planning for a market downturn is quite different from actually living through one, in the same way that crashing a flight simulator is different from crashing a real airplane. Time horizon is also important. Do not invest any money in stocks that you will need in less than five years, and do not invest more than half unless you will not need the money for at least a decade.

3. Allocate your stocks widely among many different asset classes.

Your biggest exposure should be to the broad domestic stock market. Use small stocks, foreign stocks, and real estate investment trusts (REITs) in smaller amounts.

4. It makes a difference where you put things.

Some asset classes, such as large foreign and domestic stocks, and domestic small stocks, are available in tax-efficient vehicles; put these in your taxable accounts. Other asset classes, particularly value stocks, REITs, and junk bonds, are highly tax-*in*efficient. Put these only in your tax-sheltered retirement accounts.

5. Don't rebalance too often.

The benefit of rebalancing back to your policy allocation is that it forces you to sell high and buy low. Asset classes tend to trend up or down for up to a few years. Give this process a chance to work; you should not rebalance more often than once per year.

These rules apply to tax-sheltered accounts. In taxable accounts, rebalance only with outflows, inflows, and mandatory distributions; here, the rebalancing benefit is usually outweighed by the tax consequences.

6. The recent past is out to get you.

Human beings tend to be most impressed with what has happened in the past several years and wrongly assume that it will continue forever. It never does. The fact that large growth stocks performed extremely well in the late 1990s does not make it more likely that this will continue; in fact, it makes it slightly less likely. The performance of different kinds of stocks and bonds is best evaluated over the long haul.

7. If you want to be entertained, take up sky diving.

Investors like to have fashionable portfolios, invested in the era's most exciting technologies. Resist the temptation. There is an inverse correlation between an investment's entertainment value and its expected return; IPOs, on average, have low returns, and boring stocks tend to reward the most.

8. An asset allocation that maximizes your chances of getting rich also maximizes your chances of becoming poor.

Your best chance of making yourself fabulously wealthy through investing is to buy a few small stocks with good growth possibilities; you just might find the next Microsoft. Of course, it is far more likely that you will lose most of your money this way. On the other hand, although you cannot achieve extremely high returns with a diversified portfolio, it is the best way to avoid a retirement diet of cat food.

9. There is nothing new in investing.

A knowledge of financial history is the most potent weapon in the investor's armamentarium. Since the dawn of stockbroking in the seventeenth century, every generation has experienced its own tech bust. The recent dot-com catastrophe was just one more act in finance's longest running comedy. Be able to say to yourself, "I've seen this movie before, and I think I know how it ends." The only thing that's new is the history you haven't read.

10. A portfolio of 15 to 30 stocks does not provide adequate diversification.

The myth that it does results from a misinterpretation of modern financial theory. While it is true that a 30-stock portfolio has no more short-term volatility than the market, there is more to risk than day-to-day fluctuations. The real risk is not that short-term volatility will be too high, but that long-term return will be too low. The only way of minimizing this risk is to own thousands of stocks in many nations. Or a few index funds.

www.efficientfrontier.com

'Investment bankers are not driven by philanthropy or even by an intellectual motivation to understand the world of finance. They are out to make money and will sell the public anything within the bounds of the law.'

Edward Chancellor

James B. Bittman

James Bittman is Senior Instructor at The Options Institute, the educational arm of the CBOE, where he teaches courses for public investors, brokers and institutional money managers. He is the author of three books on option strategies, and has presented custom classes all over the world.

Books

Options For The Stock Investor, Probus, 1996
Trading Index Options, McGraw-Hill, 1998
Trading and Hedging with Agricultural Futures and Options, McGraw-Hill, 2001

Trading options

---

1. Know the difference between using options to speculate and using options to invest.

Speculators are pure traders, short-term market timers with little interest in the underlying stock, and they often use a high degree of leverage. Investors, however, use options to buy, sell, protect, or increase income from stock positions, and investors do not use leverage.

2. Have a plan.

Will a purchased option be exercised or sold if it is in the money at expiration? Covered writers must know whether or not they are willing to sell the underlying stock; if not, at what price will the call be repurchased or rolled to another option? Put writers must know whether or not they are willing to buy the underlying stock; if not, at what price will a short put be repurchased, even if at a loss?

3. You need a three-part forecast.

In option trading you need a forecast for a specific price change in the underlying, for a specific time period and for a specific change in implied volatility. Developing a forecasting technique is a challenge for all traders, but options trading is unique because of the multi-part forecast required.

4. Be disciplined in taking profits and losses.

Have a profit target and close or reduce the size of your position if it is reached. Have a stop-loss point and close or reduce your position at that price. Have a time limit and close or reduce your position if neither the profit target nor the stop-loss point are reached by the end of the time period.

5. Understand and pay attention to implied volatility.

Implied volatility is the volatility percentage that justifies the market price of an option. Volatility in options corresponds to the risk factor in insurance, and implied volatility reflects the market's perception of the risk, or potential price range, of the underlying stock.

6. Implied volatility has no absolutes.

Option users must develop a subjective feel for what are 'high' and 'low' levels of implied volatility.

7. 'Buying under-valued options' and 'selling over-valued options' are not sufficient strategies.

You must focus on your three-part forecast as much as or more than the 'value' of an option.

8. 'Selling options' is not a better strategy than 'buying options'.

It is a myth that 80-90% of options expire worthless. Approximately one third, or 33%, of options expire worthless while 10-15% are exercised, and the rest are closed prior to expiration.

9. Trading means buying and selling.

Trading does not mean buying and holding! The goal of trading is to make a net profit after a series of trades. It is, therefore, essential to accept some losses and to look forward without chastising oneself for making mistakes.

10. Trading options is a learning process.

As a beginner, you should enter trades that have only small potential profits or losses, because this will ensure that objectivity can be maintained. Trades must be initiated and closed so that a 'trading rhythm' is developed. You need to develop a market forecasting technique and you should be able to explain your trade selection process in a few sentences. Almost anyone can learn to trade if they spend a few hours every week developing their technique.

bittman@cboe.com,
www.cboe.com/LearnCenter/cboeeducation

John C. Bogle

John C. Bogle is Founder of The Vanguard Group, Inc., and President of the Bogle Financial Markets Research Center.

The Vanguard Group is one of America's two largest mutual fund organizations, and comprises more than 100 mutual funds with current assets totaling more than $500 billion. Vanguard 500 Index Fund, now the largest mutual fund in the world, was founded by Mr. Bogle in 1975. It was the first index mutual fund.

For his 'exemplary achievement, excellence of practice, and true leadership', Mr. Bogle holds the AIMR Award for Professional Excellence, and is also a member of the Hall of Fame of the Fixed Income Analysts Society, Inc.

In 1999, he was named by *Fortune* magazine as one of the investment industry's four 'Giants of the 20th Century.'

Books

Bogle on Mutual Funds, Irwin, 1993
Common Sense Mutual Funds, John Wiley, 1999
John Bogle on Investing: The First 50 Years, McGraw-Hill, 2000

Common sense investing

1. There's no escaping risk.

Once you decide to put your money to work to build long-term wealth, you have to decide, not whether to take risk, but what kind of risk you wish to take. 'Do what you will, capital is at hazard,' just as the Prudent Man Rule assures us.

Yes, money in a savings account is dollar-safe, but those safe dollars are apt to be substantially eroded by inflation, a risk that almost guarantees you will fail to reach your capital accumulation goals.

And yes, money in the stock market is very risky over the short-term, but, if well-diversified, should provide remarkable growth with a high degree of consistency over the long term.

2. Buy right and hold tight.

The most critical decision you face is getting the proper allocation of assets in your investment portfolio - stocks for growth of capital and growth of income, bonds for conservation of capital and current income. Once you get your balance right, then just hold tight, no matter how high a greedy stock market flies, nor how low a frightened market plunges. Change the allocation only as your investment profile changes. Begin by considering a 50/50 stock/bond balance, then raise the stock allocation if:

1. You have many years remaining to accumulate wealth.
2. The amount of capital you have at stake is modest (i.e. your first investment in a corporate savings plan).
3. You have little need for current income.
4. You have the courage to ride out the booms and busts with reasonable equanimity.

As these factors are reversed, reduce the 50 per cent stock allocation accordingly.

3. Time is your friend, impulse your enemy.

Think long term, and don't allow transitory changes in stock prices to alter your investment program. There is a lot of noise in the daily volatility of the stock market, which too often is 'a tale told by an idiot, full of sound and fury, signifying nothing'.

Stocks may remain overvalued, or undervalued, for years. Realize that one of the greatest sins of investing is to be captured by the siren song of the market, luring you into buying stocks when they are soaring and selling when they are plunging. Impulse is your enemy. Why? Because market timing is impossible. Even if you turn out to be right when you sold stocks just before a decline (a rare occurrence!), where on earth would you ever get the insight that tells you the right time to get back in? One correct decision is tough enough. Two correct decisions are nigh on impossible.

Time is your friend. If, over the next 25 years, stocks produce a 10% return and a savings account produces a 5% return, $10,000 would grow to $108,000 in stocks vs. $34,000 in savings. (After 3% inflation, $54,000 vs. $16,000). Give yourself all the time you can.

4. Realistic expectations: the bagel and the doughnut.

These two different kinds of baked goods symbolize the two distinctively different elements of stock market returns. It is hardly farfetched to consider that investment return - dividend yields and earnings growth - is the bagel of the stock market, for the investment return on stocks reflects their underlying character: nutritious, crusty and hard-boiled.

By the same token, speculative return - wrought by any change in the price that investors are willing to pay for each dollar of earnings - is the spongy doughnut of the market, reflecting changing public opinion about stock valuations, from the soft sweetness of optimism to the acid sourness of pessimism.

The substantive bagel-like economics of investing are almost inevitably productive, but the flaky, doughnut-like emotions of investors are anything but steady - sometimes productive, sometimes counterproductive.

In the long run, it is investment return that rules the day. In the past 40 years, the speculative return on stocks has been zero, with the annual investment return of 11.2% precisely equal to the stock market's total return of 11.2% per year. But in the first 20 of those years, investors were sour on the economy's prospects, and a tumbling price-earnings ratio provided a speculative return of minus 4.6% per year, reducing the nutritious annual investment return of 12.1% to a market return of just 7.5%. From 1981 to 2001, however, the outlook sweetened, and a soaring P/E ratio produced a sugary 5% speculative boost to the investment return of 10.3%.

Result: The market return leaped to 15.3% - double the return of the prior two decades.

The lesson: Enjoy the bagel's healthy nutrients, and don't count on the doughnut's sweetness to enhance them.

Conclusion: Realistic expectations for the coming decade suggest returns well below those we have enjoyed over the past two decades.

5. Why look for the needle in the haystack? Buy the haystack!

Experience confirms that buying the right stocks, betting on the right investment style, and picking the right money manager - in each case, in advance - is like looking for a needle in a haystack.

When we do so, we rely largely on past performance, ignoring the fact that what worked yesterday seldom works tomorrow. Investing in equities entails four risks: stock risk, style risk, manager risk, and market risk. The first three of these risks can easily be eliminated, simply by owning the entire stock market - owning the haystack, as it were - and holding it forever.

Yes, stock market risk remains, and it is quite large enough, thank you. So why pile those other three risks on top of it? If you're not certain you're right (and who can be?), diversify.

Owning the entire stock market is the ultimate diversifier. If you can't find the needle, buy the haystack.

6. Minimize the croupier's take.

The resemblance of the stock market to the casino is not far-fetched. Yes, the stock market is a positive-sum game and the gambling casino is a zero-sum game . . . but only before the costs of playing each game are deducted. After the heavy costs of financial intermediaries (commissions, management fees, taxes, etc.) are deducted, beating the stock market is inevitably a loser's game. Just as, after the croupiers' wide rake descends, beating the casino is inevitably a loser's game. All investors as a group must earn the market's return before costs, and lose to the market after costs, and by the exact amount of those costs.

Your greatest chance of earning the market's return, therefore, is to reduce the croupiers' take to the bare-bones minimum. When you read about stock market returns, realize that the financial markets are not for sale, except at a high price. The difference is crucial. If the market's return is 10% before costs, and intermediation costs are approximately 2%, then investors earn 8%. Compounded over 50 years, 8% takes $10,000 to $469,000. But at 10%, the final value leaps to $1,170,000—nearly three times as much . . . just by eliminating the croupier's take.

7. Beware of fighting the last war.

Too many investors - individuals and institutions alike - are constantly making investment decisions based on the lessons of the recent, or even the extended, past. They seek technology stocks after they have emerged victorious from the last war; they worry about inflation after it becomes the accepted bogeyman, they buy bonds after the stock market has plunged.

You should not ignore the past, but neither should you assume that a particular cyclical trend will last forever. None does. Just because some investors insist on 'fighting the last war,' you don't need to do so yourself. It doesn't work for very long.

8. Sir Isaac Newton's revenge on Wall Street - reversion to the mean.

Through all history, investments have been subject to a sort of Law of Gravity: What goes up must go down, and, oddly enough, what goes down must go up. Not always of course (companies that die rarely live again), and not necessarily in the absolute sense, but relative to the overall market norm.

For example, stock market returns that substantially exceed the investment returns generated by earnings and dividends during one period tend to revert and fall well short of that norm during the next period. Like a pendulum, stock prices swing far above their underlying values, only to swing back to fair value and then far below it.

Another example: From the start of 1997 through March 2000, NASDAQ stocks (+230%) soared past NYSE-listed stocks (+20%), only to come to a screeching halt. During the subsequent year, NASDAQ stocks lost 67% of their value, while NYSE stocks lost just 7%, reverting to the original market value relationship (about one to five) between the so-called 'New Economy' and the 'Old Economy.'

Reversion to the mean is found everywhere in the financial jungle, for the mean is a powerful magnet that, in the long run, finally draws everything back to it.

9. The hedgehog bests the fox.

The Greek philosopher Archilochus tells us, 'the fox knows many things, but the hedgehog knows one great thing.' The fox - artful, sly, and astute - represents the financial institution that knows many things about complex markets and sophisticated marketing. The hedgehog - whose sharp spines give it almost impregnable armor when it curls into a ball - is the financial institution that knows only one great thing: long-term investment success is based on simplicity.

The wily foxes of the financial world justify their existence by propagating the notion that an investor can survive only with the benefit of their artful knowledge and expertise. Such assistance, alas, does not come cheap, and the costs it entails tend to consume more value-added performance than even the most cunning of foxes can provide. Result: The annual returns earned for investors by financial intermediaries such as mutual funds have averaged less than 80% of the stock market's annual return.

The hedgehog, on the other hand, knows that the truly great investment strategy succeeds, not because of its complexity or cleverness, but because of its simplicity and low cost. The hedgehog diversifies broadly, buys and holds, and keeps expenses to the bare-bones minimum. The ultimate hedgehog: The all-market index fund, operated at minimal cost and with minimal portfolio turnover, virtually guarantees nearly 100% of the market's return to the investor.

In the field of investment management, foxes come and go, but hedgehogs are forever.

10. Stay the course: the secret of investing is that there *is* no secret.

When you consider these previous nine rules, realize that they are about neither magic and legerdemain, nor about forecasting the unforecastable, nor about betting at long and ultimately unsurmountable odds, nor about learning some great secret of successful investing. For there is no great secret, only the majesty of simplicity. These rules are about elementary arithmetic, about fundamental and unarguable principles, and about that most uncommon of all attributes, common sense.

Owning the entire stock market through an index fund - all the while balancing your portfolio with an appropriate allocation to an all bond market index fund - with its cost-efficiency, its tax-efficiency, and its assurance of earning for you the market's return, is by definition a winning strategy. But if only you follow one final rule for successful investing, perhaps the most important principle of all investment wisdom: Stay the course!

---

www.vanguard.com

Lewis J. Borsellino

Lewis J. Borsellino is the founder of www.TeachTrade.Com, an educational web site for stock and futures traders.

Mr. Borsellino has traded at the Chicago Mercantile Exchange since 1981. He appears regularly on CNN-FN, Reuters Financial Television, Bloomberg TV and WebFN.

Books
The Day Trader - From the Pit to the PC, John Wiley, 1999
The Day Trader's Course: Low-risk, High-profit Strategies for Trading Stocks and Futures (Patricia Crisafulli), John Wiley & Sons Inc, 2001

The 'ten commandments' of trading

Introduction

In the 20 years I've been trading, I've discovered one truism that is valid whether you're trading stocks, fixed income or futures: trading is 90% psychological. All the rest – technical analysis, trade execution, etc. – is the other 10%.

That's not to say that technical analysis of the markets isn't important. It's vital. You can't trade without a plan based on technical analysis that encompasses support and resistance, trend lines, moving averages, momentum, volatility and the like. But you can't possibly execute that plan consistently if your mental game is off. That's where the 'ten commandments' of trading come in.

1. Trade for success, not for money.

Your motivation should be first and foremost to make a well-executed trade. If money alone is your motivation you will severely limit your chance of success. Why? Because focusing on money will raise all kinds of emotional issues, from fear to greed. It will make you afraid of losses to the point that you will abandon your discipline. It will tempt you to trade too often, too large and with too much risk. Whereas if you focus on making solid, well-executed trades - even if the result is a losing trade that you exit quickly - you will reinforce your discipline and increase your trading potential.

2. Discipline is the one quality that all traders must possess above all others.

The ability to master your mind, your body and your emotions is the key to trading. The disciplined trader - regardless of profit or loss - comes back to trade another day. A great intellect, the ability to take on risk, or even a sense that you're somehow 'lucky' mean nothing without discipline. For a trader, discipline means the ability to devise a trading plan, execute according to that plan, and to never deviate from that plan.

3. Know yourself.

Do you break out in a cold sweat at the mere thought of risking something - such as your own capital? Do you think of trading like 'gambling,' a long shot to make a million? Or can you handle risk in a disciplined fashion, knowing how much is 'too much' for both your capital and your constitution?

Trading is not for everyone. If risk makes you ill, on the one hand, or if taking a risk brings out the recklessness in you, then trading is probably not for you. But if you can handle risk with discipline, then perhaps you can find a vocation or avocation as a trader. Only you can answer that question.

4. Lose your ego.

No matter how much success you enjoy as a trader, you'll never outsmart the market. If you think you can, you're in for a very humbling experience. The market rules, always, and for everyone.

You need to silence your ego in order to listen to the market, to follow what your technical analysis is indicating - and not what your intellect (and your ego) think *should* happen. To trade effectively, you need to put yourself aside. At the same time, you cannot be so emotionally fragile that unprofitable trades shatter your confidence. Don't be crushed by the market, but don't ever think you've mastered it, either.

5. There's no such thing as hoping, wishing or praying.

I've seen too many traders staring panic-stricken at the computer screen and begging the market to move their way. Why? Because they have lost their discipline and allowed what was a small loss to turn into a much bigger one. They keep hanging on, hoping, wishing and praying for things to turn around. The reality is on the screen. When the market hits your stop-loss level (the price at which you'll cut your losses at a pre-determined level), get out.

6. Let your profits run and cut your losses quickly.

When the market goes against you and you hit your pre-determined stop, exit the trade. Period. Exit when the loss is a small one. Then reevaluate your strategy and execute a new trade. Keeping your losses small will keep you in the game. Profits take care of themselves, as long as you execute according to your plan. When you place a trade, know in advance where you'll exit for a profit. When the market reaches that level, exit the position. If your technical analysis tells you the market still has some room to move, then scale out of the position. But execute according to your plan. Remember, you'll never go broke taking a profit.

7. Know when to trade and when to wait.

Trade when your analysis, your system and your strategy say that you have a buy or sell to execute. If the market doesn't have a clear direction, then wait on the sidelines until it does. Keep your mind on the market, but keep your money out of it.

8. Love your losers like you love your winners.

Losing trades will be your best teachers. When you have a losing trade, it's because of some flaw in your analysis or your judgment. Or perhaps the market simply didn't do what you thought it would. When you have a losing trade, something is out of sync with the market. Examine what went wrong - objectively - then adjust your thinking, if necessary, and enter the trade again.

9. After three losing trades in a row, take a break.

This is not the time to take on more risk, but rather to become extremely disciplined. Sit on the sidelines for a while. Watch the market. Clear your head. Re-evaluate your strategy, and then put on another trade. Losses can shake your confidence and tempt you to become emotional (fear/greed) But if you take a break, you can gather your wits and regain your composure more quickly than if you become very emotional and angry at yourself and the market.

10. The unbreakable rule.

You can break a rule and get away with it once in a while. But one day, the rules will break you. If you continually violate these 'commandments' of trading, you will eventually pay for it with your profits. That's the unbreakable rule. If you have trouble with any of them, come back and read this one. Then read it again.

'By their nature, turnaround stocks are unpopular. That's why they have so much profit potential. If you wait until they are popular again, you will miss most of the gains. Back in 1993 when IBM dropped down to about 10 (adjusted for splits) most analysts called it a dinosaur. When it got back up to 100 a few years later, everyone loved it again.'

George Putnam III

David Braun

David Braun founded and is President of Virtual Strategies Inc., a consultancy which advises clients on proactive acquisition or divestiture programs.

The firm has acted for small and family-owned businesses, as well as Fortune 500 and multi-national companies, in a wide range of manufacturing and service industries.

Over the past 10 years, Mr Braun has lectured to over 10,000 top-level business executives, through the American Management Association and various industry organizations.

How to make gains from M&A activity

1. Invest in experienced buyers.

If you're investing in a company that is entering acquisition mode, make sure the people running it are experienced in M&A. A company that has executed a few successful deals recently is a better bet than one which has just started to think about making acquisitions.

2. Back an acquiror with a comprehensive strategy.

To maximize the chances of making successful acquisitions, an acquirer needs to have a compelling external growth strategy, with associated milestones and timeline. Avoid investing in 'one-trick ponies' – those companies looking for the one silver bullet acquisition that will propel them to where they want to be.

3. The acquisition of a great company is only as good as its integration plan.

The acquiring company needs to have a solid integration plan that solicits involvement from key management in every major functional area. Look for evidence of a '100-Day Plan' which illustrates in detail exactly how the two companies will be fully integrated 100 days after 'go live' day (the close).

4. Ignore the financials.

Well, not entirely. But avoid investing in a company that is making acquisition decisions based on its CFO saying "we can get a great price on this company." Remember, a balance sheet doesn't generate profits - people do. Accretion/dilution should not be the number one acquisition criterion. Simply stated, you can overpay for a good company and recover your earnings with time, but you can underpay for the wrong company and never recover.

5. The customer is always right.

When deciding whether consolidation makes sense for a company whose stock you own, consider its customers. The mere fact that a sector is fragmented does not make it ready for consolidation, and conversely, there are plenty of fairly concentrated industries that are still managing to consolidate with impressive multiples (e.g. banking). A good rule of thumb is to look at the industry's customer base and determine if there is *demand* for consolidation. Good industries to watch are those that have major, multinational customers that will demand a wider-spreading presence.

6. When investing in potential takeover targets, do your homework.

Don't rely on hunches, gut instinct, or market rumors. Identify companies that are likely sellers due to below average stock performance (and restless shareholders), older senior management, ownership base, etc. The market may unfairly undervalue some companies by painting them with the same brush as an entire underperforming industry group.

7. Don't be duped by a target's stock that is 'on sale'.

Avoid arbitrarily investing in a stock that seems to be underpriced in the hope that it will later be sold for a premium. Many stocks, while appearing to be bargains, are simply 'broken' or long-term underperforming stocks. Just because the stock was once trading at a much higher level it is by no means certain that the stock will ever return to its previous high.

8. An acquisition premium may already be built in to a stock price.

Do not necessarily vote *against* the sale of control in a stock you own because the offer price is not at a significant premium to the current market price. The market may already have incorporated an acquisition premium into the stock, therefore minimizing the potential for an additional premium offered by a buyer.

9. A receding economy creates novel M&A opportunities.

Many people assume that a downturn in the economy will drag M&A volume down with it. In fact, shifting market dynamics of any kind will change the complexion of deals, but not necessarily the volume. For instance, a company that has been on a buying spree to diversify its business may decide, in a tightening market, to return to its fundamental competencies and sell off a non-core business line, thus creating an acquisition opportunity for a buyer.

10. Question the Board of Directors before voting to accept an offer.

When confronted with an attractive offer, the Board of a target company may need to be reminded of its fiduciary responsibility to shop the deal around for the highest sale price possible. Many buyers will finagle their way into an exclusive offer, which may appear attractive enough to woo a Board that is eager to complete the sale.

www.virtual-strategies.com

'Stock prices are anchored to 'fundamentals' but the anchor is easily pulled up and then dropped in another place. Given that expected growth rates and the price the market is willing to pay for growth can change rapidly on the basis of market psychology, the concept of a firm intrinsic value for shares must be an elusive will-o-the-wisp.'

Burton Malkiel

Ian Burns

Ian Burns is employed in Chemical sales at Salomon Smith Barney.

His team has been ranked in the top three of all the major surveys (Reuters, II and Extel) since the Citigroup acquired Schroders, and in Extel June 2001 Ian was personally ranked second of all European specialist salesman for all sectors.

The chemicals sector

Introduction

Chemicals are the world's third largest industry, with sales in excess of US$1trillion worldwide. Significant trade flows ensure that no region is exempt from global trends. It is highly diverse with dozens of sub-sectors and tens of thousands of different products.

Chemicals are used in virtually everything, from drugs to diapers, and greatly enhance our quality of life. In western economies growth is close to GDP levels, while it can be twice GDP in industrialising markets. Growth is driven in part by the substitution of other commodities, such as glass or metals, and by the outsourcing of previously vertically integrated processes such as pharmaceutical intermediates. Each chemical has a finite life cycle, so companies need to innovate to sustain growth.

An alternate approach to growth is to follow the demand for more mature products in new geographic locations, such as emerging markets. Asia is recovering its status as the engine of growth for global chemicals, contributing about half of total incremental demand.

1. It's not for junior Buffetts - be active.

Investing in the chemicals sector has not rewarded a 'buy and hold' strategy. After keeping pace with equity markets worldwide in the 1960s and 1970s it began to underperform the bull markets of the 1980s and to do even less well in the 1990s. It offers tremendous profit opportunities, nonetheless, for active management. My confidence comes from a simplistic analysis of 52 week high and lows for the US and European companies for the past several years. The ranges (for just about every stock) are enormous and a canny investor can make substantial profits with astute timing.

2. It may be mature but it's not a sunset industry, and arguably not one sector.

Investors often argue that chemicals represents a 'sunset' industry for investment. On the contrary, it is probably the most innovative of all industries, and innovation has led to the emergence of huge sub-sector industries such as high-end electronics and fuel cells. There is nothing 'sunset' about those.

The issue for investors is a) how to profit from the innovation and b) how to judge whether the innovators are commercial or commercially managed. A major problem lies in the fact that the industry is regarded as one mass. There is such a range of business models, profit drivers and production requirements across the industry that it blurs investors' focus and leads to generalizations like that about a 'sunset industry'. Try to be 'micro' not 'macro' in your approach.

3. "Business is other people's money" - Mme de Girardin.

In this case, your money is in the hands of a management team, and management is critical in this industry. Competing for investor dollars requires able managers who lead by example, encourage an entrepreneurialis spirit, and constantly renew the company to keep pace with change (both competitive and regulatory). Investors will profit by getting to know their managers and by understanding their motivation - is it the shareholder, the corporate entity, job preservation, or the route to another job? Some parts of the chemicals industry consistently let down investors: it is worth remembering the maxim that when good management is put into a bad industry it is the industry's reputation that prevails.

4. M&A - a route to fortune? Occasionally.

One of the most successful ways of profiting in the chemicals industry has been to identify the 'next most likely' takeover candidate. But it is fraught with danger. Time works in favour of investors in quality businesses as it enhances the value of their holdings, but it may not work in favour of 'bottom fishers' holding stock in a lame victim which they hope will become a predator's prey. As time passes, value erodes.

I have watched many investors buy stocks that 'must get bid for' and even when that sometimes occurs, the passage of time has led to an erosion of corporate value and a bid price close to the investor's entry price. The M&A market is changing too, with buyers more wary of buying companies and more interested in buying businesses within a company. This helps avoid the assumption of potential environmental and pension liabilities, which are increasingly acting as a constraint for dealmakers.

5. Look beyond EPS.

Chemicals is a capital intensive industry so it is critical not to be seduced by the apparent success of a company's EPS growth. Across the sector lie many distortions in depreciation and taxation policies which investors need to appreciate to be able to make an informed decision.

6. Beware the buzzwords 'strategy' and 'innovation'.

It would be disconcerting to find a company management without a coherent strategy. However, the number of strategic changes and initiatives seems to be intensifying. Having an attractive strategy is one thing, but far more important is that the management and employees are committed to the execution of the strategy.

In sport there are many players who have a reputation for 'talking a good game' and far fewer who are winners. Look for the less showy, but most effective. Similarly there is a current trend to boast about a company's innovation. Not all companies profit from innovation. Bottom line - management is key.

7. The benefits of incest! Listen to the industry.

The chemicals industry is a huge user of its own products. It is incestuous. Customers and suppliers are common to many companies and much can be gleaned from talking to these 'related' companies to ascertain the wisdom of an investment. Listen to the chatter. Anecdotal evidence is often (always?) more valuable than a well-paid analyst's spreadsheet. Equally, listen to employees at the company which you are considering investing in. I've never known a company where unhappy people are more productive than happy ones.

If possible it's worth getting to know the employees below board level - do they share the company's aspirations, and are they happy with the way they are treated and remunerated? If not, the strategy has no chance of being executed, the best people will leave for the competition, and the cost of replacing them will soar because of the company's reputation as a poor employer.

8. "Never is there just one cockroach in the kitchen."

This quote, from Warren Buffet, is especially apt in a sector that has a long list of relative (to the wider equity market) underperformers and apparently cheap stocks. My interpretation is that a bad business is likely to remain a bad business and investors should avoid the "it cannot get any worse" school of bargain hunting. Experience has taught me that bad/cheap stocks get cheaper, and cheaper for a reason.

9. Think global.

Chemicals is a global industry, so avoid making comparisons with local (just European or just US) companies. It is fiercely competitive, and production, supply and customer dynamics are constantly evolving. This is not necessarily a negative - think about a company's ability to transfer production around the globe, and whether it is critical to be near customers, and whether or not a customer industry (eg. textiles) is migrating to a new region.

10. Watch the costs.

Many companies are making a virtue of reducing capital intensity by moving to more specialty applications. What is rarely mentioned is that these lower volume, higher priced, products require a much higher research spend, technical support and marketing budget. Just because a specialty company redefines its costs does not mean that these are not the costs of staying in business.

11. Don't wait for the 'right' price.

The whole point of buying a stock is that one has confidence in its future so trying to finesse 4-5% of the price is a mug's game. Conversely, waiting for a bad investment to 'bounce' so that one can sell closer to one's entry price is tempting the fates to send the price crashing. Once an investment decision is made, building or cutting a position should be undertaken as soon as possible.

12. "Specious in theory, yet ruinous in practice."

Edmund Burke wrote, "a thing may look specious in theory, and yet be ruinous in practice; a thing may look evil in theory, and yet in practice be excellent". In other words, experience teaches one to avoid the recommendations of others, and profit by one's own instincts. This may not be the best rule for a stockbroker to write but seems to be an appropriate piece of advice with which to conclude!

John P. Calamos

John P. Calamos has specialized in investment research and portfolio management of convertible securities for major institutional and individual investors for over 20 years.

A frequent speaker at investment seminars and conferences, he has taught graduate level courses on finance and investments and is frequently quoted as an authority on convertible securities.

Books

Convertible Securities: The Latest Instruments, McGraw-Hill, 1998.
Investing in Convertible Securities, Dearborn, 1988.
Convertible Arbitrage: Insights and Techniques for Successful Hedging, John Wiley & Sons Inc, 2003

Convertible bonds

1. The key to building wealth lies in controlling risk - a favorable risk/reward profile is critical to superior performance.

Successful investors manage risk while pursuing returns, recognizing the importance of both to the investment equation. Explore the use of convertible bonds as a unique risk-control measure. Their bond features help cushion the impact of stock market declines, while their potential participation in rising stock prices has no ceiling.

2. The upside/downside risk of convertible bonds is different from that of the underlying stock.

Historically, convertible bonds have offered about two-thirds of the upside performance and about one-third of the downside risk of the underlying common stock. One reason the two dimensions are unequal is because the bond's interest payments and fixed-income principal help moderate the downside but do not impact the upside.

3. Convertible bonds enhance yield in comparison to common stock.

That is because they often pay interest far greater than the dividends paid on the underlying common stock. Growth-oriented companies often issue convertibles because they expect their rising stock prices to change debt to equity, and these companies in particular may pay low dividends or none at all.

4. Convertible bonds' credit ratings don't tell the whole story in evaluating risk.

Credit ratings are an important consideration - but not the only one - in assessing risk. They simply evaluate the ability of the company to repay principal and interest, but in selecting a convertible, the portfolio manager also considers the potential performance of the underlying stock, the unique risk characteristics of the convertible, and the role each position plays in the portfolio's risk/reward profile.

5. The convertible market is not efficient in the short run.

Today's knowledgeable investor can still unearth inefficiencies and profit from them.

6. Any time can be the right time to buy a convertible bond.

Convertibles have both offensive and defensive traits. When the stock market is barreling forward, they participate, unlike straight bonds. And when stocks are retreating, they act more like bonds. There is no wrong time for convertibles as an asset class.

7. In taming convertibles, remember that they are social animals.

They function best in 'packs'. They probably won't function as effectively individually as they do in a portfolio that is carefully structured for overall risk/reward, as well as diversification.

8. Consider a convertible portfolio for diverse roles in your asset allocation strategy.

Convertibles are versatile. As part of a fixed-income portfolio, they can provide a competitive income stream while enhancing diversification and decreasing overall risk. As an equity alternative, they offer potential capital gains and can help protect against interest rate volatility. And since the performance of convertibles does not correlate directly to that of either the straight bond or stock markets, as a separate asset class they can enhance the portfolio's diversification.

9. There's no free lunch in convertible investing.

Convertibles offer the potential benefits of both stocks and bonds. However, there is a tradeoff - they generally pay a lower coupon rate than the equivalent straight bonds since the convertibility feature provides potential upside participation in the stock's performance.

10. Don't try this at home - convertible investing is best left to the professionals.

Unless you are trained and have the time to devote to security analysis, use managed money (mutual funds or professional investment advisors). Let experts do the work for you - but check their investment philosophy and be sure it agrees with your investment plan.

A convertible portfolio must be actively managed to help reap the benefits of its unique risk/reward characteristics. Convertible investing benefits from extensive quantitative analysis, and the pros also have access to trading opportunities that are not available to the individual investor.

www.calamos.com

'Your best chance of making yourself fabulously wealthy investing is to buy a few small stocks with good growth possibilities; you just might find the next Microsoft. Of course, it is far more likely that you will *lose* most of your money this way. On the other hand, although you cannot achieve extremely high returns with a diversified portfolio, it is the best way to avoid a retirement diet of cat food.'

William Bernstein

Thom Calandra

Thom Calandra is executive vice president of news and editor-in-chief of MarketWatch.com.

He returned to San Francisco in July 2001 after spending a year in London masterminding the successful launch of FT MarketWatch. Thom writes StockWatch, a popular daily column about U.S. investment trends, and has been named one of the 100 most influential financial journalists in the US.

General principles and the growing importance of debt analysis

1. Paint a contrarian streak across your portfolio.

Dare to be different. Everyone can't be right, as the tech sell-off is teaching us. The minority can't always be wrong. That doesn't mean you need to convert your entire wad into cash or gold. But it does mean respecting divergent opinions.

2. Understand dominant trends - they can make or save you money.

Stock markets the world over are experiencing sharper intra-day swings, for example. That's an age-old trend called volatility - which you can now trade as a security in the form of the CBOE Nasdaq Volatility Index.

3. Don't trust equity professionals - their research is besmirched.

A backlash is building against stock analysts, who essentially are paid to generate positive research for clients. Less than 10% of the pros' recommendations are 'sell' downgrades. When the 'sell' proclamations do come, it's way too late for most investors. A day of reckoning is ahead for Wall Street and London's self-serving equity analysts.

4. Trust the debt analysts.

Their financial models for companies are far more rigorous than those of the equity crowd. Start tracking corporate bond prices as barometers of your favorite companies.

5. Don't take tips.

That market tip from a newsletter or a friend has a 1-in-10 chance of coming good. Instead, be your own tipster. If your assumptions turn out to be wrong, at least you've learned a valuable lesson.

6. Be very picky with your mutual funds.

Most funds sport fees that eat into investment performance over multi-year spans. The best rationale for buying into a fund is when you cannot easily 'own' its chosen securities - like below-grade corporate bonds.

7. Understand the psychology of investing.

If you're overly confident about an idea, you may need to re-think your premises. If you're terrified, you've probably done your research and should take the plunge.

8. Got a hunch, bet a hunch.

It's tried and true. I've heard it a hundred times. Never put yourself in a position where you were absolutely correct but didn't take enough of a bet to make a difference in your life.

9. Don't short yourself.

We've heard it plenty of times and it's genuine. Most investors sell their winners too soon. Let it ride.

10. Be in the game for the long-term - meaning decades.

This is the hardest one because it takes the courage of your convictions. Since hitting its December 1989 peak of 38,915, Japan's Nikkei Index has had plenty of 50 percent rallies. But it was still a bear market. If you believed Japanese stocks were suffering for the long-term, and bet against the market, you'd have an annuity going on 12 years. This year's biggest winners are the professionals who shorted technology stocks in March and April of 2000 and still hold their positions.

---

www.cbsmarketwatch.com

Donald Cassidy

Donald Cassidy is a senior analyst with Lipper Inc., a Reuters company, doing research on money flows and closed-end investment funds. He conducts frequent seminars across the U.S.A., can be heard as a guest on radio talk shows, and has been quoted in *The Financial Times, The Wall Street Journal, Barron's, Worth, Kiplinger's Personal Finance, The New York Times,* and *Smart Money.*

Books

Trading on Volume, McGraw-Hill, 2001
When The Dow Breaks, McGraw-Hill, 1999
It's When You Sell that Counts, Irwin, 1997
30 Strategies for High Profit Investment Success, Dearborn, 1998

Which stocks to sell, and when

Principle #1: Always force yourself to move toward discomfort!

Investment/trading success cannot come from actions that make you comfortable. Buying or holding when stocks are high (following the crowd because you cannot abide 'missing the action') is a comfort-seeking decision. Likewise, fearful selling in a collapsing and low market is moving toward the comfort of cash - again at just the wrong time. Good decisions involve thoughtful analysis including pro-and-con lists. When leaping in/out rapidly, you've thought of only one side and are moving to what is apparently obvious. The crowd, a few million in size, doing the same thing thus collectively is creating temporary maximum pressure and so a predictable price-reversal point. Hold and/or buy when it is scariest and sell when the majority celebrate their brilliant conquests. Right, contrarian actions are always lonely and very uncomfortable.

Principle #2: Avoid the losers' game of owning favorite stocks for the long term (a.k.a. Heresy #1).

Rapid and relentless change (technology, regulation, internationalization, competitors' ascendancy) makes the odds of extended corporate dominance extremely low. In the five highly prosperous years 1996-2000, of more than 8,000 U.S. stocks, only 20(!) managed to avoid a single down quarter in earnings - a 99.8% failure rate. Companies rarely control the top of the hill for long; those situated there are priced very dearly. Holding them exposes your capital to sudden devastating loss at any sign of faltering momentum.

A tiny number of mutual fund managers compiles consistent above-average records. Their shares are worth holding while individual stocks of current corporate winners are at extreme statistical risk of obeying gravity. Xerox, Polaroid, Memorex, Digital Equipment, Sears, and AT&T are a few examples of the article-of-faith names of a generation ago. In the long term, there is no 'business as usual'.

Principle #3: Never buy a stock without simultaneously placing a sell order at your target.

Failing to have a target reveals fuzzy thinking. Your target should include all three of these: a *price* objective, driven by a *scenario,* in a specific *time frame.*

If your price is reached, or if the scenario does not play in the anticipated time, you must sell rather than rationalize. Don't buy stocks merely because you like the industry, respect management, or agree with their social goals. Require a driver that will push the stock higher - not those other nebulous 'reasons'. The object is profit, not good feelings!

Principle #4: Believe deeply in the 'cockroach theory' and act on it.

Like those lowly bugs, bad news for a company seldom appears solo; a first disappointment is very likely followed by others.With thousands of stocks available, why remain loyal to under-performers? Stocks are not insulted by your selling them! Move on to what is working rather than sticking with the sleeping dogs or bad ones.

Especially, stocks heavily owned by institutions take long periods to regain money managers' trust and to overcome overhanging stock held by those wishing they'd sold before bad news hit. The widely heralded 'dead-cat bounce' after a terrible fall is small and brief.

Principle #5: Untie that second hand from behind your back: become able to sell short! (Heresy #2)

I dearly wanted to list this first but feared most readers would quickly turn the page. Undoubtedly you've noticed that stocks both rise and fall. Then why be biased and seek profit in only one of two available directions? Shorting is not unpatriotic, morally wrong, or foolish - just an underutilized tool. Stocks get overpriced (fundamentally) and overbought (technically) exactly as many times as they're cheap and oversold - because prices move in waves, whose tops and bottoms are equal in number. Don't cut your opportunity to half the distance prices move. Would you fervently eschew a raincoat or umbrella because the weather is fair more days than not? Discard this self-imposed limitation!

Tactic #1: Always, always sell all large-cap and high-P/E stocks before earnings are due to be reported!

Good news is rewarded only slightly, but disappointment drives immediate, steep price declines. So holding literally stacks the payoff odds against you. Institutional ownership raises the size of selling deluges, as does a long record of prior successes.

Today's minimal commissions make stepping aside before the event very cheap insurance. Besides, learning to place sell orders readily is good practice that will make this unfamiliar activity seem more natural over time. Internet databases list expected EPS-report dates; phone the company to check.

Tactic #2: Be nimble, or the crowd will surely trample you!

Neither buying nor selling is a for-life decision; learn doing both as readily as ordering lunch when the situation requires. Instantaneous worldwide internet transmission of fact and opinion means the crowd takes virtually no time to move a stock's price. To avoid consensual victimhood, you must move rapidly. Investors/traders are paid well to anticipate change, but badly for reacting with the crowd after new facts arise. Companies change, so your opinion and position must. Today's price already reflects whatever you'll find in print or databases; you are not the first to see it!

Tactic #3: Gracefully and promptly accept unreasonable profits!

Draw a line from your buy price and date to your target price and time. When fortuitous news, a major brokerage recommendation, favorable media coverage, or market euphoria shoots a stock notably above that line, sell! Not doing so means you're now accepting a lower future return rate from today to your target

Think opportunity cost of capital. You can always buy back. When the buying crowd swells well beyond normal that condition is unsustainable, so the stock must retreat. Understanding that, why hold on? Constantly ask if you'd buy today what you're presently holding, at today's price. (Holding is buying again!) What you'd not buy, you should sell.

Tactic #4: Rid your decision process of ego's misguiding influences!

Overcome perfectionism: humans cannot always be right or routinely get the best price. Admitting mistakes early reduces money loss and ego pain. Resist temptations to 'demand your money back'. Too many investors refuse to sell unless they get back every cent paid (for what has proved not a great choice). Meanwhile, many opportunities elude those 'locked in'. Why demand getting back those last few percents in your proven laggard? Think opportunity cost, not blind loss aversion!

Forget three irrelevant facts: what you paid for the stock (the worst mental anchor), what it sold for at its all-time high (now proven a market mistake by subsequent evidence), and its high since your purchase (a strong but often wrong goal). Stocks over-run both up and down. A high was a temporary price error, not a deserved value.

Tactic #5: Watch the wider world for clues that a trend reversal is due.

Not all relevant information about markets is found in the *Financial Times, The Times* or *The Wall Street Journal*. Watch humor and advertisements (whose success requires wide, understanding consensus) for signs of a bubbly, overconfident societal mindset. Cartoons, TV sitcoms, and print and electronic-media ads reflect well-established (late) trends. Do jokes feature easy riches (time to sell), or instead people leaping from bridges and windows (panic, a bottom)? When auto and holiday-trip ads refer to our market gains, time has come to hit the exits!

don.cassidy@lipper.reuters.com

Simon Cawkwell

Simon Cawkwell (otherwise known as Evil Knievil) is Britain's most feared bear-raider. A trained accountant, he made his name exposing the fiction that were Robert Maxwell's accounts.

Over the past ten years, during the greatest bull market in history, he has made money year in, year out from shorting stock - that is selling shares he does not own in order to buy them back more cheaply later.

Books

Profit of the Plunge, Rushmere Wynne, 1995
Evil's Good: Book of Boasts and Other Investments, t1ps.com Ltd, 2002
Bear Essentials: The Secrets of Forensic Accounting and Profitable Trading, t1ps.com Ltd, 2003

Advice from a short seller

1. Never buy shares with high valuations in relation to tangible net asset value.

They can swan along and upwards for years but they have no cushion for the bad times.

2. Never short-sell stocks when they are going up.

Wait until they are going down and never hesitate to kick them down should they be so impertinent as to make an emotional appeal for help.

3. Always treat any stockbroker who is remunerated with commission as a compulsive liar.

4. Work on the assumption that all regulators are completely useless.

Except, that is, at concealing their own incompetence such that the money you pay them for their 'services' cannot be reclaimed.

5. Be very suspicious of all mining companies run by stockbrokers.

But do not hesitate to buy such companies when they are new to the market. There is an infinite supply of fools to buy after you.

6. Accept that all men always lie.

But try to lie as little as possible.

7. When a man says that his word is his bond . . .

. . . take his bond.

8. If you do not understand an investment, prepare to short it.

There will always be a large number of gormless idiots who will have to sell after you so guaranteeing you a profit.

9. Borrow when others are not borrowing. Repay when others are not.

10. Never hesitate to bet against an odds-on favourite.

Edward Chancellor

Edward Chancellor is a financial journalist and author. After reading history at Cambridge and Oxford universities, he worked for Lazard Brothers in London. He has written freelance for a number of publications, including the *Financial Times* and *The Economist*, and is currently assistant editor at Breakingviews, the award-winning financial commentary service. He also writes for Fred Hickey's *High Tech Strategist*, Smithers & Co, and *Grant's Interest-Rate Observer*.

Books

Devil Take the Hindmost, MacMillan, 1999
Crunch Time for Credit?: An Inquiry into the State of the Credit System in the United States and Great Britain, Harriman House Publishing, 2005
Capital Account: Reports from a Contrarian Fund Manager, Texere Publishing,US, 2004

Lessons from history

---

1. 'Put all your eggs in one basket and watch that basket!'

This saying comes from Mark Twain, but has been applied to stock market investment more or less verbatim by both John Maynard Keynes and Warren Buffett. Modern portfolio theory suggests that one can reduce risk by diversification. However, it also suggests that the index represents the optimal portfolio, in which case one might as well purchase a tracker fund. However, most active investors would do better to concentrate their shareholdings in a limited number of companies which they feel they understand. This can actually reduce risk.

2. 'When the ducks quack, feed them.'

This is an old Wall Street adage relating to initial public offerings. Investment bankers are not driven by philanthropy or even by an intellectual motivation to understand the world of finance. They are out to make money and will sell the public anything within the bounds of the law. In recent years we have seen a flood of second-rate IPOs, most of which are now trading at below their offer price. Research suggests that, in general, IPOs rocket upwards on the first day's trading but tend to underperform comparable companies over a three-year period. Since small investors don't receive fair allocations of the best IPOs but are landed with the duds, they should avoid the new issue market entirely.

3. 'Markets make opinions, not the other way round.'

This is another Wall Street saying, which has been revived by James Grant, editor of *Grant's Interest Rate Observer*. When markets rise, commentators find a way of rationalising the gains. Take the recent bull market. We were told that the 'valuation clocks' were broken and that companies deserved to trade on a higher price-earnings ratio. We were also told that US productivity had risen and that the US would experience a higher growth rate in the past. We were also told that Greenspan *et al* would prevent another cyclical downturn. All these comments were spurious rationalisations of an 'irrationally exuberant' market.

4. 'Buy low, sell high.'

This advice seems obvious, but investors always ignore it. The demand curve for investment assets is like that for a luxury good - the higher the price, the greater the demand. Hence we see turnover rising during a bull market (when assets are getting more expensive) and falling during a bear market (when they are getting cheaper). Investors should always be prepared to act contrary to the market, and should always be prepared to question both the optimism at the top and the pessimism at the bottom.

5. 'When the rest of the world is mad, we must imitate them in some measure.'

This observation came from the mouth of an eighteenth-century banker, John Martin, during the South Sea Bubble of 1720. It is another expression of the 'greater fool' theory, namely that you can buy over-priced shares and sell them on at a profit to some sucker. This speculative attitude has been much in evidence in recent years in the form of momentum investing. Of course, you can make money if you find a greater fool, but you also will lose your money if you don't. Would you put $10,000 into a chain-letter? If the answer is no, then avoid momentum investing. Incidentally, Martin lost all his money when the bubble collapsed and complained miserably of being 'blinded by other people's advice'.

6. 'During a bull market nobody needs a broker. During a bear market nobody wants one.'

This is another Wall Street saying, cited recently by Alan Abelson in Barron's. An unkind English version comes in the form of a question: 'What's the difference between a good broker and a bad one?' Answer: 'Not a lot.' We are now more aware than ever that most brokerage research is generally of a low quality and that broker recommendations cannot be followed profitably. This has always been the case, but the problem is exacerbated by the conflicts created by uniting brokerage and corporate finance under the same investment bank roof. Investors should avoid reading research by brokers whose parent company provides financial services for the company concerned.

7. 'Every man his own broker.'

This is, in fact, the title of the first investment book, written by Thomas Mortimer in the 1750s. It was republished several times. If you can't trust brokers, you must replace them. The problem is that the private investor is not well-equipped to do so. He doesn't have access to company management and probably can't read financial accounts with any sophistication. As a result, he is likely to make decisions on whim, many of which will be regretted later at leisure. Bull markets are periods of 'people's capitalism' when the private investor figures prominently. Inevitably, the private investor gets burnt after the market collapses and withdraws from the market, handing it back to the professionals.

8. 'Markets can remain irrational longer than you can remain solvent.'

This saying comes from John Maynard Keynes, the great English economist. He was also an acute observer of markets and a speculator. Keynes held his stock-market investments on leverage and was an active player in the commodities market. It is sometimes said that he lost three fortunes, but made four. So he died rich. The point of Keynes's comment is that your observation may be fundamentally correct but it can take the market a long time to catch up. For example, the dotcom bubble ran for almost five years from the flotation of Netscape in the summer of 1995 to the Nasdaq collapse in March 2000. Many people lost a lot of money shorting the likes of eToys and Amazon.com before the market woke up to its absurd overvaluation of the sector.

9. 'A mine is a hole in the ground with a liar standing over it.'

This saying also comes from Mark Twain. It should remind investors to be wary of all projectors, whether they are promoting gold mines, biotech or some other new-fangled technology. In general, the promise of outsize profits are followed by the reality of painful losses. You will make more money in the long run by restraining your greed. Incidentally, Twain had a personal investment maxim: 'I never spotted an opportunity until it ceased to be one.'

10. 'Be diffident when others exalt, and with a secret joy buy when others think it in their interests to sell.'

This advice comes from the English writer, Sir Richard Steele, in an article for *The Spectator* in the early 1700s. To my knowledge it is the first expression of a contrarian investment philosophy. The art of investment lies in judiciously going against the crowd. It is both intellectually more fulfilling to refute the market consensus and in the long run should be more profitable. Academic research suggests that unloved 'value shares' tend to outperform so-called 'growth stocks' over the long run.

---

www.breakingviews.com

Moorad Choudhry

Moorad Choudhry is a vice-president with JP Morgan Chase in London.

Prior to joining JP Morgan, he traded gilts and sterling Eurobonds at ABN Amro Hoare Govett and Hambros Bank. He has lectured on the bond markets at International Faculty of Finance and London Guildhall University, and is a Fellow of the Centre for Mathematical Trading and Finance, City University Business School.

Books

The Bond and Money Markets, Butterworth-Heinemann, 2001
Bond Market Securities, FT Prentice Hall, 2001
Capital Market Instruments, FT Prentice Hall, 2001

Investing in bonds

The views, thoughts and opinions expressed in this article are those of the author in his individual capacity, and should not in any way be attributed to JP Morgan Chase, or to Moorad Choudhry as a representative, officer or employee of JP Morgan Chase.

1. The oldest rule in the book: diversify. Always have bonds in your portfolio.

Not all of your investments should be looking for the quick profit. That's high risk, and therefore unnecessary. In a bull market you're buying bonds at a lower relative price, but receiving a regular income (coupon) at a time when fewer and fewer equities pay dividends; when the stock market starts falling and we start the transformation to a bear market, your investment is exposed to less downside, and as interest rates start to fall you'll also register capital gain.

2. Go with the business cycle, not against it.

Familiarise yourself with the interest rate cycle. Corporate debt spreads are at their lowest at the top of the business cycle - not the best time to buy. In reality its easier to discern a slowing down economy than a falling market. A better way of looking at this is as the 'interest-rate cycle'. As interest rates start to fall and corporate debt spreads start to widen, the market entry point becomes clearer. What's the consensus with the interest rate cycle? The UK's Monetary Policy Committee has rarely, if ever, surprised the markets. So that means the market knows roughly where interest rates are going. So if the consensus is open knowledge, you can base your buy and sell decisions on the interest rate cycle. Contrast this with equities - its anybody's guess where the buy or sell point is.

3. Everyone should have a safe haven for a portion of their savings - hold government bonds like gilts.

Gilts outperformed UK equities in 1998 and 1999, but with none of the risk of any of the equities in the FTSE 100. That's a risk-reward combination that's unbelievable and unmatchable. It almost invariably makes sense to place some funds with this kind of product irrespective of where the market or the business cycle is.

4. Buy the downgrades, sell the upgrades.

The market is usually marking down debt ahead of any formal announcement by the ratings agencies. But not all the news is priced in; after a downgrade the sharp sell-off signals a buying opportunity, as spreads have already widened considerably and widen still further. Similarly its too late to buy after the upgrade announcement, which implies a sell signal. But keep an eye on the interest rate cycle.

5. Heed the credit rating, but look ahead of it.

The formal credit rating is there for a reason, so heed it. But consider the statistical probabilities. A BBB- or BB-rated company has more upside potential, statistically speaking, than an AA-rated company, which is unlikely to go much higher. So with the higher-rated company you're looking at smaller capital gain potential.

6. The current yield spread is telling you something - heed it.

Very wide spreads are there for a reason. So if you're holding the debt, sell it. If you're not, look at buying it. Check where the equity is trading: how is it viewed? But go with the fundamentals, not media fad.

7. Don't hold corporate debt if you don't like the corporate equity.

Simple psychology of the self: if you don't like the company full-stop, you're not going to like the company's debt, and you won't feel happy holding it.

8. Don't invest going into important announcements.

Markets are unpredictable. We know that. So don't make it any harder for yourself by buying, or indeed selling, just before an important announcement such as an FOMC meeting. Sit on your hands until after the announcement and then plan accordingly.

9. Corporate bond prices are good bell-weathers of corporate health generally. Use them as a guide for all your investment decisions.

Bond market analysts will tell you that, unlike equities, the bond market is a proper market. A greater fall in a company's bond price relative to other debt of the same sector, is a good indicator of the falling positive perception of the company's overall health and financial well-being.

10. Look at established names in a slowing economy or recession.

Corporate debt spreads widen in a slowing economy or recession. However established names (such as FTSE 100 companies, etc) are often viewed positively as the economy starts to recover, and their debt is a strong contender for upside growth as the economy starts to grow again. Consider buying into the market at this point.

11. When interest rates are historically high, buy bonds.

Check recent history. If interest rates are at historically high levels (go back say, three or five years), that means they will be going down at some point. It might be next week or next year, but they are going down. Jump on board now, sit back with your coupon income, and wait. A capital gain is a certainty. Especially with new issues.

12. Don't look for the bottom of the market, or for that matter the top.

It's very difficult to pick the bottom of any falling market. Look at the business cycle and interest rate cycle, and go with it. If you've lost confidence in your holding, sell it.

My one regret: Not joining Giles Fitzpatrick's equity sales team at Hoare Govett Securities Ltd in 1993, after being offered a job by him.

www.mchoudhry.co.uk

'Be sceptical of track records. There are so many funds and forecasts that at any point in time, someone has to have been right. With enough monkeys in the room, one of them will type out Hamlet. But it doesn't mean the same monkey will then go on to write Macbeth.'

Paul Ormerod

Robert Cole

Robert Cole is editor of the *Tempus* investment column in The Times newspaper. The column analyses UK companies and their share prices, and addresses investment themes relevant to industrial sectors and overseas stock markets.

Robert contributes to a variety of other financial media, including the web site www.equityeducation.com, and also lectures in financial journalism at The City University on a part time basis.

Books

Getting Started in Unit and Investment Trusts, John Wiley, 1997

The *Tempus* ten golden rules

1. Hail the herd.

Share prices rise when there are more buyers than sellers. They fall when sellers outnumber buyers. The consensus view is not always right but the actions of many usually tell a stronger story than an individual view. However, the best investment profits go to those who anticipate change and that means investors often need to swim against the tide.

2. Valuation, valuation, valuation.

If the three important things about retailing are location, location and location, the three important things about equity investment are *valuation, valuation* and *valuation.*

Value a share price in at least three ways: by reference to the underlying assets, the company's profitability, and the dividend income. In addition, there should be a close relationship between the price of a share and the total value of its future earnings, discounted to allow for the fact that money promised is worth less than money possessed. So undertake discounted cash flow calculations.

Do not confuse the strength of a company with value of a share. Shares in good companies are not always worth buying. It all depends on price.

3. The sentimental journey.

Share prices do move for reasons other than those dictated by the laws of fundamental valuation. Swings in investors' perceptions of value, or sentiment, can be as powerful as any fundamental strength. Share prices can also move because money chases particular stocks for technical reasons. Many large investors choose to structure their share portfolios to mirror the membership of a stock market index, such as the FTSE 100. Changes to the membership list of indices can influence share prices as investors buy or sell in volume.

4. On time.

Stock market history suggest that the reliable returns are generated by long term investors - those who invest for five years or more. However, the performance benchmarks that underpin faith in the reliability of rising share prices measure, largely, success stories. Failures can harm individual portfolios in a way which is minimised by the stock market indices. Remember also that the long term is made up from a series of short terms joined together. Get short term decisions right and the long term performance will be enhanced.

5. Hedge your bets.

Never underestimate investment risk and do everything you can to reduce it. Diversify across the investment four asset classes: cash, property, bonds and shares. And then diversify within each asset class. Diversify geographically and, with shares, bonds and property, between industrial sectors. Also diversify across time. Drip feed money into equities and equity-based savings plans and stage phased withdrawals. That way you reduce the chance of falling victim to the inherent volatilities of stock markets.

6. Costs equal losses.

The costs of investment - such as share dealing fees and professional management charges - can be a serious drag. But be prepared to pay for services that enhance performance. Money spent on good information is rarely wasted because good investors are informed investors.

7. Tip top tips.

Read newspapers and stockbrokers' research for the information first, and investment recommendations second. Journalists and analysts' key skill is information gathering and this is where they add most value. Treat tips for what they are: advice, not instructions. The position of tipsters does not guarantee the wisdom of their views and ask what axes they have to grind. Are stockbrokers independent? If tipsters are so good why are they trying to make a living telling others their secrets, rather than investing themselves? Make up your own mind and take responsibility for your decisions - better decisions lie that way.

8. Keep a distance.

Do not be too proud to recognise mistakes and learn from experience. Refrain from personalising your relationship with equities. Shares do not reciprocate affection so there is no need to invest loyalty as well as cash.

9. A taxing thought.

No tax break in the world is worth anything if the underlying investment is bum. And if an investment needs a tax incentive, does it mean it cannot justify itself on its own?

10. Rules are rubbish.

The stock market does not adhere to immutable laws of behaviour. Good rules may be contradicted by other good rules in a way which is perfectly consistent in the context of the wider picture. Investors need to be flexible in the analysis of opportunity.

tempus@the-times.co.uk

'New tech is always superseded by *newer* tech. Product cycles continue to shorten, and competition will remain excruciating. As in the past, today's new tech gizmos will become tomorrow's profitless commodities.'

Gary Shilling

Antoine Colonna

Antoine Colonna is the head of Merrill Lynch's Luxury Goods Equity Research team. He joined Merrill Lynch in 1999 from Crédit Lyonnais, where he held a similar position for eight years. Antoine and his team were named #3 in Institutional Investor's Global Equity Research on the sector this year and #2 for the second consecutive year as best analyst on Reuters' European Survey on Textile & Apparel.

The luxury goods sector

Introduction

The world luxury goods market is estimated to be worth $68bn in the broad sense, including wines and spirits selling at about $20 per bottle, with the market growing at an annual rate of 8%-12%. The sector is expected to continue growing at rates in excess of GNP in most developed nations in the foreseeable future, provided that no major world conflict reduces consumer confidence and air travel.

Ready-to-wear designer clothing is the largest segment (26%), followed by Leather & Accessories (17%), Wines & Spirits (15%), Cosmetics (12%), Fragrances (12%), Watches (9%), Jewellery (5%) and Tableware (4%). Geographically, the industry is now quite well balanced between the different continents: North America 30%, Asia 36% and Europe 34%.

1. Note the strong correlation between global GDP growth and sales for the luxury goods sector.

The dynamics of the luxury goods sector are strongly correlated to the macro-economic environment. 1999 was marked by a stronger than expected rebound of Asian economies (excluding Japan) and by vigorous growth in the US. The millennium effect also boosted demand especially in segments like jewellery, watches and tableware. Equity markets exert a strong influence on the fortunes of the sector, especially in the US.

2. Value for money has always been important.

The purchase of luxury goods is often associated with the desire for higher social and/or economic status. This may well be one of the motives, but ironically customers are also motivated to buy luxury goods because they feel that they offer value for money.

Many of the brands that are seen as fashion or status icons - for example Hermes leather goods, Louis Vuitton luggage, and even Chanel's classic designs - built their reputations by offering value for money. Their high quality seemed to justify their comparatively high price. Looking forward, consumers will continue to pay very high prices for quality and for top design, but will disregard brands that cannot fulfil these criteria.

3. Value for money is becoming *more* important.

Capacity to provide goods that seem to offer value for money will be a crucial factor in determining likely levels of profitability. Some segments of the industry - for example, watches and leather goods - are much more profitable than others. Because most of the established luxury brand companies are likely to move into these highly profitable areas, customers should have a plethora of choice - and will opt for the brand which seems to offer the best quality and value for money.

4. Consolidation is inevitable.

The luxury goods market is extremely fragmented and there is powerful pressure for consolidation. The biggest companies in the sector will reinforce their market share significantly in the coming years, both through organic and external growth.

Unlike other consumer goods, it is difficult - near impossible - to replicate the established success of a luxury brand, so companies that want to establish a presence in a segment quickly have little choice but to buy their way in. Vertical integration both downstream into retail and upstream into manufacturing also enables groups to capture larger margins and exercise more precise management of the brand.

5. Control over distribution is a major factor in competitive advantage.

Over the past few years, distribution control and its corollary - 'measured product scarcity' - have progressively emerged as the key factors for success within the industry. There is a clear correlation between the performance of the most successful brands (Vuitton, Cartier, Gucci, Prada, etc.) and the degree of control they exercise over their boutiques, stores, franchises and wholesale accounts.

The benefits of strong distribution are not only in making sure the products reach the right market, but also in protecting the value of the brand and the pricing policy.

6. Traditionally high levels of profitability may come under pressure.

One of the features that singles out the luxury goods industry from other consumer businesses is the high level of profitability that most of its segments enjoy. Over the next five years, margins could come under pressure as established companies penetrate all segments and tempt younger and less well-established companies to overspend to improve their brand awareness.

Having said that, a number of companies have scope for better margins as free cashflow is often used to buy out franchisees, and the ongoing consolidation allows multi-brand conglomerates to jump-start cross-selling initiatives. This should help margins or at least balance out the possible pressure coming from higher levels of marketing spending.

7. Japanese consumers are key.

The industry's largest single geographic market is Asia, and more specifically Japan. The Japanese are the largest single body of luxury goods consumers. Sales in Japan account for an estimated 20% of total sales.

If it is assumed that Japanese people travelling abroad buy about 40% of the luxury goods sold in Europe then sales - and a similar level of profits - to Japanese consumers worldwide account for a more sizeable 32%-35% share of the total. Moreover, Japanese customers may account for up to 60% of the total market for certain goods and even more for certain markets (Hawaii, Guam, Saipan). While Japan represents the single largest market in Asia, markets in other countries, such as Korea, Taiwan and China, are growing rapidly.

8. The internet poses challenges to brand management.

Luxury goods' distribution is based on service, product scarcity and brand awareness. E-Commerce is based on price rebates, order fulfilment and volumes. For luxury goods companies, therefore, the internet will be a test in terms of increasing brand awareness while refraining from brand dilution.

Brands characterised by tightly-held distribution are well placed to control the consumer experience and be profitable online in the medium term. In absolute terms, the so-called 'low touch' product categories (ready-to-wear, basic accessories, perfumes/cosmetics, wines and spirits) are likely to sell better than 'high touch' ones (shoes, high jewellery).

antoine_colonna@ml.com

'Stocks that lead the rally to the top in late stages of bull markets aren't likely to lead the rally off the bottom in late stages of bear markets. Newer, smaller, and faster-growing companies rise to the top.'

John Rothchild

Tim Congdon

Professor Tim Congdon founded Lombard Street Research, the economic research and forecasting consultancy, in 1989, and is currently its Chief Economist.

He was a member of the Treasury Panel of Independent Forecasters (the so-called 'wise men') between 1992 and 1997, which advised the Chancellor of the Exchequer on economic policy.

Economic drivers of asset prices

Introduction

What are the ultimate drivers of asset prices? Perhaps no question in investment management is more basic or more disputed. But some rules are reliable, as they depend ultimately only on economic common sense. Five are proposed below, although they are best understood as broadly correct generalisations which need, in particular circumstances, to be interpreted with care. The first rule cannot really be disputed and the next four follow, more or less, as a matter of logic.

1. Nations cannot make themselves rich by printing more money.

This is simply an elaboration of the obvious statement, "there is no such thing as a free lunch". (Investment bank clients may sometimes think their lunches are free, but they are kidding themselves.) A crucial implication is that, however fast the money supply increases, it cannot make people better-off in the long run. The excess monetary expansion is dissipated in higher prices.

A fair generalisation is that, over periods of many decades, the growth of the money supply is related - although not identical - to the growth of nominal gross domestic product.

2. High inflation is associated with high money supply growth.

This is an extension of the first rule. As bonds have to offer a positive real return if they are to attract investors, high money supply growth is also associated with high bond yields. The crucial investment messages are, 'if money supply growth is high and rising, sell bonds' and, conversely, 'if money supply growth is low and falling, buy bonds'.

A good illustration is provided by Britain in 1972 and 1973, when the annual rate of money supply growth soared into the mid-20s ahead of an appalling bear market in gilt-edged bonds (and other asset classes, including equities and commercial property) in 1974.

3. High money supply growth is likely when banks have ample capital and can easily expand their balance sheets by extending new credit.

This is because the money supply consists mostly of banks' deposit liabilities. Further, a well-capitalised and highly profitable (an under-capitalised and unprofitable) banking system is bad (good) for bond yields, because it will try to grow quickly (contract), which will add to (subtract from) both bank credit and the quantity of money.

Japan in the 1990s exemplifies the argument. The banks suffered severe loan losses as the bubble of the late 1980s unravelled in the early 1990s. The result was a crippled banking system, a decade of stagnant bank credit and low money supply growth, and a decline in inflation which eventually became a deflation. Bond yields collapsed to the lowest ever recorded in modern times, with the yield on ten-year government debt hovering a little above 1 per cent for a few years.

4. Although high money supply leads to more inflation in the long run, it may not do so in the short run for all sorts of reasons.

Two common reasons are that the economy has a big margin of spare capacity ahead of the monetary injection or that it enjoys heavy capital inflows which cause exchange rate appreciation.

In these cases high money growth may for several quarters be accompanied by low inflation, encouraging investors to believe that the economy has achieved some sort of 'miracle'. The bubbles in the Asian stock markets in 1993 and in the USA's NASDAQ stocks in 1999 and early 2000 can be interpreted in these terms.

The rational investor has a difficult problem with bubbles like these. On the one hand, he knows that they must come to an end. (To repeat, there is no such thing as a free lunch.) On the other hand, an investment adviser who misses a big asset bubble may lose all his clients in the short run, while trying to prove to them that he is right in the long run. In monetary economics the short run and the long run are like Punch and Judy, and squabble with each other endlessly.

5. For any given rate of money supply growth, a large budget deficit is likely to do more damage to asset prices than a small budget deficit.

The reason is that the non-monetary financing of large budget deficits requires high short-term interest rates. High interest rates are unhelpful for medium- and long-dated bond yields, and so for other asset classes. The ideal conditions for a stock market boom are a falling budget deficit, low inflation, moderate but rising money supply growth, and a well-capitalised and profitable banking system. That is a fair description of the USA in the five years to 1999, which saw the biggest equity bull market in history. The most serious threat to a bull market of this kind is rising inflation, as indeed has been recorded in 2000 and 2001.

www.lombardstreetresearch.com

'Privatization has made a great impact in the UK. The impact is only starting to be felt in much of the euro area. As inefficient state enterprises are moved to the private sector, look for efficiency gains to generate attractive returns to stockholders.'

Paul Temperton

Laurence Copeland

Laurence Copeland holds the Chair of Finance at Cardiff University. His papers in academic journals cover a range of subjects including: inflation and the Phillips Curve, exchange rates and currency markets, stock and bond markets, index futures, mutual funds, Asian markets and the impact of the 1997-8 crisis.

Books

Exchange Rates and International Finance (3rd ed.), Pearson Education, 2000
Exchange Rates and International Finance (4th ed.), FT Prentice Hall, 2004

Currencies

---

1. All things in moderation, especially greed.

Don't try too hard to buy at the bottom and sell at the top. Either be a long term investor, holding through ups and downs, or be prepared to sell out when you have made a reasonable profit, even if you subsequently find you could have done better by holding on. A short term investor is a gambler, so he or she should be ready to leave something on the table when they leave.

2. Market gurus repeat themselves, but history never does.

The past often seems to provide hints about the future, but usually the hints are unreliable signposts. So exchange rates may always have risen when the central bank raised interest rates, but that doesn't mean it'll be the same this time around. Like the weather, there are always new records being set, and that means precedents are no help.

3. "Ripeness is all" (Shakespeare).

The fruit falls when it's ripe. Any later and it goes rotten. Timing is everything, in the markets as elsewhere - something economists often forget. For example, it didn't take a genius to figure out that tech stocks were overvalued long before the peak of the boom. But you could have lost a lot of money going short on the way up, and several fund managers lost their jobs because they kept out of the market bonanza. Another example is the overvaluation of the US dollar in the first half of the 1980's. So figuring out which stocks or currencies are mispriced is no help. The key to making money is knowing when the mispricing is going to be corrected (or, as is usually the case, overcorrected).

4. The more extreme the conditions, the more efficient the market.

The higher the inflation rate, the more rationally the money and currency markets behave, perhaps because the cost of getting it wrong is simply too high. So, in the extreme cases of hyperinflation, every 1% rise in the inflation rate leads almost immediately to an increase in interest rates and fall in the value of the currency.

5. Fixed exchange rates: the triumph of hope over experience.

No fixed exchange rate ever stayed fixed forever. At some point, the system offers speculators a one-way bet. Why not take it?

6. The predictive power of forward rates is more or less nil.

Forward rates simply track spot rates. The forward premium or discount is no guide to whether a currency is going to appreciate or depreciate.

7. Long calm spells, punctuated by stormy periods.

Even with a floating exchange rate, a currency market will often seem to have gone to sleep, with nothing much happening for months or years. Invariably a storm will blow up sooner or later, with a sudden sequence of high volatility days, often with no obvious news to trigger the activity.

8. The Anglo-Saxon Block.

The English-speaking currencies (Pound, US and Canadian Dollars) move together most of the time, in the Northern hemisphere at least. In particular, the Pound and the Dollar are highly correlated, and membership of the EU and the single market (and the foundation of NAFTA) seems to have made little difference to this pattern.

9. Don't bet against the dollar . . .

It's not that it will never again fall from its pedestal. It's simply that we don't know when. So, as long as the US was booming, all the pundits said the strong economy was pushing up the dollar's value. When the US economy took a dive in Winter 2000-1, what happened? You guessed right, the dollar was even stronger. A safe haven in a world threatened by an impending US recession, many pundits said. Hence, the final piece of advice . . .

10. . . . get a job as a currency guru.

The great thing about mission impossible is that nobody expects you to be successful. Failing to work miracles is not adequate ground for dismissal. The pay is good too.

www.cf.ac.uk/carbs/econ/copelandl/

Richard Cragg

Richard Cragg has over 30 years' experience in investment, spanning financial centres in three continents, and has consistently been at the forefront of opening up new and emerging markets to investors.

Books
The Demographic Investor,
FT Prentice Hall, 1998

Demographic investment

---

1. Crisis equals opportunity.

Almost forty years of falling birth rates coupled with rising life expectancy have created ageing populations throughout the developed world. Economists predict serious consequences in the decades ahead:

- Declining workforces, leading to slower output growth and wealth creation.
- Fewer workers supporting more pensioners, leading to steep rises in taxes and National Insurance to pay for rising state pensions and health provisions - or a decline in expenditure on them.

Demographic investment techniques provide the tools to turn this emerging crisis into an investment opportunity, enabling investors to devise long term pension strategies that actually benefit from ageing populations. In conjunction with other screening tools, it can help select which countries and sectors offer the best growth.

2. Manners maketh man, but money moveth markets.

Only buying and selling move share prices. Whether money is invested directly or via mutual funds and pension schemes, it has first to be generated in the form of discretionary income - what's left after paying for the house, the car and family outlays on food, clothing etc. - and this depends on your age.

3. Some age groups can save more than others.

As individuals move through life, their earnings and consumption patterns change markedly over the years. Until their first job, they are significant net consumers, and while earning capacity might then rise substantially until their mid-40s, their savings generally do not, since they have acquired partners, children and mortgages in the meantime. By their mid-50s however, despite a marked slowdown in wage growth, their discretionary income takes a Great Leap Forward, as the mortgage is paid off, school fees finish and the kids leave home. This age group is also likely to receive sizeable legacies from their parents. It is the growth of the 45-55 age group relative to the young and elderly dependents that determines changes in a population's discretionary income.

4. Goldilocks demographics - not too young, not too old.

What constitutes an ideal age profile? A country where both the workforce and the proportion of 45-55 year-olds is growing rapidly but the proportion of retirees is small relative to the workforce and not growing rapidly. Choose your countries carefully, because your pension depends on it. If you choose Japan, you'll be working until you're 100.

5. Surfing the demographic waves.

Demographics allows us to project population breakdowns for 20 years into the future with a fair degree of accuracy, enabling investors to switch from a country where savings growth is slowing into one where the savings wave that will power the next market boom is building.

6. A demographic road map.

Japan's demographic wave crested a decade ago and is still in decline. Germany and Italy become similarly dangerous after 2005, the UK and France after 2010, and the US after 2015. But the big bet from now to 2020 is China, where collapsing birth rates will create a huge bulge in the proportion of 45-55 year-olds.

7. Selecting the sectors.

In a world where annual births are static, you won't make your fortune investing in baby clothes companies. Follow the growth age groups; they're buying holidays, hollyhocks, healthcare and hearing aids. If you can select consumer items that are in growing demand from an ageing population but are benefiting from new technologies (digital hearing aids) or patent protection (drugs for diabetes, osteoporosis, cancer and heart disease), you should do well.

rcragg@nclinvestments.com

Anthony Crescenzi

Tony Crescenzi is Chief Bond Market Strategist at Miller Tabak + Co., LLC, an
institutional brokerage firm that deals with major institutional investors. His ability to dissect the markets and provide information in ways that people can understand has made him one of Wall Street's most widely quoted analysts. He appears frequently on CNBC, CNNfn and Bloomberg-TV.

Books

The Strategic Bond Investor: Strategies and Tools to Unlock the Power of the Bond Market, McGraw-Hill Publishing Co, 2002

The bond market's 'crystal ball'

1. What are the top indicators to follow for a prelude to a bull market in stocks and a strong economy?

There's a cavalcade of indicators that investors watch to try to gleam where the markets might be headed next. There are a few that I find invaluable. It is important, however, to look at them collectively, as there is no one indicator that is a crystal ball. You should follow: weekly mortgage applications, car sales, weekly chain store sales, the money supply, business inventories, the yield curve, and the spread between low-grade bonds and U.S. Treasuries or other high-grade securities.

2. What are the ten biggest factors that impact the shape of the yield curve?

There are a variety of forces that impact the shape of the yield curve. While the relative importance of each of these factors frequently changes, there are ten factors that have been and will likely continue to be the most influential for years to come:

Monetary policy and market expectations on future Fed policy
The level of economic growth
Fiscal policy
Inflation expectations
The behavior of the U.S. dollar
Flights to quality and the general level of investors' risk aversion
Perceptions about credit quality in the financial system
Competition for capital between bonds and other asset classes
Debt buy-backs by the U.S. Treasury department
Portfolio shifts to reflect the markets' level of bullishness/bearishness

3. What is the best way to gauge sentiment in the bond market?

There are several indicators that I use to gauge investor sentiment in the bond market. Over time, these indicators have reliably forecasted important turns in the bond market and hence, the stock market.

The call/put ratio on T-bond futures
The most reliable and widely tracked options to use in this regard are the bond options that trade at the CBOT. Although the supply of U.S. treasury bonds is shrinking, speculators still flock to T-bond futures to place their bets on the bond market. Using the 10-day average, a call/put ratio of over 1.4:1 has reliably signaled tops in the bond market and a call/put below 0.8:1 has reliably signaled bottoms.

Aggregate duration surveys
These surveys measure the extent to which bond portfolio managers are either long or short. Duration, a seemingly obtuse term, is simply a way to gauge risk. Portfolio managers generally maintain duration between 95% and 105% of their benchmark, usually the Lehman index. Aggregate duration at the extremes have reliably signaled turning points.

The 2-year T-note
Most don't see the 2-year as a benchmark maturity but it is. The biggest signal that the 2-year T-note gives pertains to the bond market's sentiment toward the Federal Reserve. Over time, the 2-year has been a reliable indicator mainly because of its stable relationship to the fed-funds rate, the rate controlled by the Fed. During periods when the 2-year has deviated from its historical relationship, this has pointed to the bond market's true underlying feelings about the future direction of Fed policy.

4. How can I become a better Fed watcher?

Being a Fed watcher boils down to tracking the verbiage spewed by the FOMC - that cast of 13, including Greenspan, who vote on whether to raise or lower interest rates at FOMC meetings. One of the things that I tell people to do, and that many top investors already do, is read the text of the Fed's speeches. Another is to look for key phrases that are repeated in lockstep by several Fed members. When I see a particular phrase used either verbatim or nearly so by a few members, I always sense that the phrase is a representation of current Fed policy. So, cracking this mystery is easy, since you know all of the key players and you know what they're thinking.

5. Use of the yield curve to predict economic and financial events?

The closest thing that the bond market has to a crystal ball is the yield curve. For decades it has foreshadowed major events and turning points in both the financial markets and the economy. The yield curve is basically a chart that plots the yields on bonds carrying different maturities usually ranging from 3 months to 30 years. When bond investors analyze the yield curve to try to glean its meaning, they look at the difference between yields on short-term securities compared to that of long-term securities.

First, if it is 'positively sloped' this is usually an indication that the Federal Reserve's monetary policy stance is and will likely continue to be friendly toward the markets. That is why the yield on short-term maturities is lower than on longer maturities (the Fed controls short-term interest rates). A friendly Fed is usually good news to stocks and to the economy. So a steepening yield curve generally forebodes good times for investors over a several quarter horizon.

On the other hand, a 'negatively sloped' yield curve usually indicates that Fed policy is unfriendly, with the Fed engaged in a strategy to slow the economy by raising short-term interest rates. This, of course, generally portends a gloomier set of conditions for the equity market as well as the economy. In fact, since 1970 every inverted yield curve has been followed by a period in which S&P 500 earnings growth was negative.

The yield curve is thought to be a better predictor of the economy than the stock market and can therefore give you an edge if you follow it.

6. Don't be bullish just because you're long!

Have you ever found yourself rooting for x and y to happen so that your investments might go your way? Does your portfolio rather than your investment criteria sometimes determine your next trade? In other words, do you find yourself bullish because you are long instead of long because you are bullish. If you answered yes to any of the above questions, you're not alone.

Investors seem to have a knack for letting their portfolios affect their investment decisions and seem to forget who's in charge. This was certainly the case for many dotcom investors in 2000, as there was no true basis for being bullish on these stocks. Next time you find yourself in a losing trade, ask yourself - truly ask yourself why you are long.

7. You can't put *being right* in the bank!

It's amazing how many people talk about how rich they could be "if only" they had acted when they didn't or "if only" they had been more alert when trading opportunities were passing them by. These same people think it is just their bad luck that prevents them from those really great trades that always seem to be making somebody else rich. This performance disparity is often the result of excessive rational thinking. You know the feeling. You are contemplating an investment, and contemplating, and contemplating but then for a number of supposed prudent reasons, you rationalize yourself out of the trade. The end result is inaction and, perhaps, another missed opportunity. So the next time you find yourself saying, "if only", remind yourself that you will be a successful trader "only if" you act on your ideas. Always remember: you can't put being right in the bank!

8. Assess your physical condition when trading!

Most athletes approach their competitive challenges with some form of cognitive assessment of their physical ability to compete. After all, their ultimate success or failure depends upon it. In the same way, every trader should assess the impact that their physical well-being might have upon their mental abilities during a given trading day. A tired body could result in an impaired ability to trade with the mental reflexes necessary to react and respond correctly to news, information, and events. Thus, approach the trading day like an athlete would approach a competition and assess your readiness for the day. If for any reason you feel that you're not at your level best, make adjustments.

9. Trade on your terms!

Would a driver who enjoys the challenge and thrill of negotiating a winding road at high speeds engage in such a challenge when driving conditions are poor, say, when roads are icy? In baseball, would a low-ball homerun hitter break from his upper-cutting swing to chop at high-ball pitches? Would a featherweight boxer arrange to fight a heavyweight and expect to win by KO in the first round? No chance on all counts! You should ask the very same questions when you are trading and investing.

You should pose questions such as: How do I normally fare in this type of investment? How have I fared in this type of trading environment? Should I exercise patience and wait for a better opportunity? Is the current level of market volatility a risk or a boon to my style of trading? Do I normally excel under these conditions? Or am I, perhaps, more apt to get chopped up?

You don't *have* to trade, so don't if you're not comfortable. Why risk playing under conditions that don't suit you? So don't put your pedal to the floor when you are on an icy road. Be selective. Stay away from trades and investments that don't work for you. You are in control of those black and red, buy and sell tickets. Trade on your terms!

---

www.bondtalk.com

Anthony Cross

Anthony Cross manages Liontrust Intellectual Capital Trust, a fund which invests in smaller companies using precepts which evolved from 'The Cross Report'. The Cross Report argued that intellectual capital and employee equity participation are of paramount importance in successful companies.

The investment attractions of intellectual capital

Introduction

If asked to list a company's assets, most people would probably give the accountants list of plant and equipment, property, raw materials, stocks, finished goods and cash. Whilst these assets are important, they are rarely unique and they represent a declining proportion of the value of companies. Research by Deutsche Bank shows that over the last ten years, the value of intangible assets has become a much greater proportion of total enterprise value. Fixed assets now comprise only 16% of the enterprise value of an average company compared with 42% in 1989.

So what are these intangible assets that enable companies to add value to their products and services and thereby retain pricing power? The answer is *intellectual capital*: it is frequently difficult to replicate, and its successful exploitation lies at the heart of today's growth companies.

1. Finding good investments should not be easy.

The world is becoming more competitive. More competition means that there are fewer good investments.

2. Look for intellectual capital assets, such as customer relationships and intellectual property.

They are the most important assets in companies. Competitors find it difficult to replicate these intangible assets.

3. Make sure directors and employees own shares.

Intellectual capital assets are created and exploited by employees. Equity ownership helps retain employees and aligns their interests with those of outside shareholders.

4. Target companies with proven organic growth.

Organic growth is the clearest evidence of success. Be wary of those who need to acquire growth.

5. Beware of companies that claim to be an exception to the rule.

Companies rarely miss out on wider negative industry trends.

6. Declining margins during a time of economic stability are a sell signal.

Companies that are difficult to replicate should earn superior returns but they will also attract competition.

7. Sell when directors make material equity sales.

Ignore their stated optimism for the company.

8. Protect the downside.

Think about what could go wrong as well as right and limit the size of your bet accordingly.

9. Spread your bets.

Investing is about protecting wealth as well as adding to it. Companies are valued on a multiple of optimism. When optimism turns to pessimism share prices collapse. Today's winner could be tomorrow's loser.

10. Be patient.

A good bet might take a couple of years to attract the attention of the broader market.

---

www.liontrust.co.uk

Lawrence Cunningham

Professor Cunningham is Director of The Samuel and Ronnie Heyman Center on Corporate Governance, and Professor of Law and Business at Cardozo Law School. He has taught and lectured widely in the US and to investor groups in London. He also serves as a consultant to corporate boards of directors, law and accounting firms, and regulatory and standard-setting bodies.

Books

The Essays of Warren Buffett (editor), John Wiley, 2000
How to Think like Benjamin Graham and Invest like Warren Buffett, McGraw-Hill, 2000
How to Think Like Benjamin Graham and Invest Like Warren Buffett, McGraw Hill Higher Education, 2002

The investing methods of Warren Buffett

1. Don't be the patsy.

If you cannot invest intelligently, the best way to own common stocks is through an index fund that charges minimal fees. Those doing so will beat the net results (after fees and expenses) enjoyed by the great majority of investment professionals. As they say in poker, 'If you've been in the game 30 minutes and you don't know who the patsy is, you're the patsy'.

2. Operate as a business analyst.

Do not pay attention to market action, macroeconomic action, or even securities action. Concentrate on evaluating businesses.

3. Look for a big moat.

Look for businesses with favorable long term prospects, whose earnings are virtually certain to be materially higher 5, 10, 20 years from now.

4. Exploit Mr. Market.

Market prices gyrate around business value, much as a moody manic depressive swings from euphoria to gloom when things are neither that good nor that bad. The market gives you a price, which is what you pay, while the business gives you value and that is what you own. Take advantage of these market mis-pricings, but don't let them take advantage of you.

5. Insist on a margin of safety.

The difference between the price you pay and the value you get is the margin of safety. The thicker, the better. Berkshire's purchases of the Washington Post Company in 1973-74 offered a very thick margin of safety (price about 1/5 of value).

6. Buy at a reasonable price.

Bargain hunting can lead to purchases that don't give long-lasting value; buying at frenzied prices will lead to purchases that give very little value at all. It is better to buy a great business at fair price than a fair business at great price.

7. Know your limits.

Avoid investment targets that are outside your circle of competence. You don't have to be an expert on every company or even many - only those within your circle of competence. The size of the circle is not very important; knowing its boundaries, however, is vital.

8. Invest with 'sons-in-law'.

Invest only with people you like, trust and admire - people you'd be happy to have your daughter marry.

9. Only a few will meet these standards.

When you see one, buy a meaningful amount of its stock. Don't worry so much about whether you end up diversified or not. If you get the one big thing, that is better than a dozen mediocre things.

10. Avoid gin rummy behavior.

This is the opposite of possibly the most foolish of all Wall Street maxims: *'You can't go broke taking a profit'*. Imagine as a stockholder that you own the business and hold it the way you would if you owned and ran the whole thing. if you aren't willing to own a stock for 10 years, don't even think about owning it for 10 minutes.

www.cardozo.yu.edu/heyman

Frank Curzio

Frank Curzio founded F.X.C. Investors Corp. in 1974 and has been a money manager since 1988. With over 25 years of experience in the financial industry, Mr. Curzio has become one of the most well-known analysts on Wall Street as well as one of the most quoted.

Books

Awareness of Indirection, Vantage Press, 1987

Safeguards and buying opportunities

1. Speculate with a small portion of your funds.

Preferably only 30% in aggressive situations. Invest a little to make a lot, and not a lot to make a little.

2. Do not buy on margin.

All securities involve risk. Some of the most prestigious and highest rated 'A' securities have had temporary devastating plunges. (Sears Roebuck from $61 to $15, Con Edison from $18 to $3, GM, Ford and Citicorp A rated bonds from $1,000 to $490, etc.). If a stock drops 50%, given time it may come back and may trade over your original cost.

3. The best buying opportunities usually prevail when a company reports lower earnings and when adverse economic news is widespread.

Purchase of stocks immediately after glowing earnings reports or optimistic press releases often results in buying at the top.

4. Only invest in companies audited by one of the big five accounting firms.

These accounting firms audit about 90% of the companies listed on the New York Stock Exchange (NYSE). Their clients account for most of all sales in the U.S. and approximately 90% of corporate income taxes. There are over 10,000 public corporations trading on the various stock exchanges and in the over-the-counter markets. One of the leading reasons why investors lose money is due to financial statements that are not prepared in accordance with Federal regulations (Section 13 or 15 (d) of the Securities Act of 1934). If the figures are incorrect, your investment in the stock is subjected to substantial or complete loss.

5. Watch company credit ratings.

Institutional fund managers pay close attention to credit rating from agencies such as S&P and Moody's. Increases in credit ratings ultimately result in higher quotes due to additional monies available for investment in these stocks. Decrease in ratings usually result in lower stock quotes.

6. Exploit institutional window-dressing.

The institutional funds represent approximately 80% of all monies in the U.S. market. The managers of these funds must answer to their shareholders and superiors - mutual pension funds are required to issue quarterly reports to their respective shareholders. Near the end of the quarter, stocks which were down or close to their yearly lows, are usually sold by the institutions (so they do not show as holdings in the quarterly report), causing even lower stock quotes. And stocks near their highs are purchased, thus enforcing higher quotes.

If you choose to purchase a stock because it is low, wait until after the end of the quarter. Chances are, it will be trading lower. Of course, there is no guarantee the stock will not trade even lower in the upcoming quarter. If you are going to bottom-fish, be patient. Or, if you want to sell a stock that is trading near its high, chances are it will be higher just before the quarter ends.

www.FXCNewsletter.com

Ray Dalio

Ray Dalio is President and Chief Investment Officer of Bridgewater Associates, a global investment manager with over $34 billion in assets under management. Bridgewater follows a fundamental and quantitative approach to investment decision-making. All investment criteria are thoroughly researched and systemized. Fundamental analysis is supported by advanced risk management techniques. This approach has led to Bridgewater's top decile performance.

Systemizing fundamentals

Introduction

There are some general principles that most winners of this game employ that losers neglect. If you want to win any game, you must know what the principles of the game are, and then work to develop the required skills - e.g. counting the cards and calculating odds for poker. What I describe here is my approach to playing the game, which is a mix of these general principles and my own twists on them. For me, the following are required.

1. A deep understanding of the fundamentals so that pricing inefficiencies can be identified.

Adding value (getting a return greater than that available from passive investing) requires one to see how markets are mispriced, and this requires an understanding of how they should be priced. This is required to be a winner over time. It is the equivalent of being able to count cards and calculate the odds of a winning hand in poker - it is the fundamental assessment that allows you to discern a good bet from a bad one.

Some people say that understanding the fundamentals isn't required and that one can play and win the game by playing it technically. If by technical they mean an approach that is devoid of understanding fundamental cause-effect relationships - like trend following - then I believe that they are wrong. Sometimes markets trend, and sometimes they chop, and they do so for reasons. So, without an understanding of these reasons, one will be blindly betting that markets trend more than they chop. Do markets trend more than they chop? This is one of those cosmic questions that can't be definitely answered, and certainly not without an understanding of the fundamentals that determine market behavior.

There is no escaping the need to have a deep understanding of the fundamentals so that one can sensibly assess what is cheap and what is expensive. In playing poker, I would rather place my bet based on my ability to count the cards and calculate odds than on the likelihood of a hot streak continuing (e.g. betting that I will do well because I won the last few hands).

2. Focus.

Adding value is a zero-sum game - for me to add value I must be a better player than my opponents. The markets are extremely competitive. That means that my understanding must be very deep, which requires focus. I have rarely seen investors that win over time who trade a lot of different markets. The winners I know discuss their markets with the same depth that specialists in other professions (e.g. physicians, scientists, etc.) discuss the subjects of their focus.

In addition, successful market players have the capacity to think conceptually and independently. Equipped with knowledge and perspective, they can justifiably have the confidence to stand apart from the crowd, which is essential for being able to buy low and sell high.

3. Perspective without data-mining.

Many years ago I did a lot of discretionary trading based on the flow of information I was seeing at the time. I wrote down the criteria I used to make each trade so that I could reflect on the trade later. I learned that if I specified the criteria clearly I could see how these criteria would have worked in the past, and in different countries, which gave me perspective. That perspective was invaluable.

In many cases I learned that the criteria wouldn't have worked in the past and I could see why. In other cases I learned how well my decision rule worked so that I would not abandon it when it lost (all rules lose sometime) or put too much on it because it has recently been hot and I thought it was better than it really was. As a result, I developed a good sense of what I could expect from my criteria.

I learned that I could program the computer to scan the world for opportunities, according to these criteria. And I learned a lot more. I learned to be especially wary about data mining - to not go looking for what would have worked in the past, which will lead me to have an incorrect perspective. Having a sound fundamental basis for making a trade, and an excellent perspective concerning what to expect from that trade, are the building blocks that have to be combined into a strategy.

4. Strategy.

Knowing how to identify good bets is only the first step. Knowing how to balance these bets - how much to place to on each based on their different expected returns, risks and correlations - is at least as important. This requires an understanding of probabilities, statistics, and money management principles. It requires the ability to simulate how this strategy would have worked in the past and to stress test its performance under varying conditions.

5. Substantial resources.

The days that an astute individual trader equipped with little more that his wits, being able to be a substantial winner at this game are over. Now, world class teams consisting of conceptual thinkers suppported by specialists and advanced technology set the standard of play. While technology has radically advanced the average level of play, in markets as in warfare, it has served to widen the gap between the resource-rich and the resource-constrained players.

---

www.bwater.com

'Buy and hold strategies generally are less rewarding than trading strategies. The cliché that *markets can't be timed* may be right for some investors all of the time, and for all investors some of the time, but there are times when market prices are far above or far below their long run equilibrium prices.'

Robert Aliber

Alexander Davidson

Alexander Davidson used to work as a share dealer, specialising in small, high-growth companies. Disillusioned with the biased advice that some City firms gave clients, he quit his job to write *The City Share Pushers*, a best-selling exposé which was made into a TV documentary and formed the basis of a motion on City practices in the House of Commons. Davidson now writes for *International Financing Review*, which specialises in new issues, and *Vanguard Investor*, which specialises in high tech stocks.

Books
The City Share Pushers
How to Win in a Volatile Stock Market, Kogan Page, 2000
Stock Market Rollercoaster, John Wiley, 2001

How to avoid being a victim of stock manipulation

1. Do not over-trade.
It will cost you a fortune in commission costs. This is why most day traders lose money.

2. Never buy only on share tips.
Journalists often write these as a favour to PR agencies. They make the tips sound enticing, but the skill is often in the writing, not in the analysis or insight. Also, be wary of analysts' recommendations, which are typically biased or outdated.

3. Be prepared to stag new issues.
If you invest in a new issue in shares, be prepared to sell out immediately after flotation if the institutional investors do.

4. Avoid penny shares in most cases.
Avoid penny shares unless you really understand the company and have a strong reason for investing. Small companies are more subject to market

manipulation than their larger counterparts. They are relatively illiquid, with large spreads.

5. Do not take your broker's recommendations at face value.

Many brokers have very limited qualifications and no real ability to understand a company, but simply bluff their way.

6. Never buy from share dealing firms abroad.

Dubious share promoters from abroad are still trying to get your money, sometimes initially via the internet. Put the phone down on them and don't visit their web sites. If you deal, do not feel obliged to stick to the oral agreement.

7. Don't rely on technical analysis.

It makes money for the gurus but does not work except to a limited extent in short term trading situations.

8. Avoid a poor investment proposition in a fashionable industry.

Do not be seduced into buying shares simply because they are in a fashionable industry. A broker can usually present a stock's poor fundamentals in an attractive light. If the PE ratio is very high, he may say that this is normal for growth stocks. If it is low, he may say that this is an undervalued stock.

9. Be wary of stock recommendations on internet message boards.

Use internet chat room and message boards only as pointers for conducting your own research. They are full of manipulators trying to persuade you to buy and sell stocks because it suits their purposes.

10. Always think for half an hour before buying or selling.

Give any stock recommendation half an hour's thought before you commit yourself, and make sure you have enough facts about the company at your finger tips.

alexanderdavidson@lineone.net

Nigel Davies

Nigel Davies read law at Oxford University and then qualified as a chartered accountant. He worked in the transport industry for 3 years in Hong Kong with Jardine Matheson, before entering stockbroking in 1986. His career since has covered many roles from equity sales to Head of Research.

He is currently head of the transport industry group at WestLB Panmure.

The transport sector

Introduction

The transport sector accounts for only 3% of European stock market capitalisation, but between 10 and 15% of European GDP. The difference represents the continental European operators which are still state or municipally owned. There are also thousands of small operators in segments such as trucking. Privatisation has only really fully happened, Royal Mail excepted, in the UK.

The sector splits into unrelated sub-sectors, including: airlines, infrastructure (e.g. airports, seaports, railways), passenger transport (e.g. trains, buses), shipping, and logistics. Each sub-sector has a totally different market structure and dynamics. Airlines and shipping are global businesses, urban buses local. Some are consolidated, others fragmented. All face legislation and regulation risks.

1. Buy cyclical stocks - particularly airlines - when next year's P/E ratio is 50x, sell when 5x.

The lower the P/E ratios for airline stocks, the greater the stock market's conviction that current consensus earnings forecasts are near the top of the cycle and therefore about to start falling. Low P/E ratios point to potential downgrades ahead as the cycle turns down. They suggest it is a good time to sell. High P/E ratios for airline stocks are caused by negligible earnings - even losses - and tend to exist around the bottom of the cycle. It is often a good time to buy as the cycle is near the bottom and may be close to turning up.

2. The share prices of regulated business are anything but boring and predictable.

Regulated businesses are perceived as dull, boring and predictable monopolies, and not the sort of businesses to have profits warnings. Not true. Shareholder returns are hugely geared to company management achieving demanding targets set by their regulator. Management excellence, rather than competence, is the requirement. Investment, before this is proven beyond reasonable doubt, can be hazardous.

3. Recently privatised businesses acquire disastrously.

Cash generative, and with a desire to diversify away from their often unexciting core businesses, these companies are in too much of a hurry to make acquisitions overseas of similar businesses. BA with its investment in US Air, BAA with Duty Free International, AB Ports with American Port Services and Stagecoach with Coach USA are all examples in the UK transport sector, and all were damaging to shareholder value. There are as many examples in other sectors.

4. Americans will stop travelling overseas at the slightest excuse.

Bombing of Tripoli 1986, Gulf War 1991, US economic slowdown, weak dollar, bombs in London, Foot and Mouth in Europe 2001, you name it, American tourists stop travelling outside the US. The stock market always underestimates this and a surprisingly high number of industries depend on them.

5. Bottom line sensitivity to a 1% change in GDP growth, a $1 per barrel move in the oil price, and a 1% price increase must be defined.

Transport companies are highly geared operationally. They have high fixed costs with marginal revenue often going straight through to the bottom line. They are very sensitive to GDP growth and their high operational gearing means they tend to exaggerate changes in GDP, both up and down. Surprises, both pleasant and unpleasant, therefore originate nine times out of ten from macro economic developments outside management control.

6. Be aware of the extended investment cycle.

The economic cycle is often exacerbated by too much new capacity being ordered/built on the back of over-confidence during the good times, which, given the long time lags involved in construction, often then comes on stream as the cycle is starting to turn down.

7. GDP growth has a multiplier effect on the propensity of things to move around more.

Most transport sub-sectors are growing above GDP growth because the propensity of goods and people to move about tends to grow at a multiple of underlying GDP of anything between 1.5x and 6.0x, depending on sub-sector. The logistics industry is growing even faster as companies out-source to third party providers, functions previously undertaken in-house.

8. The IT revolution is having a big impact on certain sub-sectors.

The IT revolution has created enormous opportunities in certain transport sub-sectors. Airlines for example, by encouraging on-line booking through their websites, are able to dis-intermediate travel agents who have traditionally charged 7-8% commission on ticket prices. Logistics companies that have best harnessed the new technology have established enormous competitive advantage over those who have not in the management of global supply chains, both B2B and B2C.

9. Barriers to entry are critical: these dictate pricing power.

The supply side revolution in the US and the UK means good businesses are soon copied, bringing competing new entrants and lower returns. Today's niche becomes tomorrow's commodity. Scarcity of suitable land makes ports, airports and railways powerful local monopolies and, if unregulated, safe investments geared to economic growth.

10. Detailed analysis of y-o-y change in a company's net cash position is neglected at one's peril.

Companies have huge leeway to make their profits what they want them to be. Any sensible FD will maintain a stockpile of provisions available for release as and when required. Earnings growth is therefore a meaningless number because it is measuring the difference between two numbers both of which have been manipulated. Cash is fact, not opinion, and therefore more difficult to manipulate. Analysts focus on P+L, rarely on detailed cash flow despite the recent requirement for a company to reconcile movements in its net debt.

---

www.westlb.com

'All great bull markets are rooted in easy money . . . The corollary is that a bull market cannot persist in the face of tightening liquidity.'

Martin Barnes

Steven I. Davis

Steven Davis is CEO of Davis International Banking Consultants, which provides strategic advice to European and U.S. Banks. Before setting up DIBC, he spent 20 years with J.P. Morgan and Bankers Trust. He has written six books on banking, most recently - *Bank Mergers: Lessons for the Future.*

The banking sector

1. Look for strong CEO leadership.

In a rapidly consolidating banking world, mergers and restructuring are the order of the day. Change management skills and the ability to drive a large, increasingly complex organisation are thus at a premium, and banking is not known for wealth in such leadership skills.

2. Be deeply suspicious of claims for strategy-driven deals.

Consultant jargon of 'revenue synergies', 'cross selling opportunities', 'penetrating new markets' and the like should be taken with a giant dose of salt. Banking clients change behaviours - and banks - much less frequently than newcomers would like, and the track record for buying into new markets is pathetic.

3. Be equally suspicious of commercial banks acquiring investment banks and fund managers.

So-called value added businesses like these are clearly destined to grow in the long term, but their success is a function of a limited number of highly motivated, self confident professionals whose partnership culture does not sit well with that of a commercial bank top management. Unless true integration is achieved - which doesn't happen very often - mutual frustration and ultimate divorce are highly likely.

4. A good bank investment becomes an even better one when there is a quoted minority/majority held by outside investors.

As the banking world consolidates, the pressure to buy up outside holdings in core businesses increases. Some of the best investments we have made have been in such quoted minorities/majorities when the parent decides at last to pick the fruits of his investment.

5. The best indication of stockholder value commitment lies in the historical record.

Lip service is universally paid to stockholder value, but the real litmus test is how the bank's management has allocated resources in the past and the results obtained. Historical RoEs, cost/income ratios, and the success of expansion moves are the best test of a management's concern for its stockholders.

6. Problem banks are usually worse than the figures indicate.

In almost every banking basket case, the ultimate reality is far worse than indicated on the surface. Management knows it's in trouble and usually tries to cover up its problems with more lending and position-taking. And at the same time necessary investment in systems and people usually doesn't take place.

7. Look for banks with large, established client bases.

Ultimately a bank's core strength is its client base, which in a consolidating and competitive market is the target of innumerable competitors. These clients rarely shift banks or go elsewhere except for specialist products as long as they feel that their bank is reasonably responsive to their needs.

8. Defendable specialist niches are rare, but when they exist they are extraordinarily attractive.

Everybody loves true sustainable competitive advantage, but finding it in the rapidly commoditizing world of banking is not a simple task. Global custody, which is the domain of a handful of US banks who have out-invested their competitors, is one of these.

9. In a consolidating banking world, holding the stock of a well-positioned bank gives you a double advantage.

In Europe and to a lesser extent other markets, there is a virtually infinite demand for acquisition candidates which offer entry into an attractive business segment or market. As long as this seller's market exist, a premium over market is virtually assured. And if it doesn't, organic growth should ensure an attractive return anyway!

www.dibc.co.uk

Philippe Delhaise

Philippe Delhaise is President of Hong Kong-based Capital Information Services, a consulting company specializing in financial and strategic risk management.

Books

Asia in Crisis - The Implosion of the Banking and Finance Systems, John Wiley, 1998

Asia in Crisis: What Went Wrong and Why, John Wiley & Sons (Asia) Pte Ltd, 1999

Valuation of Asian bank shares

---

1. Standard valuation theories do not apply to Asian banks.

- with a few exceptions in Hong Kong and Singapore.

2. Do not invest in Asian banks for their book value.

There isn't much of it! Except for banks in Hong Kong and Singapore, together with a few isolated cases in some other countries, most banks in Asia have minimal or negative equity.

3. Published accounts do not tell the truth.

Many banks conspire with regulatory authorities to conceal their problems. This is a result of years of uncontrolled growth, culminating in the Asian crisis of 1997, but Japanese and Korean banks were already very weak early in the 1990s while Taiwanese banks started suffering only recently.

4. Banks in Asia have seldom created value for their shareholders.

Let alone in a way commensurate with the (usually high) risk profile of the institutions. This remark does not, of course, hold true for bank founders who went public at grossly overpriced levels in the early 1990s, but that's another story.

5. Only Singapore and (especially) Hong Kong banks have generally combined good profits with low risk, resulting in real value creation.

Prior to the 1997 crisis, banks in Hong Kong, the Philippines and Thailand enjoyed comfortable profits, thanks to unnaturally high interest margins. Singapore, Malaysia and the Indonesian private sector also had reasonably good profits. Most of the banks outside Hong Kong and Singapore faced disaster when their profits and equity were wiped out by delinquent loans.

6. Quite why the shares of so many listed banks in such countries are still worth anything is beyond understanding.

It has to do with the way the market prices them: if it can hold on to its license, a bank remains a potential source of future dividends. Yet the goodwill attached to that license will depend very much on artificial measures taken by Asian governments to salvage the banks, since the present value of future cash flows seldom exceeds the current loan losses.

7. Asset management companies will transfer wealth from the many to the few: from taxpayers to bank shareholders.

The key to strategic buying of bank shares will be to anticipate such huge wealth transfers.

Thomas DeMark

Tom DeMark, Sr. has spent over 31 years testing, trading, and teaching his ideas in all types of markets. Known for his mechanically driven, objective approaches to trading the markets, he has created numerous successful market timing models and indicators, which help traders to spot tops and bottoms in the markets.

Books

DeMark on Day Trading Options, McGraw-Hill, 1999
New Market Timing Techniques, John Wiley, 1997
New Science of Technical Analysis, John Wiley, 1994

Trading with technical analysis

1. The trend is your friend UNLESS it is about to end.

2. Markets bottom, not because of astute buyers, but because of an absence of sellers.

3. Markets top, not because of astute sellers, but because of an absence of buyers.

4. Anticipating trend reversals enables traders to purchase calls at the narrowest premiums and cheapest prices, and to purchase puts at the narrowest premiums and cheapest prices.

5. Uniformity in calculating price retracements requires:

   a) the identification of the highest price high since price traded previously at the current price levels, in the case of an upside retracement, and

   b) the identification of the lowest price low since price traded previously at the current price levels, in the case of a downside retracement.

6. Trading disqualified trendline breakouts far exceed the benefits derived from trading qualified trendline breakouts in the direction of the ongoing trend. Typically, price slippage and skidding occur when trading with the trend and when trading against the trend and anticipating price exhaustion zones, more reasonable price fills and trading opportunities arise.

7. The determination of accumulation and/or distribution is best calculated by relating the current price with the market's opening rather than the prior price period's close.

8. Duration, or the amount of time an oscillator remains overbought or oversold, determines a market's susceptibility to a rally rather than oscillator and price divergences.

9. Markets tend to operate in a trading range 70-75% of the time and trend 25-30% of the time. Consequently, any moving average time period should be equally effective in a trending market and no moving average is effective in a trading range market. Conversely, oscillators that identify areas of overbought and oversold are most effective in trading range or sideways markets.

10. Exponentially calculated oscillators can contaminate price data since these values remain within the data series until the security suspends trading. On the other hand, arithmetic averages are removed once the time period expires.

---

www.tomdemark.com

David DeRosa

David DeRosa is the president of DeRosa Research and Trading, Inc. He is also an Adjunct Professor of Finance and Fellow of the International Finance Center at the Yale School of Management.

He writes a thrice-weekly column for Bloomberg News on international finance and world politics.

Books

In Defense of Free Capital Markets, Bloomberg Press 2001
Options on Foreign Exchange, John Wiley, 2000, 2nd ed.
Currency Derivatives, John Wiley 1998 (editor)
Managing Foreign Exchange Risk, Irwin 1996
Managing Foreign Exchange Risk: Advanced Strategies for Global Investors, Corporations, and Financial Institutions, McGraw-Hill Publishing Co., early 2007

General principles and the dangers of financial engineering

1. Don't confuse trading with investing.

I think of investing as a long-term process of wealth accumulation. If you want to speculate that is fine, but you should have a predefined portion of your total portfolio reserved for that activity. Use stop-loss orders and buy options to hold potential trading losses to non-catastrophic levels.

2. Avoid investment 'products' . . .

Financial engineering is more the friend of the broker than it is of the investor. Often these products are laden with fees. They are hard to understand, too, in a risk context. Get as close as possible to the primary securities as possible.

3. . . . except build your core portfolio with index funds.

I am a huge fan of common stocks held in diversified portfolios for the long haul. One exception to my remark about investment products is index funds. They are tax efficient and cost efficient.

4. Don't be fooled by high yields or high coupons.

Investors frequently expose themselves to great risk by seeking superior cash returns in emerging markets debt and distressed sectors. Often the risk-return trade off for these sectors is pitifully inadequate.

5. Sovereign risk can be just as lethal as private sector risk.

Many investors learnt the hard way in the decade of the 90s that sovereign risk can be significant when they saw their Mexican bonds, Brady bonds, and Russian bonds suffer steep and sudden loses.

6. Never trust mechanical risk models.

As I was quoted in Roger Lowenstein's book on Long-Term Capital Management, 'statistical risk models are lighthouses for the soon to be shipwrecked'. In the same way, don't be overly concerned about track records and Sharp ratios when considering investing with a professional investment advisor.

7. Never make an investment that is predicated on a fixed exchange rate regime's survival.

Fixed exchange rate regimes are prone to explosive convulsions, as we saw in Thailand, Indonesia, Mexico, Europe (the famous Exchange Rate Mechanism crises), Brazil, and Russia.

8. Never try to 'catch a falling knife'.

Markets may at times overreact but there is no way to know what is real and what is exaggeration.

9. Avoid naked options.

Never write naked puts or calls unless you are a professional option trader.

10. Be very cautious about the use of leverage.

In a market panic, margin calls will force you to liquidate at prices and times not of your choosing.

www.derosa-research.com

Joe DiNapoli

Joe DiNapoli is a veteran trader with over 30 years of trading experience. He is also a dogged and thorough researcher, an internationally recognised lecturer, and a widely acclaimed author. He is President of Coast International Software, Inc.

Books

Trading With DiNapoli Levels - The Practical Application of Fibonacci Ratios to Investment Markets, 1998
The Fibonacci, Money Management and Trend Analysis Home Trading Course, 1989

Trading and the importance of a plan

1. Loss of opportunity is preferable to loss of capital.

There was a time when I felt it was my duty to be personally involved in every wrinkle of the S&P. I've traded this market since it's inception in 82. It took quite a while for me to realise that picking safe, readable, and high probability winning trades was the way to go.

2. Use Logical Profit Objectives for all positions.

The concept of using and executing LPOs is one of the most important I know of. It keeps your percentage of winning trades high and gets you back to the computer the next day. Everyone enjoys a pay day. With the correct concepts this is something you can do.

3. Place your Logical Profit Objectives in the market ahead of time.

Markets are squirrelly animals. If you know how to calculate your profit objectives, get them in the market ahead of market action. If you wait for the alert to go off, hoping to capture more, it's likely the market will move away from your exit before you have time to execute your order.

4. Enter markets on retracements.

Don't buy new highs or sell new lows. Wait for the market to come to you. Precalculate your entries and be patient. If you miss the move another bus will come by shortly.

5. Above all, follow your trading plan.

Having a clearly defined trading plan is the single most important aspect of profitable speculation. Never trade without one and once you have it, following it is more important than any single profit or loss.

6. Trade quietly.

With the exception of a mentor, tell no one about your positions, profits, or losses. Especially those close to you, like your wife, husband, or friends. This self-gratification process or sharing process puts you under psychological pressure to win on every trade and can be a primary reason for failure to follow your plan.

7. Don't carry a sizeable position while traveling.

It will catch you!! The laptop won't work. The hotel internet connection will break. The cell phone battery will run out. The plane won't land! I know you'll try it anyway. It's good for the markets, we need to spread the money around a bit.

8. 'You are only one trade away from humility.'

For over 15 years this tattered hand-written sign, scrawled with bold black strokes with a magic marker, has hung over my trading table. A swelled head does not belong on a trader's shoulders.

9. Add to your knowledge before attempting to add to your wallet.

This seems obvious but somehow many newbie traders think they can become pros with little more than a computer and hope. In this business hope is a four letter word. I hear the following a dozen times a month. "I only wish I came across you before I blew 50-500 grand." I was here. Others like me were here. They thought it was easy and needed to find some humility. Now they're ready to progress.

10. Develop your sense of humour.

You'll definitely need it.

11. Help other traders whenever you can.

This is more practical than philosophical: giving keeps the ego in line and when you need help, and you will, you'll find it!

www.fibtrader.com

Bob Dischel

Dr. Dischel is a partner in Weather Ventures Ltd in the US and Global Weather Exchange in Europe, where he provides meteorological analysis and forecasts, and develops risk management programs for weather-sensitive enterprises. Bob left a position as a Managing Director in the Portfolio Department of a multi-billion dollar US Insurer to begin his weather risk market activities in 1997. He is certified by the American Meteorological Society as a Consulting Meteorologist and is a member of the National Council of Industrial Meteorologists.

The weather risk market

1. Weather is bigger than the Fed.

Weather-indexed derivatives link cashflows to the weather. These derivative securities grow in value only with the occurrence of weather events measured at specific sites over periods of a few weeks or months. While the weather affects economic events on many scales - certainly business performance - economic events do not affect the weather or the final value of a weather derivative. If there is a correlation between weather derivatives and other markets, the driver is the weather.

2. The right kind of weather forecast is never wrong: unfortunately, it is never entirely correct.

Meteorologists prevaricate as they skirt simple statements, as I just did. Forecasters must hedge their opinions because weather is changing even as we watch, so the right kind of forecast is one that offers the odds of coming events. For example, forecasting an 80% chance of rain also allows for a 20% chance of no rain, and a forecast of rain amounts is even better. Chances are good that the real event was represented within the forecast range of events, but the winning forecast will be the one that gave the real event a high probability.

3. People's opinions may rule weather trading but Mother Nature and Father Time decide who wins.

Weather derivative prices change as each new seasonal forecast is issued and market players use this new information to tilt the odds in their favor.

The usefulness of a seasonal forecast depends on many conditions, including global events like El Nino. But weather, as we all know, can be uncertain, so winning is not just about forecasts - it's about estimating the probabilities of future weather. We can choose to look forward or backward to form opinions, but the weather event that actually happens establishes who pays - and this is not open to opinion.

4. A one-season visit to the weather market is a crapshoot.

Enter the weather market only for the long term. Weather and climate are moving targets ensuring year-to-year volatility. Market players struggle to understand how much last season's average weather says about this coming season's weather. The climatologist (and any statistician) knows that in the absence of a confirmed trend, decades of history tell more about the future than a few recent years. It is simplistic to look only at the warmer-than-normal few years of the 1990's when last winter (2000-2001) smashed US long-term records for low temperatures. Was this a broken trend or increasing variability?

5. Mother Nature may come uninvited to the company picnic but you can keep her out of the shareholder's meeting.

Most weather-sensitive businesses bet on the weather even though they don't have to, as when they don't hedge the weather. For them, not hedging keeps weather risk high. When a business hedges its weather exposure well, it 'takes the weather bet off the table' and is free to focus on its business competencies; these usually do not include managing weather. Now that there is a choice, will equity analysts and shareholders continue to accept 'bad weather' as an explanation for poor company performance?

6. Resist taking money off the table from an in-the-money position if it was meant as a hedge.

End-users should always hedge a weather exposure if it is economical to do so, even if the forecast indicates a favorable season. First, it surprises no one that forecasts can be wrong. Second, weather hedging can free up capital reserves for important activities like growth or better service to customers. Having hedged for protection, the hedge becomes valuable only in an adverse season, precisely the event that required protection. If the hedge is winning, it is because the business is losing to the weather. If it's working - don't fix it.

7. Diversity in weather greatly exceeds diversity in weather derivatives.

Today's end-users, mostly energy producers and distributors, are naturally short temperature in winter and long temperature in summer: cold winters and hot summers generate sales. To hedge their natural position against mild seasons, they need to lengthen temperature in winter (a temperature call) or shorten temperature in summer (a temperature put). Absent natural counterparties, the market absorbs these hedges into risk capital. When a mild season is forecast, end-users and everyone else want the same side of the market, driving prices up. If prices get too high some end-users mistakenly choose not to hedge, leaving the speculators, all wanting to bet the same side of the weather odds. This lack of diversity won't change until new products, specifically considering precipitation, bring end-users from other sectors of the economy.

8. Price is important, but value is more important.

End-user or portfolio manager, your view of value is based on your weather exposure, your risk preferences and your opinions on future weather. The market price and your perspective on the value of a weather derivative can be quite different. If the value of a derivative to your enterprise exceeds the market price - go for it. However, remember that the weather market is not yet a liquid market and often the position you take is yours until expiration, so if you pay too much, you tilt the probability of a favorable outcome away from your hand.

9. Black and Scholes pricing is valuable in many markets, but in weather, it is simply wrong.

The basic idea of the Black-Scholes analysis is to hold a position in an option that is equal and opposite to a position in the asset from which the option's price is derived: to build a risk-neutral portfolio. We cannot do this because the weather on which the derivative's price is based cannot be owned. This isn't all bad. It means no one can manipulate the market by cornering the weather, and portfolios can still be balanced with other assets, just not with the weather itself.

10. It can rain on one side of the street and not on the other - so what?

Climate is geographically diverse leading to weather basis risk. Site-to-site correlations break down with increasing distance, the presence of mountains, coastlines, and of course, cities. This geographic basis risk is troublesome for the end-user looking to hedge a local business, but it makes opportunity for a speculator for the very same reason: weak correlations offer diversity. As to the rain across the street - how much will the histogram of rain measured over a month on one side of the street look like the histogram for the other side? Very much like it, I think.

bobdischel@weatherventures.com,   www.weatherventures.com

'The pain people feel from losing $100 is much greater than the pleasure they get from winning $100. Be careful that this does not lead you to cling on to losing investments in the hope that they'll return to profit.'

Gary Belsky

Richard H. Driehaus

Richard Driehaus is widely regarded within the investment industry as an expert in the specialty of aggressive growth investing.

He founded Driehaus Securities Corporation in 1979, followed by Driehaus Capital Management, Inc. in 1982. He is the architect of the firm's investment philosophy and is primarily responsible for all domestic portfolio management and investment analysis within the firm.

In early 2000, Mr. Driehaus was named in Barron's "All-Century" team of the 25 individuals who have been the most influential within the mutual fund industry over the past 100 years.

Mr Driehaus was one of the portfolio managers profiled in *The New Market Wizards* (Jack Schwager, HarperBusiness 1992) and in *Investment Gurus* (Peter Tanous, New York Institute of Finance, 1997). He has contributed a chapter on growth investing to *Expert Financial Planning: Investment Strategies from Industry Leaders* by Robert Jaffra, John Wiley, 2001.

Investment paradigms worth avoiding

Introduction

Paradigms are beliefs that most people have. Unfortunately, they are often outdated and really no longer true, yet people tend to hold on to these paradigms. In fact, they search for evidence to support them and reject information that conflicts with their beliefs.

Mistaken Paradigm 1: 'Buy low and sell high.'

Perhaps the best known investment paradigm is 'buy low, sell high'. I believe that more money can be made by buying high and selling at even higher prices. I try to buy stocks that have already had good price moves, that are often making new highs and that have positive relative strength. These are stocks that are in demand by other investors.

What is the risk? Obviously, the risk is that I'm buying near the top. But, I would much rather be invested in a stock that is increasing in price and take the risk that it may begin to decline than invest in a stock that is already in a decline and try to guess when it will turn around.

Mistaken Paradigm 2: 'Just buy stocks of good companies and hold onto them.'

Another mistaken belief: 'just buy stocks of good companies and hold on to them; that way you don't have to pay close daily attention.' I would say: 'buy good stocks of good companies and hold on to them until there are unfavorable changes.' Closely monitor daily events because this will provide the first clues to long-term change. Remember, just as the business value does not equal the stock price, things are always changing, and yesterday's good company may not be today's great investment.

Mistaken Paradigm 3: 'Don't try to hit home runs; you make money hitting a lot of singles.'

I couldn't disagree more. I believe you can make the most money hitting home runs. But, you also need a discipline to avoid striking out. That is my sell discipline. I try to cut my losses and let my winners run. Perhaps that's a paradigm too, but it is one that works.

Mistaken Paradigm 4: 'A high turnover strategy is risky.'

Most people believe high turnover is risky. I think just the opposite. High turnover reduces risk when it is the result of taking a series of small losses in order to avoid larger losses. I don't hold on to stocks with deteriorating fundamentals or price patterns. For me, this kind of turnover makes sense. It reduces risk.

Mistaken Paradigm 5: 'An investment process must be very systematic.'

Many people believe an investment process needs to be rigidly systematic. I believe a good process involves discipline, but must be flexible enough to respond to changing market conditions. Let me give you an example:

At the end of November 1991, the Dow Jones Industrial Average was trading at 2895 and the market's price to earnings ratio was 23. The price-to-book ratio was a lofty 2.7 and the market's yield was only 2.8%. A rigid, systematic value-based process would have told you to get out of the market with at least a portion of your assets. After all, the market was higher relative to those valuation measures than it had been 90% of the time, on a historical basis.

But, I believed that there were other relevant factors that suggested the market could go much higher. This was not a time to rigidly adhere to valuation disciplines. People who stayed fully invested benefited. From that time, through January, 2000, the Dow Jones Industrial Average quadrupled.

Don't invest because of what you think should be happening. Invest because of what is happening.

Mistaken Paradigm 6: 'You must have a value-based process.'

Often when I talk to consultants, they like to see a very systematic, value-based process. They think that each stock has to be submitted to some type of disciplined, precise and uniform evaluation. But the real world is not that precise. I'm convinced that there is no universal valuation method. In fact, in the short run, valuation is not the key factor. Each company's stock price is unique to its place in the market environment and to its own phase in its corporate development.

Mistaken Paradigm 7: 'The best measure of investment risk is the standard deviation of return.'

Another paradigm and one that I deal with frequently is that 'the best measure of investment risk is the standard deviation of return'. In other words, volatility. But volatility only measures risk over the short-term yet a long-term perspective is far more important. For most investors, a major long-term risk is portfolio underperformance due to insufficient exposure to high returning, more volatile assets. In my opinion, investment vehicles that provide the least short-term volatility often embody the greatest long-term risk.

Mistaken Paradigm 8: 'It's risky to place your money with a 'star system' manager.'

I disagree! In any industry, performance is achieved by the stars. Working with a diversified group of investment management stars is probably the safest way to invest. Great ideas, inventions and works of art have always been created by individuals, not groups or committees. This is also true in the investment business: good long-term results have been achieved by talented individuals.

www.driehaus.com

'Buying on fundamentals is fine, but you need to be patient. The long term normally wins in the end. Always remember that fundamentals are bad for selling. Charts will get you out much faster.'

David Linton

Dru Edmonstone

Dru Edmonstone is Head of Smaller Company Research at Durlacher, the research driven European technology investment bank.

He is also Editor of *The AIM Bulletin*, Durlacher's monthly research publication dedicated to companies listed on the Alternative Investment Market, and a weekly commentator on Bloomberg TV and www.nothing-ventured.com.

Investing in AIM companies

Introduction

Investing in AIM companies is high risk, but no more so than investing in smallcaps listed on the main market. The risk-averse mentality of the City means that fund managers leave smallcaps, and in particular AIM stocks, under-researched and overlooked. This provides an opportunity for private investors able to distinguish between leaders and laggards.

1. Only invest in companies with trading records of more than three years.

The value of an extended track record is that it enables you to see how the company has responded to a variety of macroeconomic conditions within a full business cycle. The perceived adroitness of management in poor economic conditions is usually a pre-cursor to above average growth in the ensuing upswing in the economy. If you are risk averse to start-up or seed companies, invest only in companies with trading records of more than three years.

2. AIM stocks can suffer from lack of comparability.

Many AIM stocks, particularly in the technology sector, suffer when it comes to market valuation because it is often difficult to compare them with any similar quoted business. It is quite common for stocks to trade at a significant discount to their main market cousins until their performance forces an upward market rating - often precipitated by a strong set of results relative to main market competitors. In cases where there does not appear to be quoted competition, research the company's product in terms of its perceived dominance in the market place.

3. Stick to simple, short-term forecasts.

Avoid rocket science valuation methods and forecasts spanning the next 3 to 5 years. Concentrate instead on the next 12 months and the plain English behind the numbers. If your investment decision rests with the forecasts, use the numbers given by the house broker, whilst ignoring their Buy recommendation. Nominated Brokers and Advisers can no longer afford to make mistakes with regards to profit projections. They know that the City is a very unforgiving place.

4. Watch directors and institutional share dealings.

Try to establish the level of proprietorial share activity. Generally speaking, internal investors and the large institutional shareholders whom they try to please are closer to the everyday operations of the business than external investors are ever likely to be. This does not mean that their judgement is necessarily better, but their views on the short-term future of the company will generaly be sound. Note, however, that institutional share dealings are also influenced by factors which may have nothing to do with the prospects of the company - such as portfolio weighting, compliance with corporate governance rules, and acceptable levels of profits on original cost.

5. Stay away from stocks which have less than 25% of their share capital in public hands.

Some companies have been floated on AIM with as much as 90% of the issued share capital kept in private hands. Restricting the number of external investors in this way results in huge disparities between the supply and demand of shares and their bid and offer prices. Getting into these stocks may be easy enough; getting out of them is likely to prove a problem, particularly in a bear market.

6. Research the track record of the company's advisers.

Levels of due diligence, at the expense of admission fees, have improved dramatically since the Stock Exchange conducted its first annual review of Nominated Advisers. However, some advisers, and indeed brokers, are better than others! Try to ascertain the previous succes/failure ratio of a company's advisers before investing, particularly when considering investing in a new issue.

7. Consider sector prospects.

Although AIM is principally a stock picker's market, at times it does demonstrate clear sector trends (the demise of the multimedia and internet sectors being good examples). An in-depth knowledge of a particular sector will assist in spreading the investment risk, and investors should therefore acquaint themselves with as much of their 'selected' AIM sector research as possible, whilst comparing the performance trend to the equivalent Official List sector.

8. Detailed appraisals of the management team and their past track records are an analytical necessity.

For some owner/managers the entrepreneurial drive in building up a business becomes dissipated once the business has achieved critical mass. The leap from running a private organisation to managing a public company is not always an easy adjustment and one that is often reflected in the performance of the share price. Investors should therefore evaluate whether or not the management team is ready and willing to take on the additional responsibilities associated with a quoted company. The experience and future role of the non-executive directors is also an important consideration.

9. Don't expect dividends!

The dividend policy is a normal feature of AIM prospectuses, as most investors have some requirement for yield, if only in the long-term. However, AIM is not predominately an income market. Whilst some AIM companies do pay dividends, most of the rapidly growing ones will omit the dividend in favour of retained earnings and the resultant rise in the share price reflecting the growth in productive assets.

10. Consider how the company is affected by the economic cycle.

The correlation between the macro economic cycle and AIM companies is often very weak, as innovative companies are creating new markets, which initially are tiny relative to long established technologies and sectors. Nonetheless a weakening macro economic trend will disproportionately dampen willingness to back 'entrepreneurship' in AIM companies. Looking at the AIM market as a whole, there are some companies whose exposure to poorly performing economies, such as those in the Far East, will have a significant impact on their share price.

---

www.durlacher.com,   www.nothing-ventured.com

'Avoid technology companies with a sales-dominant corporate culture. All too often, accounting irregularities and questionable practices creep in sooner or later, ultimately leading to restated results, a loss in investor confidence and an overnight collapse in the share price.'

Conor McCarthy

Marc Faber

Dr Marc Faber writes and edits *'The Gloom, Boom & Doom Report'* - a monthly newsletter regarded as an essential alternative investment manual. He is a regular contributor to *Forbes* and contributes to several websites, such as Financial Intelligence and Asian Bond Portal.

Books

Tomorrow's Gold: Asia's Age of Discovery, Clsa Ltd, 2005

Contrarian advice from Dr Doom

Rule #1: There is no investment rule that always works.

If there was one single rule, which always worked, everybody would in time follow it and, therefore, everybody would be rich. But the only constant in history is the shape of the wealth pyramid, with few rich people at the top and many poor at the bottom. Thus, even the best rules do change from time to time.

Myth #1: 'Stocks always go up in the long term.'

This is a myth. Far more companies have failed than succeeded. Far more countries' stock markets went to zero than markets which have survived. Just think of Russia in 1918, all the Eastern European stock markets after 1945, Shanghai after 1949, and Egypt in 1954.

Myth #2: 'Real Estate always goes up in the long term.'

While it is true that real estate has a tendency to appreciate in the long run, partly because of population growth, there is a problem with ownership and property rights. Real estate was a good investment for Londoners over the last 1,000 years, but not for America's Red Indians, Mexico's Aztecs, Peru's Incas and people living in countries which became communist in the 20th century. All these people lost their real estate and usually also their lives.

Problem rule #1: 'Buy Low and Sell High.'

The problem with this rule is that we never know exactly what is low and what is high. Frequently what is low will go even lower and what is high will continue to rise.

Problem rule #2: 'Buy a basket of high quality stocks and hold.'

Another highly dangerous rule! Today's leaders may not be tomorrow's leaders. Don't forget that Xerox, Polaroid, Memorex, Digital Equipment, Burroughs, Control Data were the leaders in 1973. Where are they today? Either out of business or their stocks are far lower than in 1973!

Problem rule #3: 'Buy when there is blood on the street.'

It is true that bad news often provides an interesting entry point, at least as a trading opportunity, into a market. However, a better long term strategy may be to buy on bad news which has been preceded by a long string of bad news. When the market no longer declines, there is a chance that the really worst has been fully discounted.

Rule #2: Don't trust anyone!

Everybody is out to sell you something. Corporate executives either lie knowingly or because they don't know the true state of their business and the entire investment community makes money on you buying or selling something.

Rule #3: The best investments are frequently the ones you did not make!

To make a really good investment, which will in time appreciate by 100 times or more, is like finding a needle in a haystack. Most 'hot tips' and 'must buys' or 'great opportunities' turn out to be disasters. Thus, only take very few investment decisions, which you have carefully analyzed and thought about in terms of risk and potential reward.

Rule #4: Invest where you have an edge!

If you live in a small town you may know the local real estate market, but little about Cisco, Yahoo and Oracle. Stick with your investments in assets about which you may have a knowledge edge.

Rule #5: Invest in Yourself!

Today's society is obsessed with money. But the best investments for you may be in your own education, in the quality of the time you spend with the ones you love, on your own job, and on books, which will open new ideas to you and let you see things from many different perspectives.

---

email - contrary@pacific.net.hk

Frank J. Fabozzi

Frank J. Fabozzi is editor of the *Journal of Portfolio Management*, an Adjunct Professor of Finance at Yale University's School of Management, and a consultant in the fixed-income and derivatives area.

From 1986 to 1992, he was a full-time professor of finance at MIT's Sloan School of Management. Frank is a Chartered Financial Analyst and Certified Public Accountant who has edited and authored many acclaimed books in finance.

Books

Frank Fabozzi has written and edited many books on fixed income and equity markets. His *Handbook of Fixed Income Securities*, published by McGraw-Hill, is now in its seventh edition.

Bond investing

Introduction

The investment world can be divided into retail investors (i.e. individual investors) and institutional investors (e.g. insurance companies, mutual fund managers, depository institutions). The investing rules below focus on the institutional investor. One can probably trace some well known financial fiascos by institutional investors to a violation of one or more of these rules.

1. Know your benchmark.

Institutional investors manage money relative to a benchmark. The benchmark may be either some market index or future liabilities that are contractually determined. The institutional investor should clearly understand the characteristics of the benchmark. A strategy that is appropriate for one institutional investor may be disastrous for another because of different benchmarks. Moreover, understanding the benchmark means that the primary risks that drive returns are identified and they are the risks that the institutional investor can focus on to control risk and attempt to outperform the benchmark.

2. Securities are only appropriate relative to a strategy.

The fundamental principle of modern portfolio theory is that the risk of an individual security is not its risk in isolation but the contribution of risk to a portfolio. This means that given the benchmark and given the strategy that is consistent with that objective, an investor should focus on how much an individual security adds to the risk of the strategy.

At professional conferences I have heard two portfolio managers from the same investment management firm give two very different views of the same bond structure. Both were right given that one managed money relative to a bond index and the other relative to actuarially determined liabilities.

3. For bond investors, modeling risk is an important risk that should never be underestimated.

For bond investors, the valuation of bonds introduced into the market in the last two decades have been difficult to value. Their valuation depends on several assumptions. To value these securities and to assess how they will perform under different scenarios in order to control risk, it is necessary to assess the impact of these assumptions to cope with modeling risk.

4. Hedging is not the same as risk control.

Too often institutional investors state they want to hedge risk. Hedging risk means eliminating risk and unless markets are inefficient, the elimination of risk means that the potential return will be approximately equal to the risk-free return. Institutional investors who manage portfolios want to control the primary risks associated with the benchmark based on their view of the primary risk factors.

5. For bond funds, understand what duration means and how it is measured.

A commonly used measure of interest rate risk for a bond portfolio is duration. Unfortunately, too often duration is interpreted as some temporal measure (i.e., in terms of years). Duration is simply a measure of the sensitivity of the change in the value of a bond (or a portfolio) to a change in interest rates.

A useful working definition is that duration is the approximate percentage change in the value of a bond (or a portfolio) for a 100 basis point change in rates. So, for example, a duration of 4 for a bond means that the value of the bond will change by approximately 4% for a 100 basis point change in rates.

For portfolios that include complex securities (that is, securities that have considerable cash flow uncertainty), the calculation of a bond's duration is difficult and therefore there is modeling risk associated with the computed duration.

6. Yield is not return.

A yield measure calculated for a bond - yield to maturity, yield to call, or cash flow yield - is only a measure of the potential return from investing in a bond under limited circumstances.

7. Understand why a yield spread exists.

The practice in the bond market is to calculate the yield on a security and then compare that yield to a benchmark security. The difference is called the yield spread. An investor should understand what characteristics of a security (i.e., what risks) the yield spread is seeking to compensate the investor for and determine if that spread is adequate given the risks.

8. Always perform attribution analysis when evaluating managers.

In analyzing the performance of a portfolio manager it is important to decompose the actual return into the reasons why that return was generated. This activity is called attribution analysis.

9. Watch with great concern money managers with far superior returns than the rest.

A client employing the services of several money managers to invest in a specific sector (e.g. bonds) should be most concerned with the manager that generated a return that is considerably better than the rest. Using attribution analysis the client can determine the reason for the superior performance and should clearly understand the risks accepted by the manager. The client may find that the particular risks (or equivalently, bets) are not the ones that the client wants to accept in the future.

www.frankfabozzi.com

'The most highly paid people in the country work on Wall Street. They become highly paid because they persuade people to buy and sell securities. It would be hyperbole to say that they had no interest in the fate of the transaction - but only a little bit.'

Robert A.G. Monks

Alan Farley

Alan Farley is a private trader and publisher of the Hard Right Edge, a comprehensive online resource for trader education, technical analysis and short-term trading tactics. His methods have been widely featured in the financial press, including *Barrons, Smart Money, Tech Week, Active Trader, TradingMarkets.com* and *TheStreet.com.*

Books
The Master Swing Trader, McGraw-Hill, 2000
The Master Swing Trader: Tools and Techniques to Profit from Outstanding Short-term Trading Opportunities, McGraw-Hill Education, 2001

Swing trading

1. Forget the news, remember the chart.

You're not smart enough to know how news will affect price. The chart already knows the news is coming.

2. Buy the first pullback from a new high. Sell the first pullback from a new low.

There's always a crowd that missed the first boat.

3. Short rallies, not sell-offs.

When markets drop, shorts finally turn a profit and get ready to cover.

4. Don't chase momentum if you can't find the exit.

Assume the market will reverse the minute you get in. If it's a long way to the door, you're in big trouble.

5. Trends test the point of last support/resistance.

Enter here even if it hurts.

6. If you have to look, it isn't there.

Forget your college degree and trust your instincts.

7. The trend is your friend in the last hour.

As volume cranks up at 3:00p.m., don't expect anyone to change the channel.

8. Avoid the open.

They see you coming, sucker.

9. Price has memory.

What did price do the last time it hit a certain level? Chances are it will do it again.

10. Beat the crowd in and out the door.

You have to take their money before they take yours, period.

www.hardrightedge.com

Niall Ferguson

Niall Ferguson is Professor of Political and Financial History at Oxford University and Visiting Professor of Economics at the Stern Business School, New York University.

Books

The Cash Nexus, Allen Lane, 2001
The House of Rothschild, Penguin 2000

Lessons from the Rothschilds

Introduction

When I began work on the history of the Rothschild family I was not myself an investor. Naturally, I hoped that studying the correspondence of the nineteenth century's richest dynasty would reveal to me the secret of their success and endow me with the Midas touch. I certainly learned a great deal in the bank's immense archives, but I remain unsure as to whether the rules by which the Rothschilds operated then have any validity today. Of course, members of the family still offer professional financial advice through a variety of firms bearing the Rothschild name. Anyone who seriously wants to know how to invest their money today should contact one of them. As an historian whose biggest investment is a seventeenth-century Oxfordshire farmhouse, all I can offer is past Rothschild advice, which may or may not be perennial.

There are at least two pieces of folklore about Rothschild investment strategy. One, often attributed to Nathaniel, the first Lord Rothschild, is that investment should be like a cold shower: 'Quick in, quick out'. This is the very opposite of today's 'Stocks for the Long Run'. But I doubt that was ever said, at least not in earnest.

Another apocryphal story is that the Rothschilds invested a third of their wealth in securities, a third in real estate and a third in objets d'art. That certainly was not the case: big though their houses were (and they were the biggest private residences built in the nineteenth century) and no matter how dazzling their collections of Old Masters, their immense securities portfolios were always worth a lot more.

So what did the Rothschilds really say about investment? As they were primarily though not exclusively bond-issuers and traders, much of what they wrote in their voluminous correspondence is relevant to investors in government securities, not equities.

1. Look for governments in trouble.

Mayer Amschel Rothschild, the founder of the bank, used to tell his sons: 'It is better to deal with a government in difficulties than with one that has luck on its side.' That sounds like another way of saying a government in real financial trouble will pay higher yields and commissions. (Note: That should not be read as a recommendation to buy Ukrainian government bonds today.)

2. Spread the sugar . . .

The Rothschilds were bond wholesalers as much as investors, so it is worth listening to what they had to say about trading. In 1836 James de Rothschild, Mayer Amschel's youngest son, gave his nephews some advice about how to sell securities on the Paris stock exchange:

'When you are buying or selling rentes, try not to look at making a profit, but rather your aim should be to get the brokers used to the idea that they need to come to you . . . [O]ne initially has to make some sacrifices so that the people then get used to the idea to come to you, my dear nephews, and as such one first has to spread the sugar about in order to catch the birds later on.'

3. . . . or spread the fear.

But if sugar didn't work, James had an alternative strategy: 'If one can't make oneself loved then one has to make oneself feared,' he told his nephews, a rule he himself had been taught by his father.

4. Insider dealing rules.

The Rothschilds were of course able to act in ways that nowadays might invite allegations of 'insider dealing'. It was said of James's brother Nathan, for example, that 'If he possessed news calculated to make the funds rise, he would commission the broker who acted on his behalf [initially] to sell half a million.' Then, when the price had gone down and the rest of the market was looking the other way, Rothschild would buy in a big way. Only then would the 'news' break, driving up the price to new heights.

Of course, this kind of activity was easier in the days before the telegraph (Bloomberg screens and CNBC were undreamt of). The Rothschilds' private couriers were generally first into town with any hot news from abroad. So the Rothschilds could easily steal a march on less well-informed investors. They were also adept at cultivating influential politicians, who had a habit of revealing their intentions to the Rothschilds in return for a cut of any ensuing speculation.

5. Know when to hold back.

The next generation lacked the hard-nosed ethos of their ghetto-born fathers. Nathan's son Nat was exceedingly risk averse, though his advice against investing in railways may strike a chord with those modern investors who were lured into the market for UK railway privatisation shares in the 1990s:

> 'I am against [investment in railways] because I am afraid of the anxiety, bother & trouble which it will surely occasion us - the moral responsibility of it will rest entirely on us, & I wd sooner leave to others the profit which the shares are likely to bring than engage in a concern of such magnitude without the possibility of attending to it properly. I think the best thing is . . . not to have anything to do with them.'

6. Sell too soon.

As might be expected, the Rothschilds were frequently badgered for free investment tips. Asked if he had a formula for financial success, the first Lord Rothschild habitually replied, 'Yes, by selling too soon.'

7. Don't go bust.

The above caution had its disadvantages and helps explain why the Rothschilds - still in terms of capital the biggest bank in the world in 1905 - were overhauled by joint-stock banks in the twentieth century. When Sir Edward Guinness sought to float the famous brewing company on the stock market in 1886, the London Rothschilds refused to handle the £6 million flotation, which was snapped up by Barings and yielded the rival bankers a handsome profit. Yet when asked by a journalist if he regretted turning the business down, Lord Rothschild replied: 'I don't look at it quite that way. I go to the House every morning and when I say "No" to every scheme and enterprise submitted to me, I return home at night carefree and contented. But when I agree to any proposal, I am immediately filled with anxiety. To say "Yes" is like putting your finger in a machine: the whirring wheels may drag your whole body in after the finger.' Risk averse, yes - but then one of the secrets of success in banking is not to go bust.

8. Be a rich man.

Buy my favourite Rothschild story is an old German-Jewish joke: 'Herr Baron, Herr Baron,' asks the archetypal stock market hanger-on, 'What will the markets do tomorrow?' 'If I knew that,' replies Rothschild, 'I'd be a rich man.'

www.history.ox.ac.uk

'A major pitfall to any investment strategy is the discrete start of the investment program. If all funds are committed at the start of the program, the overall performance of the investment program will depend significantly on the specific entry point. Build up positions over time.'

Richard Olsen

Kenneth L. Fisher

Ken Fisher is best known for his 'Portfolio Strategy' column in *Forbes*. He is the sixth longest running columnist in *Forbes'* 83 year history. He is the founder, Chairman and CEO of Fisher Investments, Inc., an $8 billion dollar money management firm with offices in Woodside, CA, and in London, serving large corporate and public pension plans, as well as endowments, foundations and high net worth individuals.

Ken has written three major finance books and been published and/or interviewed in virtually every major American finance or business periodical.

Books

Super Stocks - Dow Jones Irwin 1984
100 Minds that Made the Market - Business Classics 1993
The Wall Street Waltz - Business Classics 1987
The Warren Buffett Way, (Bill Miller, Robert G. Hagstrom) John Wiley & Sons Inc, 2005
Common Stocks and Uncommon Profits and Other Writings, ohn Wiley & Sons Inc, 2003

Engaging The Great Humiliator

---

1. Engage The Great Humiliator without ending up humiliated by it.

The market is effectively a near living, near spiritual entity that exists for one goal and one goal only - to embarrass as many people as possible for as many dollars as possible for as long a time period as possible. And it is really effective at it. It wants to humiliate you, me and everyone else. It wants to humiliate Republicans and Democrats and Tories. It is an equal opportunity humiliator. Your goal is to engage The Great Humiliator without ending up humiliated by it.

2. Never forget - you are really Fred Flintstone.

If you always remember you have a stone age mind genetically trying to deal with post-industrial revolution problems, you will better understand your cognitive difficulties in seeing the market correctly. We got our brains from our ancestors and they are both genetically identical to those that existed before markets did, but also the ways we process information are almost identical to they way information was processed thousands of years ago. When you think of a tough stock market problem in terms of how would a stone age person think of this, it takes you to rudimentary evolutionary psychology, which is closely linked to behavioral finance and leads quickly to being able to see yourself better and better understand your problem.

3. The Pros are always wrong.

For decades people have presumed that the little guy is wrong and the sophisticated pro is more likely to be right. The concept is cute but is inconsistent with finance theory. The reality is that professional consensus is always wrong. Why?

The market is a discounter of all known information. That is core finance theory. Everyone has information, but on average professionals have a lot more access to information than normal people. Professionals as a group have access to all essentially known information. So, if you can figure out what professionals as a group believe will happen you know what has been discounted into current pricing from all known information and therefore cannot happen. It is theoretically and empirically perfect.

The pros as a group are a perfect guide to what won't happen. Knowing what won't happen doesn't tell you what will but eliminates a big part of the possibility spectrum and gives you a leg up on figuring out what may happen.

4. Nothing works all the time.

Sometimes growth is hot. Sometimes it's not. Sometimes value leads. Sometimes small caps do. Sometimes foreign stocks lead and sometimes domestic stocks do.

Investors have layered their thought processes on top of thousands of years of a prior process we did well that we now call collecting. Thousands of years ago people collected food, stone points for spears, firewood and much more. Now people collect for fun because our brains are adept at it. Collectors collect consistent with their biases and their access to information and or stuff.   Their collections tell you more about who they are than the stuff.

In equities they collect in categories consistent with their biases, like value, growth, etc....   The value guy and growth guy both think their categories are basically and permanently better. But in the long run they all end up with almost exactly identical average annualized returns, and *must* - it is core to how capitalism's pricing mechanism works.

5. Most investors will go to hell or die not understanding why.

If you don't fathom number 4, above, and actually believe that some category of equities is basically better or worse than others, you are not alone. Most investors, being collectors, believe that, including most professionals, most of whom are collectors.

But to say some equity category is basically better permanently is to say that you either disbelieve in capitalism, in which case you are sure destined to hell, or that you don't fully fathom its pricing mechanism.

In the long term supply is much more powerful in setting securities prices than demand and the only marginal costs of new supply are distribution. All other costs can be amortized over large unit volume to drive them to zero if the price of the equities is high enough. What that means is that as soon as investment bankers see any excess demand for any equity category they busily go about the process of starting to create new supply to meet it. To the extent they do so, which may take some time, they pull that category's pricing back into line with all other categories. When you look at 30 year average annual returns of equity categories they are all essentially identical and always will be. It is core finance theory.

6. Heroes are myths.

The great investors of the past were mostly innovators, but because they were if they were alive today they wouldn't do it now the way they did it then. That was then; this is now. Almost everything from the past is obsolete now.

Think of it like being Intel. If Intel made semiconductors now like it did 15 years ago, it would be broke. You have to keep learning, changing, adapting and adopting the latest and newest capability. If you don't you will get left behind. If you don't believe that, watch me leave you behind. Hence it is a mistake to say things like, "I want to be an investor like Ben Graham (or any past guru) was" - because they wouldn't do it like they did themselves - *now*.

7. Pray to The Luck God.

In behavioral finance theory the ultimate sin is accumulating pride and shunning regret. Accumulating pride is a process that associates success with skill or repeatability. Shunning regret associates failure with bad luck or victimization. Accumulating pride and shunning regret is something people have done in our normal lives for more than 25,000 years, since *Homo Sapiens* first walked as modern man. It motivates us to keep trying in non-financial activities and is surely good.

But in financial activities it cause us to become overconfident and enter into transactions for which we have no particular training, background, experience or special knowledge and when we enter into overconfident decisions we get bad luck - we become unlucky.

To become lucky reverse the process and learn to shun pride and accumulate regret. Then you assume success was materially luck, not skill and not particularly repeatable. You assume failure was not bad luck or victimization but your own lack of skill and hence mandating introspective lessons to self-improve. When you do that you make less overconfident decisions and become fundamentally lucky instead of unlucky. This is just using finance theory to get lucky.

8. Market timing is terrible unless you time it right.

Most of the time the market rises. Unless it is a real bear market, all attempts at market timing backfire and become very costly. But when you actually encounter a real bear market, recognizing it and taking corrective actions is near life saving. But it is hard to do because you have to build and maintain the skills for so doing while not deploying them for years and sometimes many years during bull markets. Usually people who don't use skills for a long time eventually lose them. Not very many folks can do this.

9. A bear is bullheaded until you can't bear it.

The change in psychology that is the sign of a shift from a bull market to a bear market is that early in a bear market downdrafts are met with increased optimism. In a bull market, because the market has been rising more than folks expected, every correction is short, sharp and strong and met with near hysteria from panicky investors who fear the bull markets up-move will be largely retraced on the down side. They didn't expect or understand the up-move so they fear wild stories about things that could make it vanish.

But after a long bull market they have learned to always buy the break, and that long-term investors always come out ahead. And then as the market drops they see it as an opportunity and become more optimistic (which you can measure by watching professional investor sentiment), and spend their cash, using up their spare liquidity and leaving none to support stocks later.

10. When you get really good: quit.

Kids aren't so good as investors. They don't know anything yet. They are impulsive and have very short senses of time. Old investors aren't very good either. They get rigid and can't change with the winds. The best investors get best between the ages of about 35, after they've gotten some real experience, and peak by about 60 or maybe even a little earlier, by which time they start slowing down.

Different people are different but I've never seen a really old investor who hadn't pretty well lost most of his prior skill set. Part of what makes a great investor is his ability to adapt but when you get too old you lose that ability. So if you've been really good, and hit it really well, plan in advance when to quit and when you get there, just stop making decisions. Let go.

---

www.fi.com

'Ignore almost all bullish comment in newspapers about takeovers, especially hostile ones. Most of these deals destroy value, though you will not hear this from hacks, because writing about these life-or-death contests is too much fun.'

Robert Peston

George Fontanills

George Fontanills heads Pinnacle Investments of America, Inc., a hedge-fund and money management company. The trading strategies used by Pinnacle are published on www.optionetics.com.

Books
The Options Course, John Wiley, 1998 (updated)
Trade Options Online, John Wiley, 1999
The Stock Market Course, John Wiley, 2001
The Index Trading Course, John Wiley, 2006
Options Course: High Profit and Low Stress Trading Methods, John Wiley, 2005

Attaining a winning trader's edge

1. Understand the psychology of the trade; never believe that you are smarter than the markets as the markets will always win.

2. Acquire the knowledge on how the markets truly work, then test and retest your ideas and concepts until you feel confident.

3. Develop a working knowledge of what types of entry and exit orders work best.

4. Understand how to manage risk by employing the use of options strategies.

5. Pick a strategy that matches the market conditions.

6. Manage the strategy; you should always know what your next reaction point will be and what prompts you to take it.

7. Watch what moves; to be successful, you have to become a media hound.

8. Integrate fundamental, technical, and sentiment analysis into a real-world trading approach that enables you to best understand market performance.

9. Specialize in one sector and one strategy at a time.

10. Give yourself the winner's edge by always continuing to actively pursue the learning process.

'Certain technical indicators, such as relative strength, may be useful in emerging markets, but for the most part there is not enough reliable historical data for proper technical analysis. Technical analysis may have its day in emerging markets, but that day has not yet arrived.'

Mitchell Posner

Martin Fridson

Martin Fridson is Managing Director at Merrill Lynch, where he edits *Extra Credit: The Journal of High Yield Bond Research.* He was formerly principal and manager of Credit Research at Morgan Stanley.

Books

Investment Illusions, John Wiley, 1993
It Was a Very Good Year, John Wiley, 1998
How to Be a Billionaire, John Wiley, 1999
Financial Statement Analysis: A Practitioner's Guide, John Wiley, 2002
Unwarranted Intrusions: The Case Against Government Intervention in the Marketplace, John Wiley, 2006

A streetwise approach to stock selection

---

1. Matching the averages is not a bad outcome.

Over the long run, an index of small-cap stocks has far outperformed the best active mutual fund managers. In past decades, you could not buy a fund designed to replicate that index, but today you can.

2. Investors will not wake up one day and realize that the stock you're considering is too cheap.

Stock price surges require some sort of stimulus, such as an unanticipated pickup in demand or a takeover bid.

3. The stocks of highly admired companies are not bargains.

Investment counselors figure they cannot get into trouble by investing your money in a company that has gone from success to success. The problem is that all of the other investment counselors reason the same way, causing the stock to be overpriced.

4. The best oil exploration deals never get sold outside of Texas.

Organizers of limited partnerships can ordinarily raise all the money they need among their close friends, assuming they have genuinely good prospects. If you are a stranger with a modest sum to invest, the fact that you are being offered the 'opportunity' to participate is a reason to be skeptical.

5. Beware the stockbroker's blue light special.

Be careful if your broker calls to pitch you on a new investment product. The brokerage house may have created a special sales incentive and urged the salesforce to call every customer. The product is not necessarily something that fulfills your objectives.

6. Meeting a quarterly earnings target does not guarantee that a company is on a good track.

Over short periods, plenty of gimmicks are available to management to pump up the reported income figures. Overstating earnings today ensures a shortfall in the future.

7. When a red flag goes up in the area of financial reporting, assume the worst.

The company's investor relations officer is always ready with a plausible explanation for an alarming surge in receivables, revenues that are completely out of line with the industry trend, or a late filing of a quarterly statement. These excuses are notoriously unreliable.

8. Put a value of zero on a company's claim to be recession-proof.

Investment bankers coach the chief executive officers of cyclical companies to reassure investors that their particular market niche is impervious to economic downturns. At some point after the deal closes, as a rule, the economy declines and the earnings of all of the supposedly rock-steady companies go down in unison.

9. Consider IPOs from the corporate finance point of view.

Do not assume that some bright entrepreneur came up with a good business idea and then looked for a way to finance it. Investment bankers may have created the company to exploit a hot stock market or a flaw in the accounting system that enabled them to fabricate huge earnings.

10. There is always a first time.

Do not buy a stock on the premise that if some economic indicator has declined for three years in a row, it must be poised for a rebound, simply because it has never gone down four years in succession.

David R. Fried

David Fried is editor and publisher of The Buyback Letter and BuybackLetter.com, both devoted to finding opportunities among companies that repurchase their own stock.

His business and investing experience has helped him develop a unique ability to analyze a company's prospects and develop strategies to take advantage of buyback information. Mr Fried also offers investor advisory and money management services based upon these strategies.

Profiting from buybacks

Introduction

A buyback stock is stock of a company which buys back a significant number of their own shares. For 50 years, buyback stocks have outperformed the market - sometimes spectacularly so.

A major study of the U.S. stock market over a 10 year period of time found that in each four year period, value buyback stocks (buyback stocks with high book-to-market ratios) generated returns 45% higher than other stocks, 24% annually vs an annual return of 15% for the average stock. Over a 10-year period this out-performance means that $10,000 invested in the S&P 500 would grow to $40,400 while the same $10,000 invested in buyback value stocks would grow to $79,200, an out-performance of about 388%!

1. Buybacks increase the value of your shares.

Buybacks benefit stockholders in a number of ways. By decreasing the number of shares outstanding, they increase the purchasing company's earnings per share. As earnings per share increase, the price of the stock generally rises. This increases the value of the shareholders' current holdings without requiring any additional investment, and without the taxes that would be incurred if the company had paid the same money out as dividends. Additionally, buyback companies provide shareholders with a margin of support under their stock by stepping in and buying shares when their price falls. This often causes its shares to rebound faster after a market correction, as there are fewer shares available when demand returns.

2. No-one understands a company better than the company itself.

When companies buy back their own stocks, it's an enormous vote of confidence in the stock by those who know it best - the company's senior executives. No one else knows more about the firm's financial situation, it's market share, business plans, research and development programs, or new products. Those executives usually keep their plans, tactics, and research behind closed doors. However, a stock buyback tips you off that the stock is primed to go up.

3. But buybacks are not that simple.

First, not every company that announces a stock buyback actually follows through and executes the buyback as announced. Sometimes the actual number of shares purchased is far fewer than announced - converting a major buyback into a minor, insignificant one you should simply ignore.

Other times, a company cancels their stock buyback entirely, often with no public announcement. In such cases, the only way you'll know for certain that a buyback has taken place is by looking at a company's quarterly and annual reports.

4. It's important to understand a company's motivation for the buyback.

While one company's motivation for repurchasing shares may be to use them for the exercise of stock options, another firm may be repurchasing because it feels its shares are under priced and represent a good investment. In fact, 90 percent of buyback announcements do not disclose the reason or the motive behind the announcement.

5. Not all buyback companies are equal - focus on the value stocks.

In general, buyback companies outperform companies that do not buy back their own stock. But the overall best performance is seen with buyback companies that have the optimum fundamental ratios. Baskets of stocks with low price-earnings, low price-sales, low price-book ratios and high yields tend to outperform baskets of stocks with high price-earnings, price-sales, and price-book ratios and low yields.

When a share repurchase effect is added to the mix this effect is even more pronounced. Academic research shows ('Market underreaction to open market share repurchases' - Ikenberry, Lakonishok and Vermaelen) that buyback stocks outperform accross all valuations. However the biggest outperformance comes from the stocks with the lowest fundamental values.

6. Avoid the companies that announce buybacks, but never follow through.

Some companies are habitual offenders. They make buyback announcements to signal that they believe their shares are undervalued, but never follow through with their announced plans.

7. Some companies buy back stock only if and when their shares are bargain-priced.

Sky West Airlines is an example of this type of company. Sky West only repurchases shares when they are close to book value. If the share price rises much beyond that level, the company won't buy its shares back. Companies like Sky West give the opportunity to make good profits over a two or three year period - so long as you can buy shares close to the price at which the company itself purchases them.

8. Follow the companies committed to long-term buyback programs as a way of building shareholder value.

These companies can be counted on to fulfill their promise when they announce a stock buyback. It's this group that has the most appeal for long-term investors. A prime example is Coca-Cola, perhaps the ultimate buyback company. Since beginning its buyback program in 1984, Coke has repurchased 966 million shares (adjusted for splits). In their annual report, Coca-Cola states that it has "always viewed its stock as a consistent bargain for long-term holders." During the period from 1984-1996, Coca-Cola's stock buyback has turned 14% annual gains in profitability into 18% annual growth in per-share earnings.

9. The corollary to buyback investing is to avoid companies that are issuing additional shares.

A study by Loughran and Ritter ('The New Issues Puzzle') found that the average annual return of issuing companies in their sample was 7% a year, compared with a 15% return from a comparable sample of non-issuing companies. The study's conclusion: "Investing in firms issuing stock is hazardous to your wealth."

www.buybackletter.com

'Trust the debt analysts. Their financial models for companies are far more rigorous than those of the equity crowd.'

Thom Calandra

Foster Friess

Foster Friess is best known as the founder of Friess Associates and its flagship mutual fund, Brandywine.

Kiplinger's listed Brandywine as one of the top three no-load growth funds in America for results in the 10 years through 1997. *The Wall Street Journal* highlighted Brandywine as one of only eight funds with over $1 billion in assets to outpace the Wilshire 5000 Index by at least 15 percentage points in 1999 and 2000. What about 1998? That might be the Fund's best year because Foster and his team adhered to their investment disciplines, forgoing short-lived gains to avoid the eventual implosion of the dot-com and tech-stock bubble. *Money* magazine concluded: "Today, after the collapse of many high-priced stocks, Friess' caution looks a lot like prescience."

Investing in growth companies

1. Never invest in the stock market; invest in individual businesses.

The benefits of focusing on the strength and promise of individual companies outweigh the effects of more difficult to predict broad factors such as interest rates, foreign currency values and general market trends. For more than 26 years, we have capitalized on the historic relationship between earnings performance and stock prices by isolating rapidly growing companies that sell for reasonable multiples of forward earnings.

2. Buy earnings, not dreams.

Three things ultimately determine a company's value: the first is earnings, the second is earnings and the third is earnings. Sure, other factors drive stock prices, but our strategy is committed to the earnings power of individual companies. We require three years of earnings history and three years in after-tax income before a stock crosses our researchers' radar screens, keeping us out of short-lived trends like the recent dot-com debacle.

3. Prefer modest P/E ratios over high P/E ratios.

We typically avoid over-researched, big-name, highly visible, high-P/E companies - the Microsofts, WalMarts and Home Depots of the world. If a shoe maker grows earnings 40 percent a year in a mature industry and sells at 10 times estimates, we'd find it much more exciting than an optical networking company that grows earnings 30 percent with a forward P/E of 50.

4. 'Pigs at the Trough'.

Replace good ideas with great ones. Like a pig that has eaten its fill is displaced by a hungrier pig at the barnyard trough, potential holdings must earn their way into the portfolio by having more upside potential than an existing holding. Our system of forced displacement allows us to nimbly maneuver toward companies with earnings strength despite broad changes that often catch other investors off guard.

5. Don't buy 'market leaders'.

Find a #7 company in an industry headed for the # 3 spot because its recognition increases and its P/E expands. There's more money to be made in finding tomorrow's winners than in chasing yesterday's.

We were early buyers in Cisco in 1990, one year after it went public, and the second largest holder of Dell years back. When they become household names with hefty prices relative to their earnings growth, we sold for lesser knowns with substantially more earnings upside per dollar invested.

6. Don't subscribe to the 'I Love Lucy' investment strategy.

Lucy believed the 10 cents a jar she and Ethel lost on their kitchen-based jam business could be 'made up on volume.' The strategy didn't work for them, it didn't work for the dotcoms and it will never work.

In 1998 and 1999, analysts hyped internet start-ups preaching 'earnings don't matter' in the 'new economy,' focusing instead on price-to-sales ratios and website 'hits'. Only companies that turn an innovative idea into a consistent profit-generating business deserve our attention.

7. Don't let the tax tail wag the investment dog.

Gains can and do evaporate. We operate under the premise that shareholders would rather make money than risk losing it in order to avoid a tax bill. Brandywine's taxable shareholders made over $3 billion dollars in 1999 and 2000. Sales of Nortel, Nokia and other technology stocks near all-time highs on signs of deteriorating fundamentals saved $1 billion.

8. Indexing makes no sense.

Investing in a pre-constructed basket of stocks, including the sick and outrageously over-valued ones, has never made sense to us. There are just too many variables. After a tremendous run-up in the 'Nifty-Fifty,' the S&P 500 peaked in 1973, failing to reach that level again for nine years. In the 24 months ended March 31, the S&P 500 as a proxy for index investors fell 8 percent while Brandywine grew 40 percent. Our challenge is to uncover fundamental developments, both good and bad, before others pick up on them.

9. Embrace entrepreneurship through teamwork.

Make the ultimate measure of success how well clients and shareholders perform. The Friess research team structure is unique. Our seven research teams are not in competition. They cooperate, sharing information from each contact they make in a real-time database and alerting others to potential opportunities. Team decisions are surprisingly selfless. There have been years when the largest bonus did not go to the person with the best raw performance, but to someone who helped other teammates excel.

10. Accentuate the positive.

Anyone who doesn't admit to making mistakes in the investment business hasn't been in it long enough. Foster is motivated by Philippians 4:8, which says, 'Whatever is true, whatever is noble, whatever is right, whatever is pure, whatever is lovely, whatever is admirable - if anything is excellent or praiseworthy - dwell on such things.' We refer to mistakes as 'adjustment opportunities,' or AOs, since each AO provides insight into how we might address the situation better next time.

www.bfunds.com

'It is easy to get to a high value for a company – just underestimate the capital investments that it will need to make.'

Nick Antill

Tony Golding

Tony spent 24 years in the City, mostly with Flemings, as an investment analyst in a stockbroking firm, in fund management (as head of research) and, latterly, in investment banking.

Tony left Flemings in 1998 to write *'The City: Inside The Great Expectation Machine - Myth And Reality In Institutional Investment And the Stock Market'*.

Books

The City: Inside The Great Expectation Machine, FT Prentice Hall, 2000

Interpreting broker research and recommendations

1. Don't take broker research recommendations at face value.

Be as sceptical as you would if you were buying a used car. You know that the salesman is likely to be more interested in doing the deal than worrying whether it will run smoothly for the next year, or even two!

2. 'Buy' recommendations are always in the majority.

'Hold' is also common but 'sell' recommendations are virtually in the hens' teeth category. Which is fine in a bull market when a rising tide floats all boats. But this built-in 'buy bias' clearly doesn't make sense when share prices are falling and brokers continue to urge purchase all the way down.

3. Broker recommendations have always had a strong 'buy bias'.

No analyst wants to risk offending the company he is researching as he is heavily reliant on it for information. The problem is that this 'buy bias' has become significantly worse in the last few years. The main reason is the increasing involvement of analysts with investment banking work, mostly new issues and advising on acquisitions.

4. It is an unfortunate fact that investment banking is much, much more profitable than buying and selling shares for investment institutions.

So increasingly research is used by investment banks to make corporate clients - or potential corporate clients - feel warm and cuddly. Institutions have responded to this lack of objectivity by setting up their own internal research. They now use equity analysts primarily for information (on the company and its sector) and not much for advice on whether to buy, hold or sell.

5. What is written and what is said are two very different things.

A fund manager can call an analyst to ask him what he really thinks of a stock. You can't! Often analysts would like to be more objective but - in public at least - have to go along with their employer's 'house view'.

6. The larger the investment bank or stockbroking firm that employs the analyst making the recommendation, the less likely it is to reflect what the analyst really thinks.

In big, integrated investment banks the pressures to toe the line are intense though some - those with a tradition of independent research - give their analysts greater freedom.

7. When judging the objectivity of recommendations, look at where the fees are earned.

Objective recommendations (including a willingness to use the dreaded 'sell' word!) are much more likely to come from firms that rely exclusively or heavily on trading shares for their living and do little or no investment banking.

8. The bottom line is: the private investor needs to take care.

Treat recommendations with due scepticism. For many analysts working in investment banks, getting the share-price right is no longer their primary motivation.

www.bedfordpark.demon.co.uk/city

Julio Gomez

Julio Gomez is CEO of the company which carries his name and which is a leader in the field of 'customer experience measurement' in e-commerce. In the investment world, the Gomez ratings of online brokers are highly influential both within the industry and among the traders and investors who use broker services.

Selecting an online broker

1. Seek and ye shall find.

A virtual who's who of clicks and bricks and pure-play financial services offer online investment services catering to almost every customer segment and lifestyle need. Like a pair of shoes, you'll need to pick a broker that best fits your needs. This process begins with a basic understanding of your investment profile ('hyperactive investor', 'serious investor', 'life goal planner' and 'one-stop-shopper') and what you value most in an online relationship with a financial services firm (customer confidence, on-site resources, overall costs and relationship services). Then look to see if the broker has the products you need. For example, not all sites offer no load and no fee mutual funds. Some offer options trading, short selling and cash management services. Others don't.

2. Parsimony is paramount.

Opening an account should be an easy and straightforward exercise. The account application form should be intuitive and self-explanatory, with a reasonable amount of context-sensitive help to define investment and technical jargon as questions arise. If this isn't the case, it can be indicative of more serious internal business process and customer service shortcomings. Investors who want to trade ASAP, will want to select a broker that handles real-time account transfers via check or credit card.

3. Multiple touch points are critical.

Win or lose, online investing can be a solitary endeavor, particularly if you choose a 'go it alone' strategy with a discount or deep discount firm. Even the most self-directed investor, however, will at some point need to contact his brokerage firm. It's therefore essential to have multiple channels for reaching your firm: in person at an office, over the phone or via the net. Reputable firms provide contact information at key junctures of their sites.

4. Customer service differentiates leaders from laggards.

Whether you're a first-time investor or a seasoned pro, you may need technical help and other educational materials. Online FAQs, web-based e-mail and telephone support are essential starting points. New approaches are emerging in the form of instant online chat and voice services that enable near instantaneous interaction with customer service reps. Though customer service varies with market activity and firm size and staffing, a golden rule goes something like this: it shouldn't take more than five minutes to reach a customer service rep and five minutes to resolve your question.

5. An educated investor is the best investor.

Even deep discount firms have come to the realization that they must offer third-party research from reputable providers and investment planning tools to placate everyone from newbie through veteran investors. Quotes, charts, news, screening tools, and life-event calculators are starters. These tools should generally allow investors to transact directly from the pages on which they reside.

6. What you see is what you get.

You wouldn't shop in a store with cluttered aisles. Nor would you put your money in a bank whose vault lacks proper safeguarding. Seeing isn't always believing, but you'll get some sense of the client experience by surfing the public areas of the site. One way to get a good feel is to put the site's trading demo through its paces. If it's easy to use, understandable and fast enough, chances are the site proper is the same way.

7. The price must be right.

Fees and commissions must be acceptable to you and your financial circumstances. The only way to gauge this is to know what you're getting for the money spent. Low commission sites normally connote frills-free services. That's fine if you're confident in your investment instincts, have your own trading formula or have access to a wealth of educational tools and educational guides at personal finance portals or other web sites, personal financial management software packages or print publications. Investors who require a little more hand-holding - online or offline - should consider sites with a deeper array of financial planning calculators and research and the opportunity of working with a registered investment advisor. There's a cost associated with this type of service, of course, either in higher commission rates or fee-based services tied to the number of transactions or assets under management.

8. Jacks or better ante.

Clearly you have some cash to play with if you're considering opening an online brokerage account. To past muster you'll need to meet the broker's minimum deposit or minimum balance requirements. They vary based on the size of the broker and the market segment targeted. Make sure you read the fine print of the online broker's terms & conditions agreements: many brokers are now hitting clients with inactivity fees.

9. Security starts at the home (page).

Online trading is no less secure than trading over the telephone, but you shouldn't trust just anyone with your hard earned cash. You should only trust those firms that properly secure their sites - you can tell by the 'https' in your browser's address field or the padlock that should appear in the systems tray when you access a so-called secure site area. Also make sure you read the firm's security policy - which hopefully is accessible from the homepage. The firm should clearly articulate its security processes (relating to the site's underlying technology and the firm's business practices). Pay careful attention to fraud guarantees - which like health insurance you hope you'll never need to avail yourself of. Make sure the firm is a member of SIPC (Securities Investor Protection Corp.), or the equivalent (if such exists) in other markets, which protects up to $500,000 in assets.

10. Character witnesses are critical.

As with any business deal where money changes hands, you want to know how reputable your prospective broker is before signing on the dotted line. Sure you've seen their commercials, but what do real people like you think? Does the firm pay lip service to privacy or does it jealously guard your personal data like a trusted bodyguard? You might want to consult knowledgeable friends or online message boards. The National Association of Securities Dealers Web site (nasdr.com) offers regulatory insights and details actions pending and taken against specific firms.

---

www.gomez.com

'Never invest in a company on the basis of a single patent. In few industries can a single patent transform a company.'

Bruce Berman

Philip Gotthelf

Philip Gotthelf publishes the Commodex System and Commodity Futures Forecast Service. His writing has appeared in *Futures* magazine, *Investing, Stocks and Commodities, Top Farmer, Barron's, Forbes, The Wall Street Journal* and *Fortune*, among others. He is a regular guest on CNBC, MS-NBC, and CNN.

Books
Precious Metals Trading: How to Profit from Major Market Moves,
John Wiley & Sons Inc, 2005

Precious metals trading

1. Precious metals are not 'investments' in the traditional sense.

Since they have no intrinsic yield like stock dividends or bond interest, any profit must result from an accurate price forecast. Therefore, precious metals should be considered 'trading vehicles' similar to other commodities and international currencies. When trading metals, the objective is to determine the trend and its associated time frame. A trend is defined as a consistent and observable price direction over a reasonable time. Metals generally exhibit long term or secular trends over several months. These price patterns can usually be accurately identified using moving averages between 20-days and 60-days.

2. Precious metals fall into two categories: monetary and industrial.

Gold essentially stands alone as a *monetary* precious metal. Silver, platinum, and palladium are *industrial* precious metals. The category for any precious metal is determined by the amount of metal consumed for industrial purposes, i.e. industrial demand.

Palladium represents the most industrial precious metal with virtually none used for 'investment' or jewelry. Most palladium is used for catalytic processes. Platinum rates second as an industrial precious metal with most demand coming from catalysts, too. However, there is a modest amount of platinum purchased for hoarding (bullion) and more, still, for jewelry. Silver is hoarded as bullion, coins, and medallions. However, its number one use is for film and photographic processes. Although gold has many industrial applications in electronics, chemistry, and processes, its primary application is as a store as value. It is mostly a 'monetary' metal. Always view a precious metal objectively within its respective category.

3. Precious metals maintain parity with currencies.

Precious metals reflect the value of currency as parity or the ratio of currency to metal defined as price. Metals maintain easily identifiable parity that allows cross currency trading against a precious metals standard. If a currency is 'pegged' to metal (i.e. gold), its gold parity becomes constant. When trading metals, always be aware of cross parity relationships between popular currencies like the U.S. Dollar, European Currency Unit, and Japanese Yen. A dramatic change in cross parity represents an element of risk and exposure.

4. If metals are currency, they cannot be traded for profit.

Although unlikely, there is always the possibility of a return to a metals currency standard (i.e. Gold Standard). If currency value is fixed to metal, the metal cannot appreciate or depreciate against the currency and it loses all speculative potential. Be careful what you wish for if it is a return to a metals standard. It forecloses opportunity.

5. Metals can fall below production costs.

In particular, precious metals that are byproducts of base metals production are highly sensitive to base metal values. If copper soars, silver can suffer because silver is a byproduct of copper. Never trade the long side based upon a presumption the price is close or below production costs.

6. Precious metals do not always track inflation.

Precious metals have lost ground to derivative vehicles as a hedge against inflation or changing interest rates. The old rule that gold and silver react to inflation is, itself, inflated since inflation can be hedged using currency futures, related options, forwards, and interest rate futures strategies. Never assume inflation automatically boosts precious metals.

7. Metals are subject to structural change.

Few trading vehicles have undergone as much 'structural change' as precious metals. In reality, these commodities have very limited price histories since they have been linked to currency parity over the past several hundred years. Structural change is defined as a change that completely alters a commodity's fundamentals. For example, the demise of a gold or silver standard was a structural change allowing values to float. The development of digital imaging that does not consume silver is a structural change for silver demand. The commercial development of platinum-based fuel cells is a potential structural change for this metal. Gold divestiture by central banks is a structural change in gold hoarding. Always look for structural change and never trade against it over any prolonged period.

8. Never seek a predetermined top or bottom.

Always attempt to follow a trend rather than pick a top or bottom based upon price levels alone. History proves silver can fall well below $5 that was previously viewed as a 'floor'. Palladium can soar beyond $1,000 per ounce seen in 2001 . . . virtually unthinkable before it happened. There are no tops and almost no bottoms.

9. Precious metals do not always move in tandem.

In the past, precious metals tended to trend in similar directions under similar fundamental assumptions. In the new precious metals market, each dances to a different drummer. Silver fundamentals are not the same as gold and these can move inversely. Platinum and palladium can be diametrically opposite based upon substitutability. Always analyze each metal on its own merits.

10. Metals are good business.

Falling metals prices do not automatically translate into weak corporate performances. Gold stocks can remain strong in a weaker gold market. Always look at the whole picture. Few companies produce a product that has intrinsic value like gold and other precious metals. Thus, gold mining stocks can offer double security in crisis times because of the underlying presumption of value. Gold companies are increasing efficiencies (dropping production costs) in pace with gold price trends. It is wise to have some of the precious metals sector represented in any diversified investment portfolio.

11. Wonders never cease.

In 1989, Professors Pons and Fleischmann announced Cold Fusion using palladium. Prices soared. Cold fusion was debunked. Prices crashed. Never rule out wonderous processes that incorporate precious metals. The platinum fuel cell could become the 'engine of the future'. Palladium could prove Cold Fusion a reality. We may perfect extracting gold from sea water. Always be prepared to accept and react. There's a reason humankind gravitates toward precious metals like gold, silver, and the platinum group. We simply don't know why . . . yet.

www.commodex.com

'If you want to be entertained, take up sky diving. There is an inverse correlation between an investment's entertainment value and its expected return.'

William Bernstein

Jeremy Grantham

Jeremy Grantham co-founded Grantham, Mayo, Van Otterloo & Co. LLC (GMO) in 1977.

GMO is an institutional investment management firm with over $20 billion under management. Jeremy Grantham serves as its chief investment strategist and oversees its quantitative products and investment strategies.

The firm runs over 35 equity investment products both traditionally and quantitatively managed for the U.S. and foreign markets including emerging countries.

Investment management

1. Indexing is hard to beat, and relative passivity is not a vice.

The investment management business creates no value, but it costs, in round numbers, 1% a year to play the game.

In total, fund managers are the market and given the costs they collectively must underperform. The U.S. stock market is approximately efficient - 95% or more of all market moves are unknowable noise and perhaps 5% are manageable (or predictable).

2. Historically, equity investors have over-paid for comfort and excitement.

Paying up for comfort (stability, information, size, consensus, market domination, and brand names) and excitement (growth, profitability, management skills, technological change, cyclicality, volatility, and most of all, acceleration in all these) as growth managers do for example, is not necessarily foolish, for their clients also like these characteristics.

Conversely, when a value manager is very wrong - as he will be sooner or later - he will be fired more quickly than a growth manager.

3. One of the keys to investment management is reducing risk by balancing Newton (momentum & growth) and regression (value).

Bodies in motion tend to stay in motion (Newton's First Law). Earnings and stock prices with great yearly momentum tend to keep moving in the same direction for a while, perhaps because economic cycles are, on average, longer than a year.

Be aware that everything concerning markets and economies regresses from extremes towards normal faster than people think (e.g., sales growth, profitability, management skill, investment styles, and good fortune).

4. Ability to handle illiquidity is a major advantage for long-term investors.

Because everyone's time horizons are shorter than they should be, liquidity is overpriced. A long-term investor should always try to exploit the other guy's short-term horizon and be paid for taking illiquidity.

5. Confidence factors are the primary influences on price levels in the U.S. market, not fundamental factors like growth and real interest rates.

Confidence is primarily affected by inflation, volatility of the economy and corporate profit margins (not growth) and the importance and make-up of confidence has been remarkably stable for 100 years or more.

Because rising margins drive confidence and p/e's up and sales growth does not, market cycles tend to double count: rising margins x higher p/e's followed by falling margins x lower p/e's. Therefore, the market deviates far more from economic trend than strictly financial logic would allow. Trading noise further adds to this non-economic volatility.

6. The single most important advantage for traditional investors vs. quants is a tight focus.

Quants will never win in U.S. Electric Utilities. For quants, the relative advantages are complexity and speed of price moves (however because quants can handle more variables they can't resist using them -they can easily end by throwing in the kitchen sink and drowning in detail and data mining). In addition, liquidity problems and risk control are also more easily addressed by quants. Quantitative models tend, like chess models, to get a little better every year. While traditional managers can only handle so much data. (But unlike chess models, quants do not have to beat Kasparov but only the average market player.)

7. Asset allocators must be picked on faith.

With a 60% hit rate it takes a good manager only 1.5 years to prove he can pick stocks because of many decisions a year, but 55 years to prove he can pick stocks vs. bonds (assuming only one decision every 3 years).

8. Investment managers are harder to pick than stocks.

Clients have to choose between facts (past performance) and the conflicting marketing claims of several potential managers. As sensible businessmen, clients will usually feel they have to go with the past facts. They therefore rotate into previously strong styles which regress (since opportunities by style regress, past performance tends to be negatively correlated with future relative performance), dooming most active clients to failure. 90% of what passes for brilliance or incompetence in investing is the ebb and flow of investment style (growth, value, small, foreign).

www.gmo.com

'Why look for the needle in the haystack? Owning the entire stock market is the ultimate diversifier. Buy the haystack!'

John C. Bogle

Robert V. Green

Robert V. Green is an accomplished investor, entrepreneur, and business writer. He was the founder and President of Numetrics, which created a personal portfolio management product for individuals. He was also the president and founder of 401(k) Today, the first internet based advisory service for participants in 401(k) plans. He writes about investing at Briefing.com, where he does original research on companies and follows trends in technology.

Handling the emotional side of investing

1. There is no such thing as a good stock.

There are only good companies. When someone tells you "this is a good stock" you need to look beyond the stock chart. *Why* is the company a good company? How will it grow its business? If you can't answer these questions, you don't know what you own.

2. Have a premise.

When you buy a stock you must have a premise. A premise is a reason why that particular stock will go up. For best results, the premise will be one that explains why the company's line of business will increase, and why the marketplace will value that business at current or higher multiples. Without a premise, you don't own an investment, you just own a stock.

3. Think trends. Buy stocks.

If you really want to invest in big growth stocks, you need to invest in secular trends. Secular trends are events unrelated to either the economy or individual company events. The advent of the PC, the birth of the internet, and the desire for wireless phones, are all secular trends. The biggest investment winners are those companies which are ideally placed to reap the benefits of large secular changes. Microsoft and Intel rode the transition to PCs as computing power became cheaper and cheaper. Nokia, Motorola, Qualcomm, and Ericsson all found themselves unable to keep up with demand in the mid 1990s, when wireless phones finally reached the critical price points. If you want really big winners, find the trend, then find the stocks.

4. Know your risk tolerance.

The biggest mistake most investors make is to buy positions with more risk than they can really tolerate. This is where most people got hurt in the internet bubble burst. They had no idea they owned risky stocks. If you can always tolerate, both financially and emotionally, the complete loss of your entire position, you obviously will be okay. But most people aren't in that position. Figure out how much downside you can live with without having to sell. Figure this out before you buy the stock.

5. Don't average down to feel better.

'Averaging down' is often a way to lose more. If you believe in the company, and the price goes down, you may want to invest more. But if you, like many others, purchase more simply to lower your 'break even' stock price, you are making a mistake. If you find yourself calculating new 'average price per share' points, you might be averaging down for the wrong reason.

6. Don't miss the train to shave a dime.

If you are investing in a major trend through a stock, and have a multi-year investment horizon, what difference does a few cents per share make on your purchase? Many investors try to place buys with limit orders just below the ask, and wind up missing the purchase. If you really want a stock, particularly a big position, place a limit order at the ask, or even slightly higher. You will at least get the order. This is especially important if you are trying to buy far more shares than the current ask size. If you are right about the trend, you will never miss the extra ten cents per share.

7. Don't buy hot and watch cold!

Many investors buy a 'hot stock' and immediately look for big gains. When they don't happen, the stock falls away from the daily attention list. Pretty soon it starts to edge downward, and, emotionally, the investor stops watching it. Pain avoidance is common to us all. But you can't let pain avoidance prevent you from watching your stock. If you do, you often take a look two months later and find the stock is far from hot, and you are now presented with a really painful decision.

8. A hold is as good as a buy!

There is no such thing as a 'hold' decision. If you wouldn't buy the stock again today, assuming you had additional money, you should either sell, or admit that you are confused. Resolve the confusion. The hold condition often happens when you have owned a stock for years, are way ahead of your basis, and are basically happy. But what is driving the stock today? What will make the price rise in the future? Why would you buy the stock today, assuming you didn't own it? If you don't know, you don't have a premise for this stock. See rule 2.

9. Don't be an inadvertent long-term holder!

When your premise doesn't work out, or you no longer believe in the stock, you must sell, even if it means a loss. Holding on just to 'get my money back' is the single biggest reason for losing more money. Who owns all those stocks that have lost 98% of their value in 2000? A good percentage is owned by people who turned into long-term holders inadvertently, when they made the decision to just stick it out.

10. You will lose money!

You won't be right every time. If you are going to be an investor, you need to become accustomed to losing money on some positions. This rule is the natural consequence of living up to rules 5, 7, and 9. Taking losses is often the only way you can save your capital from further losses.

copyright: The RVG Corporation

---

www.briefing.com

'Historically, convertible bonds have offered about two-thirds of the upside performance and about one-third of the downside risk of the underlying common stock.'

John P. Calamos

Herb Greenberg

Herb Greenberg is senior columnist for TheStreet.com. Before joining TheStreet.com he was a columnist for 10 years at the *San Francisco Chronicle*, and a reporter for the *Chicago Tribune*. He also spent a year as an analyst at an arbitrage partnership.

Avoiding problem stocks: lessons from *Lernout & Hauspie*

Lernout & Hauspie, a Bulgarian developer of voice recognition software, found a fast audience with Wall Street with its sexy story: *software that will eliminate the need to type*. But the sizzle was more than the substance, causing the company to catch the eye of shortsellers who began probing its underbelly. Not only was it run by Gaston Bastiaens, known in Silicon Valley for the fast rise and fall of Quarterdeck, but it was engaged in various related party dealings that questioned the quality of its financial results. The company denied there were problems, but in the end Lernout filed for bankruptcy and within months the company's co-founders and former CEO were arrested on securities fraud charges. The stock, which once traded as high as $72 USD in its high flying days, now trades for just pennies.

1. Don't be fooled by a supposedly hot new technology that is a better story than a business.

Lernout & Hauspie is the poster child for this. Speech-recognition technology is likely to be big one day, but in all likelihood it will be a low margin product that is given away.

2. If one analyst drops coverage of a company, veering from a crowded pack, find out why.

This could be the first sign of trouble.

3. Don't ignore stories about shortsellers who are raising critical issues about a company.

This is often the first sign of trouble.

4. Take note if a company picks a public fight with shortsellers and/or refuses to return calls to reporters.

This IS the sign of trouble!

5. Beware of companies that say they are immune from issues hurting their competitors.

In very few cases is this so.

6. Beware of companies that rely heavily on related-party or too-close-for-comfort transactions, no matter how well they're disclosed.

In Lernout's case there was a wide web that, in the end, helped inflate revenue and reduce expenses.

7. Don't be fooled by companies that boast investments by well-known companies like Intel and Microsoft.

Both held big stakes in Lernout & Hauspie.

8. Don't get fooled by a rapidly rising stock price.

It doesn't necessarily reflect underlying fundamentals and sometimes means nothing more than . . . the stock is rising! Lernout's went from $20 to $72 in a flash, making its investors feel like geniuses.

9. Be leery of any company in which the analysts raise their target price while cutting earnings estimates.

It simply doesn't make sense unless they're trying to hype it to issue stock.

10. The minute you think you're a genius - that you have it all figured out - start looking over your shoulder.

You are about to get blindsided.

---

www.TheStreet.com

Bill Gross

Mr. Gross is a founder and Managing Director of Pacific Investment Management Company (PIMCO) and has been associated with the firm for 30 years. As Chief Investment Officer of PIMCO he oversees the management of over $220 billion of fixed income securities. He is the author of numerous articles on the bond market, and has frequently appeared in national publications and media.

Morningstar named Mr. Gross, and his investment team, Morningstar's Fixed Income Manager of the Year for 1998 and for 2000. When presenting the award to Mr. Gross, Morningstar stated that he had earned the award by "demonstrating excellent investment skill, the courage to differ from consensus, and the commitment to shareholders necessary to deliver outstanding long-term performance."

Books
Bill Gross on Investing, John Wiley, 1997
Everything You've Heard About Investing Is Wrong, Times Books, 1997

Cost reduction and other essential lessons

1. Where are the customer's Gulfstreams?

Instead of yachts, the brokers and money managers own Gulfstreams these days – but no difference. The point is you must work intensely to keep your investment expenses as low as possible. Reduce commissions and trades. Make sure your mutual fund expenses are .5% or less annually. Keep the money in your pocket and out of the hands of those who need it the least.

2. Stocks don't always outperform bonds.

Stocks are the best liquid investment for the long term, but not for all terms. From 1930-1955, Treasury Bills outperformed the stock market. Same thing from 1960-1974, as well as for much of the first part of the Nineteenth century. Stay diversified consistent with your ability to weather an equity thunderstorm or two - and remember, slow and steady sometimes wins the race.

3. When you think you've found 'the answer' – think again.

Formulas, models, and anything that assures you that the next twenty years will resemble the last twenty years are all hokum. Examples of historical sure thing dinosaurs include a focus on money supply statistics, the Philip's 'unemployment' curve, and relevant factors which determine P/E ratios and currency levels. By the time you've got it figured out, somebody else probably has too and the predictive ability disappears.

4. The long term is the right term.

Short term fixation on economic and market movements is confusing and often leads to emotional reactions to sell at bottoms and buy at peaks. By focusing on longer term, more stable trends (demographics, globalization, political shifts) an investor gives himself a better chance to follow the right road map.

5. Turn over your portfolio at a snail's pace.

Turnover can eat into an investors profits in several ways. First of all, commissions add up and depending upon your broker can be 1%+ annually. Secondly, rapid turnover plays into the hands of Uncle Sam by providing him capital gains to feed off of. Slow and methodical changes are best for these and the reasons stated in #4 above.

6. Risk and return are Siamese twins.

Risk and return are attached at the hip. You rarely can get high returns unless you increase your risk levels. Conversely you rarely can invest in a low risk portfolio unless you sacrifice return. If you think today's equity markets offer double-digit type annual returns, you're going to have to take a lot of risk to get them. Remember NASDAQ 5000!

7. "It's different this time" is generally a losing proposition, but when it *is* different watch out.

Economic, business, and investment cycles invariably repeat, if only because human nature itself is so consistent. Investors and business people become overly optimistic at just the wrong times. The same goes for pessimism at market bottoms.

Thus the perpetual cycle is born. Every once in a while though, something dramatic changes the routine – a new technology, a change in politics, a catastrophic series of human errors. Be on the lookout. Sometimes it *is* different, but not often.

8. Beware of the snake oil and its salesmen.

Wall Street and Main Street are full of hucksters – hocking their opinions like touts at the nearest racetrack, except in this case with apparent sophistication and worldly knowledge. Know that they almost always are working for themselves and not you. Analysts' recommendations are primarily meant to line their own pockets not yours, so filter what they have to say very carefully.

9. A guru not busy being born, is busy dying.

There are very few authentic gurus in this world of investments. I've seen almost all of them come and go for nearly 30 years now. Their moment in the spotlight is rarely longer than the proverbial 15 minutes. Listen to only a few chosen experts and then with the knowledge that they are fallible and made of plaster, not marble.

www.pimco.com

'Avoid the losers' game of owning favorite stocks for the long term. Rapid and relentless change makes the odds of extended corporate dominance extremely low.'

Donald Cassidy

Steve Harmon

Steve Harmon is one of the technology industry's most-recognized analysts and investors. He was named by *Worth* in its list of fifteen top visionaries (1999); by CBS.MarketWatch as one of four 'Best of Wall Street' analysts (1998), and by *Smart Money* as one of three rising stars in technology investing (2000).

Harmon is CEO of High Velocity Ventures (www.highvelo.com), which consults entrepreneurs and venture capitalists in building businesses, and investors understand the shifts in technology with research and information about private and public companies.

Commonsense lessons on technology stocks

1. Earnings matter.

Don't pay for promises, pay for actual earnings. Things change too fast to pay for next year's performances. If a company lacks earnings it's higher risk. Debate whether or not you're comfortable with that but limit your exposure anyway by making it a small part of your overall investment strategy. Every other metric in the world is only a piece whereas earnings makes the whole.

2. Don't be wowed with the technology.

Be wowed with the business model, management team, market share, technology and most of all, cash flow and earnings. The best technology doesn't always win. Xerox PARC developed most of the key improvements for PCs and networks but yielded none of the benefit directly to Xerox the company.

3. Forget the peaks, study the valleys.

Just because a stock is 50% off its high doesn't mean it's a bargain. Don't believe the newspaper headlines. As investors we learn more from mistakes sometimes than success. Study a company's ups and downs and economic cycles - and study its P/E, not how far has it fallen from its 52-week high. How far is it off a low and is the low in line with a 'reasonable' valuation?

Reasonable being 10x to 30x earnings depending on the growth rate, or versus historical average P/E.

4. Listen to what the executives say, but more importantly, listen to what customers say.

Look at inventory pile up or order backlog. Are customers still buying its leading product or has another company moved in for competition? For example, in the ISP industry ask your local ISP what servers, routers and switches they use and why. Ask about pricing and performance.

5. Learn the difference between 'betting' and 'investing'.

A large part of what tanked the market in 2000 was that most people seemed to be speculating. Federal Reserve chairman Alan Greenspan and the Federal Reserve with its interest rate hikes were not speculating.

Research every company you want to invest in from a wide variety of sources, as well as the sector each is part of. I use several great resources including EDGAR, Zacks, First Call, Multex, Market Guide, Hoovers, a number of finance web sites, S1 filings, 10Ks, 10Qs, S&P, Media General, CSI, Bloomberg and more.

6. Diversify investments.

Stocks. Bonds. T-Bills. Real estate. With stocks, examine low, medium and high risk stocks and know why you own any one of them. Know what the company does and how economic cycles help or hurt the company. Limit your exposure to high risk stocks. If you cannot afford to lose your investment don't invest in high risk stocks.

7. Cash - how much does the tech company have?

Can it pay the bills for several years without selling equity or debt? Does it have a cash-flow positive business? Earnings to sustain itself? How much cash is on hand? Working capital? Thousands of companies don't have enough cash because they were funded by external financing - rather than sales and earnings - and investors are no longer interested in footing the bill.

8. Stock options.

Many tech companies issue stock options and it may dilute the shares outstanding (and earnings) dramatically. Typically 25% to 30% of tech companies are owned by employees. They all want to convert their options to cash some day. This option overhang is seldom computed by most analysts or investors. Look in the company filings and IPO documents to see what the total fully-diluted shares outstanding are.

9. Establish buying and selling discipline.

Always employ a stop-loss to limit your downside. Typical is making it 20% from the cost of the shares or the closing price if the stock climbs. On selling, if the stock has risen a set percentage - whatever you're comfortable with - sell some or all. Consider selling enough to cover your cost basis at the very least. Take profits. You may miss more climb but at least you have limited downside. Or if management shuffles happen quick or earnings fall short, consider selling.

10. Never get emotionally attached to a stock.

Love the company's cash flow or earnings but not the stock. Just because your father owned AT&T doesn't make it a great investment. Or a stock that did well before may not be a perpetual winner. In technology the industry changes rapidly and you must keep up with those changes.

'A common investment paradigm is "don't try to hit home runs - you make the most money by hitting a lot of singles". I couldn't disagree more.'

Richard Driehaus

John Hathaway

John C. Hathaway is a partner and managing director of Tocqueville Asset Management, a registered advisor. He manages the Tocqueville Gold Fund as well as separate portfolios for individual and institutional clients.

Investing in gold

1. An investment in gold should be based on macroeconomic considerations.

If one expects or fears rising inflation, destabilizing deflation, a bear market in stocks or bonds, or financial turmoil, gold should do well and exposure is warranted.

2. Understanding the internal dynamics of the gold market can be helpful as to investment timing issues.

For example, the weekly position reports of commodity trading funds or sentiment indicators offer useful clues as to entry or exit points for active trading strategies. Reports on physical demand for jewelry, industrial, and other uses compiled by various sources also provide some perspective. However, none of these considerations, non-monetary in nature, yield any insight as to the broad market trend. Reports of central bank selling or lending may influence the market in the short term but cannot counteract macro economic factors.

3. Excessive reliance on trading strategies to generate returns can be dangerous and counterproductive.

Returns from a 'buy and hold' strategy should be more than sufficient to compensate for the inherent volatility. Many who have tried to outsmart this market by hyperactive trading have underperformed. Success is dependent in large part on the occurrence of 'fat tail' events that lie outside the parameters of trading models.

4. Every investor should have some gold.

A reasonable allocation in a conservative, diversified portfolio is 0% to 3% during a gold bear market and 5%-10% during a bull market.

5. Equities of gold mining companies offer greater leverage than direct ownership of the metal itself.

Gold equities tend to appear expensive in comparison to those of conventional companies because they contain an embedded option component for a possible rise in the gold price. The share price sensitivity to a hypothetical rise in metal price is related to the cash flow from current production as well as the valuation impact on proven and probable reserves.

6. Watch out for companies that have hedged their gold exposure.

Although a rising tide may lift most boats, financial statements should be reviewed with special attention to hedging arrangements that could undermine participation in higher gold prices or even jeopardize financial stability. The carnage of the last twenty years has simplified the task of individual stock selection because so few have survived the gold bear market. But individual stock selection is less important than identification of the primary trend.

7. Don't get caught up in gold fever.

Even though gold itself is a conservative investment, 'gold fever' attracts a crowd of speculators, promoters, and charlatans who only want to separate investors from their money. Avoid offbeat 'exploration' companies with little or no current production and gargantuan appetites for new money.

8. Bullion or coins are a more conservative way to invest in gold than through the equities.

There is also greater liquidity with bullion for large pools of capital. Investing in the physical metal requires scrutinizing the custodial arrangements and the creditworthiness of the financial institution. Do not mistake the promise of a financial institution to settle based on the gold price, for example, a 'gold certificate' or a 'structured note' (i.e. derivative), for the actual physical possession of the metal. Insist on possession in a segregated vault, subject to unscheduled audits, and inaccessible to the trading arrangements or financial interest of the financial institution.

9. Gold is a controversial, anti-establishment investment.

Therefore, do not rely on conventional financial media and brokerage house commentary. In this area, such commentary is even more misleading and ill-informed than usual.

10. Don't settle for too little.

Should outlier events now deemed unimaginable by consensus thinking actually occur, the price target for gold would be several multiples of its current depressed price. Gold represents insurance against some sort of financial catastrophe. The magnitude of the upside is a function of the amount of paper assets that would be converted to gold irrespective of price.

www.tocqueville.com

'In a world where annual births are static, you won't make your fortune investing in baby clothes companies. Follow the growth age groups; they're buying holidays, hollyhocks, healthcare and hearing aids.'

Richard Cragg

Alan Hicks

Alan Hicks has spent over 20 years in foreign exchange with major banks, specialising in FX options since 1983. Since 1996, he has been running courses in over-the-counter financial derivatives and, more recently, has concentrated his time on the fast expanding financial spread betting market in the UK. He is an active trader in his own right using FSB to procure income and for hedging his investment portfolios.

Books

Managing Currency Risk Using FX Options, Woodhead, 2000
Foreign Exchange Options, Woodhead, 2nd ed., 1997

Financial spread betting

Introduction

Don't be frightened by the word 'betting' in financial spread betting (FSB). Investing through FSB is not the same as betting at the racetrack (the risk /return profile is completely different). The FSB market can be viewed as an over-the-counter (OTC) equivalent to a cash-settled financial futures contract and, as such, may offer a more efficient, cost effective method of profiting from stock (and other market) movements.

There is no need to use a broker. Users reap the benefits from dealing in an OTC market - you talk directly to the market makers and you can specify your own contract size (not restricted to contract specifications or share size amounts). This has the immediate effect of reducing the costs associated with using a broker in exchange listed markets such as stock and futures exchanges.

1. Deal outside Exchange market hours.

Many of the FSB firms operate when the underlying cash markets are closed; some firms operate 24 hours for certain markets such as stock indices. This means you can make investments (or get out of bad positions) ahead of the crowd. Don't be put off by wider bid-ask spreads if you strongly believe that the market will open higher or lower - a few points lost in the spread will look tiny compared to a market open price driven by a wall of money waiting for the first price!

2. FSB prices can be a leading indicator for the underlying.

Many stockbrokers give forecasts of where a particular stock, or market, might open or close but such advice is not backed by any fact - it is just waffle to entice buy and sell orders where they can collect their commissions. FSB prices are not just forecasts - they are real dealing prices - the smart money is already on. Evidence the recent flotation of Friends Provident in the UK. The traditional stockbrokers were estimating the first day's price to be in a range of 210-270, when the FSB market was dealing 220-225. The FSB price, being backed by actual transactions, was the more accurate indicator.

3. Open accounts with at least three FSB firms.

FSB firms will usually have a bias to buy or sell a particular stock or index based on their position (whether they are already long or short), and perception of the direction of the next price move. This means you will sometimes get different prices from different FSB firms - which is great because it has the net effect of reducing the bid-ask spread - but does mean that you will need more than one account.

Calling different FSB firms need not be an onerous task as most display their prices on the internet. Use the internet price as a guide, then call the dealer (either by telephone or by a dealing system, if provided) to get a dealing price - there may, or may not, be a difference depending on the FSB firm concerned and the trading software employed. Thus, it is possible to talk to two (or more!) firms at the same time if markets are moving fast.

4. Understand the forward value.

FSB is based on the underlying future value of a particular stock or index. Thus you will not normally get the cash price of the asset as related in the relevant stock exchange price. This means that the FSB price will normally be higher than the cash price. But do not be put off if buying this 'high' price - you have not paid the cash to buy the stock in the first place, and will benefit from the interest accrual over the time the position is held (less any dividend that might be paid).

5. Understand the tax considerations.

Profits from FSB in some countries - including the UK - are tax free, so it makes a lot of sense to invest through this method. In the UK, FSB also avoids stamp duty and broker/exchange fees. However, FSB losses are not deductible for tax purposes and this should be borne in mind when arbitraging (see below) or hedging. Thus, you should always look for the FSB 'leg' of any strategy to be where the profit should accrue.

6. Arbitrage opportunities.

It is possible to arbitrage price differences between the FSB market and other derivatives such as CFDs (Contracts for Differences) and financial futures and options. Or, if you are very quick, between the FSB firms themselves (don't forget, FSB is an un-brokered OTC market). However, you will need to have several accounts and manage the resultant cash flows that make arbitrage capital intensive. In addition, the tax implications will make arbitrage somewhat complex as losses on betting may not be offset against capital gains in other markets.

7. Always ask for a two-way price.

Never disclose your direction - whether you intend to buy or sell - before you get a two-way (bid and offer) dealing price. This rule applies to all markets but especially to OTC markets such as FSB. The very nature of the product implies that you will get a two-way price automatically, so it is normally down to the investor making the mistake of disclosing their intentions. If, by chance, the FSB dealer asks whether you want to buy or sell, respond by saying, "I will let you know after you make me a two-way price".

8. Show your interest.

This is the opposite statement to that above and only applies after receiving a two-way price. FSB is an OTC market - you are dealing direct with your counterparty - so there is nothing wrong in asking if the firm can meet a specific price for you. A typical conversation might go like this: -

Investor: "May I see your September Vodaphone please?"

FSB firm: "152-155"

Investor: "Any interest to offer me at 154 in £50?"

Whether or not you get the 'improvement' is up to the FSB dealer but, in all cases, you will get an instant yes or no. Note that the act of showing your interest (in this example to buy £50 per point - equal to buying 5,000 shares in Vodaphone Plc) is not a limit order - the ensuing 'yes/no' means you have either bought the shares at 154 or nothing has been done at all - no order has been left in either event.)

www.fenics.com

'The entire financial industry exists to sell product. If you don't understand this basic maxim, you'll be misled time after time.'

Timothy Vick

Yale Hirsch

Yale Hirsch is Chairman of The Hirsch Organization, an independent investment research and publishing organization. Hirsch publishes two monthly newsletters, the annual Stock Trader's Almanac, other books and special reports, and a daily market timing hotline. Its focus has always been on the individual investor and all of its recommendations are suited to individual investors, including those with small stakes. Much of Hirsch's research is also used by professionals, especially his famous recurring market pattern studies and discoveries.

A stock trader's almanac

1. As January goes, so goes the year - only three significant errors in 51 years.

Since 1950, the January Barometer has predicted the annual major trend of the stock market with amazing accuracy. Based on whether Standard & Poor's composite index is up or down in January, most years (excluding six flat years 1956, 1970, 1978, 1984, 1992 and 1994,) have, in essence, followed suit. Of three significant errors 1966, 1968, and 1982, Vietnam affected the first two. However, there were no errors in odd years when new congresses convened. Bear markets began or continued when January's had a loss. The six flat years switched directions in the year's final months.

2. Invest in the market between November and April each year.

My 'best six months' discovery racks up 99.6% of all gains compared to 0.4% for the other six months of the year. Since 1950 an excellent strategy has been to invest in the market between November 1st and April 30th each year and then to switch into fixed income securities for the other six months of the year. I discovered this strategy in 1986. Investing $10,000 and reinvesting proceeds during all November-April periods since 1950 would have gained $415,890, outperforming May-October's puny $1,743. As sensational as these results are, they can be more than doubled with a simple timing oscillator.

3. Gains in third and forth years of Presidential terms triple those of first and second years.

Stock prices have been impacted by the presidential election cycle for 170 years, gaining 722.4% in the second halves of presidential terms vs. 251.7% in the first halves. Nine major bottoms occurred during the last ten midterm-election years.

4. If Santa Claus fails to call, bears may come to Broad and Wall.

Santa tends to come to Wall Street nearly every year, bringing a short, sweet, respectable rally within the last 5 days of the year and the first 2 in January. This has been good for a gain of 1.7% on average in the past half century, a theoretical 80% annual rate of return. Santa's failure to show usually preceded bear markets or times stocks could be purchased at much lower prices later in the New Year. The bear market that began in 2000 was preceded by a 4.0% loss during the holiday period.

5. We tend to pay the piper in post-Presidential election years.

Politics being what it is, incumbent administrations during election years try to make the economy look good to impress the electorate and tend to put off unpopular decisions until the votes are counted. This produces an American phenomenon - the Post-Election Year Syndrome. The year begins with an Inaugural Ball, after which the piper must be paid. Americans have paid, and paid, and paid in the past. It is rare indeed when a victorious candidate succeeds in fulfilling his winning campaign promise of peace and prosperity. In the past 22 post-election years, 3 major wars began, 4 drastic bear markets started, and 10 less severe bear markets occurred or were in progress. Only in 1925 and the previous 3 post-election years were American blessed with peace and prosperity.

6. Buy stocks at mid-term election-year lows.

In the last ten mid-term election years, bear markets began or were in progress six times in a row before the onset in 1982 of the biggest bull cycle in Wall Street history. A hypothetical portfolio of stocks bought at midterm election-year lows since 1914 has gained 50.2% on average when the stock market reached its subsequent highs in the following pre-election years. A swing of such magnitude is equivalent to a move from 10,000 to 15,000. Pretty impressive seasonality! There is no reason to think the quadrennial Presidential Election/Stock Market Cycle will not continue in 2002-2003. In which case the Dow could possibly gain 5000 points from its 2002 mid-term bottom to its high in pre-Presidential election year 2003.

7. First trading days of the month sizzle.

Between September 2, 1997 (Dow 7,622.42) and July 6, 2001 (Dow 10,252.68) the Dow Industrial average gained a total of 2,630.26 points. During this 47-month period, first trading days of the month gained an incredible 2,662.51 points. In stark contrast, all the other remaining trading days (923 of them) lost 32.25 points. What this means is that the average gain for each of these 47 first trading days was 56.7 points, compared to a loss of a third of a point per day for the other 923 days. On an annualized basis that's roughly 265% vs. a negative return for the entire year for all other days.

8. So-called summer rallies are a farce - it is the weakest of all the seasons.

In any year when the market is a disappointment, you hear talk of a summer rally. Such a big deal is made of the 'summer rally' that one might get the impression the market puts on its best razzle-dazzle performance in the summertime. Nothing could be farther from the truth! Not only does the market rally in every season of the year, but it does so with more gusto in other seasons. Winters in 38 years averaged a 13.7% gain as measured from the low in November or December to the first quarter closing high. Spring was up 10.6% followed by fall with 10.3%. Last and least was the average 9.6% 'summer rally'.

9. The only 'free lunch' on Wall Street is served in December.

Several shrewd observers note that many depressed issues sell at 'bargain' levels near the close of each year as investors rid their portfolios of these 'losers' for tax purposes. Stocks hitting new lows for the year in late December tend to outperform the market handsomely by February 15th in the following year. Select stocks that are making mid-December lows by first eliminating preferred stocks, closed-end funds, splits, new issues, etc. Then buy stocks that are down the most. They do tend to bounce back more than the market after tax-selling season is over.

10. Down Triple-Witching Weeks trigger more weakness in the week after.

Triple-Witching Week (TWW) refers to expirations in three vehicles: S&P futures; put and call options on other indices; and options on stocks. Down TWWs often lead to a down market the following week. Since 1991, of 13 down TWWs, 11 were also down in the following week.

---

www.stocktradersalmanac.com

'The biggest mistake individual investors make is concentrating their portfolios, and the greatest sin of all is holding an excessive portion of your wealth in the stock of the company you work for.'

Richard Thaler and Russell Fuller

John C. Hull

John Hull is the Maple Financial Group Professor of Derivatives and Risk Management and Director of the Bonham Centre for Finance in the Joseph L. Rotman School of Management at the University of Toronto. He is an internationally recognized authority on financial engineering and has many publications in that area. Recently his research has focused on interest rate options, credit risk, and market risk. He was voted *Financial Engineer of the Year* in 1999 by the IAFE.

Books

Options, Futures and Other Derivatives, FT Prentice Hall, 1999
Fundamentals of Futures and Options Markets, FT Prentice Hall, 2001
Hull-White on Derivatives, Risk Publications, 1996
Risk Management and Financial Institutions, Prentice Hall, 2006
Options, Futures and Other Derivatives, Prentice Hall, 2006

Option valuation and trading

1. To make money trading options you must take a different view from most other market participants - and you must be right.

An example illustrates the point here. Suppose you think there will soon be some news leading to a big change in a company's stock price (This could be the result of an attempted takeover or the outome of a major lawsuit). You might try a straddle trading strategy. This involves buying a call and a put with the same strike price and time to maturity. If the news is favourable to the company, you expect the call to provide a big payoff; if it is unfavourable to the company, you expect the put to provide a big payoff. The strategy works well if few other people have the same idea. But, if most other market participants also expect a big price change, the prices of calls and puts will be bid up and there will be no easy profits.

2. Do not imply the volatility from the price of one option on a stock and use it to price another.

This used to be recommended, but it is now recognized that the market does not use the same volatility to price all options. (This means that the market does not agree with the assumptions underlying Black-Scholes.) In equity markets the volatility used to price an option is a decreasing function of strike price. For example 28% might be used to price a low-strike-price option on the S&P 500 while 20% is used to price a high-strike-price option on this index.

3. As a rough approximation, the price of an at-the-money option increases with the square root of its time to maturity.

This rule is related to a more general result that states that our uncertainty about the future value of a market variable increases (at least approximately) as the square root of how far ahead we are looking. Our uncertainty about the value in four months is approximately twice (not four times) our uncertainty about the value in one month.

4. When we use the risk-neutral valuation principle we are not valuing options on the assumption that investors are risk neutral.

Risk neutral valuation is the most important principle in option pricing and is very widely used. It states that we get the right price for an option (or any other derivative) if we assume investors are risk neutral. The price is correct in situations where investors are risk averse as well as in situations where they are risk neutral.

5. Never trade a product without fully understanding it and evaluating the risks.

This might seem a somewhat obvious rule. In fact, many of the well-publicized derivatives disasters of financial and non-financial companies were caused by individuals who failed to follow the rule.

6. When you speculate with options, you are taking a position not only on what will happen but when it will happen.

Options have limited lives. How often does it happen that an investor buys a call option on a stock and finds that the stock price shoots up during the week after the end of the life of the option?

7. Option pricing models such as Black-Scholes are nothing more than sophisticated interpolation tools.

They should be used with caution by investors. Professional traders price options as follows. Each day they observe the prices of a number of actively traded options in the market. They use Black-Scholes to calculate implied volatilities for these options. They then interpolate between the implied volatilities to get a table showing the implied volatility as a function of strike price and time to maturity. This table is used to price other options during the day.

8. When uncertainty increases in the market the volatilities of short-dated options increase by more than the volatilities of long-dated options.

The volatility of an asset is what analysts refer to as mean reverting. It tends to be pulled back to its long run average (normal) level. When market uncertainty increases the volatility increases, but after that it tends to be pulled back to normal levels. The implied volatility of an option can be thought of as what investors expect the average level of the volatility to be over the life of the option. For a long-dated option, this is less than for a short-dated option in the situation considered.

9. Keep your eyes open for valuable option add-ons.

Options are sometimes added to other products by financial institutions. For example, a bank when offering a mortgage may quote a rate and say that it is good for two months. (If rates improve you get the improved rate.) British insurance companies have in the past offered annuities where the interest rate used to calculate the annual amount is guaranteed to be not less than a certain level. Often the option is considered a cost of doing business and not properly priced into the product.

10. Never forget to factor transaction costs into your calculations when considering option trades.

Transaction costs can be high for options. One type of transaction cost is the broker's commission. Another hidden transaction cost is the market maker's bid-offer spread. If the bid is $4.75 and the offer is $5.25, our best estimate of the market price is $5.00 and there is a $0.25 (= 5%) transaction cost every time you trade. Commissions are required when options are exercised. Sometimes, when transaction costs are taken into account, it is more favourable to sell an option than exercise it.

www.rotman.utoronto.ca

'Research has shown that companies in which the post of Chairman and Chief Executive were held by the same person had more than a 50% higher chance of going bust than other listed companies. Maxwell (who had his two sons as Joint Managing Directors) and Asil Nadir at Polly Peck are two classics, but there are plenty of others.'

Alan Sugden

John Husselbee

John Husselbee is a Director at Henderson Global Investors, where he is responsible for portfolio construction and fund selection for a complete range of multi manager, mutual fund portfolios. John has over 10 years experience, both at Henderson Global Investors and Rothschild Asset Management, researching and selecting fund managers to include in his retail portfolios. He sits on the AUTIF Performance Committee as well as the advisory panel for the Investment Week Mutual Fund Awards. John writes a regular monthly column for Bloomberg Money and is a regular guest on Bloomberg TV.

Selecting a mutual fund manager

1. Never use an old map to find new countries.

One thing I firmly believe is that consistent performance doesn't exist. The past is only a guide. I prefer to use it as such and then look a little deeper. I want to find out how and why a fund has achieved a top ranking and then establish whether those reasons can be imposed upon current market conditions and future market prospects.

2. It's not all about returns.

It may be a simple observation but a fund's objective is a key issue for me. And the objective is not simply to make lots of money. Each fund has a stated objective, quoted in their scheme particulars, and guidelines on how it aims to achieve it. Does the objective match your own? Is the manager's style, which can be gleaned from the types of company he holds (larger companies or smaller companies, for example), appropriate? A clear understanding of the objectives and management style and consistency of approach will assist in predicting how the fund will behave in the prevailing market conditions.

3. Experience brings its own rewards - let the apprentices practice with someone else's money.

The fund manager's experience is extremely important. And that means experience relevant to the fund he is managing. Look at the manager's track record for both his current fund and any previously managed funds. This information can be easily obtained. I'm happier investing in managers who have mastered their craft in varying types of market conditions. This is particularly relevant given the extended bull run we've seen recently. There are many managers out there who have no experience of managing money in bear markets.

Loyalty and length of tenure are also attractive qualities in a fund manager. As well as providing a clear track record, they can also highlight whether a manager's own objectives are in line with the fund's.

4. You can get a better view from the big house on the hill.

The larger investment houses can bring a great deal to the party. In many instances the investment house dictates asset allocation and has particular views which the fund manager is bound to follow. This will naturally have a big effect on how the fund is managed and how it performs. So remember you're buying the house as well as the manager.

The larger houses can also provide a great deal of resources to the fund manager, particularly in the form of global economic and company information. The manager of a large house will gain greater access to the companies he invests in. Such first hand information will certainly benefit you as an investor. These houses can also provide an element of security and inspire confidence.

5. Elephants can't gallop.

The size of a fund matters and can bring with it problems for the manager. Good managers very often become victims of their own success. Cash pours in from investors hoping to share in the success of the top performing funds. Trying to invest large amounts of money can dilute a manager's ideas.

Make sure the size of the fund sits well with the fund's objectives. A smaller companies fund, for example, is going to have difficulty investing £1 billion. A word of warning though: small funds can flatter an average fund manager so don't go small for the sake of it.

6. Show me what's up your sleeve!

Investing money isn't a magic show. You should expect complete transparency. There should be a clear flow of information, revealing exactly what a manager is up to. The companies he invests in, the transactions that take place and the reasons why decisions have been made. You can only make an informed decision if you have all the information to hand. The manager should have no secrets. If he's hiding something then he's got something to hide.

7. Beware the siren's call.

Don't let the clamour of sales and promotions distract you from the core essentials of investing. Be confident in the reasons why you are investing. Everyone's looking to promote Number One figures and you'd be amazed how many Number One funds there are out there. Look behind the figures and check the timescales and the management. A Number One fund is no good to you if the manager has since left. And watch out for the press-fuelled thematic bandwagon. It could entice you onto the rocks of an investment you're simply not suited to.

8. Be sure you understand what you're letting yourself in for.

Investing is a risky business. In fact it is the business of managing risk. Always understand that if you're chasing big returns they come at a price. Risk and return is a clear trade-off so make sure you're comfortable with the ratio.

9. A little knowledge is a dangerous thing.

You can't beat in depth research. Quality information makes the decision process less emotive. Look deeper - it's worth it.

10. Knowing when to sell.

You should review your circumstances and expectations regularly and see if your current portfolio still sits comfortably within them. If it doesn't, make changes.

Remember, poor performance may be temporary so understand why before making a decision. If a manager has left - what's the new one like? If the manager isn't doing what he said he would - what is the impact on you?

Most of all, take control. Ensure that you are getting what you want from your investments. They are yours, after all.

www.henderson.com

'Each day, millions of managers the world over systematically destroy shareholder wealth, sometimes in huge amounts. Why? It is not because they are incompetent. Nor because they are dishonest.

It is because they are responding rationally to the compensation systems used by the vast majority of corporations which reward them for over-investing in mature industries, over-spending on labor-saving automation, and over-paying for acquisitions.'

Joel Stern

Roger Ibbotson

Roger Ibbotson is chairman and founder of Ibbotson Associates, a leading authority on asset allocation, providing products and services to help investment professionals obtain, manage and retain assets. The company's business lines include asset allocation, investment consulting and planning, analytical and wealth forecasting software, educational services and a widely used line of NASD-reviewed presentation materials. Mr. Ibbotson is also a professor in the practice of finance at the Yale School of Management.

How to manage your asset allocation

1. Invest in stocks for the long run.

Several studies suggest that future stock returns will be much lower than past returns. In fact, one study even suggests that the future equity risk premium is negative, meaning that stocks will not beat bonds in the future.

Our research shows, however, that of the 11 percent that the market returned each year over the past 75 years, only 1.25 percent was from an increase in the P/E ratio - the rest was from actual earnings growth. While changes in P/E ratios are largely responsible for returns in the short term, they are highly volatile and unpredictable. In contrast, growth from corporate earnings accounts for returns in the long run and is relatively stable. There is good reason to believe that stocks will continue to provide significant returns over the long run.

2. Asset allocation is the most important of all investment decisions.

On average, investors don't beat the market, which means that the asset allocation mix accounts for 100 percent of the return on an average portfolio. Of all the decisions investors make, therefore, the asset allocation decision is the most important. Typically, 40 percent of the return difference between one fund and another is explained by asset allocation differences, while the remaining 60 percent difference is explained by security selection, timing and fee differences between the funds.

3. Diversify across and within asset classes.

The extended superior performance of large cap growth and technology stocks through the last half of the 1990s lulled investors into a false sense of security. If 2000 taught us anything, it's that hot stocks and asset classes are difficult to predict and equally hard to time. Returns, historically, tend to come in spurts that make momentum investing and market timing unreliable investment strategies. Investors should heed the old adage, 'Don't put all of your eggs in one basket.'

4. Invest globally.

Although the correlation between the U.S. and international markets is rising, that's no reason to reduce international exposure. The United States only accounts for approximately half of the world's market. Americans traditionally allocate far too little to international markets, cutting off a huge portion of the investment universe. The correlation is still relatively low and continues to provide substantive diversification to investors' portfolios.

5. Minimize costs.

The costs associated with purchasing investments are certain, but the returns of those investments are not. And, over time, high returns in one year tend to cancel out low returns in another, but costs just compound. Differences in fee structures explain much of the performance difference between two funds over the long run. Paying close attention to the cost structure of an investment will increase total return.

6. Limit the impact of taxes.

Know how different types of gains are taxed and hold them in the appropriate accounts. To capitalize on the full benefits of tax-deferred or exempt accounts, make the maximum contributions and hold highly taxed assets (such as taxable bonds, dividend-producing equities or mutual funds with high trading activity) in these accounts to defer realization of capital gains as long as possible. Hold long-term investments in taxable accounts.

7. Keep a composite record of your total wealth and accounts.

It's easy to fixate on the big winners and the big losers in one's portfolio rather than the portfolio as a whole. Every portfolio should have winners and losers - that's the sign of a well-diversified portfolio. If you concentrate on the total performance, you will stay focused on your long-term goals.

8. Evaluate and rebalance your portfolio regularly.

Investors should evaluate their portfolios each year to determine if their asset allocation has significantly changed due to the price appreciation or depreciation of their investments. Rebalancing will help keep an investor on track to achieve his or her long-term goal and can help reduce risk. Investors with an allocation in technology stocks, for example, who did not rebalance annually during the tech runup took a much bigger hit during the decline than those who rebalanced.

9. Plan your investments to cover your liabilities.

We sometimes lose sight of the goal of investing, which is to accumulate wealth to finance various consumption needs. Whether it's retirement or college tuition, investors must consider how far away the liability is in time, the rate at which it is increasing and the likelihood that the chosen investment vehicle will be able to meet the liability when it's due.

10. Invest over your life cycle.

Reduce your allocation to equities as your investment horizon decreases. However, don't get out completely. People are living longer and facing many costs, like healthcare, that are rising faster than inflation. Even retirees need to have a portion of their portfolios allocated to stocks in order to finance retirement.

www.ibbotson.com

'As attractive as the concept might sound - generally something like *buy global winners to capture the benefit of international markets without the risk* -- the reality is that one does not get the diversification advantage of foreign stocks with multinationals.

Domestic MNCs tend to have a beta close to 1.0 with their home market, and large-cap global MNCs are usually the most highly correlated both with each other and with large developed markets.'

Steven Schoenfeld

Mark Ingebretsen

Mark Ingebretsen writes a weekly column on trends in online investing for TheStreet.com. He is working on his second book recounting the rivalry between the New York Stock Exchange and the Nasdaq. It will be published by Random House in January 2002.

Books

The Guts and Glory of Day Trading, Prima 2001

Using the web to perform due diligence on a stock

1. Create a watch list.

With a watch list you can monitor a stock's daily performance before buying. Also, you can use that watch list as a base for doing fundamental research on the stock. Yahoo Finance! (http://finance.yahoo.com) allows you to do both. Many other financial web sites give you the same kind of fundamental information you'll find at Yahoo! Finance but Yahoo's pages load the fastest. And they let you explore SEC filings, options prices, recent analyst upgrades and downgrades.

2. Find out what people are saying about the stock.

A web site called Validea.com (www.validea.com) tracks what financial reporters and analysts have had to say about your stock recently. Not only that, the site details the track record of each pundit. You can also ferret out opinions on a stock by searching the archives at the financial news site TheStreet.com (www.thestreet.com). The search window appears on the site's home page. For technology stocks, CNet (www.news.com) is especially helpful, since it leads to reviews of a company's products from a wide-ranging group of magazines, both general interest and technical.

3. Get a second opinion.

Quicken.com (www.quicken.com), VectorVest (www.vectorvest.com) and ValuEngine (www.valuengine.com) all have free stock analysis software on their sites. Simply enter a ticker symbol and the number crunching software will give you an opinion on, for example, what the stock's fair value might be, or what its growth prospects are. Compare this information with what analysts have said about the stock.

4. Analyze the stock's sector.

As much as 80 percent of a stock's movement can stem from movements by the sector as a whole. The web site ClearStation (www.clearstation.com/cgi-bin/Itechnicals) shows you how the stock's sector has been performing. Using a list of fundamental and technical indicators it compares the sector performance to its component stocks.

5. Determine the trend.

Will the stock likely rise or fall in the near term? Using technical indicators the web site BuySellorHold (www.buysellorhold.com), gives you a quick read on the trend and points to short-term support and resistance levels.

6. Know the risk of ownership.

At RiskGrades (www.riskgrades.com) you can simply enter a ticker symbol, specify a period - say, six months - and then view a graph of the stock's volatility as compared to the market. Another useful site called BigCharts (www.bigcharts.com) again lets you specify a period, and then see a chart detailing how the stock traded that week.

7. Develop a plan.

At what point should you buy the stock? When would it be most advantageous to sell when factoring in such things as dividends, and tax consequences? The free calculators at FinanCenter.com (http://www.financenter.com) let you quickly perform calculations like these.

8. Monitor your performance.

A web site called Gainskeeper.com (www.gainskeeper.com) will automatically track your cost basis in a stock, calculating the effect of dividends, splits, spin offs, etc. The site will also automatically generate a Schedule D used for reporting capital gains on a U.S. tax return. Fees for this service start at US$49 per year.

---

www.thestreet.com

Edmond Jackson

Edmond Jackson writes 'Taking Stock, the diary of a private investor' for *The Sunday Telegraph,* and a daily Notepad at www.Citywire.co.uk. He eschews formal investment systems - preferring to take a flexible and pragmatic approach to investing, with a particular focus on the processes of change. He regards a sense for dynamics - at the economic, company and stock market perception levels, and how they interrelate - as key. Business moves on, investment ideas must adapt.

General principles and intrinsic value of companies

1. Weigh risk/reward to buy and sell astutely.

Have a sense for the upside/downside parameters in a stock and try to quantify them, roughly. This basic ratio can be applied to almost any investment situation. If you can't get a grip on it, steer clear.

2. Develop a rationale for sectors & stocks - keeping an open mind.

Summarise the reaons why you are buying/holding selected stocks, and ask yourself if the course of events reinforces or detracts from that rationale. Things rarely turn out as one expects, so be ready to evolve your rationale in the light of new information.

3. Look beneath the surface and identify key issues.

A company's disclosure is liable to be coloured by the directors' agenda at the time of reporting, or the PR advisers doing a good job. When you are assimilating words and numbers in a company's releases, get quickly to the heart of the matter - and how it affects your rationale.

4. Assess intrinsic value - a dynamic concept.

Such a benchmark for a stock is the price at which it ought to trade if all relevant factors are considered: earning power, quality of management and assets, etc. Economic change means that intrinsic value needs regular re-appraisal.

5. Identify market bias - when to back or buck it.

It is hard to define intrinsic value objectively: every judgement in the stockmarket depends on the players' varying perspectives. There is nearly always some kind of bias, like an infectious trend in social psychology. Or just plain old greed and fear. Discerning when the trend has sense or nonsense, and its relation to underlying values, is vital.

6. Growth stocks can deliver hefty gains and losses.

A 'lockaway' growth stock, to hold and watch multiply, is the first choice of most investors. Yet rapid growth of a business introduces all manner of strains, especially competition. Acquisitions are a classic problem area. Add in the factor of stock market bias and you have a recipe for boom-to-bust.

7. Turnarounds & cyclicals are valuable when your timing is right.

The economic cycle can generate opportunities when the risk/reward ratio is particularly favourable in these stocks. There is also a steady supply of sound yet unexciting businesses where new management can be a catalyst for 'recovery-to-growth' - frequently a profitable theme.

8. Takeovers and divestments offer special opportunities.

Arbitraging market disparities in announced terms is one, conservative approach, in 'event driven' situations. Enterprising investors should keep a watch list of potential targets. Once an attractive risk/reward profile is perceived, dealing volumes and/or relevant news can be the necessary trigger for the stock to converge on intrinsic value.

9. Re-appraise stocks in terms of opportunity cost.

Besides company and market factors, there is the issue of 'what better choices for my money?' A stock may rate a satisfactory hold - yet selling down is logical if you find a better alternative. One's optimum level of portfolio activity needs to consider tax and transaction costs.

10. Have the courage of your convictions - to deal effectively.

With experience, an intuitive link develops between your ideas and actions - so that you balance a patient, disciplined approach, with courage to seize the day. Nurture and listen to your own intuition.

edmondj@msn.com

Simon M. Johnson

Simon Johnson is in charge of Mid and Small Cap Consumer Services research at UBS Warburg. His team's corporate client base encompasses groups such as Jarvis Hotels, First Choice Holidays, Greggs and Carpetright. He recently joined UBS Warburg from CSFB where he headed up the Leisure & Hotels research team.

The leisure sector

Introduction

The quoted leisure sector is very much a UK phenomenon. With a highly fragmented industry base, a wide variety of leisure outlets, concepts and an element of fashion retailing, specific company analysis is critical. There are, however, some very clear investment guidelines.

1. Be aware of the economic cycle.

While spending on eating out, health, fitness and other leisure pursuits is undoubtedly in long-term secular increase, it is also highly discretionary and one of the first to go in an economic downturn. Cut holdings as the economy falters and do not buy until you are confident of recovery. Some bottom-end operators may benefit from 'trading down', but generally people 'trade out' until better times return.

2. Look for a replicable concept.

Better a concept that has had 50 previous successful openings than one that has to be re-invented every time. Not only is this cheaper (design costs spread out over a larger base), but it also reduces risk. Managers of the most replicated and successful concepts can tell within days if a new location is working, and if it isn't, can do something about it quickly.

3. Be aware of fashion.

Leisure is a fashion retail business. The supertanker concept of today may be marooned by next week. As a result, paybacks need to be quicker the higher up the design curve a unit is. Most preferable is a 'timeless' concept that can be refreshed rather than needing remodelling.

4. Be aware of the costs of refurbishment.

As leisure tastes evolve, so do amenity requirements and these cost more to include than a simple refurbishment of the existing site. London's Waldorf

Hotel was considered a luxury hotel when it opened because it had 1 bathroom for every 4 bedrooms. If it had been maintained over the years only to its original standard it would now be a Youth Hostel!

5. Allow for the property element.

Returns in the industry are notoriously difficult to calculate, as a valid part of the calculation is the asset appreciation of many freehold businesses. This is particularly true of the longer living elements such as hotels and pubs. If such businesses give good returns before capital appreciation, then so much the better. Rising property values then come free!

6. Look out for legislative step-changes.

Leisure is regulated by a whole swathe of legislation. Occasionally, legislative changes throw up huge new opportunities. The Beer Orders in 1991 changed the landscape of UK pubs forever, and the implementation of many of the recommendations in the Budd Report on Gaming and Gambling in 2001 could have similar impacts for casinos, betting shops and bingo clubs. However, make sure such recommendations are going to be implemented!

7. Buy on consolidation, sell on disaggregation.

Leisure companies in the 1980s and early 1990s paid up for leisure concepts and businesses when conglomerates were seen as the way forward. The same groups had to write down the value of those businesses when they came to sell them in the late 1990s.

8. Be wary of claims of 'synergy benefits'.

Leisure remains a single site concept, with high personnel costs attached to each unit. Central structures and raw materials make up a relatively small part of the overall costs and therefore claims of synergies between units should be viewed with a degree of scepticism.

9. Trust your eyes and instincts.

Do you like a concept? Do you tell your friends about it? Could every town support one? If so, it might be worth further investigation. Look also for spin-off benefits or problems. If there are no good movies on at the cinema, it will not only be the cinema that is suffering, but also the bar and restaurant chains next door.

10. Listen to the story with a critical mindset.

If it sounds too good to be true, it almost certainly is. Few people manage to reinvent the leisure wheel!

Philippe Jorion

Phillippe Jorion is a Professor of Finance at the University of California at Irvine. His recent work addresses the issue of forecasting risk and return in global financial markets, as well as managing exchange risk with derivative instruments.

Books

Value at Risk Fieldbook, McGraw-Hill, 2000
Value at Risk, Irwin, 2000 (2nd ed.)
Big Bets Gone Bad, Harcourt Brace, 1995
Financial Risk Manager Handbook, John Wiley & Sons Inc, 2005

Value at Risk

---

1. Balance returns against risk.

If you want no risk, invest in cash. You sure cannot get greater returns without assuming some risk. Your goal should be to get the just reward for the risks you elect to take. But you need to measure your risks.

2. Use Value at Risk (VAR) for an intuitive sense of risk.

VAR is a first-order measure of downside risk. It is the maximum loss over a target horizon that will not be exceeded at some confidence level. Say you have $1 million invested in a diversified stock portfolio. You would then say: "Over the next year, the VAR at the 95% confidence level is approximately $330,000." You would expect this loss not to be exceeded in 95% of cases, or 19 years out of 20. But in one year out of 20, there will be a larger loss. If you are uncomfortable with this risk profile, you should alter the asset allocation. But at least this will be an informed decision.

3. Risk should be measured in a portfolio context.

What looks like a volatile investment, say in an emerging market, may have little effect on the total portfolio risk. Actually, if foreign equities move in opposite cycles to domestic stocks, portfolio risk is reduced. Limiting the amount invested in more speculative assets can also control risk. Portfolio risk is best measured with VAR.

4. Beware of chasing winners.

Picking losers among mutual funds is a bad idea, but picking winners can be dangerous too. Winning portfolios may be heavily exposed to the same risk factor, say the high-tech industry. If so, loading the portfolio with winners will create undue risk concentration. A downturn in this industry will hurt badly.

5. Risk is a double-edged sword.

Beware of traders that enjoy sizzling returns. Risk is the dispersion in unexpected outcomes, and not only the occurrences of losses. Countless investors have missed this point, as they failed to realize that the performance of traders, such as Nick Leeson or Robert Citron, really reflected greater risks. Extraordinary performance, both good and bad, should raise red flags. Ask questions, if only to imitate them.

6. There is no such thing as 10% or more excess return with no risk.

Anybody making such a statement either has not measured risk or did not measure it well. Robert Citron maintained that his fund was "safe". He managed to lose $1.6 billion out of $7.5 billion invested. He did not measure his risk. The partners at LTCM maintained that the fund had a daily volatility of $45 million only. They managed to lose $4.4 billion out of $4.7 billion. The real risks were misunderstood.

7. Watch for large short positions in options.

These created most financial blowups. Short options positions collect regular premiums but take a large hit once in a while. Victor Niederhoffer was a legend in the hedge fund business, returning an average of 32% annually from 1982 to 1997. In 1997, he sold naked out-of-the-money puts on the S&P and was wiped out as the market dived. LTCM's positions amounted to a huge short option position, a bet on volatility and liquidity risk. Similarly, selling earthquake insurance is profitable until the big one hits.

www.gsm.uci.edu

Ajay Kapur

Ajay Kapur is a Managing Director at Morgan Stanley in Hong Kong and the firm's Asia/Pacific equity strategist. He is ranked as #1 equity strategist in 2001 by Institutional Investor and the Greenwich (US) survey.

Prior to working at Morgan Stanley, he was the Asia equity strategist at UBS Securities, the Chief Economist at Peregrine Securities in Hong Kong, and an economist for WEFA Group in the USA.

Investing in Asian equities

1. Ride the cycle - don't freewheel.

Asian equities are trading, not trending markets. Buy and hold, and you will fold. Corporate profitability in Asia is extremely cyclical, being linked with the global business cycle. Margins are compressed by replicated capacity, more assertive labor and a lack of franchises - hence, the need for the cycle to be positive.

2. When global growth is low, let the Asia money flow.

Asia's cyclical equities bottom with global growth (time to buy), and peak when global activity is strongest (time to bye-bye). Follow the US yield curve, the NAPM new orders index, the Australian dollar, and the stock/bond relative performance to track expected moves in global activity, in addition to global monetary growth and interest rates.

3. Country beats sector. Don't go out without your passport.

In Asia, unlike Europe, country prevails over sector in stock-picking. The region is a patchwork of different monetary and fiscal policies, political cycles, development levels and regulatory risks. Lesson: know the country.

4. Know the price of everything. Don't pay $1.50 for $1.

With the exception of technology, value triumphs over growth in secular fashion in Asia. There is no value-growth cycle, unlike in the US. Why?

Investors overpay for the latest growth concept, or fashion, that emerges. Competition and capital raising attracted by the latest fashion crush excessive enthusiasm and multiples for growth stocks in Asia.

5. If the barn-door is open, don't scramble through the skylight.

In other words, don't ignore the big and obvious. Larger companies have higher returns on equity, a lower cost of capital, longer histories, greater survival skills, stronger political connections, rent-seeking abilities, and also attract the best talent. Small gems can be mined, but are only for those with time and a tolerance for pain.

6. Crises don't just happen. Be a macro maven.

You wouldn't check into a luxury hotel that violated fire safety regulations and construction codes and was located in an earthquake-prone zone. Likewise, you'll want to avoid the financial crises that convulse Asia about once a decade. Monitor lending booms, the ratio of short-term external debt to international reserves, the current account balance, and the (generally) under-regulated non-bank financial sector where the mischief usually begins.

7. Don't follow the herd - it may be heading to the slaughterhouse.

The herd instinct is extremely powerful in Asia. Both local retail and foreign institutional investors fall prey to it. Tracking investor sentiment is extremely profitable, if you remember that happy masses precede crashes. Bubbles come and go in Asia with regularity. Know when to get off by monitoring volatility, small cap relative performance, the ratio of market capitalization to money supply and inflows to equity mutual funds.

8. Cool today is cruel tomorrow. Leave the fads to the amnesiacs.

Restructuring, mega-growth, and unbounded prosperity from the latest fad/theme resonate at market peaks, are conveniently forgotten at troughs, and are shamelessly repeated in the next upswing. The plot lines are similar, a few characters change. Stories based on large populations hungry for the next cool product should be treated with suspicion.

9. When the political wind changes, expect the windfalls to stop.

Do not underestimate the impact of politics, corruption and malpractice on stock performance. Many Asian democracies are young, the rule of law is tender, and political transitions are tricky. Cronyism and sharp practices often lead to excess returns in the short term, but can inflict large losses when political winds shift. Diversify across political factions.

10. Follow the central banks. That's where the money is.

Track the central bank balance sheet, not just company balance sheets. Asian equity markets move closely with the liquidity cycle. Track the gap between narrow money growth and nominal activity - when rising, it is positive for Asian equities, when contracting it is negative.

www.morganstanley.com

'The IPO market is never in equilibrium. It's either too hot or too cold. Buy in the cold periods.'

Jay Ritter

John Kay

John Kay has been described as "the most important business analyst in Britain, bar none". He is well known for his incisive and entertaining columns in the *Financial Times*, his regular audio and TV broadcasts, and is much in demand as a speaker and consultant.

Books

The Business of Economics, Oxford University Press, 1996
Foundations of Corporate Success, Oxford University Press, 1993
Everlasting Light Bulbs: How Economics Illuminates the World, The Erasmus Press Ltd, 2004
The Hare and the Tortoise: An Informal Guide to Business Strategy, The Erasmus Press Ltd, 2006

Business economics

1. *Myth* - 'Profits are higher in fast growing industries.'

They're not, because everyone else knows they are fast growing. Returns are often higher in unfashionable activities, like tobacco. Best are industries that grow faster than expected - whether expectations are high or low.

2. *Myth* - 'Most industries are concentrating around a few global companies.'

Some are, some aren't. The overall trend of concentration has been down over the last twenty years - even in automobiles.

3. *Myth* - 'A company can get the middleman's profit by vertical integration.'

But it will have to pay for it - you don't save the highwayman's toll by buying his business. Vertical integration pays only when a company can use it to extend its market power, or take control of assets that are specific to its business.

4. *Myth* - 'Diversification increases the quality of business earnings.'

Sorry, but a company's shareholders can diversify more cheaply than it can. Brokerage commissions are a lot less than takeover premiums.

5. *Myth* - 'New technologies increase profits.'

If new technologies are generally applicable, then competition means that the benefits will go to consumers. Not just most of them, all of them. New technology has always been better news for customers than shareholders.

6. Look at industry specifics, not assertions about trends.

Few generalisations about industry structure stand up. You need to understand the specific nature of competitive advantage in each industry.

7. Competitive advantages come from distinctive capabilities.

The only way to make profits above the cost of capital in the long run is to do something others can't - and *still can't* after they see the benefits to the company that can.

8. *Myth* - 'First mover advantages are key - the early bird catches the worm.'

Not often, in business. There are very few industries in which being first is the basis of a sustained distinctive capability. How many of us have Ampex video recorders?

9. *Myth* - 'Market share is key to profitability.'

High market share is associated with higher profitability. But that doesn't mean higher market share causes higher profitability. Sustainable competitive advantage is the source - the only source - of both higher market share and higher profitability.

10. Beware financial engineering.

Over the long run, the only place shareholder value can come from us cash generated by operating businesses.

www.johnkay.com

Karl Keegan

Karl Keegan heads the European Biotechnology research team at UBS Warburg in London.

Before that, Karl was a biotechnology analyst at Dresdner Kleinwort Benson, and a researcher at SmithKline Beecham Pharmaceuticals.

The biotechnology sector

1. The valuation of biotech companies is fraught with difficulty.

The diverse nature of biotech business models, the relative newness of the company, the lack of many tangible assets, the limited financial histories available and the spectacular growth forecasts make any such attempt demanding. As such it is almost impossible to get the balance right between quantitative and qualitative analysis.

2. There is no one 'correct' way to value the sector.

Various valuation tools can be used to assess the potential, products and/or technology of a biotechnology company. There is no one correct way to value the sector, given the diversity of the companies under examination and the markets in which they operate. We assess the quality of the management (and their ability to do deals), the potential of the company and the quality of the science and technology underpinning its business.

3. Use all the quantitative methods at your disposal.

- *Comparable company analysis* (either EV/revenue or EV/EBITDA)
    Pros - it provides an idea as to what investors are prepared to pay.
    Cons - it's crude and there are few true comparators.
- *Discounted future earnings* (EBITDA in 2005, for example)
    Pros - it's EBITDA-based, so few assumptions are needed.
    Cons - it's very dependent on the discount rate used.
- *Discounted portfolio valuation* (of the product pipeline)
    Pros - it's good for early stage companies and current drugs.
    Cons - it underestimates the value of more mature biotechs.

• *Discounted cash flow* (for the mature, profitable companies)
  Pros - it's the most fundamental valuation methodology available.
  Cons - it overvalues early stage companies and is heavily dependent
  on exit multiple/terminal growth rates.

4. Forget tech. Focus on the people.

Management continues to be a key, if not the most important, variable in
determining the success of a biotechnology company. Sustainable success
can only be achieved by those companies led by individuals who can
manage risk and not merely avoid it. Understanding the risk profile of drug
development is a key attribute of the successful manager.

5. Watch out for news flow.

The sector is very sensitive to the impact of news flow, thus contributing to
the volatility in share prices. The absence of financial parameters increases
this sensitivity. 'Buy on the rumour, sell on the news' is not too far from the
truth.

News flow is comprised of clinical, scientific and financial press releases.
However, the nature of scientific endeavour is leaky at best, and this feeds
the city rumour mill, in addition to the growing number of internet bulletin
boards. Furthermore biotech is now media-friendly - witness the huge
number of articles in 2000-2001 detailing the progress and politics of the
mapping effort and the personalities behind it. The downside of this was
that genomics became a buzzword that too many companies tried to use in
their positioning, and the term became commoditised.

6. Understand the technical risks.

To be successful, a drug has to make it through clinical trials and a regulatory
process. The level of risk you take as an investor is partly linked to the stage
of clinical trials that a drug is in, but also to whether the concept and any
drug based on that concept is proven 'in man'.

For instance, Genset's anti-obesity drug, Famoxin, is an entirely new
concept. To date, the only direct proof of its efficacy is the reduction of
weight in mice fed on a fatty diet. The only evidence to support it being
successful in man is the existence of a famoxin-deficient obese population in
man. This does not make it any less exciting or interesting – but it does make
it higher risk.

By contrast, the anti-TNF approach to modifying rheumatoid arthritis is
well established, with the anti-TNF drugs currently on the market having
sold in excess of US$1bn collectively in 2000. As such, anyone developing

another TNF binding protein can be sure that the approach has a high chance of proving efficacious. Here, the technical risks relate more to side effects than efficacy.

7. Understand the commercial risks.

Investors need to focus as much on commercial success as technical probabilities. Ultimately, technical risks can be reduced to a binary decision: is the drug approvable or not? In contrast, the commercial risks are much broader and consist of a spectrum of possible outcomes.

Is there room for five similar products on the market?

Does a latecoming product have the technical superiority, or the marketing power behind it, to make a dent in the market-share of a first-to-market product?

Does the biotech company have a GP sales force or the resources to create one?

Can it license its product to another company which has the right marketing channels?

With biotech, as with other industries, the product itself is only half the story. To be successful the company needs a mix of commercial strengths too. And the particular obstacles it has to overcome will depend in part on the therapy area it is launching its drugs into.

8. Recognise the different types of biotech business.

All financial investors want to maximize return while minimizing risk, but they differ in their tolerance of risk. Biotechnology can be arbitrarily split into companies that have a platform model, a therapeutic focus, or a hybrid of both. The risks and rewards associated with each are mapped in the table below.

	Platform technology ➡	Hybrid ⬅	Therapeutics
Risk	low/medium	balanced	high
Revenue generation	near term	near term	medium/long term
Upside potential	low	high	low
Revenue stream	consistent	consistent	lumpy
Break even	near to medium term	medium term	long term

Hybrids usually combine the technology platform approach with a product story in an attempt to maximise reward and minimise product-specific risk.

9. View cash as a tool, not as an indicator of value.

Cash is irrelevant in valuing an ongoing business, because the likelihood of management giving it back to you is very remote. The fact that many biotech and internet companies trade at or below the value of their cash reserves reflects the fact that as they develop their businesses they burn cash, and there is an appreciable risk of them running out of cash before revenues flow. Cash can give an investor comfort as to how much life there is in a company ahead of the next financing but it should be viewed as a tool that the company is expected to use by transforming it into value added technologies/pipeline advancements.

10. Don't be fazed by the technology.

Biotechnology by its very nature is technical but it is not overwhelmingly so. A common danger for both investors and analysts is to become overly fixated on the technology/drug in question. It is really important that investors be able to step back and look at the company in terms of a sustainable model. Of course there are issues and instances where a certain level of expertise will be required but in the main, biotechnology can be assessed by using common sense. Does the business model make sense and can management deliver on its promises?

11. Be careful not to check in to the Roach Motel.

"You can check in but you can't check out" neatly summarises the issue of liquidity for biotechnology stocks. It is almost always possible to buy stock if you wait long enough, but selling stock can be a much more difficult issue. Liquidity and market capitalisation are two key checks that investors should assess very early in their decision making.

www.ubs.com

Brian Kettell

Brian Kettell gained his experience of financial markets working for Citibank, American Express and Shearson Lehman and was most recently Director of Training and Assistant Vice President for the Arab Banking Corporation in Bahrain. He has published 11 books on financial markets and has taught at the London School of Economics, London Guildhall University and the City University of Hong Kong. He has run training programmes for clients which include Chase Manhattan Bank, Morgan Stanley, Kleinwort Benson, Nomura, Banque Indosuez and Barclays Capital.

Books

Economic for Financial Markets, FT Prentice Hall, 2000
Fed Watching for Dealers, FT Prentice Hall, 1999
What Drives Financial Markets, FT Prentice Hall, 1999
What Drives Currency markets, FT Prentice Hall, 1999
Economics for Financial Markets: Making Sense of Information in Financial Markets, Financial Times Prentice Hall, 2001
The Valuation of Internet and Technology Stocks: Techniques and Investment Analysis, Butterworth-Heinemann, 2002

Fed watching

1. Remember the central role of nominal/real GNP quarterly growth.

The Fed Watcher must project and interpret developments other than Federal Reserve policy that are likely to affect future economic conditions and interest rates. The semi-annual Humphrey-Hawkins Testimony sets out the Fed central targets and projections for nominal GDP, real GDP and the Personal Consumer Expenditure (CPE) Price Index. If the nominal GDP growth appears to be overshooting the target there is pressure for the Fed funds rate to rise. Similarly if there appears to be undershooting there is pressure for the Fed funds rate to fall.

2. Track the yield curve if you want to predict business cycle turning points.

It has been recognised for some time that the yield curve, which shows the term structure of interest rates prevailing in an economy at any point in time, contains information that can be used as an indicator of economic prospects. This is because the term structure reflects both the settings of the instruments of monetary policy, as shown in the level of short-term interest rates, and the market's expectation of future short-term rates, and hence of future growth and inflation.

Historical experience shows that on several occasions prior to recessions, long term interest rates dipped below prevailing short term rates, a phenomenon known as an inverted or negative yield curve. Since 1960 the yield curve has been inverted prior to all five recessions. The extent to which the yield curve is tilted away from its normal 'shape' has been identified by many researchers as a valuable indicator of forthcoming recession.

3. Watch what the Fed watches - not what you think it should watch.

In tracking and anticipating the trend for interest rates, begin with a close reading of the most recently released Federal Open Market Committee (FOMC) minutes. Try to understand the Committee's concerns and the balance of opinion among its members. The FOMC minutes will emphasise different measures of inflation such as non-farm payroll employment or the consumer price index, different monetary aggregates or the behaviour of nominal gross domestic product that will influence a policy change. These indicators should be watched closely.

4. Keep an eye on the 3-month Euro-Dollar futures contract.

This contract is amongst those financial instruments most sensitive to Fed funds rate changes and indicates what investors think three-month deposits will cost when the market expires. It is expressed as: 100 - the annualised interest rate. So if the 3 months contract is priced at 95.00 this indicates an expected 3-month interest rate of around 5%. Clearly if the contract price rises above 95.00 interest rates are expected to fall and if the contract price falls below 95.00 then interest rates are expected to rise.

5. Use Taylor's Rule as a guide to changes in Fed policy.

John Taylor, an economist at Stanford University, suggested short-term nominal interest rates should be equal to the sum of four elements:

The first is the real short-term rate that is consistent with 'neutral' monetary policy - i.e. one that is neither expansionary nor contractionary.

The second is the expected inflation rate.

The third, in the simplest and most common version of the Taylor rule, is that 0.5 percentage points should be added to, or subtracted from, short-term rates for every percentage point by which the current inflation rate is above or below its target.

The fourth is that the same adjustment should be made for the 'output gap' - i.e. for every percentage point by which GDP is above or below its long-term trend level. The idea is that output above trend is a signal of inflation on the way; below trend, the reverse.

Several studies have found that central banks have, in effect, been following the Taylor rule for some time.

6. Pay attention to what the Fed does - not what it says.

This may sound rather obvious but it is not necessarily the case that the Fed does what it says it will. Former Fed Chairman Arthur Burns (1970-1978) and G William Miller (1978-1979) both talked of the need for restrictive action but did very little. It must be said however that the same charge cannot be made against either Paul Volcker (1979-1987) and Alan Greenspan (1987 -).

7. View potential Fed policy shifts as a reaction to, rather than a cause of, undesired economic/monetary conditions.

Alan Greenspan has frequently referred to the economy being the patient whilst the Fed is the doctor. If the patient is hyperactive the doctor should take the appropriate action. As former Fed Chairman William McChesney Martin (1951-1970) famously commented, "The role of the Fed chairman is to take away the punch bowl just as the party is starting."

8. Remember that ultimately the Fed is a creature of Congress.

Although insulated in the short-term from partisan political pressures it is not insulated in the longer term. The limits of its independence are clearly delineated. The Fed was created by an act of Congress and, like any agency so created, can be changed or terminated altogether by Congress. What Congress creates it can also destroy!

So although the Fed receives its mandate from Congress regarding what it should try to achieve with monetary policy over time, these decisions are subject to Congressional Review. Former Chairman Martin liked to describe the Fed as "independent within the government, not of the government".

A new US president is likely to be able to choose several governors for the Fed during his or her term of office. Through the choice of nominees, the president can influence the direction of monetary policy. President George W. Bush is in the unusual opportunity of influencing the selection of a large number of governors.

9. Follow the trends in FOMC Directives.

At each meeting the FOMC issues a policy directive, the language of which determines whether the directive was symmetric or asymmetric. One of the most important decisions reached at Federal Open market Committee (FOMC) meetings is whether to ease or tighten monetary policy. The FOMC transmits its decision to the Federal Reserve Bank of New York (where open market operations are actually executed) in a domestic policy directive that guides monetary policy in the subsequent weeks.

Policy directives express the preference of the FOMC for the implementation of monetary policy during the period until the next FOMC meeting. Symmetrical directives express no bias toward either greater ease (a lower federal funds rate) or toward greater restraint (a higher federal funds rate).

Asymmetrical directives do express a policy bias. By writing an asymmetrical directive, the FOMC empowers the chairman to raise or lower the federal funds rate target during the intermeeting period.

10. Fears of inflation provoke faster changes in monetary policy than do fears of unemployment.

The reasoning behind this rule comes from Alan Blinder, former Vice Chairman of the Board of Governors of the Federal Reserve, in his publication 'Central Banking in Theory and Practice (1998)'. He discusses the extent to which monetary policy should take the form of a 'pre-emptive strike' when faced with fighting either inflation or unemployment. Blinder argues that the lags in monetary policy could be longer for inflation fighting than for unemployment fighting, calling for earlier pre-emption in the former case. He then cites empirical evidence that supports his views.

---

bkettell@hotmail.com

Max King

Max King manages the Piccadilly Growth Trust, Capital Opportunities Trust, and an emerging companies OEIC for J.O. Hambro Capital Management. Prior to that he spent 10 years building Finsbury Asset Management, a derelict investment trust group, into one of the best performing and most successful independent boutiques in London.

General principles and politicians' promises

1. Fight the consensus, not the fundamentals.
The true contrarian does not oppose the consensus for the sake of it, but because the herd has charged in the wrong direction.

2. Nobody waves a flag at the top (or the bottom) of the market.
Don't expect a clear signal when the market or the price of an individual stock is about to change direction. The reason why such a change happens is only obvious with the benefit of hindsight: at the time, being a contrarian is lonely. This particularly applies to brokers' analysts, who rarely risk their reputation by recommending a purchase or a sale until the price has moved 50%.

3. Don't fight your prejudices.
They may be illogical and wrong, but you will never be happy with an investment decision that goes against a prejudice. Like superstitions, they are often based on fact.

4. 'It is not strength that determines the survival of the species, or even intelligence, but ability to adapt to change.'
This is a quote from Charles Darwin, and it applies very well to investors. Good fund managers do not stick rigidly to a style or a strategy, but are able to adapt when the need arises, sometimes even reinventing their whole approach.

5. 'History repeats itself first as a farce, then as a tragedy.'
This is a quote from Marx, although Mark Twain's observation that 'History doesn't repeat itself, but it rhymes' is equally good. If you want to predict the future, look to the lessons of the past.

6. Don't confuse brains with a bull market.

Everybody makes money in a bull market, and just because that includes you doesn't mean you are a skilled investor. Likewise, it is important not to let your analysis of a company's value be influenced by its price movement, particularly if you own it.

7. Keep your distance from management.

Managers are always biased to optimism about their own companies, because they are locked in by their jobs. Investors can afford to be objective, because they don't need to own the stock, and their perspective compensates for their lack of detailed knowledge. Meeting management is useful, but you have to be sceptical and you have to make up your own mind.

8. The graveyards of Wall Street are filled with people who were right too soon.

Timing is critical in investment, and being too early can be almost as unrewarding as being wrong. However, Rothschild's answer to being asked the secret of his success - "I never buy at the bottom and I always sell too soon" is also worth remembering, particularly the emphasis on selling on the way up, not the way down, which most analysts forget.

9. A long term investment is a short term investment which has gone wrong.

This is a trader's dictum, not an investor's, but it is still useful. It is always tempting to hang on to shares which have gone down in value, but recovery happens for a reason, not by some law of physics. The quip is a handy way of responding to ignorant people who try to distinguish between long term investment (good) and short term investment (bad).

10. Don't invest in politicians' promises.

Politicians love making promises to 'encourage savings', 'promote investment in transport infrastructure', 'put more resources into education and training' etc. However, these promises are often abandoned, countermanded by a contrary objective or merely empty, so that politicians regularly achieve the opposite of what they intended. Making an investment in a supposed beneficiary of a government decision is highly dangerous, because helping private sector companies make money is bottom of any government's list of priorities, while getting them to spend money on the government's behalf for no return is pretty high up.

www.johcm.co.uk

George Kleinman

George Kleinman, is President of Commodity Resource Corp. He has been trading futures and commodities since 1977 for himself and on behalf of clients. CRC specializes in financials and metals futures. George is Executive Editor of *Trends in Futures*, the flagship newsletter of *Futures*.

Books

Commodity Futures and Options (2nd ed), FT Prentice Hall, 2000
Mastering Commodity Futures and Options: A Step-by-step Guide to the Products, Applications and Risks, Financial Times Prentice Hall, 2000
Trading Commodities and Financial Future: A Step-by-Step Guide to Mastering the Markets, Financial Times Prentice Hall, 2004

Commodities

1. Overtrading - your greatest enemy.

W. D. Gann termed overtrading the 'greatest evil'. He felt it was the cause of more losses than anything else, and who are we to disagree with one of the masters? The average novice trader really doesn't have a clue as to how much money is needed to be successful, and he or she invariably buys (or shorts) more than prudence dictates. His analysis may be correct, but due to too big a position there is a forced liquidation when the margin clerk calls. How often does the money run out just at that critical time when it is ripest to enter? The overtrader is exhausted and misses the profit opportunity he had once seen clearly in those more optimistic days.

2. When in doubt get out!

If the market has not started to move in your favor within a reasonable amount of time, get out. Your judgment will deteriorate the longer you hang on to a losing position and at extremes you will do the wrong thing. One of the old timers once said something to the effect, "I am prudent enough not to stand in the middle of the railroad tracks while I try to decide if the headlight I think I see is a freight train or an illusion."

3. Never average a loss!

Averaging a loss may work four times out of five, but that fifth will wipe you out. It is a bad habit to get into. Look at it this way: if you make a trade, and it starts to go against you, then you're wrong (at least temporarily). Why buy or sell more to potentially compound the problem? Stop the loss early before it is eternally too large, and don't make it worse.

4. Money management is the key.

You do not necessarily need a high win to loss ratio, but your average win must be higher than your average loss if you want to succeed. To do this, there must be (at least some) 'big hits'. Some trades you will need to maximize. You need these big wins to offset the inevitable numerous (and hopefully small) losses which are going to happen. I've found by being able to just cut losses early, by even a small incremental amount per trade, say $100, this can make a major difference to the bottom line. Waiting a 'few more ticks' is generally not a recipe for success and it is bad practice to cancel or extend a stop loss order. My experience has been that 99 times out of 100 canceling a stop is the wrong thing to do. It's OK to cancel a profit-taking order at times, but the sooner a loss is stopped the better.

5. The trend is your friend.

So, don't buck it. The way to make the big money is to determine the major trend and then follow it. If the market will not go your way, you must go its way. When you are in a bear market, and the major trend is down, the plan should be to wait for rallies and sell short; not try to pick the bottom. In a major bear market, you can miss the bottom several times on the way down and end up losing all your money. The same applies (in reverse) in a major bull market. In my experience, the big money is made by going with the trend, not against it.

6. Never let a good profit turn into a loss!

This one has ruined many hopes. If you have a decent profit in any position, and you are absolutely sure it is going to grow larger, at the very least place a stop where (in the worst case) you'll break even. If the market is any good, the stop won't be hit. Should the market continue to move in your favor, keep moving the stop to lock in at least some profit. The objective is to always protect your principal in every way possible, and when you are fortunate enough to start accumulating paper profits, at least lock a portion of them in.

7. The market's reaction to the news is critical.

It's not the news, but how the market reacts to the news that's important. You see, it's the news that sets the public perception. Be alert for divergences between the news and market action. It all has to do with expectation versus reality. Look for the divergence between what's happening and what people think is supposed to happen. When the big turn comes, the general public will always be looking the wrong way. This is why the best trades are the hardest to do. The news will always sound the most bullish at the top, and appear to be the most hopeless at the bottom. If the news is good, but the market has stopped going up, ask yourself why, and then heed the call.

Bottoms can be the most confusing. The accumulation phase, where the smart money is accumulating a position, can be marked by reactions, choppy action, shakeouts and false reversals. After the bottom is in place, many traders will be looking for the next break to be a buyer. But it never comes, the train has already left the station and you need to have the courage to hop on.

8. If the market is not confirming your opinion, lose your opinion and listen to the market.

No doubt you will be wrong innumerable times in your trading life. Being wrong is not a problem, it is more like a certainty. Not admitting you're wrong, not taking the loss when it is manageable is the big problem and will eventually lead to ruin. I have seen it so many times, and it does not matter how big or well capitalized the trader is; intractable opinions have brought down some of the biggest operators throughout history. No human can be, only the market is, always right!

9. Pyramid properly.

The big money can only be made by pyramiding a good position in a trending market. You have an excellent opportunity to use leverage with your unrealized profits to create a larger position than otherwise possible. Pyramiding takes both courage and self-control and be advised, there is a right way and a wrong way to pyramid. The masters recommend you never reverse pyramid (that is add a greater number than your initial position as the market moves your way). Your first risk should be your greatest risk. It is generally better to decrease the size of your position through the ride, not increase it. In this way, you have the opportunity to increase your profitability without dramatically increasing your risk.

10. Be aggressive ...

Be aggressive when taking profits and/or cutting losses if there is a good reason to be so. A good trader acts without hesitation. When something is not right, he will liquidate easily and early to save cash and worry. Never think too much. Just do it! And don't limit your price - go at the market! Many times a market will give you one optimal opportunity to act and that's it!

---

www.commodity.com, geo@commodity.com

'You can overpay for a good company and recover your earnings with time, but you can underpay for the wrong company and never recover.'

David Braun

Richard Koch

Richard Koch was a consultant with the Boston Consulting Group, a partner with Bain & Co, and a co-founder of LEK Consulting before becoming a private equity investor on his own account. He was behind the rescue of Filofax in 1990, was the original backer of the Belgo restaurant chain before it went public, and has had major investment successes with Plymouth Gin and Capstone Publishing.

Books

Selecting Shares That Perform: 10 Ways to Beat the Index, Financial Times Prentice Hall, 2005
Living the 80/20 Way: Work Less, Worry Less, Succeed More, Enjoy More, Nicholas Brealey Publishing Ltd, 2004
Smart Strategy Rev, Capstone Publishing Ltd, 2004
The 80/20 Individual: How to Build on the 20% of What You Do Best, Currency, 2005
The 80/20 Revolution: Why The Creative Individual Is King And How YOU Can Create Wealth And Wellbeing, Nicholas Brealey Publishing Ltd, 2002
Smart Things to Know About Leadership, Capstone Publishing Ltd, 2002
The Power Laws of Business: The Science of Success, Nicholas Brealey Publishing Ltd, 2001
The Natural Laws of Business: Applying the Theories of Darwin, Einstein, and Newton to Achieve Business Success, Currency, 2001
The Financial Times Guide to Strategy, Financial Times Prentice Hall, 2000
The FT Guide to Selecting Shares that Perform, FT Prentice Hall, 2000
The Third Revolution, Capstone, 1998
The 80/20 Principle, Nicholas Brealey, 1997

Finding your own approach to stockpicking

---

1. Do it your way.

Follow an investment approach that matches your personality and psyche.

2. If you don't succeed, give up.

Keep an accurate record of your investments, and if you don't beat the index, give up and buy a tracker fund.

3. Don't copy Noah.

Don't end up with a zoo of stocks. Have a small portfolio where each investment is a significant position for you.

4. Stick to one investment approach.

This must be your own philosophy, reflecting your skills and personality. Differentiate your approach from everyone else's.
Unless it is unique, you won't out-perform.

6. Know yourself.

Don't try to be something you aren't. Evolve your own investment niche.

6. Go for the breeders.

Only buy stocks if there is potential to multiply its value. If the prospective gain is less than 100% over 2-5 years, pass.

7. Stop losses.

Always sell stocks that decline by 15%.

8. Gear up gains.

Buy more of stocks that beat the index by more than 50% in any year.

9. Gather outsider information.

Get price sensitive information on your investee or potential investee companies - by doing your own independent outside research.

10. Follow the Pleasure Principle.

If it's not fun, stop doing it. If it is fun, do more of it. And if it is fun, *make up your own rules.*

Joe Krutsinger

Joe Krutsinger is President of Joe Krutsinger, Inc., the trading system design consulting firm. He began his futures and options career over 25 years ago with ContiCommodity. He has worked in every facet of the industry and continues to be a prolific developer of trading systems.

Books

Trading System Secrets - Selecting a Winning System, TL, 1999
Trading Systems - Secrets of the Masters, Irwin, 1997
The Trading Systems Toolkit, Probus, 1994

Trading systems

1. If you want to keep getting what you're getting, keep doing what you are doing!

One of the reasons you buy a trading system or a set of trading systems is to replace and/or supplement your current methodology. Why not get what you paid for? Many would-be systematic traders follow a system until they have three losers in a row, and then put it on the shelf. *Almost* every strategy will experience 3 losing trades in a row, so those traders are destined to fail! Give your new approach a chance to work. This is the most important rule I know!

2. While becoming expert, rent expertise.

The best way to have expertise is to become an expert. Until you are expert, the second best way is to rent an expert. Going to seminars, buying software and trading systems can allow you to 'ramp up' faster. We don't all tune our own automobiles, or fix our own teeth; why should we feel we must write our own trading systems? Once you have a system that is comfortable and profitable to you, you can 'edit' it and add your own twists. Ask yourself this - is it easier to write a book from scratch, or edit a manuscript?

3. If you can't run with the BIG DOGS, stay on the porch.

Trading *isn't* for everyone! I design racing cars, (trading systems); I don't race them! (manage money). I know my limitations. Do you know *yours?* Is the thrill of victory worth the possible agony of defeat? Are you trading small while learning, or do you trade to 'beat the bank!' Do you trust yourself, or do you need validation by the 'talking heads' on cable TV? Do you have the time for day trading (5-10 hours per day with a system), or the discipline for *daily* trading? (5-10 minutes per day with a system)? When you learned *your* business, did you learn everything at once, or did you learn one or two things thoroughly, and go from there? There is no shame on the porch. The Big Dogs can be and will be rough!

4. Eagles don't flock.

Avoid trading clubs, chat rooms, bar side gossip, newsletters, magazines, newspapers, and other traders. Keep your own counsel. Once you have developed or purchased your trading system, follow the rules, take every trade, and keep a diary of your trades. When you are winning, who *really* wants to hear about your latest conquest? When you are losing, who will really feel sorry for you and console the 'poor' trader? Do 'other' people really have your best interests at heart? Do you really care whether they win or lose? Learn your game and keep your cards close to the vest! Trading is a lonely business.

5. Do the hard thing. Buy High; Sell Higher! Sell Low; Buy Lower!

Everyone wants to do the 'easy' thing; buy at the low and sell at the high. If the market is going lower, perhaps there is a reason. Don't stand in front of the train, stand on the platform, wait for it to stop, and as it starts to go the other way *then* jump on board! It is very hard to wait. Do the hard thing! By buying high (breakouts) and selling higher (liquidating after a certain time or price target has been hit), you can do what the crowd won't do (win.)

6. Take the milk with the cream.

If you have a strategy that is right 50% of the time, it's also wrong 50% of the time. If a strategy has flat performance for several months, you will get bored, and probably abandon it right before the big trade. One of the best systematic traders in the world, Richard Dennis, has been attributed as saying: '90% of my trades are breakeven, 5% are above average losers, 5% are *huge* winners. The system helps me stay in the game waiting for the huge wins.'

In the Midwest, where I live, often buyers want only the best (the cream), and want to leave the rest (the milk) for others. I contend that you must take both the good and the not so good in order to enjoy the peace of mind and the discipline that systematic trading brings to the table.

7. When in doubt, stay out, and if you are IN - GET out!

You have instincts and they are good! (How do I know? If you have the money to trade you have made some good instinctive financial decisions!) Systematic trading is nothing more than cheap discipline. If you feel, for any reason, that you should not get in a trade, don't! (And if you are *already* in, exit.) No one likes your money better than you do! A system is nothing more than a piece of equipment. Like your morning alarm clock, when it rings *you* must decide to get up or hit snooze!

8. 'Badges? We don't need no stinking badges!'

Unlike many careers, (lawyers, doctors, teachers), traders do not need nor should they seek validation from 'someone out there' telling you are 'AOK' to trade! Many losing traders run from method to method, guru-to-guru, desperately seeking approval. Be your own accreditation agency. When *you* feel you are ready, you *are* ready!

9. Buying a race car doesn't make you a NASCAR star!

If it were that easy, who would drive the cabs? In effect, I design and manufacture the trading equivalent of a NASCAR race car. If you chose to buy one or more of my systems, great! I will run you through the basics of its design and show you how to run it and tune it. I will be there to help you if it needs 'fixed', but *you* are the driver. If you hit the wall, you are injured; I am safely in the infield. Practice on paper. Test everything. Beware. If it were that easy, no one would be driving taxicabs!

10. Talk is CHEAP; it takes money to buy whiskey!

The second most important axiom in my mind is this one. Paper trade, research, and forward test. Eventually, you must *really* trade! The best way to start trading is to trade smaller than you would normally. If you are going to trade 300 shares eventually, trade 100 for the first 90 days of systematic trading! After a big success, don't immediately increase your trading size! It is very important to really trade all of the signals, even if you only trade 1 share! Simulations, even the best on tick-by-tick data, will normally be twice as good as real trading. Rule of thumb: If a simulation makes $50,000 in a year, would you *really* do the strategy if you only made $25,000 in real-time?

If yes, then: Gentlemen, START YOUR ENGINES!

---

www.joekrut.com, www.TheSystemTrader.com, www.eTrackRecords.com

'Always sell all large-cap and high-P/E stocks before earnings are due to be reported!'

Donald Cassidy

Mike Kwatinetz

Mike Kwatinetz is a founding partner of Azure Capital Partners, an investment advisory firm focused on technology.

He was formerly the global head of Credit Suisse Boston's Equity Technology Research Group. Kwatinetz has been named No. 1 PC Hardware Analyst by *The Wall Street Journal* and by *Institutional Investor* for four of the past five years and No. 2 Software Analyst for the past two years.

Books

The Big Tech Score, John Wiley, 2000
[The rules below are reproduced from The Big Tech Score with the permission of the author and the publisher, John Wiley & Sons, Inc.]

Investing in technology companies

1. Look for a CEO under fifty.

Technology is a very fast-paced business. While age shows a certain amount of maturity and experience, I've found that a lot of CEOs begin to falter once they hit a certain benchmark. Take Digital Equipment. The company's founder, Ken Olsen, was one of the smartest people in the entire industry - but at a certain point, he lost track of where the market was heading. The PC revolution swept in and Olsen ignored it.

2. Look for a 'virtual enterprise'.

With new technologies it's often crucial to get up to critical mass as quickly as possible, because getting the numbers up creates an advantage both for customers and for the product. By licensing its operating system to every PC manufacturer, Microsoft made its operating system pervasive, which in turn encouraged software developers to write programs for it, which in turn attracted more users - a 'virtual enterprise' of partners. Apple, by contrast, refused to let its system run anywhere but on its own products, and has always remained an 'exclusive' product.

3. Look for an 'increasing feedback loop'.

Put another way, is it a product where the more people use it, the more valuable it becomes to *all* users, and the more valuable it becomes to all users, the more people get involved with it?

AOL's buddy list allows users to type in the email addresses of a list of friends, and AOL then notifies them whenever any of those friends are online. In the first year it was offered, the service grew so popular that many people signed up with AOL just so they could use it. As more people signed up, the value of the Buddy List increased further. This became a huge competitive advantage for AOL.

4. Make sure the product cannot easily be replicated.

Meaning either that it would be so costly or time-consuming for a competitor to replicate it that it doesn't make sense to try, or that the product is protected by copyright, patent or trademark legislation.

Texas Instruments holds many of the original patents on computer memory chips, and gets a royalty for almost every memory chip that hits the market. Xerox, on the other hand, developed the graphical user interface (GUI), Ethernet and the laser printer but didn't patent anything. As an investor, it's important to determine not only how good a technology is, but also how easily it can be copied.

5. Favour strong brand names.

Few competitive advantages are as difficult to fight as a brand name. An economic advantage can be overtaken eventually, a patent may be lifted, but a great brand can be sustained for years. Note that a brand can do more than retain market share. It also allows the company to launch new markets. Amazon started as an online bookseller. A few years later, it branched into CDs, DVDs, videos etc. Because it had such a strong brand, it has a sea of loyal customers, already comfortable with its site.

6. Use forward earnings estimates, not historical ones.

A company's value should be judged on its future prospects, not on its performance last year. Let's say you're thinking of investing in a company whose earnings per share were $5 last year, putting it on a P/E of 15. That may sound fine, until you learn that a competitor is about to release a product that is likely to bankrupt the product within a year. Basing your evaluations on historical earnings is ludicrous, especially for companies in the fast-changing technology industry, yet that is precisely what most investors do.

7. Use the P/R ratio where the P/E ratio is impossible.

If a company has no earnings, you cannot value it using the P/E (Price/Earnings) ratio. Such companies are obviously higher risk, and you shouldn't have more than two of them in your high-growth portfolio. But you can still value them using the P/R ratio: market capitalisation divided by consensus forecast revenue.

You may be invited to invest in public companies which not only have no earnings, but have no revenue. My advice: stay away.

8. Check for all three growth drivers.

For real long-term growth opportunity, a company needs three factors in its favour: it has to be in a market that is growing rapidly; it has to growing its market share rapidly. And it has to be creating products or services which propel it into new markets. Be wary of the company that already has a large market share in a static market and which cannot branch out, because however good it is, the potential for growth is limited.

9. Put your companies through the stock screener test.

Apart from rookie companies with the potential to be superstars, any stock you hold should have revenue of at least $100 million, and have grown revenues at least 25 per cent each year for the past three years. Its rate of growth decline should not be unreasonable. On this last point, growth rates invariably slow as companies get bigger, so a slowing growth rate is not necessarily a reason not to invest. But the rate of slowing should be within certain parameters. The formula for deciding what rate is acceptable is described in detail in *The Big Tech Score*.

10. Check whether the company has met brokers' consensus earnings forecasts in the past.

Some companies are conservative in the guidance they give analysts, beating the quarterly estimates time after time. Others give optimistic guidance, then consistently come up short. Others have no bias at all. Try to incorporate this factor into your stockpicking: a company that has a history of doing better than estimates is likely to be cheaper in reality than its P/E suggests. And a company that routinely does worse, more expensive.

www.azurecap.com

'Timing is everything. It didn't take a genius to figure out that tech stocks were overvalued long before the peak of the boom. But you could have lost a lot of money going short on the way up, and several fund managers lost their jobs because they kept out of the market bonanza.'

Laurence Copeland

Dean LeBaron

Dean LeBaron, founder of Batterymarch Financial Management in 1969, pioneered the application of computer technology and modelling techniques, first in the US market and then in international and emerging markets. Batterymarch is recognized as one of the first foreign entrants in the nascent securities markets of Brazil, India, Russia and China.

Books

Dean LeBaron's Treasury of Investment Wisdom: 30 Great Investing Minds, John Wiley & Sons Inc, 2002
Mao, Marx and the Market, Wiley, 2001
Dean LeBaron's Treasury of Investment Wisdom, Wiley, 2001
Dean LeBaron's Book of Investment Quotations, Wiley, 2001
The Ultimate Book of Investment Quotations, Capstone, 1999
The Ultimate Investor, Capstone, 1999

Habits

Sole Rule: Don't have rules - it's too hard to break them. My guiding precepts are habits, which others might call rules or addictions, but, like all addictions, I might try to break them when circumstances warrant . . . with varying success.

1. Observe the views of others, especially the most prestigious and widely recognized, but do not follow their prescriptions.

2. Ignore earnings and follow the cash.

3. Recognize that corporate control is worth everything or nothing; there is no point in between.

4. Learn more about enterprises from competitors than from the enterprises themselves.

5. Avoid company visits, since they are usually successful promotions.

6. Observe commercial bankers, who usually know the inside story and are a source of hints.

7. Ignore investment bankers and their advice.

8. Recognize that prestige is inversely related to future investment success.

www.deanlebaron.com

'Investors frequently expose themselves to great risk by seeking superior cash returns in emerging markets debt and distressed sectors. Often the risk-return trade off for these sectors is pitifully inadequate.'

David DeRosa

Steve Leuthold

Steve Leuthold is the founder and Chairman of Leuthold Weeden Capital Management and a portfolio manager for three of its funds. He has been an investment strategist, manager and researcher for more than thirty years. He is also Chairman of The Leuthold Group, an investment research organization, where he leads a team that uses quantitative historical research to develop sophisticated investment models.

Books

The Myths of Inflation and Investing, Crain Books, 1980
Index Funds, The Risks And Pitfalls, 1977

Managing your mother lode . . .
your serious money

1. Know thy self.

When investing, everyone has strengths and weaknesses. It is particularly important to recognize the weaknesses and continue to be aware of them. Then you can defense against them. Examples: 'I hate to admit I'm wrong', 'I'm a sucker for sexy tech stocks', 'I'm inherently pessimistic'.

2. Discipline is essential.

Establish your own personal set of investment disciplines, carefully considering your own investment shortcomings. Write them down. Carry them with you. Follow them. Revise your disciplines only after considering the revisions for a period of time (in a de-emotionalized state).

3. Manage risk as well as return.

When deciding on an investment, always consider how much you might lose, as well as how much you might make. Compare the potential risk with the potential reward. Does it make sense if the potential gain is 25%, but if things go wrong the risk is 50%? Apply this kind of analysis to an entire market (bonds, stocks, real estate), as well as to individual issues.

4. Cash is not trash.

Cash reserves reduce overall portfolio risk in declining markets. But more importantly, cash reserves provide the investor with the ammunition to take advantage of the unexpected opportunities that develop in markets - see the next rule.

5. Market crisis is market opportunity.

Your emotions say sell, sell, sell. But your personal disciplines previously established say BUY! However, if you have no cash reserves, the opportunity is lost.

6. Bonds can be best.

Over the next year, if yields fall to 6%, a 20-year bond now priced to yield 7% will provide a total return of over 20%, twice the historical return achieved by the stock market. What of the risk? If yields rise to 8% instead of falling to 6%, the total return loss from the bond is less than 2%. And, with bond yields rising, the stock market could be down much more.

7. Stock market new valuation eras have always been temporary.

When Wall Street starts using the term 'new era', saying it's really different this time for the stock market . . . well, that's the signal to consider asset class options like cash and bonds. While bubbles can inflate beyond most all expectations, they always ultimately burst.

8. Not even Microsoft is forever.

Virtually every blue chip growth company ultimately has matured and become a no-growth company. No company's earnings growth will ever be permanent. Of America's 100 leading companies in 1920, only 1 is on the list today (GE). Thus, you can't just buy today's leaders, put them away, and expect them to still be leaders 20, or even 10 years from now.

9. Short term trading is a loser's game.

Over 90% of non-professional short term traders will end up losers, if they stay in the game. Even those with winning trades two-thirds of the time will mostly end up losers since losses on losing trades are usually at least twice as large as the average gains realized. The few that are successful, professional or not, typically will ultimately 'burn out'. So, even if successful, the ultimate price can be high. Many of those who do win still end up as life's losers.

10. History is experience ... learn from it.

History is not a Xerox machine, and does not repeat itself exactly. Simply put, history is mankind's past experience. It is said, experience is the best teacher, but it is much less painful to learn the hard lessons from the experience of others. In terms of human nature, investor psychology in the horse and buggy days is little different than today. Society may have changed, but human nature has not. Fear and greed continue to be the dominant market forces.

---

www.leutholdfunds.com

David Linton

David Linton is the founder of Updata plc, a market leader in the provision of software and services to private and professional investors. He writes regularly in the financial press, and appears weekly on Bloomberg. He sits on the Parliamentary Information Technology Committee.

Trading and the importance of stop losses

1. Cut losses, cut losses, cut losses, let profits run.

Most investors underperform because they sell all their good stocks and hold onto all their bad ones. If you buy a share and it starts falling heavily, get out. Equally, if it starts going up, wait for it to come off the top before selling. Even if you only get your stock picks right some of the time, you can easily be ahead on this strategy.

2. Buy stocks that are going up.

It sounds ridiculously simple, but it's true. Stocks that are rising tend to keep rising while those in a downtrend continue to fall. Unless there are clear signs of a reversal, the trend is your friend.

3. Hindsight is a wonderful thing. Use it!

No investor can know the top or bottom of a cycle until it has happened. When you find yourself saying "I should have bought there", buy. Likewise, "I wish I had sold there", is a great sell signal.

4. Don't be eager to buy on buy signals. Be eager to sell on sell signals.

Don't anticipate a signal, wait for it to happen clearly. Recoveries don't normally happen overnight, you need very clear signs that the worst is over. Support levels are always tested. Get used to it. If they are clearly breached, that's different. Get out!

5. Know your sectors.

Often investors are not in the wrong stocks, but in the wrong sectors. Scroll through all the sector charts at least once a month and establish which ones are going up and which are not. When you realise you are invested in all the wrong places, rebalance your portfolio.

6. Don't trade against the trend.

Going for a short term trade against the direction of the longer term trend is very dangerous. The odds are against you.

7. Never take a tip. Time them at least.

Most tips come to nothing. You can increase the odds by establishing levels on a chart where the price is breaking out. This can often happen months after the tip. Set an alert. If it is breached then you may be onto something.

8. Fundamentals are good long term. Charts are better short term.

Buying on fundamentals is fine, but you need to be patient. The long term normally wins in the end. Always remember that fundamentals are bad for selling. Charts will get you out much faster.

9. Tell me something I don't know.

Investors are bombarded with information they already know. The key is to spot things happening that the crowd hasn't yet seen. If it is obvious, it is obviously wrong!

10. Take the emotion out.

Emotion is the investor's biggest enemy. It is the place where fear and greed meet and conspire to blur your judgement. If you are finding a decision difficult you are already dangerously close to being in the grips of the emotional taking over from the rational. When in doubt - do nought if you are out, get out if you're in.

www.updata.co.uk/pa

Burton Malkiel

Dr. Burton G. Malkiel is the Chemical Bank Chairman's Professor of Economics at Princeton University. He is a past president of the American Finance Association and is a member of the American Economic Association.

One of his books, *A Random Walk Down Wall Street*, is in its seventh edition, and he has written or co-edited eight other titles, the most recent of which are *Global Bargain Hunting: An Investor's Guide to Profits in Emerging Markets*, with J. P. Mei, and *The Index Fund Solution*, with R. Evans.

Books

A Random Walk Down Wall Street, W.W. Norton, 7th edition, 2000
Global Bargain Hunting, Simon & Schuster, 1998

Essential truths of risk and reward

---

1. Investment rewards can only be increased by the assumption of greater risk.

This fundamental law of finance is supported by centuries of historical data. Stocks have provided a compounded rate of return of 11 per cent per year since 1926, but this return came only at substantial risk to investors: total returns were negative in three out of ten years. Higher risk is the price one pays for more generous returns.

2. Your actual risk in stock and bond investing depends on the length of time you hold your investment.

Holders of a diversified stock portfolio in the years 1950 to 2000 were treated to a range of annual total returns which varied from +52% to -26%. There was no dependability of earning an adequate return in any single year. But if you held your portfolio for 25 years in the same period, your overall return would have been close to 11% whichever 25 years you were invested. In other words, by holding stocks for relatively long periods of time, you can be reasonably sure of earning the generous rates of return available from common stocks.

3. Decide how much risk you are willing to take to get high returns.

J.P. Morgan once had a friend who was so worried about his stock holdings that he could not sleep at night. Morgan advised him to "sell down to his sleeping point". He wasn't kidding. Every investor must decide the trade-off he or she is willing to make between eating well and sleeping well. Your tolerance for risk informs the types of investment - stocks, bonds, money-market accounts, property - that you make. So what's your sleeping point?

4. Dollar-Cost Averaging can reduce the risk of investing in stocks and bonds.

Dollar-cost averaging simply means investing the same fixed amount of money in, for example, the shares of a mutual fund at regular intervals - say, every month or quarter - over a long period. It can reduce (but not avoid) the risks of equity investment by ensuring that the entire portfolio of stocks will not be purchased at temporarily inflated prices.

5. Stock prices are anchored to 'fundamentals' but the anchor is easily pulled up and then dropped in another place.

The most important fundamental influence on prices is the level and duration of the future growth of corporate earnings and dividends. But earnings growth is not easily estimated, even by market professionals. In times of optimism, it is easy to convince yourself that your favourite corporation will enjoy substantial and persistent growth over an extended period. In times of pessimism, many security analysts will not project any growth that is not 'visible' and hence will estimate only modest growth rates for the corporations they follow. Given that expected growth rates and the price the market is willing to pay for growth can both change rapidly on the basis of market psychology, the concept of a firm intrinsic value for shares must be an elusive will-o-the-wisp.

6. If you buy stocks directly, confine your purchases to companies that appear able to sustain above-average earnings growth for at least five years and which can be bought at reasonable price-earnings multiples.

As difficult as it may be, picking stocks whose earnings grow is the name of the game. Consistent growth not only increases the earnings and dividends of the company but may also increase the multiple (P/E) that the market is willing to pay for those earnings. The purchaser of a stock whose earnings begin to grow rapidly has a potential double benefit: both the earnings and the multiple may increase.

7. Never pay more for a stock than can reasonably be justified by a firm foundation of value.

Although I am convinced that you can never judge the exact intrinsic value of a stock, I do feel that you can roughly gauge when a stock seems to be reasonably priced. The market price earnings multiple (P/E) is a good place to start: you should buy stocks selling at multiples in line with, or not very much above, this ratio. Note that, although similar, this is not simply another endorsement of the 'buy low P/E stocks' strategy. Under my rule it is perfectly alright to buy a stock with a P/E multiple slightly above the market average - as long as the company's growth prospects are substantially above average.

8. Buy stocks with the kinds of stories of anticipated growth on which investors can build castle in the air.

Stocks are like people - some have more attractive personalities than others, and the improvement in a stock's P/E multiple may be smaller and slower to be realized if its story never catches on. The key to success is being where other investors will be, several months before they get there. Ask yourself whether the story about your stock is one that is likely to catch the fancy of the crowd.

9. Trade as little as possible.

Frequent switching between stocks accomplishes nothing but subsidizing your broker and increasing your tax burden when you do realize gains. My own philosophy leads me to minimize trading as much as possible. I am merciless with the losers, however. With few exceptions, I sell before the end of each calendar year any stocks on which I have a loss. The reason for this is that losses are deductible (up to certain amounts) for tax purposes, or can offset gains you may already have taken. Thus, taking losses can actually reduce the amount of loss by lowering your tax bill.

10. Give serious thought to index funds.

Most investors will be better off buying index funds (funds that buy and hold all the stocks in a broad stock market index) rather than buying individual stocks. Index funds provide broad diversification, low expenses and are tax efficient. Index funds regularly beat two-thirds of the actively managed funds with which they compete.

www.princeton.edu

'A good rule-of-thumb is: the larger the investment bank or stockbroking firm that employs the analyst making the recommendation, the less likely it is to reflect what the analyst really thinks.'

Tony Golding

Joe Mansueto

Joe Mansueto founded Morningstar, Inc., a leading provider of investment information and analytical tools, in 1984.

Morningstar.com is listed among the top investing sites by *The Wall Street Journal, Barron's, SmartMoney, Money, Worth* and *Kiplinger's Personal Finance,* and is also named among the top 50 Web sites by CIO magazine.

Mansueto received the Distinguished Entrepreneurial Alumnus Award from University of Chicago Graduate School of Business in 2000.

Value investing and funds

1. Apply a private company mentality to public company investing.

Private company owners rarely buy or sell equity and, when they do, they know the value of their equity. A similar approach works well with public company investing: know the value of what you're buying and treat your holding as you would a family business by rarely trading it. Also, private company owners think about the worth of their shares at most once or twice a year. You'll do better with your public company investing if you adopt a similar mindset and don't obsess with daily fluctuations in value.

2. If it's overly complicated and you don't fully understand it, avoid it.

Only invest in things you understand and feel strongly about. If you don't have conviction when you buy it, there's a greater likelihood you'll sell at the first sign of bad news. As with most things, simplicity is a virtue in investing.

3. Invest for the long term.

Most real wealth is built from owning excellent companies for long periods of time. Frequent trading leads to frequent tax bills and frequent transactions costs, both of which can reduce long-term returns significantly. Give the exponential effects of compounding time to work for you. Take a look at your portfolio: how many holdings have you owned for five years or more?

4. As long as you don't lose money, you won't have to worry much about making money.

If your portfolio earns 50% one year and then loses 50% the next year, you're even, right? Wrong. Your two year return is still a negative 25%. To achieve a high return over a long period of time, focus more on minimizing mistakes. Ask yourself "what is the downside risk on this investment?" and leave a comfortable margin of safety. You needn't hit a homerun on every investment, but avoiding large losses will do wonders for your overall return.

5. Buy great companies at reasonable prices.

Look for companies that have high returns on capital, strong balance sheets, sustainable competitive advantages and shareholder-oriented management. Be patient and try to buy them when they are selling at a discount to their real worth. These opportunities don't come often, so buy meaningful amounts when they do.

6. Don't worry about forecasting the market.

Focus on a company's prospects and its valuation, not the overall market. No one knows where the market is headed over the next year, so don't concern yourself with it. And tune out the noise from those who claim - rather loudly, sometimes - that they do. If you're right in your company selection, you'll be fine in the long run.

7. Think different.

To do well as an investor, you need to have the insight and courage to invest differently than the crowd. It's easy and comforting to invest in what's currently popular and doing well - like technology stocks in 1999 and 2000. Being contrarian and following the less traveled path will lower your risk and give you the opportunity to outperform.

8. Search for a few great managers and stick with them.

On average, fund managers approximate the market because they *are* the market (or at least a significant part of it). Still, there are a few brilliant managers who consistently do far better than average. Search them out and invest with them for long periods of time.

9. Don't pay active management fees for passive management by buying closet index funds.

Many funds don't stray far from the component make-up of their passive benchmarks. This guarantees they'll never have terrible relative performance and hence increase the odds of holding onto their investors. In these cases, you're better off investing in index funds and lowering your expenses.

10. Consider index funds for all or part of your portfolio.

You'll certainly do better than the average fund by owning an index fund. The Vanguard 500 Index Fund, for example, has outperformed 80% of its peers over the last fifteen years. The compounding effect of your management fee savings translates into meaningful sums over the years. And you'll pay less to the tax man as well, since index funds have very low turnover.

www.morningstar.com

'Don't be fooled by companies that boast investments by well-known companies like Intel and Microsoft. Both held big stakes in Lernout & Hauspie.'

Herb Greenberg

Conor McCarthy

Conor McCarthy is the Dublin-based founder and editor of *Techinvest,* a monthly newsletter for investors interested in technology stocks. Each issue of *TechInvest* provides news and information on technology companies quoted on the London market, and gives buy/hold/sell ratings.

Technology stocks - attractions and dangers

1. Look out for fallen favourites.

Fallen favourites are stocks which have declined a long way over a period of time following earnings disappointments. They tend to fall to levels that take leave of the underlying fundamentals and fail to take account of recovery prospects. However, it is important to check that the balance-sheet is not over-stretched. If there is net cash, so much the better.

Patience is essential - it is almost impossible to time the turning-point for recovery situations. It is also important not to buy in the early stages of the price fall. Wait for the first signs of stability to appear in both the business and share price.

2. Calculate annual R & D expenditure per share and compare it to the share price.

If the PRR (price-research ratio - share price divided by R and D per share) is 5 or less it is nearly always worth buying the shares. This applies particularly to recovery situations. As long as an exploration company has the wherewithal to drill holes, there is always the possibility it will strike it lucky. The same goes for an out-of-favour technology company. As long as it can continue to invest in R and D there is the chance it will come up with a blockbuster product. The lower the PRR the more development bang you get for your buck.

3. Use Relative Strength to detect significant changes in a stock's performance relative to the market.

In particular, I like to use 10 and 20 week moving averages of Relative Strength. Relative Strength is particularly useful when buying into recovery stocks or when considering sales of long-term winners. The larger the market capitalisation of the stock the more useful Relative Strength is. For small cap stocks, price movements are too erratic and random for Relative Strength signals to be reliably useful.

4. Never plan to hold a stock forever.

Be prepared to take part-profits if the price gets too far ahead of the underlying fundamentals. Sell if newsflow disappoints in a big way.

Use stop-losses, but only in certain situations. They are most helpful when protecting profits after a huge rise in the share price. Use of a stop-loss in early-stage recovery situations is rarely a good idea. Simplistic stop-loss rules, such as sell on a 20% price drop, should be avoided. Instead, chart patterns, trading volumes and moving averages should all be used to help identify suitable stop-loss points.

5. Recurring revenue streams, the larger the better, are very attractive.

They provide predictability of sales and profits going forward and reduce the likelihood of nasty earnings surprises. Companies that change to a business model which steadily increases the recurring proportion of revenue are likely to undergo a market rerating.

6. Watch for management changes.

Top-level management changes at a company that has gone stale nearly always lead to a revitalised performance, although not necessarily immediately. The new management team normally experiences a honeymoon period with the stockmarket which nearly always sees the share price outperform even before the new team delivers improved results.

7. If investing in early-stage companies, go for those with a realistic chance of playing a significant role in a fast-developing emerging market.

Ideally, the management team should have at least one previous small company success under its belt in delivering enhanced shareholder value.

8. Look for medium-stage companies with a dominant share of a high growth market.

For medium-stage tech companies, that is those that are already profitable but far from mature, look for companies with a dominant share of a high growth market and with a product or service that provides significant cost benefits to customers.

9. Avoid companies with a sales-dominant corporate culture.

All too often, accounting irregularities and questionable practices creep in sooner or later, ultimately leading to restated results, a loss in investor confidence and an overnight collapse in the share price.

10. Look for companies with a PEG (current year prospective P/E divided by the growth rate for the following year) of less than 1.

This enables comparisons to be made between stocks with varying multiples and growth rates. If two stocks have more or less equal PEGs, go for the one which looks most likely to achieve market expectations.

www.techinvest.ie

'Risk is the dispersion in unexpected outcomes, and not only the occurrences of losses. Extraordinary performance, both good and bad, should raise red flags.'

Philippe Jorion

Duff McDonald

Duff McDonald is Executive Editor in charge of public market coverage for Red Herring Communications, both in print and on RedHerring.com. He is also New York Bureau Chief for the company's editorial operations.

Business technology

Introduction

We at Red Herring are devout followers of venture capital, of the great liquidity event known as the IPO, and also of the democracy of the public equity markets. We are drawn to companies that change the way we live - at work, at home, or somewhere in between. Find one, and odds are good that it's a technology or telecommunications company.

Once considered narrow, monolithic sectors, technology and communications together made up nearly a quarter of the overall market capitalization of the S&P 500 in mid-2001. Combined, those companies had trailing 12-month revenues of $1 trillion. Even after a tumultuous year, 8 of the 20 most highly capitalized companies trading on U.S. exchanges were heroes of the networked era - including Microsoft, Intel, AOL Time Warner, IBM, Verizon Communications, and Cisco Systems. And 8 of the top 20 performing stocks over the past five years were technology companies.

The future could bring a similar imbalance: as a group, technology and telecommunications companies are projected to post annual earnings growth of more than 20 percent over the next several years - more than half again as much as any other sector. But that number even includes giants like IBM that lumber along churning out earnings growth rates in the high single digits and low teens. The majority of companies expected to post long-term annual earnings growth of 100 percent or more are technology, healthcare, or telecommunications companies.

Of course, these stocks tend to be expensive. And volatile. Catch the swing at the wrong time - as many have done recently - and you've got big losses on your hands. Follow strict principles in investment process, though, and you have the opportunity to profit handsomely. Our principles follow.

1. We believe in disruption.

Change, as John F. Kennedy so succinctly put it, is good. New technologies driving new functionality in our PCs, networks, our cell phones, our automobiles, and even our bodies are the lifeblood of the Red Herring ethos. And we want to invest in the companies driving those changes.

At the right price, we like software makers like BEA Systems, i2 Technologies, Mercury Interactive, or Veritas Software; biotechnology companies like Illumina; and fledgling energy companies like Ballard Power Systems. That doesn't necessarily mean that we're focused on Silicon Valley-like upstarts to the exclusion of all else. Texas Instruments, for example, pulled off one of the greatest about-faces in corporate history when it transformed itself from a sluggish maker of pocket calculators into the world's leading manufacturer of digital signal processors for cellular phones.

2. But we also believe in market power.

Despite the market's recent punishment of technology kingpins like Cisco Systems and EMC, investors would do themselves a grave disservice to forget about the big guys and focus exclusively on the next hot stock. Technology, by its very nature, lends itself to the creation of monopolies. That, in turn, translates into the ability to set the standards, and to reap outrageous profit margins.

Legal woes aside, Microsoft's gross margins of 80 to 90 percent are still to die for. Not surprisingly, the stocks of companies in this position - colloquially referred to as gorillas - tend to be expensive. But unless we see serious trouble on the horizon, we tend to be inclined to pay a premium for leadership. Other candidates in this category include database leader Oracle, wireless vanguard Nokia, and semiconductor equipment maker Applied Materials.

3. We believe in convergence.

Technology in and of itself contains endless investment opportunities - PCs, cell phones, internet, whatever. But when technology meets something like health care, things get really interesting.

By their very nature, investments in companies that are trying to retool the human body can be quite speculative. But they can also be among the most rewarding: companies like Immunex, IDEC Pharmaceuticals, and MedImmune all delivered returns of more than 1,500 percent over the past five years.

Slightly less profound, but still offering awesome investment possibilities, is the convergence of technology and entertainment. Technology and finance also make a fine pair.

4. We believe in diversification.

If there's anything that technology investors like more than originality, it's a good old-fashioned bandwagon. In recent years, we've seen B2C, B2B, P2P, Internet infrastructure, optics and others being the drivers of said bandwagon. While we're not one to argue with great ideas, it's important to withstand getting hypnotized by the latest buzzword and to diversify technology investments.

Taking a step back, it's also important to diversify outside of technology itself, if only because the sector's stocks continue to move in a loose unison.

5. We believe in being reasonable.

When investors lost all sense of rationality at the height of the internet bubble and proclaimed the importance of profits an anachronistic concept, we voiced our dissent. It's okay to forsake profits to establish one's business, but one's business should still be about making profits. Companies that merely demonstrate an ability to spend money at investors' expense are not on our short list of purchase candidates

As reasonable investors, we also place less importance on the results of a single quarter than momentum investors do. If a company misses earnings expectations for reasons other than extreme ineptitude, we're inclined to consider purchasing a battered-down stock. Likewise, one quarter of outperformance doesn't justify the opposite treatment, and we see extreme optimism as a chance to take profits.

6. We believe in a medium-term perspective.

We try to take a longer-term perspective on the purchase of a stock than whether or not next week's press release will be positive or negative. That said, it's important to remember that technology is about change—and even once-omnipotent companies can be yesterday's news if they don't keep innovation as their mantra (think Novell or Corel).

For that reason, we are fans of the medium-term, or a two- to five-year horizon, a span in which we feel we can comfortably understand the possibilities. In the shorter-term, stock market movement is just noise; the shape of things ten years from now is just too difficult to contemplate. So while we advocate a buy-and-hold approach, we're not afraid to let go. That said, we believe that technology is showing the way to the future, and technology stocks should do the same in a portfolio.

www.redherring.com

'When bears rule the street, it pays to own things that pay you to own them. This includes stocks that pay high dividends, preferred stocks, REITS, convertible bonds, and balanced mutual funds that own a mixture of the above assets. If it takes years for stock prices to rise, you might as well get some return while you wait.'

John Rothchild

Colin McLean

Colin McLean is Managing Director of Scottish Value Management, an Edinburgh-based investment management group established in 1990. SVM manages portfolios for US and European institutions, in addition to the SVM Highlander Fund, a Europe long/short hedge fund, five investment trusts and a range of offshore funds. Funds under management exceed €1bn.

Value investing and the unreliability of share prices

1. Find your own zone of comfort - and stick to it.

Buy stocks you can live with, and structure portfolios to keep you comfortable with the risks. If you cannot stand day-to-day share price volatility, you will only end up selling out a stock at the worst time and lowest price.

2. Share prices are not so smart.

Share prices will not tell you what real risks a company is running, or how good it is. Shares with low volatility can suddenly change their pattern, or even steadily destroy value in the long term. A fall in the share price does not mean it is now cheap; a rising share price does not make a company good.

3. Focus on the stocks you own.

With hundreds of companies on the stockmarket to choose from, half of which will outperform, you can afford to miss out on a lot of winners. Focus on the stocks you hold that might turn out to be losers, rather than worrying about missing out on performing stocks you don't own.

4. Not all sales are created equal.

A low market capitalisation relative to sales is not necessarily cheap. Some industries will never earn more than 2% on sales, others 30%. Some will generate free cash flow from sales, others can fail to make a satisfactory return on the working capital involved. Lots of sales are not the same as value - look at operating profit.

5. Buy smaller companies for growth.

Given the lower liquidity and more limited research coverage, it is dangerous to buy small companies unless they are likely to become big ones. Companies moving up into the next stockmarket division, such as from small cap to the FTSE Mid 250, often attract new investors. It is the key way in which liquidity in smaller and medium sized companies can improve, and a re-rating be achieved.

6. Be wary of companies with large convertible issues.

This often indicates that a company cannot issue further equity, possibly because its shares are below the price of the last issue, or does not have a satisfactory bond rating. Also, companies offering shares as deferred consideration on a takeover believe it is a cheap way of buying businesses. But if their share price falls, meeting these obligations can prove very expensive.

7. Watch executive share sales.

Director buying is a less useful guide as boards often try to emphasise this signal. However, selling by chief executives or finance directors still works well as a warning. Striking share options early is also a danger signal.

8. Read the annual accounts.

Beware of unconventional accounting practice or overdesigned accounts. Some companies can try too hard to impress investors. If you have questions, write to the chairman before the AGM.

9. Don't use earnings per share to determine growth rates.

Establish the underlying real growth of companies by looking at growth in turnover, volume or customer numbers.

10. Establish the business drivers and value catalysts.

Understand the business model, and the key factors involved in a company making money. Check for specific evidence of success of this. Think like a trade investor. Identify the catalyst that is likely to see value recognised by the stockmarket or a bidder.

www.scottish-value.co.uk

Lawrence McMillan

Lawrence McMillan is the editor of *The Options Strategist* newsletter. He is the author of several articles on options and investment trading, including *Hedged Options Strategies*, a weekly investment newsletter. Mr McMillan currently manages money and trades his own account.

Books

Options as a Strategic Investment, Prentice Hall, 1993
McMillan on Options, John Wiley, 1996
McMillan on Options, John Wiley & Sons Inc, 2004

Axioms for option traders and short-term traders

---

1. Always use a model before trading an option.

It's okay to buy an overpriced option, but you must be aware that it is overpriced. Once aware of that fact, act accordingly to limit losses if the option begins to lose its 'pricey-ness'. There are plenty of cheap or free versions of the Black-Scholes model available. Don't trade without access to one of them.

2. Don't buy more software than you need.

Many traders load up on expensive software that is so difficult to use, they don't even get any benefit from it. Option traders sometimes spend thousands on fancy software and then wind up using only the Black-Scholes model portion of it. Again, as stated in rule 1, there are plenty of cheap or free versions of the Black-Scholes model available. The same thing goes for technical analysis. Fancy systems that over-analyze are not beneficial. Stick to simpler things such as support, resistance, and moving averages - all of which are available for very low cost (even, free) on internet charting services.

3. Trade all markets.

There are many excellent trading opportunities in futures and indices as well as stocks. Traders who ignore the futures and index markets are missing out on plenty of good trades.

4. Use technical analysis to make sure you're going with the trend.

No matter whether you're a long-term or a short-term trader, technical analysis can identify the trend. That is, don't buy a stock in a steep downtrend. If you like the stock, wait until it stabilizes somewhat - forms a base or whatever, perhaps rises above a resistance level - and *then* buy it. Trying to catch a 'falling knife' is foolhardy and unnecessary.

5. Always use a stop.

Whether you're a long-term investor or a day-trader, you must use a stop. Not to do so is foolish. The only people who were wiped out when the internet stocks fell by 80% or more were those who didn't use stops. Long term investors often make the crucial mistake of figuring that time will bail them out, and thus they don't use stops. But if you get your cash out of a losing position, it can work better for you in some other stock - rather than sitting around waiting for your 'dead money' to come alive once again. Corollary: once you're stopped out, don't look back. Take a stock off your 'watch screen' once you've been stopped out. You'll only torture yourself if you see it go back up right after you're stopped out, and that might cause you to ignore your stop in the next trade - a potentially fatal error.

6. Don't use stop orders with your options.

If you're good at selecting stocks, futures, or indices to trade, then use your expertise properly. Use the chart of the underlying as your guide on when to enter and exit the position. So, if you own options, you shouldn't put a stop order in for the option itself, but instead keep an eye on the underlying and use a MENTAL stop for your option - based on where the underlying is trading.

7. Take partial profits.

If you're fortunate to have a profit in a position, take some of it. Not only does this take some of your risk off the table, but it also allows you to think more clearly about how to handle the position going forward. Once you have booked some profit, you'll be surprised at how you'll be able to let profits run.

8. Let the rest of your profits run.

The easiest way to do this is to use some simple moving average as a trailing stop. For example, suppose you're long, and the underlying begins to move up. Whether you're long options or stocks, it makes no difference. Use the 20-day moving average, say, as a trailing stop - probably even a closing trailing stop. That is, you stay long unless the underlying closes under its 20-day moving average. Then you can easily let your profits run. As long as the underlying stays above its 20-day moving average, you'll stay long and you can capture some huge moves this way. As a corollary: don't use targets! - they force you to cut your profits short.

9. Go against the crowd.

Most option traders are wrong at major turning points. Make it your business to find out what they're doing and do the opposite. If they're all bullish, then *you* should be bearish. If they're all bearish, it's time for *you* to buy. Option sentiment is quite evident through the put-call ratios. Monitor them and you'll find that you can identify major turning points for the market as whole, and stocks, futures, and indices.

10. Most important: only trade in accordance with your philosophy.

No matter how good a trading system looks or how successful its inventor has been, it will not work for you if it doesn't fit with your own personal investment philosophy. If it causes you to have sleepless nights, or if you can't take your eyes off the screen, then it's probably too intense for you. Find a strategy that lets you be comfortable when you trade.

www.optionstrategist.com

'In many foreign markets, the dominant mentality is a trading one. Insider trading is permissible and rife, turnover is very high, stories abound, and the locals are mainly interested in running a stock up 25 percent and dumping it.

There's no way you can outtrade the locals, so the secret is to become a long-term investor, to adopt a different time scale. Then, their edge washes out over time.'

Ralph Wanger

Rajnish Mehra

Rajnish Mehra is Professor of Finance and Chair of the Department of Economics at the University of California. He is a visiting professor at the Graduate School of Business, Chicago, and is an associate editor of The Journal of Economic Dynamics and Control.

The equity premium

1. The equity premium - what is it?

For over a century, stock returns have been considerably higher than those for T-bills. The average annual real return (that is to say, the inflation adjusted return) on the U.S. stock market over the last hundred and ten years has been about 7.9%. Over the same period, the return on a relatively riskless security, like a government bond was a paltry 1%. The difference between these two returns, 6.9 percent, is termed the 'equity premium'. This statistical difference is even more pronounced over the post war period, with the premium of stock returns over bonds being almost 8%.

2. What is the equity premium puzzle?

Since stocks are 'riskier' than bonds, investors require a larger premium for bearing this additional risk; and indeed, the standard deviation of the returns to stocks (about 20% per annum historically) is larger than that of the returns to T-bills (about 4% per annum), so, obviously they are considerably more risky than bills! But are they?

Stocks and bonds pay off in approximately the same states of nature or economic scenarios and hence according to standard asset pricing theory they should command approximately the same rate of return, or at most, a 1% return premium over bills! Since the observed mean premium on stocks over bills is considerably and consistently higher, we have a puzzle on our hands.

The equity premium puzzle is a quantitative puzzle in that standard theory is consistent with our notion of risk that, on average, stocks should return more than bonds. The puzzle arises from the fact that the quantitative predictions of the theory are an order of magnitude different from what has been historically documented.

3. Statistics, damn statistics . . .

The observed premium is not just a statistical artifact. Given that we have over a hundred years worth of good data, it is highly unlikely that the 'true' premium is small or zero when the observed premium is 7%.

4. The US and other markets.

The pattern of excess returns to equity holdings is not unique to U.S. capital markets. Equity returns compared to the return to debt holdings in other countries also exhibit this historical regularity. The annual return on the British stock market was 5.7% over the post war period, an impressive 4.6% premium over the average bond return of 1.1%. Similar statistical differentials are documented for France, Germany, Italy and Spain.

5. Great fluctuations of the equity premium year-by-year.

The 'ex-post', or 'realized', equity premium is the actual, historically observed difference between the return on the market, as captured by a stock index, and the risk free rate, as proxied by the return on government bills. This premium has varied considerably over time, being positive in some years and negative in others.

6. Investment planning with the equity premium.

The related concept, the 'ex-ante' equity premium, is a forward-looking measure of the premium - that is, the equity premium that is expected to prevail in the future or the conditional equity premium given the current state of the economy.

To elaborate, after a bull market, when stock valuations are high relative to fundamentals, the ex-ante equity premium is likely to be low. However, it is precisely in these times, when the market has risen sharply, that the ex-post, or the realized premium is high. Conversely, after a major downward correction, the ex-ante (expected) premium is likely to be high while the realized premium will be low.

The ex-post premium (i.e. the realized) premium can be negative. However, the forward-looking premium MUST be positive. If it were negative investors would not hold stocks and perhaps even short them. Can the whole market do that? No. What will happen is that the price would go down so that, looking ahead, the premium is positive.

7. Investment planning horizons are key!

The documented equity premium is for very long investment horizons. It has very little to say about what the premium is going to be over the next couple of years. Market watchers and other professionals who are interested in short term investment planning, will wish to project the conditional equity premium over their planning horizon. This is by no means a simple task.

8. Time and tide . . .

The ex-post equity premium is the realization of a stochastic process over a certain period and it has varied considerably over time. Furthermore the variation depends on the time horizon over which it is measured. There have been periods when it has even been negative. It is important to remember that not only is the mean 7% but it comes with a standard deviation of almost 20%!

9. The equity premium is dead! Long live the equity premium!

There is the point of view, held by a group of academicians and professionals who claim that at present there is no equity premium and by implication no puzzle. Before we dismiss the premium we need to examine the evidence. The data used to document the equity premium over the past hundred years is probably as good as any economic data we have - and a hundred years is long series when it comes to economic data. Even if the conditional equity premium, given the current market conditions is small, this in itself does not imply that either the historical premium was too high or that the equity premium has diminished.

10. Stocks payoff in the long run.

Based on what we know, we can make the following claim: over the long investment horizon the equity premium is likely to be similar to what it has been in the past and the returns to investment in a diversified equity portfolio will continue to substantially dominate that in bills for investors with a long planning horizon.

www.econ.ucsb.edu/~mehra/mehra.htm

'If you are wondering when to bank a profit, wait until all the brokers say buy and the stock is tipped in the Sunday Newspapers. It can be promoted no more and it is then time to get out.'

Tom Winnifrith

Viren Mehta

Dr Viren Mehta formed his own investment advisory group in 1989 specialising in the pharmaceutical and biotechnology industry investment, after working in related areas for Merck & Co, Wood MacKenzie, and S.G. Warburg. As a 'boutique' Wall Street firm, Mehta Partners has honed a specialty niche both with its science (R&D) expertise and an integrated global perspective aimed at understanding the critical success factors in the global pharmaceutical and biotechnology sector. Mehta Partners provides asset management, institutional research, and strategic advisory services to pharmaceutical and biotechnology investors worldwide.

The innovative therapeutics sector

Introduction

I use the term 'new science' to refer to all the scientific progress that has been unfolding since the mid-1970s, including recombination biology, combinatorial chemistry, high throughput screening, genomics, proteomics and so forth.

This evolving new frontier will continue to yield new drugs, or 'innovative therapeutics' that go well beyond treating just the symptoms. During the next generation, if not sooner, these innovative therapeutics will capture two if not three percent of the industrialized world's GDP as compared to the one percent today.

What is most exciting is that this growth may well come without increasing the overall healthcare spending and, with a bit of luck, may in fact help reduce total healthcare spending over time by replacing many of the expensive but ineffective healthcare services of today. The biopharmaceutical (pharma and biotech) sector accounts for about three quarters of the healthcare sector market value and lends itself much more readily to fundamental analysis than the rest of the sector - thereby justifying this 'innovative therapeutics' focus.

1. Invest globally and across all market caps and stages of maturity.

This reduces volatility and increases performance because no one group has a monopoly on the next flash of inspiration. Also different markets and currencies follow divergent trends - Global (multinational profitable companies), Emerging (specialty profitable companies), and Rising Stars (unprofitable biotech companies) often participate in opposite rotation cycles. Such diversified investing also enables a more comprehensive valuation framework that is critical for investments based on fundamental analysis, perhaps the safest way to invest in this sector.

2. Focus on 'innovative therapeutics'.

Companies discovering and developing more cost-effective drugs based on new science account for about three quarters of the health care sector market valuation and their share prices are driven much more by their fundamental progress than the rest of the sector. Also, drugs account for about one percent of the GDP in the industrialized countries today, but this figure should rise to two percent, and possibly three percent, in a decade - at the expense of the other segments of the health care sector as better drugs replace much less cost-effective modes of healthcare.

3. Invest for the long term, but take advantage of near term volatility.

Innovative therapeutics take a shorter time to get to market nowadays than they used to, but discovering, developing, and marketing a new drug is still a long term and risky business. Invest a majority of your portfolio for the long term when fundamental value is definable and an inflection point is at hand, then avoid the temptation to sell your winners.

The 'inflection point' in this sector is almost always driven by the emergence of a significant innovative therapeutic product on the horizon. However, the investment window is usually between the first confirmation of the product's potential and its market approval. Unless the company has a solid stream of products, experienced investors are exiting by the time doctors find out about the drug.

The convergence of information technology and new science is causing greater volatility, and thoughtful near term fundamental longs and fundamental shorts around hypes, falsehoods, and missed milestones can yield large gains.

4. Find proven management teams.

Only one in sixteen products entering the clinic, or human testing, succeeds in the marketplace. Having the skills to manage through the failure that is a normal part of this sector is critical. In the exciting but high risk phase of transition from 'old' to 'new' science, an able and scientifically astute management team makes all the difference.

5. Invest primarily in products, and only very carefully in tool-kit or technology companies.

Products usually have a long life cycle, create global enterprises, and build substantial equity value. Tool-kit and technology companies, by contrast, sell their time, and their skills quickly become commoditized.

Combinatorial chemistry, for example, was rapidly commoditized, with a random chemical compound now going for pennies compared to dollars during the early days of this technology. Similarly, gene sequencing is a technology today that is already becoming a commodity. Proteomics is all the rage today, but it is only a matter of time before it too will be a set of tools a dime a dozen. The real value of these tools and technologies will accrue to those who are first to identify validated biological targets and, better still, product candidates with solid patents that have a good chance of becoming innovative therapeutics.

This of course is easier said than done, and fewer than one in ten that try will succeed as a product company.

6. Invest in products with sophisticated marketing.

Innovation alone can only go so far in a free market environment, and a unique marketing platform is critical for achieving full potential of any product.

7. Invest only very selectively in money-losing biotech companies.

And only if they have critical innovative scientific pathways with an attractive patent portfolio, and adequate cash balance to survive for at least two years. Also, watch for dilution - thanks to maturing options and warrants - especially when a company is about to enter sustainable profitability.

8. Prepare to invest in emerging markets.

Today, 10% of the world population consumes 90% of drugs. Many emerging markets are maturing in their economic policies, thus increasing wealth among the middle class who will demand newer, better drugs - even at western prices. Both local and multinational companies will benefit for decades to come.

The key word here is 'prepare' as the liquidity, transparency, and regulatory issues are not at a stage where investors can feel comfortable. Multinational companies are too large to register this opportunity as yet in their share price, so high quality domestic companies in selected major emerging markets (Brazil, Mexico, India, selected Eastern European countries, and perhaps China and Russia) will need to be analysed for these opportunities once they mature over the next one to five years.

9. Double up in good names when the sector goes out of favor.

The market's penchant for sector rotation is the best friend of fundamental, long term investors, and at appropriate times justifies an over-weighted position.

10. Sit out the sector (or short it) when valuations reach silly heights.

Avoid the hype and remain true to your convictions. Take the time necessary to develop a first hand feel about the breakthroughs of the new science that will benefit both your personal and financial health.

www.mpglobal.com
www.mpfunds.com

Paul Melton

Paul Melton edits *The Outside Analyst*, the only monthly newsletter that actually compares stocks globally. Since its inception in 1986, this wholly independent publication has earned a reputation for sound research.

Melton specialises in sourcing the world's bargain equities, screening earnings estimates each month for more than 15,000 companies in over 40 countries.

Books
Investor's Guide to Going Global with Equities, FT Prentice Hall, 1996

Navigating the world's markets

---

1. Chart a course.

Lucius Annaeus Seneca (4BC-AD65) left you this warning: "When a man does not know what harbor he is making for, no wind is the right wind." There are investment strategies to suit all tastes and pocketbooks. The key is to decide which approach best suits your circumstances, special skills, unique sources and, above all, your character. Then stick to your plan.

2. Leave your home port.

Antoine Marin Lemierre (1723-1793) wrote: "It is a profound mistake to think the horizon the boundary of the world." Not everyone can beat the averages. But sailing out of your home port decidedly improves your odds.

First of all, going global gives you more opportunity to find bargains. If no equities meet your criteria in a particular market, move on to another. There's always a bull market somewhere. Secondly, going global makes your portfolio more stable. The risk of your home market remains the same, whether you own two stocks or twenty. That's because stocks in a single market tend to move up or down together. However, just as you can diversify away the specific individual risk of each stock, you can reduce the market risk of your total portfolio by going into uncorrelated markets.

For optimal global equity diversification, select some twenty-five stocks, or their equivalents, from different countries and industries, placing more emphasis on country diversification than on industry diversification. Diversify to hedge your ignorance. (John Maynard Keynes, Warren Buffett, and William J. O'Neil would all disagree, saying it's better to own few stocks about which you know a great deal. If you're a full-time investor and truly in their league, you can afford to ignore diversification.)

3. Remember that one port can be as good as another.

To the global navigator, all countries are equal. Yet, to paraphrase Orwell, some countries are more equal than others. So weight countries as equally as possible. Though equal weighting, as typified by the MEGA benchmark in Going Global with Equities, is clearly the best point of departure, it by no means rules out further adjustments. Quite the contrary. Each country's part of the total score should be further attuned to risk and reward. The two steps to doing this: first, adjust your weightings to minimize the chance of correlated market movements, then tilt that mix towards the most promising markets and shares.

4. Fish where they're biting.

The bumblebee's philosophy was neatly expressed by Publilius Syrus in the 1st century BC: "It is better to have a little than nothing." Bees ignore rare events and pay attention to common events. A U.S. researcher set out an artificial meadow of reliable blue flowers, each containing a small amount of nectar, and chancy yellow flowers, some containing nothing, some a jackpot of nectar. The bees - in this universe of specific risk - quickly learned to avoid the chancy flower and home in on the known quantity. They clearly preferred steady small rewards to the chance of hitting it big.

Humans, on the other hand, are optimists who believe rare events will happen more frequently than they actually do. So don't chase the giant marlin by paying too much for the prospects of huge profits from a new industry, the potential of a big minerals find, or the current fast growth of a technology firm. Go for earnings stability and settle for smaller fish that are easier to catch.

5. Tack into the wind.

As Henry Wadsworth Longfellow noted: "Things are not what they seem." Perceived risk and actual risk do not coincide. If markets were perfectly rational and efficient, returns would relate to market risk: the risk you cannot diversify away within a single market. But markets are people, and people are not perfectly rational. People expect greater return for greater perceived risk, and price an equity accordingly. Share prices fluctuate much more widely than values. Popular equities are often overvalued and unpopular ones undervalued Hence, one way to create steady profits is to follow strategies that exploit these recurring discrepancies between the risk the crowd sees in an equity and its expected market risk. So buy shares perceived as risky.

Market cycles are like the seasons. When the winter winds blow, blue and yellow flowers wilt alike. But if you've gone global, you have a portfolio for all seasons. In choosing your holdings, this diversity gives you the opportunity to seek market risk for more potential reward. For individual stocks, the best proxy for market risk is the dispersion of analyst estimates. The wider such estimates are scattered, the higher the return you can expect. Typically the strategy will produce some spectacular flops more than offset by spectacular gains. Though this may seem the antithesis of the bumblebee's approach, your global portfolio of apparently 'risky' wallflowers will have a much higher probability of success. The bumblebee would envy you.

6. Limit ballast.

William Wordsworth put his finger on the problem of information overload back in 1807: "The world is too much with us." We react consciously to only a fragment of the data being thrown at us. Research suggests we tend to become more confident and less accurate as we process increasing amounts of information. So avoid information overload.

As most people can handle no more than seven pieces of information at once, it is wise to employ no more than seven criteria for choosing each stock. (Barry Ziskin uses only seven criteria to pick stocks for his Z-7 Fund. These include: earnings stability, good working capital ratios, acceptable cover of long-term debt obligations, a share price of less than 10 times estimated current earnings, and institutional ownership of less than 10%.)

7. Check regularly for leaks

"Beware of small expenses," said Benjamin Franklin: "A little leak will sink a great ship." For every euro, dollar, or yen, skimmed from your investment capital today, you lose far more as you sail on. Those funds are gone forever. They can no longer help increase your assets. Money spent on commissions and expenses is money that fails to grow. The key to evaluating investment fees is to perceive that such expenses represent capital that would otherwise have been invested. The hidden cost of investment fees is their future cost: cumulative curtailment of your return. So hold down turnover and fees.

Expert tennis is a winners game because the ultimate outcome is determined by the actions of the winner. Conversely, amateur tennis is determined by the actions of the loser, making it a loser's game. The amateur seldom beats his opponent, but he beats himself all the time. The victor gets a higher score because his opponent loses even more points. Most investment managers fail to beat the market because due to the rising costs of trading they are playing a loser's game. The average spread on the Nasdaq rose from less than 3% in 1984 to almost 6% in 1992. Suppose we estimate that in most markets institutional investors incur spreads and commissions some 60% lower than those on Nasdaq, say 3.5% Now here's a key question: If equities return an average annual 9% return, turnover averages 30% a year, and dealer spreads and commissions on institutional transactions (one way) average 3.5% of the assets involved, how much does a professional manager have to outperform a market to deliver net returns 20% above its index? The answer boggles the mind: over 43%. And that ignores management and custody fees! Using the same estimates, the active manager must beat a market gross by 23% just to equal the market net.

The moral? Think twice before doing anything, because chances are it is a mistake.

8. Maintain the lifeboats.

When asked what he had done during the Terror of the French Revolution, the Abbé Sieyes replied, "I survived." Rule 8 will help you to do likewise: Limit your downside. Use stops, which, in the long run, limit losses to reasonable size and let profits run. A stop can be used not only to protect against loss, but also to lock in a profit. The idea is to place a "trailing stop" under a stock that's on the rise. You can think about raising that stop when your paper profit nears 20%. Your aim is to separate random and normal short-term sell-offs from really bad news. Bear markets are a fact of life, so ultimately a local index will turn down and trigger your trailing stop, often letting you realize substantial profits. When several stops are triggered in a single market, implying a major downturn, buying puts in that market is likely to produce gains.

9. Sell your catch before it spoils.

"Experience," wrote Oscar Wilde, "is the name everyone gives to their mistakes." So set strict rules on when to sell. You can ignore the history of any equity in your portfolio. Just ask yourself the simple question: "Would I be willing to buy it now at today's price?" If not, you should sell. Sell after a stock has gone up 50%, or after the first two years, whichever comes first. Sell if the dividend is omitted, or if earnings decline so sharply that the stock sells 50% above your target purchase price. Don't be afraid to take a loss; mistakes are part of the game.

10. Don't give up the ship too soon.

A song of the thirties embodies this investment axiom: "The fundamental things apply, as time goes by." Trust time rather than timing. Time is on your side. Currency-cost averaging, regularly investing the same amount of euros, yen or dollars, is a system that makes anyone an expert market timer. You may not get all your money in at the cheapest point, but you won't be committing your whole wad at the top either. By investing a fixed sum each month, the number of shares you acquire depends on the level of a market from month to month. If the market rises, the price of shares goes up and each investment buys fewer. But if the market falls, the price of shares goes down and each investment buys more of them. If you regularly invest a fixed amount over a number of market cycles, the larger number of low-cost shares in your portfolio will lower the average cost. This system is especially useful in purchasing volatile country funds, such as those in emerging markets.

Time is your friend in another way. The wise investor diversifies not merely in space (geographically), but also in time. Patience is the key. You get the chicken by hatching an egg - not by smashing it. Long-term investors almost invariably come out winners. Obviously, many individual shares lose money in the long run. But a diversified equity portfolio, especially one mirroring various markets, will rise on the back of the long-term upward trend. You get most of the benefits of time diversification within ten years. Global and time diversification make an unbeatable combination for minimizing your chances of loss and meeting your long-term expectations of gain.

'Never put yourself in a position where you were absolutely correct but didn't take enough of a bet to make a difference in your life.'

Thom Calandra

Michael Molinski

Michael Molinski is president of Investing Across Borders, a financial media company dedicated to global investing. He is a former International Editor at CBS MarketWatch and a veteran foreign correspondent from Bloomberg News. He holds an MBA from Columbia University in New York and was a recipient of the prestigious Knight-Bagehot fellowship for business journalists.

Books

Investing in Latin America, Bloomberg Press, 2000

Global investing and the small investor advantage

---

1. Diversify.

This is the golden rule of global investing. Diversification is why you're going global in the first place. But it doesn't stop there. Putting half your portfolio outside your home country doesn't necessarily mean you're sufficiently diversified. It's important to split up your investments between different regions of the world, between developed countries and emerging markets, between different asset types, industries and investment styles.

2. Pay attention to correlation.

This follows from Rule #1, but it's important enough to emphasize. Avoid investing in countries whose stock markets are closely correlated with each other. Look for stocks in countries that have low correlation coefficients (R-squared) relative to the market of your home country (assuming most of your portfolio is invested in your home country).

3. Don't ignore risk.

Risk can be measured and quantified, either by looking at volatility (standard deviation), relative volatility (beta) or risk-return measures such as the Sharpe Ratio. Get to know these terms. Even if you don't fully understand them, you can use them to compare potential investments. Understanding risk is especially important when investing outside your home country. Find out what risks your investments are subject to such as currency risk, political risk, or regulatory risk, and weigh them against the stock's potential returns.

4. Never forget why you picked a stock.

In today's volatile investing world, it's easy to get caught up in rallies or get spooked in bear markets. But when you're faced with the decision of whether or not to sell a stock, the most important question to ask yourself is, 'Why did I pick it in the first place?' Do the reasons still hold water? If not, dump it!

5. Don't use currency hedges.

It's a natural assumption that when one invests in a country whose currency is prone to devaluation, you should consider buying currency futures or hedging your investments in similar ways. In most cases, though, that assumption is wrong. Your global investments are, in and of themselves, hedges against a downturn in your home country's stock market and against the stability of your home-country currency. Besides, currency hedges are expensive and require constant monitoring and frequent transactions. Your time and money are better spent elsewhere.

6. Look under rocks.

One of the principal reasons for investing abroad is that markets in less-developed countries are less efficient. It's easier to find stocks whose prices may not reflect all the information that is out there about that company. Perhaps the investor who most personifies this rule is Templeton's Mark Mobius, who has spent his life digging up bargains in the far corners of the globe. We don't all have his travel budget, but we can spend time combing the web for bargains.

7. Do your homework.

The internet has made it possible for an investor in Des Moines, Iowa or Toledo, Spain to research and invest in companies from Kuala Lumpur to Sao Paulo. You wouldn't buy stock in a company down the street if you didn't know something about what the company does, would you? The same goes for global investing. What does the company make? What are its financial fundamentals? Who manages it? Who are its major shareholders? What are its strategic advantages? Who is its competition?

8. Exploit the small-investor advantage.

It's a myth that large investors have an advantage over small investors. Especially when investing in far-off places, small investors can have several benefits, many of them having to do with liquidity. Emerging market stocks, for example, are often so lightly traded that big pension funds and mutual funds won't spend the time researching and investing in them. Institutional investors also tend to put limits on the 'high-risk' portion of their portfolios. And in times of crisis, it's much more difficult for a big pension fund to sell off its $10 million stake in that Chinese cement company than it is for Joe Smith to sell off his $10,000 stake.

9. Buy bonds.

Don't limit yourself to equities when investing abroad. Global bonds can diversify your fixed-income portfolio, and can bring much higher yields than the bonds of U.S. or major European countries - sometimes without a significant amount of added risk. Price inefficiencies also exist in the bond market, and investors willing to do their homework can find bargains in emerging market bonds.

10. Buy mutual funds.

I'm a big believer in mutual funds, both in indexed products and in professionally managed portfolios. If you don't have the time and energy to spend researching global stocks, let someone else pick them for you. Your costs will almost invariably be lower than if you tried to build your own portfolio of global stocks. In picking funds, though, be sure to pay attention to costs, tax implications, risk and the track record of both the fund and its managers. Spread the foreign portion of your portfolio across more than one fund. For example, you might buy three funds: a broad-based international fund, a regional fund in an area of the world that you believe will outperform, and an emerging markets fund.

www.investingacrossborders.com

'Myth # 6: *First mover advantages are key - the early bird catches the worm.* Not often, in business. There are very few industries in which being first is the basis of a sustained distinctive capability.'

John Kay

Robert A.G. Monks

Robert Monks is the world's highest profile shareholder activist. He founded Lens, the institutional activist investment fund which since 1992 has achieved returns in excess of the S&P 500 average throughout its life and has exceeded them by over 100% during the last three year period.

Books

Corporate Governance, Blackwell Publishers, 2003
The New Global Investors, Capstone, 2001
The Emperor's Nightingale, Capstone, 1998

General principles and Senators from Tennessee

1. Sometimes it snows in July.

We should never forget how little we know. Barraged by data, extrapolations and seeming numeric certitude, the reality is that no one on earth will ever possess more than .01% of the facts necessary for a genuinely rational decision. The only constant is change. We cannot over invest in the past; the past is not always prologue for the future; the unexpected is to be expected.

2. If you don't understand the concept, it is not understandable.

Particularly in a time when huge value is created through technological innovation, the temptation is strong just to 'go along' when everyone else nods in agreement about the brilliance and financial promise of a particular breakthrough. This is a mistake. If you do not understand the concept, either it is poorly articulated, or - even worse - it is imperfectly understood. In either case, do not part with your money.

3. The children (or designated heirs) of a great CEO are about as likely to excel as are any of Beethoven's children to write great symphonies.

Upper middle class values favor artistic genius, but will settle for professional success. There is no place on the scorecard for mere businessmen. The fact is that business is an 'art' and there are geniuses in this category. No one expects that the child or the protegee of a master will themselves be a master, but hubristically, there is a tendency to forget this in business. Beware of investing in a company run by 'son' (or 'daughter') of 'great man'.

4. Sell short the stock of any company with a former or future Senator from Tennessee on its board.

In light of the service of the following Tennessee Senators on the following boards: Howard Baker - Waste Management, Fred Thompson - Stone & Webster, Albert Gore, Sr. - Occidental Petroleum. This rather rude aphorism is a reminder that distinction in one walk of life cannot be taken as an automatic qualification in another. Celebrities can be good directors - even former Senators - but the question must be posed as to what their appointment to a board says about the board's view of itself. If you need Henry Kissinger's wisdom, engage him as a consultant.

5. Before you utterly repudiate 'short termism' beware lest 'long termism' turns out to be a euphemism for forever.

Many of the best managers make decisions that tend to under stress profits in the short term in the interest of long-term value maximization. The trick is to differentiate between them and the preponderance of managers failing to hit the numbers who use this nomenclature as an excuse. An investor must insist on the achievement of intermediate benchmark objectives.

6. Invest in companies where outside directors have large personal stakes.

Nobody likes to lose money. No matter how smart, how principled, how otherwise successful an outside director is, nothing will assure the application of their ability to 'your' company more than a substantial personal investment. This is to be distinguished from granting themselves options - if there is any justification for that one-way street, it should be restricted to full time officials.

7. Only invest in conglomerates which have 'genius' CEOs.

This is a short list. Litton Industries with Thornton and Ash, ITT with Harold Sidney Geneen, Berkshire Hathaway and Warren Buffett, Jack Welch and GE, Dennis Kozlowski and Tyco International. The market values enterprises under their stewardship at a premium, thus enabling the continuing acquisitions that assure growth. Without the market perception of genius, the premium disappears and the discount is almost a self-fulfilling prophecy for the decline and eventual liquidation of these once beautiful creatures.

8. Do not buy personal service businesses.

There is endless evidence that the key employees who create and maintain the relationships on the basis of which huge revenues are produced appropriate the 'surplus' in personal service businesses. How many times have we witnessed the sale of a boutique money manager or investment banker to a large institution only to be followed within five years by the sale back of the same property for 10 cents on the dollar? There is no 'there' there.

9. Wall Street sells better than Main Street buys.

The most highly paid people in the country work on Wall Street. They become highly paid because they persuade people to buy and sell securities. It would be hyperbole to say that they had no interest in the fate of the transaction - but only a little bit. The huge Wall Street fortunes of the last decade were in substantial part gleaned as commissions from unloading on a credible public the mangiest bunch of IPOs since the Dutch Tulip Bulbs.

10. Affronting the public is bad business.

No matter how much money Exxon, Mobil or Philip Morris spend and give to persuade the public of their attentiveness to public concerns, the perception that they have inadequate concern for the environment and make products hostile to human welfare will in the long run depress the value of their stock. P/E multiples are an implicit calculation of the risk that current earnings and cash flows can be maintained and enhanced for an indefinite number of years. Discounts are applied - or will be applied - to industry P/Es for companies and managements that are perceived as being contumacious.

---

www.lens-inc.com

'*You can check in but you can't check out* neatly summarises the issue of liquidity for biotechnology stocks. Be careful not to check in to the Roach Motel.'

Karl Keegan

David Morgan

Mr. Morgan has been a private silver analyst for over twenty years and adheres to the Austrian School of Economics. He hosts www.silver-investor.com, and issues a private email newsletter for serious investors on a monthly basis.

Books
Get The Skinny On Silver Investing, Morgan James Publishing llc, 2006

Investing in silver

1. When all else fails, there's silver.

No one likes to be labeled a prophet of doom, but the simple truth is that silver is the world's money of last resort. Should a severe economic collapse occur, leaving paper assets worthless, silver will be the primary currency for purchase of goods and services. (Gold will be a store of major wealth, but will be priced too high for day-to-day use.) Thus, every investor should own some physical silver - and store a portion of it where it's accessible in an emergency.

2. Start small - and keep it simple.

Too many investors, upon deciding to beef up the metals portion of their portfolio, buy too much physical silver at once - and in the wrong forms. Beginning metals investors should concentrate on pure bullion bars or coins, in smaller sizes, looking to pay a minimum premium over the actual metal value. Avoid commemorative coins, decorative items, jewelry and other collectibles, all of which carry large premiums and have limited resale markets.

3. Boost the buying power of your dollars with mining shares.

If you're a typical investor, you can't expect to be an expert on silver and the silver market - but you can invest in the people who are. Once you've established a core holding of physical silver, leverage both your knowledge and your buying power by purchasing the stocks of silver mining companies. These shares are highly responsive to changes in silver prices, frequently producing much higher percentage returns than the metal itself.

4. Dollar-cost average to lower your costs - and increase your discipline.

Dollar-cost averaging is an ideal way to implement Rule 2. By making same-dollar purchases at regular time intervals, you wind up buying more metal when prices are low and less when they're high. This approach helps you develop discipline, erasing the 'trader' mentality that infects many market participants and instead fostering an 'investment' philosophy. Dollar-cost averaging also eases some of the sting when prices move against you, allowing you to view the downturn as an improved buying opportunity rather than a disappointing loss.

5. Don't get a raw deal from your dealer.

Because of the specialized nature of the physical metals markets, selection of a well-established dealer with a quality reputation is essential. A good dealer will provide timely execution of your trades at fair prices with reasonable fees. Note, as well, that the lowest price is not necessarily the best price. In the past, some dealers who squeezed their price margins too low in order to attract clients were unable to make delivery, leaving those clients holding the bag.

6. What's yours is yours - so keep it that way.

While it's wise to keep some of your silver where you can get to it easily, it's also important to keep the bulk of your metal in a safe place - especially as your holdings increase. However, if you establish an account with a brokerage warehouse or other public storage facility, you should make sure your holdings are kept segregated and that you can inspect them when you wish.

7. Silver speculation's like cough syrup - good in small doses, but too much can make your portfolio sick.

Depending on your individual goals and your personal tolerance for risk, a small portion of the assets you commit to silver can be used for speculation, perhaps in futures contracts or options on futures. Never forget, however, that this type of trading is speculation, *not* investment.

8. A little information can mean a lot more dollars.

You do not need to be a student of the silver market to profit from your metals investments. However, you will greatly increase your chances of success - and the size of your potential profits - if you understand the fundamental factors that drive silver prices and pay regular attention to current supply and demand considerations.

9. Collecting silver is an art - but not really an investment.

Owning fine silver items - including rare coins - can provide great enjoyment and personal satisfaction. Like paintings and other artworks, they are beautiful and often quite valuable - and, if you are astute at buying and selling, they can generate large profits. In spite of this, however, always view such holdings as collectibles, *not* as investments. When you need your silver - or simply want to cash in - you don't want to have difficulty selling or be forced to forfeit a large aesthetic premium, both of which are likely with silver rarities.

10. More than 10 percent is too much of a good thing.

No matter how good the market looks, or how worried you are about the future of civilized society, you must always remember that silver should make up only a small portion of a well-diversified portfolio. I recommend committing no more than 10 percent of the average portfolio to silver, regardless of how strong you feel about the potential of the metals markets.

www.silver-investor.com

'Investors who tune out the majority of financial news fare better than those who subject themselves to an endless stream of information, much of it meaningless.'

Gary Belsky

John M. Mulvey

John Mulvey is a Professor of Operations
Research and Financial Engineering at
Princeton University. His specialty is strategic
financial planning and dynamic optimization.
He has implemented financial risk management
systems for many companies, including Pacific
Mutual, American Express, Towers Perrin,
Merrill Lynch, American Re-Insurance,
Siemens, and Lattice Financial.

Books
Worldwide Asset and Liability Modeling, Cambridge Univ. Press, 1998
Financial Engineering, AOR, co-editor, 1994

Portfolio optimization

Note: Thanks are in order to Ron Madey at Towers Perrin for initial
discussions regarding the investment rules

1. Invest for a purpose.
Investors should link their assets, liabilities and goals in an integrated
fashion. For example, a couple saving for retirement should put together a
savings and investment plan with a view of their consumption requirements.
Uncertainties should be addressed in the planning process.

2. Risk is not achieving one's goals.
Traditional portfolio theory suggests that risk is equated with volatility or
standard deviation of investment returns. However, a young investor with a
long horizon will take on less risk by investing in equities, as compared with
an elderly person (also investing in equities) who needs liquidity this year.
Measuring risk requires an understanding of the investor's goals.

3. Long-term investors should employ multi-period portfolio models.
The Markowitz mean variance model is generally posed as a single period
model. This approach, while simple, misses an important dimension since it
is a static approach to investing. It is better to conduct a dynamic analysis in
which the investor re-balances his portfolio at the beginning of each period.
Dynamic analysis will give difference recommendations than a static model.

4. Take advantage of volatility pumping.

Within a dynamic investment model, the most aggressive side of the efficient frontier consists of a set of high returning assets (see graph). The

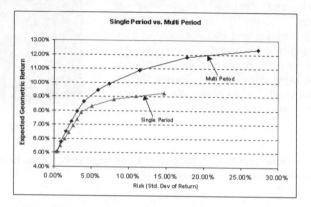

investor must re-balance his portfolio to the target mix at the beginning of each period. This fixed-mix approach can provide higher returns than any single asset category by taking advantage of the market's natural volatility. In fact, highly volatile assets with high growth are sought after. Historical returns show a similar result (see graph below).

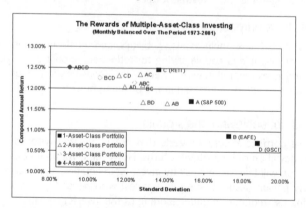

5. Asset allocation is critical for long-term performance.

High net worth and institutional investors focus on asset allocation as a critical aspect of investment planning. Any investor can readily employ a passive index approach to investing within an asset allocation framework. The passive portfolio provides a benchmark for active management. Active managers are paid to beat their benchmark. In many cases, the active managers do not beat their benchmarks due to high fees and other causes.

6. Find robust recommendations.

A portfolio model is dependent upon a set of parameters, such as the equity risk premium. These parameters are determined by analyzing historical returns in conjunction with current market conditions and expert opinion. Blending these aspects together can be difficult. Recommendations of a portfolio model should be stress tested. The final recommendations should be robust with regard to the assumptions.

7. Optimal portfolios should make sense.

The recommendations of an investment model should be explainable in common sense terms. How does the model react to changing market conditions? What are the projected ranges on the upside and the downside? Any model suggesting an outcome that is too good to be true is likely to be flawed. Optimization will attempt to exploit any advantage, without regard to the practicality of the strategy. Care must be given to the output of an investment model.

8. Protect the investor's surplus.

Investors should diversify their assets in concert with their liabilities and goals. For instance, a pension plan must make contributions when their assets fall below the market value of their liabilities. These contributions can be difficult to make when the economy is experiencing a recession. Similarly, an individual investor should protect their own surplus by finding assets that are correlated to their long-term goals.

9. Avoid computer black boxes.

Periodically, there are proposals to develop deep 'mathematical' methods for forecasting the returns on financial assets, such as stocks, bonds, and currencies. These computer systems depend upon a complex set of equations that involve feedback, highly nonlinear functions and other exotic techniques. The investor is told that model is too complex for understanding the underlying approach. Beware of these black box systems. Investors should be able to understand the underlying methodologies.

10. Implementing a strategic plan requires persistence.

The goal of a planning system is to develop insights towards a plan of action. The investor must implement their financial plan and stick with it during both good and bad periods. Changing strategies during strong market moves generally leads to poor performance.

www.princeton.edu/~mulvey

'As difficult as it may be, picking stocks whose earnings grow is the name of the game. Consistent growth not only increases the earnings and dividends of the company but may also increase the multiple (P/E) that the market is willing to pay for those earnings. The purchaser of a stock whose earnings begin to grow rapidly has a potential double benefit: both the earnings and the multiple may increase.'

Burton Malkiel

John Murphy

John J. Murphy is co-founder and president of MurphyMorris, Inc., which provides commentary and analysis for investors at www.murphymorris.com. Formerly a Director of Technical Analysis for Merrill Lynch, he was the technical analyst for CNBC-TV for 7 years. He is the author of the bestselling Technical Analysis of the Financial Markets.

Books

Technical Analysis of the Financial Markets, NYIF, 1999
The Visual Investor, John Wiley, 1996
Intermarket Technical Analysis, John Wiley, 1991

Murphy's laws of technical trading

Introduction

John Murphy's ten laws of technical trading explain the main ideas to beginners and streamline the trading methodology for experienced practitioners. The precepts define the key tools of technical analysis and show how to use them to identify buying and selling opportunities.

1. Map the trends.

Study long-term charts. Begin a chart analysis with monthly and weekly charts spanning several years. A larger scale 'map of the market' provides more visibility and a better long-term perspective on a market. Once the long-term has been established, then consult daily and intra-day charts. A short-term view alone can often be deceptive. Even if you only trade the very short term, you will do better if you're trading in the same direction as the intermediate and longer term trends.

2. Determine the trend and follow it.

Market trends come in many sizes - long-term, intermediate-term and short-term. First, determine which one you're going to trade and use the appropriate chart. Make sure you trade in the direction of that trend. Buy dips if the trend is up. Sell rallies if the trend is down. If you're trading the intermediate trend, use daily and weekly charts. If you're day trading, use daily and intra-day charts. But in each case, let the longer range chart determine the trend, and then use the shorter term trend for timing.

3. Find the low and high of it.

The best place to buy a market is near support levels. That support is usually a previous reaction low. The best place to sell a market is near resistance levels. Resistance is usually a previous peak. After a resistance peak has been broken, it will usually provide support on subsequent pullbacks. In other words the old 'high' becomes the new 'low'. In the same way, when a support level has been broken it will usually produce selling on subsequent rallies - the old 'low' becomes the new 'high'.

4. Know how far to backtrack.

Measure percentage retracements. Market corrections up or down usually retrace a significant portion of the previous trend. You can measure the corrections in an existing trend in simple percentages. A fifty percent retracement of a prior trend is most common. A minimum retracement is usually one-third of the prior trend. The maximum is usually two-thirds. Fibonacci retracements of 38% and 62% are also worth watching. During a pullback in an uptrend, therefore, initial buy points are in the 33-38% retracement area.

5. Draw the line.

Draw trend lines. Trend lines are one of the simplest and most effective charting tools. All you need is a straight edge and two points on the chart. Up trend lines are drawn along two successive lows. Down trend lines are drawn along two successive peaks. Prices will often pull back to trend lines before resuming their trend. The breaking of trend lines usually signals a change in trend. A valid trend line should be touched at least three times. The longer a trend line has been in effect, and the more times it has been tested, the more important it becomes.

6. Follow that average.

Follow moving averages. Moving averages provide objective buy and sell signals. They tell you if existing trend is still in motion and help confirm a trend change. Moving averages do not tell you in advance, however, that a trend change is imminent. A combination chart of two moving averages is the most popular way of finding trading signals. Some popular futures combinations are 4 and 9 day moving averages, 9 and 18 day, 5 and 20 day. Signals are given when the shorter average crosses the longer. Price crossings above and below a 40 day moving average also provide good trading signals. Since moving average chart lines are trend-following indicators, they work best in a trending market.

7. Learn the turns.

Track oscillators. Oscillators help identify overbought and oversold markets. While moving averages offer confirmation of a market trend change, oscillators often help warn us in advance that a market has rallied or fallen too far and will soon turn. Two of the most popular are the Relative Strength Index (RSI) and Stochastics. They both work on a scale of 0 to 100. With the RSI, readings over 70 are overbought while readings below 30 are oversold. The overbought and oversold values for stochastics are 80 and 20. Most traders use 14 days or weeks for stochastics and either 9 or 14 days or weeks for RSI. Oscillator divergences often warn of market turns. Those tools work best in a trading market range. Weekly signals can be used as filters on daily signals. Daily signals can be used for intra-day charts.

8. Know the warning signs.

Trace MACD. The Moving Average Convergence Divergence (MACD) indicator (developed by Gerald Appel) combines a moving average crossover system with the overbought/oversold elements of an oscillator. A buy signal occurs when the faster line crosses above the slower and both lines are below zero. A sell signal takes place when the faster line crosses below the slower from above the zero line. Weekly signals take precedence over daily signals. An MACD histogram plots the difference between the two lines and gives even earlier warnings of trend changes. It's called a histogram because vertical bars are used to show the difference between the two lines on the chart.

9. Trend or not a trend?

Use ADX. The Average Directional Movement Index (ADX) line helps determine whether a market is in a trending or a trading phase. It measures the degree of trend or direction in the market. A rising ADX line suggests the presence of a strong trend. A falling ADX line suggests the presence of a trading market and the absence of a trend. A rising ADX line favors moving averages; a falling ADX line favors oscillators. By plotting the direction of the ADX line, one is able to determine which trading style and which set of indicators are most suitable for the current market environment.

10. Know the confirming signs.

Include volume and open interest. Volume and open interest are important confirming indicators in futures markets. Volume precedes price. It's important to ensure that heavier volume is taking place in the direction of the prevailing trend. In an uptrend, heavier volume should be seen on up days. Rising open interest confirms that new money is supporting the prevailing trend. Declining open interest is often a warning that the trend is near completion. A solid price uptrend should be accompanied by rising volume and rising open interest.

'Basing your evaluations on historical earnings is ludicrous, especially for companies in the fast-changing technology industry, yet that is precisely what most investors do. Use forward earnings estimates, not historical ones.'

Mike Kwatinetz

Alan M. Newman

Alan Newman has been the editor of HD Brous & Co., Inc.'s *Crosscurrents* since the first issue was published in May of 1990 and is also editor of www.cross-currents.net. Mr Newman is the firm's technical market analyst and is a member of the Market Technician's Association.

How to win the stock game

1. The stock market is like any other game; you have to know how to play in order to win.

Learn *all* the rules, such as placing limit orders, stops, good-till-cancelled orders etc. Does your firm accept 'stops' on OTC stocks? Some do. Find out everything you can about the ground rules as well.

2. Just like in other games, you are allowed to win when other investors lose.

Buying stocks is one way to profit, but there are losers in even the best bull markets. Short selling - selling stocks you don't own - is a way to make money in a falling market and can ramp your profits considerably. In fact, playing both sides at the same time affords what is known as a 'market neutral' or 'hedged' stance. Theoretically, a market neutral or hedged stance means less overall risk.

3. Stop playing the game if you are losing!

Know your pain threshold and don't linger in a bad position, especially one that is moving rapidly against you. It may get worse. Much worse. Never freeze like a deer caught in car headlights in the middle of the road. When in doubt, *exit the position.*

4. Sometimes, ignore rule #3 - particularly when your gut feeling is that you will be vindicated in the end.

In these cases, if you cannot run the risk of being 100% wrong on the position, then you *must* change the odds to 50% by exiting half the position. Then, you will only be 50% right, but you will never be 100% wrong. If the position moves in the direction you initially anticipated, you will profit. If the position moves further against you, you will lose less.

5. NEVER average down!

See rules #3 and #4 above. If the position is going against you, it is probably for a very good reason (e.g. it is a stinker that you should no longer own). Why add to the punishment by increasing the size of the position? If the position moves further against you, lowering your average cost only accomplishes one thing - you lose more money!

6. Don't be afraid to pyramid your winning trades.

Conversely (to rule #5), if your confidence increases, don't be afraid to pyramid your winning trades. Investors of all stripes generally have very good hunches and intuition, especially when decisions are based on fundamentals they are familiar with, like a new product. If the product proves successful, it may ensure the company's growth for longer than initially expected. If your confidence increases as a result, consider ramping up your position.

7. Never risk more than 5% of your capital on any trade and always maintain a modest cash reserve to take advantage of a new situation.

If you are already extended when a good new idea pops up, extending yourself further by buying with borrowed money can only increase your overall risk if the market turns against you.

8. A background in fundamentals never hurts.

If you don't read the financial journals, at least read the newspapers. If you are not up on current events, you should be.

9. Your best investments may come from your own experience and common sense.

Bear in mind that listening to others ideas is *not* the same as your own experience or common sense! Chances are that you are at least as smart as the broker who is recommending the stock!

10. Winning streaks are fun, but they all end way too soon.

When it gets too easy, pull back and trade less. That's usually when the trend changes so fast it will rip your head off. On the other hand, losing streaks can seem to go on forever. When you're on a losing streak, pull back and trade less or stop altogether for a week or two. Smell the flowers. Read a book. Call up an old friend. A fresh perspective will usually work wonders. Last but not least, remember, it's only money.

www.hdbrous.com

David Newton

Since 1990, David Newton has been Professor of Entrepreneurial Finance and the founder and head of the Entrepreneurship program at Westmont College in Santa Barbara, CA, prior to which he taught for five years in the MBA program at Pepperdine University in Los Angeles. He worked for two years in investment banking in Boston in the early '80's, and has been a consultant to more than 100 fast-growth emerging ventures in the areas of start-up business plans, small firm financial strategy, venture capital, IPOs, and firm valuation.

Books

How to Be an Internet-Stock Investor, McGraw-Hill, 2000
How to Be a Small-Cap Investor, McGraw-Hill, 1999
Entrepreneurial Ethics, Kendall-Hunt, 1997

Investing in small-cap stocks

1. Today's youngsters will one day grow up!

The 'big' publicly-traded firms that dominate the DJIA and SP500 were *all* at one time small-cap stocks. They just happened to turn into big companies over time. That same kind of growth is still available for investors willing to do the careful review of today's smaller, less-popular and less-watched firms. Granted, not every small-cap today will be a mid-cap or large-cap industry leader tomorrow, but recognising future industry potential means that dozens of today's $200M capitalization companies may one-day be $5+ billion caps when they finally hit full stride.

2. See through an 'entrepreneurial perspective'.

Investors have to think like an entrepreneur and view small-cap companies with the same entrepreneurial eyes employed by venture capitalists and early-stage investors. Don't look for some 'quick-fix' rapid return. Instead, nurture an entrepreneurial approach to spot solid opportunities, and then embrace a vision for potential extraordinary results. Ask questions like, "How will this firm reshape its industry?" and "Why will this company do it better than the others?" The result can often be several-fold increases in share prices for investors who gave these small 'upstart' challengers the breathing room to state their case, implement their innovation, and compete head-on with the established firms in the best industries and growth markets.

3. Keep sifting that profile colander.

It is imperative that investors systematically put new small firm prospects through a rigid and multifaceted review process, to continually screen the best industries for the most promising investment opportunities. Treat the external environment like a pool of interesting new ventures, each pitching their business model and management team to you for possible investment. So you'll need to keep regular incoming deal-flow in order to yield a consistent pattern of new equity investments throughout each fiscal quarter. Do this quarter by quarter, and year by year, and over time, this constant sifting will yield a nice cache of golden nuggets with extraordinary value.

4. "I'll Be Watching You" - because nobody really is.

Understand this! If equity markets are weak-form efficient, then your systematic approach to research, homework, interviews, and due diligence will amount to far more than most other investors and analysts do with these same small-cap firms. And the overall picture that unfolds when all the data is in will likely be quite proprietary versus the generic near-consensus that typically happens in reviewing the large-caps. Good contacts, attending trade shows, talking with industry people, tracking product and service advances over time . . . these all yield insights into the small up-and-comers where virtually no one else is doing any regular monitoring and review. So "every breath they take, every move they make, you'll be watching them", and that's what makes small-caps well worth the effort.

5. Out of sight, but not out of mind.

Give the small-cap stocks some time to develop their great investment flavour. Like a fine wine sitting in a cellar, or a great sauce simmering on the back burner, great taste comes with patience. Stop chasing every short-term trend that surfaces, because you'll probably end up buying after the upward movement, and selling before the peak anyway. Instead, invest systematically in an ongoing process over time, and then give these small firms ample time to put out roots, mature, and bear fruit. Just seven short years ago, those 10-foot Valencia trees in my backyard were scrawny 8-inch saplings with two leaves in a half-gallon bucket. Today they're laden with hundreds of sweet ripe oranges three times a year. You cannot rush success, and your time is wasted chasing every new 'hot-tip'. But patience cultivated over time is an invaluable small-cap investor virtue.

6. Follow the bread-crumb trail to a great investment pathway.

Spend time regularly reviewing the 8-10 year track record of investments made by twenty or so public small-cap stock mutual funds. What companies were they investing in 1992, 1994, and 1997? Look up those same companies today and calculate each fund's batting average, by taking the highly successful firms today divided by the total small-caps invested in over the entire period under review. Now, take a closer look at today's small-cap investments in those same small-cap funds, and target reviews for individual firms from funds with the highest success averages. It's fairly likely that many of the these small-caps will be well worth some additional homework on your part.

7. Diversity is the spice of your investment life.

Small-cap investing is not simply about technology companies. There are hundreds of great emerging companies across every sector of the economy, and in each of the dozens of industries that comprise those sectors. Be sure to represent numerous 'types' of smaller, emerging firms in your portfolio. A little-known manufacturer today may be acquired tomorrow by a global distributor at 6 or 7 times its current price. A tiny parts provider today could become the leader in its market niche over the next few years. And a small-cap engineering company might turn its patented speciality design into hundreds of strategic partners within five years. Good diversification across several strong industries will always provide a wider and more robust range of opportunities for company growth and share price appreciation.

8. VCs live with losers. You can too!

Thinking like a venture capitalist is the only way to approach systematic small-cap investing. Not every small-cap investment can be expected to provide huge returns. In fact, for every 10 firms in the portfolio, 3 small-cap stocks will most assuredly lose significant value while 4 others will probably end up in the general vicinity in which they were originally purchased, even after holding them for a long time. So deal with it; the VCs do. However, 2 other firms will perform very well over time, and 1 of those original 10 will be the star that soars geometrically ten or twenty fold in value. The expectations should be this: the net result of the combined performance on every 10 stocks purchased should be a positive return and significant, but not every individual stock will be a star performer.

9. "Hey buddy, can you spare some information?"

Smaller companies often do not show up on the radar in industry or consumer marketing reports. They are generally left out of the most noteworthy stock guides, or at best, have relatively little company information or news releases when compared with the 'big names' in their investment sector. But that also becomes your advantage, because you can uncover information that is not widely known if you're willing to attend a few trade shows and product fairs, or speak with purchasing managers and company officials directly. And don't rule out a site visit to the firm's HQ. Less formal research and review may produce insights that are not common knowledge throughout the equity markets.

10. Hang out with the 'players'.

You've heard that 'misery loves company'. But on the flip side of that adage, 'risky opportunity loves confirmation'. One such confirmation about a small-cap that passes your own systematic screening process, is that it has also been 'approved' by larger institutional investors (commercial banks, investment banks, insurance companies, broker-dealers, pension funds). Check to see if any common shares in your target small-cap firm are held by noteworthy institutions and if so, what is their relative percentage stake among all the equity holders. If a small firm is not closely watched, but a few institutions have decided to take a position, then they must know something, either better than your information or the same thing you've uncovered. This could serve as the affirmation boost you need to hear, and confirm that your thorough due diligence is probably trustworthy after all.

www.westmont.edu

Victor Niederhoffer

Victor Niederhoffer is a private speculator specializing in futures and options trading.

Books

The Education of a Speculator
John Wiley, 1996
Practical Speculation, John Wiley, 2003
Fifty Years in Wall Street, John Wiley, 2006

Laurel Kenner

Laurel Kenner is a financial writer in New York City.

Formerly head of US stock market coverage at Bloomberg News, she previously reported on police, politics and aerospace during her 17-year news career.

Rules for a life-time

1. Be humble.

The market is always creative in finding a way to make you eat crow - raw, squawking and fully feathered. Always have enough in reserve to meet any conceivable market eventuality.

2. Don't get fixed in your ways.

The cycles are ever-changing. Just when you've found the perfect stream, the fish will stop biting, the weather will change, and other fisherman will appear, reducing the catch.

3. Count.

If a question is important, it deserves to be tested. That involves counting, and taking account of variability and uncertainty. Conventions for settling how much of a difference is enough to differentiate the result from randomness must be decided in advance. Read Stephen M. Stigler's *Statistics on the Table: The History of Statistical Concepts and Methods*, or anything by Francis Galton.

4. Buy-and-hold works.

Almost all portfolios of NYSE issues held for 10 years or more show returns of at least 8%. See Jeremy Siegel's *Stocks for the Long Run* or Louis Engel's *How to Buy Stocks*.

5. Be patient.

Don't throw in the towel when things look worst, or pyramid when things look best. Stocks have a substantial tendency to reverse over all periods. See what the trend followers are doing, and do the opposite.

6. Follow the insiders.

Corporate officers and directors make an extra 3 percentage points on their buys and an extra 3 percentage points on their sells. They must disgorge any profits they make on shares held for less than a year. If they buy their company's stock, usually it's for a good reason, unless it is to lure you in with meaningless purchases.

7. Read good books.

The ideas in Shakespeare, Cervantes, Twain, Rand, Galton, Darwin and Hugo were canonical when published, and will continue to be so.

8. Play games.

Checkers and chess are better for market wisdom than browsing through the internet, both for you and your kids.

9. Be skeptical.

In no field are there more cranks and charlatans than in the market.

10. Pay attention to wise people.

The average reader who writes to us is much smarter and better versed on his subject than we are. Knowledge changes too fast and the level of specialization is too high for any Duo to be anything but behind the form, unless they pay close attention to you.

Michael Niemira

Michael P. Niemira is a vice president and senior economist for Bank of Tokyo-Mitsubishi in New York, and previously worked as an economist for PaineWebber, Chemical Bank and Merrill Lynch.

He has taught a class on economic forecasting at NYU's Stern Graduate School of Business and on interpreting economic statistics at the New York Institute of Finance.

Books

Trading the Fundamentals, revised edition, McGraw-Hill, 1998
Forecasting Financial and Economic Cycles, John Wiley & Sons, 1994

The economic backdrop of investing

1. A roller coaster is no fun for the consumer.

The 'Katona effect' is named for the late founder of the University of Michigan's Survey Research Center, George Katona, and is a little-known hypothesis which holds internationally among industrialized countries. It describes a relationship between consumer spending growth and the volatility in the overall price level. As price volatility in the economy increases, consumers spend less and save more, and vice versa.

The Katona effect is a clear window on when consumer's spend - which is particularly important since the strength of consumer spending affects the bond market prices and the valuation of retail sector stocks.

2. 'Technology has mastered the inventory cycle' - wrong!

Curiously, it is widely felt that high-tech supply chain management has provided greater control over the aggregate inventory cycle. Maybe someday, but the reality is far from that now. On the contrary, U.S. inventories are increasingly more volatile relative to final sales. This raises an important question on the taming of the business and industry cycles: are shorter cycles emanating from demand spurts likely to be amplified by inventory management and in turn increase economic volatility? Probably so.

3. Don't believe everything central bankers, economists or journalists say or write.

Although this axiom probably has greater acceptance when applied to economists, investors should be just as critical in evaluating all pronouncements and articles in the financial press. Too often a good story is better than a factual one. *Ask for the proof!*

Case in point - the stock-market wealth effect: the econometric support is not strong, nor is the survey-based evidence. George Katona summarized the basic challenge to the logic for that seemingly popular view. Katona explained that as household financial wealth grew, economists turned their attention to how the increase in wealth affected consumption and savings (simple enough). Economists interchanged 'wealth' for 'income' in standard consumption analysis, since 'in principle, consumer expenditures may be paid either out of income or from liquid assets.' But the problem with that view, Katona pointed out, is that it is in essence built on a faulty logic that 'money burns holes in people's pockets' and 'incentives to save were supposed to weaken with an increase in wealth'.

4. Rumors of the death of the business cycle are greatly exaggerated.

In 1897, Mark Twain said it best: "reports of my death are greatly exaggerated." So too is it with the business cycle. Just when the popular sentiment - led by a handful of unseasoned economists - questions the existence of the business cycle, one shows up to correct the misperception.

Although the business cycle is extremely important to investment decisions, the 'growth cycle' is far more important to watch. Growth cycles can be measured as deviation from trend growth or as cycles in growth rates - both have a stronger statistical relationship with the stock market. Growth cycles precede the so-called classical business cycle, which provide yet another reason to watch them.

James W. Oberweis

James W. Oberweis is President of Oberweis Securities, Inc. Senior Vice-President of Oberweis Asset Management, Inc. and Portfolio Manager of the Oberweis Mid-Cap Portfolio. The Oberweis Funds specialize in rapidly growing companies in the micro-cap, small-cap, and mid-cap asset classes.

Mr. Oberweis edits *The Oberweis Report* advisory letter which was ranked by Hulbert Financial Digest as the #2 performing investment advisory letter for the 10 year period ended 12/31/2000.

Investing in very fast growing companies

1. Look for consistent, rapid growth in sales - preferably internally generated and 30% or greater.

If you are looking for stocks with great investment potential, we recommend beginning with the most successful companies. If consumers or corporate purchasing agents are buying 40%, 50%, or 100% more of a company's products each year, then the company is a super-success in the marketplace. Whether they produce hamburgers, computers or widgets, one of the best indications of the success of their products is the rate at which sales are growing. Surprisingly, the industry in which a company operates should not be a critical factor. In fact, companies able to grow at rapid rates in industries with average growth rates are sometimes the best prospects. This indicates to us that the company clearly is doing something better than its competitors. We prefer internally generated growth rather than growth through acquisitions.

2. Look for similar consistent growth in pre-tax income and earnings per share.

Similar consistent rapid growth in earnings is also required. A corollary is that the company must have earnings. It is frequently possible to increase sales in the short run by significantly cutting prices. But if such price reductions diminish or eliminate profit margins, such growth may not be in the long-term best interests of the shareholders. Be wary of companies and sectors experiencing rapid growth, but where that growth is not feeding through to increased earnings, as we saw with airline companies in the 1960s and internet companies in the late 1990s. While you may miss some opportunities in the short run, investing in companies with increasing annual profits will increase the probability of owning long-term successful businesses. We have seen far too many times the promise of future earnings fail to materialize.

3. Look at net income, of course, but pre-tax income is also very important.

If profit growth is resulting primarily from lower tax rates, such growth is not sustainable. There must also be similar growth in earnings per share. It is always possible for a company to increase its earnings by selling more shares and using the proceeds to pay off debt or even investing in T-bills. From the shareholders' point of view, this only makes sense if earnings per share are enhanced over the long run.

4. Buy stocks whose P/E ratios are not greater than half of the company's rate of growth.

Once you have identified a list of companies that meet the revenue and earnings growth minimums you must still make a value judgment. Is the current price reasonable in relation to the company's growth prospects? Are there even more attractive investment opportunities? Which is a better buy - a company selling at 20 times earnings growing at 30% per year or a company selling at 30 times earnings growing at 60% per year? Many investors - institutional as well as individual - would assume the first stock is a better value since it is selling at a lower price/earnings (P/E) ratio. All else being equal, I would argue that the second is more attractive since it is selling at a lower ratio of P/E to growth rate.

5. Look for companies with products or services that offer the opportunity for substantial future growth.

Looking forward also requires you to make a value judgment concerning a company's products or services. Was its recent growth due to a *temporary* or a *sustained* increase in demand for its products? For example, exceptionally low interest rates over the past several years have led to an increase in demand for construction and substantial profit increases for construction-related firms. However, are construction companies experiencing this growth due to solid, long-term increasing demand for their products? Probably not. When interest rates reverse course, you can bet your last dollar that demand for construction will slow as well.

A further desirable characteristic is that the product of service offered by the company should be capable of substantial future growth *without* attracting too many competitors, too quickly.

6. Pay particular attention to recent trends in quarterly sales and earnings. Look for companies whose rate of growth is expanding.

This (and the following rule) focus on the most recent quarterly results - perhaps the most important numbers when evaluating a company's direction - and how the market values the company in relation to its sales.

Investors should focus not on the year-over-year earnings gain but rather on the consecutive quarterly increase for non-seasonal, non-cyclical companies. In other words, if a company reports 1995 Q2 EPS of $.15 vs. $.10 a year ago, that report sounds great - a 50% increase. But if the first quarter was $.16 vs. $.08, then the second quarter was actually $.15 vs. $.16 in the prior quarter, indicating a slowing in the company's growth sequentially.

For seasonal companies, such as retailers, compare a company's latest quarter year-over-year growth rate with the prior quarter's growth rate, rather than comparing absolute numbers. The ideal situation is a company whose earnings and revenues grew at 25% or 30% last year, are growing 35% or 40% this year, and are accelerating towards 45% or 50% for next year. In these rare situations, the stock frequently rises not only because of the earnings growth but also due to multiple expansion - the PE becomes larger as investors begin to recognize the company's faster growth rate. Obviously such situations are wonderful for investors.

7. Watch for a reasonable price-to-sales ratio based on the company's growth prospects and profit margins.

A price/sales ratio of 2 means that the total market value of the company is twice its annual sales. Companies with fast growth and/or high profit margins should have a higher P/S ratio than companies with a lower growth rate or lower margins. When a company's P/S ratio exceeds 5, either the company must have excellent growth prospects or very attractive profit margins or the stock may be overpriced. A P/S below 1 may indicate modest growth prospects, lower margins, or an undervalued stock. These two guidelines help determine whether a stock is an attractive buy at any particular time.

8. Carefully review the company's balance sheet.

Try to understand why and how the company is growing so fast. Sometimes unusual items may be discovered, such as a huge increase in receivables or inventories, unrelated to the sales increase. Pay particular attention to footnotes in order to identify unusual items, which may indicate future problems. Don't be afraid of leveraged companies. Leverage tells us how a company is financed, not whether a business is successful. A successful, growing business can be financed primarily through equity, debt, or any combination thereof. In the case of a very successful company, some leverage may be a positive rather than a negative factor, but note that this leverage does increase the risk level.

9. Believe the tape!

A final check is relative strength. If a company shows consistent rapid growth in both earnings and revenues, has attractive P/E and P/S ratios, strong recent trends, and a product or service which offers excellent future growth prospects, yet its stock is underperforming the market, don't buy it. If everything looks good fundamentally, the stock should be rising faster than the market.

An easy way to check its relative performance over the last 12 months is to look at its relative strength. The number tells us how a particular stock is performing compared to the market. If everything looks strong fundamentally for a particular stock, but it has a low relative strength, something may be wrong. Your analysis may be missing something or insiders may know something you don't.

Generally it's best under such circumstances to wait awhile before buying the stock. If the fundamentals are as strong as you believe, the relative strength should begin to improve and you can buy the stock then, even though you may miss the first few points of a move. But frequently by waiting you may learn more and find you have avoided a disaster. For this reason, no matter how good a company looks on paper, if its stock is declining in a steady or rising market, don't buy it.

10. Diversify.

Finally, it's especially important when investing in emerging growth companies to follow the Golden Rule of Investing - Diversify, diversify, diversify. If you follow these guidelines over long periods of time, at least 5 to 10 years, I believe you will be able to achieve above average investment results.

---

www.oberweis.net

Terence Odean

Terrance Odean is an Assistant Professor of Finance at the Graduate School of Management at the University of California, Davis. His research on how psychologically motivated decisions affect investor welfare and securities prices has been cited in numerous publications including *The Wall Street Journal*, *The New York Times*, *The L.A. Times*, *The Washington Post*, *Time*, *Newsweek*, *Barron's*, *Forbes*, *Business Week*, *Smart Money*, *Bloomberg Personal*, *Worth*, and *Kipplinger's Personal Finance*.

Lessons for investors from behavioral finance

---

1. Trading is hazardous to your wealth.

In a study of monthly positions for over 66,000 households with accounts at a large discount brokerage, Brad Barber and I found that the twenty percent of investors who traded least actively outperformed the twenty percent who traded most actively by an average of 5.5 percentage points a year. We believe that many active traders are overconfident in their ability to pick stocks.

2. Before you trade, consult your wife (if you have one).

Consistent with the overconfidence hypothesis, Brad Barber and I found that men - who tend to be more overconfident than women in areas such as finance - traded on average 45 per cent more actively than women. Both men and women tended to reduce their returns through trading, but men did so annually by 1 percentage point more, on average, than did women.

3. If you need to sell, sell for a loss.

When I studied the common stock trading patterns for investors at a large discount brokerage, I found that they are far more likely to sell their winners than their losers. This is backwards. While, in general, investors should avoid active trading, if they need to sell stock to raise cash they should sell their losers - at least in taxable account. In this way, they get a tax write off now and postpone realizing capital gains. If the loss is sufficient, they should consider selling simply to capture the tax benefit. (By the way, on average, those losers don't bounce back. The losers people clung to on my sample subsequently underperformed the winners they sold.)

4. Do the things you can do, not the things you can't.

Many investors concentrate on picking winning stocks. For the most part they can't. I've found that, on average, the stocks investors sell subsequently outperform the stocks they buy - even before subtracting transactions costs. Most investors would be better off forgetting about picking winners and paying attention to doing the things they can actually do. Controlling trading costs, managing taxes, and diversifying.

5. When the market is crashing, go to the beach.

Don't make long-term investment decisions in a panic. In a calm moment, evaluate your portfolio. Decide whether your mix of stocks, bonds, and other assets is appropriate for your goals and emotional and financial ability to sustain losses. If you need help figuring this out, get it. This is a much more fundamental decision than which stocks to pick. If a market downturn churns your stomach, go for a walk. When the market, and your stomach, have settled, re-evaluate the risk profile of your portfolio.

6. Diversify, diversify, diversify.

Mutual funds are the optimal investment for most investors. Buy funds with no-loads, low expense ratios, and low turnover. Index funds are a good choice for many people.

7. Get 90% of the thrills with 10% of the risk.

If you really enjoy trading common stocks consider putting 90% of your common stock portfolio into mutual funds and treating the remaining 10% as an 'entertainment' account. If you keep the entertainment account small enough that you can comfortable sustain some losses, you can go ride the rollercoaster of risky stocks to your heart's content.

8. Give your portfolio an annual check-up.

Don't follow your portfolio returns day to day. If you do, short-term market losses may chase you out of the market. If you have an appropriate, well-diversified portfolio, it doesn't need constant tune-ups.

www.ucdavis.edu

Michael O'Higgins

Michael O'Higgins is President of O'Higgins Asset Management, Inc., an independent investment management firm which manages portfolios for high net worth individuals, institutions, and investment companies.

Books

Beating the Dow, HarperBusiness, 2nd ed., HarperBusiness, 2001
Beating the Dow with Bonds, HarperBusiness, 1999

Beating the Dow

1. Get paid for taking risk.

Historically, investors have been paid handsomely for taking the risk of owning stocks. If the earnings yield, also known as the earnings/price ratio, is below the yield on AAA Corporate bonds, avoid stocks and put your money into long term 0% coupon U.S. T-Bonds.

2. If the price of gold is rising, don't buy bonds.

The price of gold has correctly predicted the course of long term U.S. interest rates in 26 of the last 32 years. If gold's price has risen over the past year, avoid bonds.

3. When buying stocks, stick to the 'Dogs of the Dow'.

The 10 highest dividend paying DJIA components have consistently beaten the Dow by wide margins with below average risk.

4. Low price 'dogs' do even better.

A strategy of buying the 5 lowest dollar price of the 10 highest dividend yielders, has compounded at close to 20% per year since 1972 compared to 13% for the Dow and the S+P 500.

5. Asset allocation is your most important decision.

Long term studies have concluded that 85% of investment success is due to asset allocation. By using the above described strategy, an investor would have earned annual returns of over 22% versus under 13% for the major stock averages since 1968.

---

www.ohiggins.com

'Virtually every blue chip growth company ultimately has matured and become a no-growth company. Of America's 100 leading companies in 1920, only one is on the list today (GE).'

Steve Leuthold

Richard Olsen

Dr. Richard Olsen is founder and CEO of the Zurich-based Olsen Group, a pioneer in the development of online financial forecasting systems and trading models for applications ranging from trading to investment and risk management.

Books

Introduction to High Frequency Finance, Academic Press, 2001

The trading edge and quantitative tools

1.You are your best advisor.

One of the biggest pitfalls in trading is to rely too heavily on the guidance of other people. It is important to formulate your own personal view of the world and make investment decisions in tune with this view.

2. Be clear about your competitive edge.

Everyone has a personal competitive edge. The competitive edge might be as little as being more removed from the market than other players and thus not having to contend with the distractions of short term price movements. Some of the most successful investors have taken a very broad brush view of the world and have generated huge returns by making some long-term bets.

3. Use quantitative tools.

Market prices are determined by the interaction of groups of investors trading on very different time scales. The actual impact of fundamental factors depends on the market dynamics. Typically, market observers take a far too simplistic view of the interaction between market dynamics and fundamental events. Only sophisticated quantitative models, that are similar to weather forecasting models, can systematically analyse market conditions and generate forecasts of consistent quality. See our forecasting services at http://ois.olsen.ch or www.oanda.com.

4. Trade in liquid markets.

Markets are not continuous and it is dangerous to assume that positions can be liquidated at any time. For this reason, investors should stay away from illiquid markets, except if their investment horizons are very long term.

5. Follow a top down approach.

In establishing an investment strategy, it is important to take a top down approach starting with defining the investment philosophy, formulating the decision process and allocating the assets to the markets and underlying instruments.

6. Build up positions over time.

A major pitfall to any investment strategy is the discrete start of the investment program. If all funds are committed at the start of the program, the overall performance of the investment program will depend significantly on the specific entry point. If the investor is lucky, his performance will have a positive bias, otherwise, he will be negatively impacted by the start of the program.

7. Stick to your time scale of trading.

Another major pitfall is that investors change their trading horizons depending on the profits and losses of their positions. If an investor accumulates losses, he tends to extend his trading horizon in the hope of recouping his losses. He should not do so. He should stick to his initial strategy and close out his position. There are many other investment opportunities waiting for him provided he has not lost his money.

8. Watch out for transaction costs.

Transaction costs are far more important in the overall performance of an investment strategy than typically understood. The reason is simple: Transaction costs are 'certain' costs, whereas trading returns are uncertain. It is easy to control transaction costs, whereas it is difficult to enhance the success of your trading decisions.

9. Use tactical tricks, such as limit orders and stop losses.

Performance of any investment strategy is increased by setting limit orders in opening positions and maintaining a strict stop loss regime. In this way, the investor can turn to his advantage the short-term overshooting of markets. Quantitative forecasts are an ideal tool to set limit orders and position stop losses.

www.oanda.com

Paul Ormerod

Paul Ormerod is a founding director of Volterra Consulting which calls on the skills of economists, mathematicians, physicists and statisticians to find innovative solutions to a wide range of business issues.

Books
The Death of Economics, Faber & Faber, 1995
Butterfly Economics, Faber & Faber, 1998
Why Most Things Fail: And How to Avoid It,

Rules for sceptical investors

1. Be sceptical of macro-economic forecasts.
They only seem to work when everything is quiet. Forecasters have a very bad track record in predicting genuine booms and slumps. They sometimes fail to forecast a recession even when it has actually started.

2. Be sceptical of anyone who claims to predict interest rates or exchange rates.
One of the most well established facts about markets is that these cannot be forecast over time with any useful degree of accuracy - if they could, we'd all be millionaires.

3. Be sceptical of arguments that just because an interest rate/exchange rate is high, it is more likely to fall than to rise.
At some point, the Euro will certainly rise against the dollar, but people have been predicting a rise ever since it fell after its launch in Jan 1999. At any point in time, a rise is as likely as a fall, no matter what the level is.

4. Be sceptical of track records.
There are so many funds and forecasts that at any point in time, someone has to have done well/been right. With enough monkeys in the room, one of them will type out Hamlet. But it doesn't mean the same monkey will then go on to write Macbeth.

5. Be sceptical of analysts' reports on companies.
They usually know no more than a well informed reader of the quality business press. Monitor the press with a bit more care for a while, and see

for yourself how many times analysts predict profit warnings in advance, and how many times they simply re-write the company's press release.

6. Be sceptical of dynamic, new CEOs modernising and transforming the core elements of a business.

Most people think that this improves a company's prospects. It might do eventually, but companies going through major changes actually experience increased risk of failure.

7. Be sceptical of arguments that sheer size reduces a company's vulnerability to new competition.

The tendency to believe that the powerful will always be powerful is very deep seated. The Soviet Union looked invulnerable, but disintegrated in the space of a few years. The same applies to companies. IBM looked to have a lock on computer markets, but almost went under. Even in much more staid markets such as retailing, successful companies can implode quickly.

8. Investment is about risk management not prediction.

Here's a prediction: if anyone really can make consistently successful forecasts, he or she a) won't be reading this book and b) will have retired in complete luxury. For the rest of us, we need to decide for ourselves about the level of risk we are willing to accept. It's nice to be able to boast about the quick profit you have just made on a stock. But serious investment is much more mundane. It's about managing risk.

9. Diversify, but make sure you really are diversified.

Diversify, diversify, diversify is the slogan. But be sure you really are diversifying. It's how the companies or bonds perform that matters, not their name, or the location of the issuer. Holding GE and American Express might look like a diversification play, but it probably isn't, and not just because they are both in the USA.

10. Track what the trackers track.

Tracker funds are often a good way to invest in a low cost way, but the diversification you get is only as good as the index they track. And several of the indexes are dominated by assets which often move in step with each other, so the real diversification you get is much less than you might think. The NASDAQ in recent years for example has been dominated by the movement of 'technology' stocks, and many of its members have moved up and down in step with each other.

www.volterra.co.uk

Lois Peltz

Lois Peltz is the president and chief executive officer of Infovest21, an information services company, located in New York City.

Books

The New Investment Superstars,
John Wiley, 2001

Selecting a hedge fund manager

---

1. Money should just be their way of keeping score.

Look for managers who are motivated by what they do - not by big bucks. The best managers make a total commitment. They are motivated by a job well done and gain satisfaction in finding things that others don't. They love the intellectual and emotional challenge of the markets.

2. It's like getting a report card every day.

Select a manager who has a strong work ethic, is intense, and is as demanding of himself as of the other people on his team.

3. Look for continuity of organization.

Search for a manager who has developed a team approach rather than a star system where he alone is the decision-maker. Many of the best organizations are built around teams and specialists, divided by industry, region, trading strategy and/or type of situation. Having a specialist, decentralized organization helps keep talented key employees on board because they have a degree of decision-making authority and responsibility as well as a stake in the firm. In those organizations where a star approach exists, key employees eventually leave to start their own fund where they have more authority, decision-making power and responsibility. Key personnel leaving doesn't lead to a strong, lasting organization.

4. Require them to eat their own cooking.

Select those managers who put a significant amount of their own assets into their hedge funds. This means they have strong conviction in their own talent. It also means their own net worth is highly correlated to the performance of their funds and thus, they have a huge incentive to generate excellent performance.

5. Make consistency a virtue.

Find a manager who has a long track record and has generated consistently excellent returns during various market cycles. Examine years such as 1990 and 2000 which were negative years for the stock market (as measured by the S&P) as well as 1994 and 1998 which were difficult years for hedge funds.

6. Acknowledge the survival of the fittest.

At various times, all managers have gone through adverse times. Look for managers who are willing to learn from their mistakes. It is not so much about being right all the time as being able to adapt and find a strategy that works. Losses are expected because ideas are being tested. The best managers worry when losses are larger than expected/predicted or when risk levels are exceeded.

7. Be sure that they are controlling the downside.

Search for managers who put as much emphasis on controlling the downside as generating returns to the upside. Specific risk management tools to examine include strategy diversification, maximum allocation per position, number of positions in the portfolio and degree of leverage, as well as stress testing and the ability to reduce allocations quickly.

8. Technology is their friend - or should be.

Run from those managers who are afraid of technology. Technology is here to stay. Smart managers acknowledge the importance of technology information and rapid adoption of technology gives them an edge. They are able to harness information coming in and use it to their advantage.

9. When opportunity knocks, do they open the door?

Look for managers that view the world as having rapidly shifting opportunities. Opportunistic managers allocate capital where the opportunities are.

10. Be wary if the manager's goal is to be the *largest* hedge fund.

Be wary of managers whose primary goal is to grow assets as large as they can in order to collect management fees. The best and brightest managers are often closed to new investment, acknowledging that being the largest hedge fund is not their main objective - having the best performance is.

www.infovest21.com

Robert Peston

Robert Peston is an award-winning journalist with 18 years experience in national and international publications.

He is editorial director of Quest (www.csquest.com), an online provider of valuation tools and commentary for fund managers and professional investors.

He also writes the 'Peston's People' column for *The Sunday Times* and is a regular television and radio broadcaster.

Books
Brown's Britain, Short Books, London, 2005

Interpreting the news flow

1. You will not be awake earlier than the market.

Most of what you read in newspapers, magazines or on the internet - especially those dedicated to business and investment - has already been discounted by the stock market before you are ready to deal. Or to put it another way, the efficient market theory works 99 per cent of the time.

2. One per cent of media coverage is pure gold, but which one per cent?

There are opportunities to make quick profits if you can identify a golden 1 per cent of stonkingly good price sensitive information that the market has missed. But ask yourself this - if the market has missed that 1 per cent, why should you do any better? You could of course join the ranks of insomniac, unwashed disciples of internet bulletin boards, but is that any way to live?

3. The good stuff is really dull.

The most valuable price sensitive information is to be found where you least expect. Look out for apparently dull comments on business issues from politicians or regulators. These could presage price sensitive changes in the regulatory environment. Or scour the apparently tedious industry supplements of newspapers like the FT. Frequently these contain fresh information on a company's trading performance or sector trends.

4. Sell all columnists for short term gains.

Investment commentary in newspapers is particularly useless as a source of advice on how to make short term capital gains. If the writer has spotted a share price anomaly, the market will have corrected it by the time you finish the column.

5. Buy columnists for long term advice.

The media can help you with your long term investment decisions. Perceptive columnists can help you to identify the better quality companies to be bought and held for a period of years.

6. Socialism rules.

Don't assume that the most avowedly right wing, free market newspapers have the best business coverage. In the UK, the left-of-centre Guardian, for example, has recently had a run of market-moving scoops.

7. Strange but true.

In spite of their reputation, 99 per cent of the supposedly speculative stories in Sunday newspapers is true. However once again you have the 1 per cent problem. How can you be sure which ones are the stinkers?

8. Silence speaks volumes.

If there is no statement of denial from a company within 24 hours of a speculative story, chances are that it is true.

9. The company declined to comment.

If a story contains the phrase "the company declined to comment", it normally means precisely the opposite. In most cases, the company has commented and confirmed a story, but does not wish to be on the record.

10. Irrational exuberance.

Ignore almost all bullish comment in newspapers about takeovers, especially hostile ones. Most of these deals destroy value, though you will not hear this from hacks, because writing about these life-or-death contests is too much fun.

www.csquest.com

Thomas A. Petrie

Thomas A. Petrie, co-founder of Petrie Parkman & Co., a Denver and Houston based energy investment firm, is a former Managing Director and Senior Oil Analyst of The First Boston Corporation.

Prior to joining First Boston, Mr. Petrie was an Oil Analyst with Wainwright Securities and Colonial Management in Boston. For eight consecutive years, Mr. Petrie was ranked the number one oil analyst in the exploration/independent sector by *Institutional Investor* magazine's annual survey of money managers. During his career, Mr. Petrie has also been an active advisor on more than $100 billion of energy related mergers and acquisitions, including many of the largest.

The energy sector

1. Geopolitics matter.

The variable effectiveness and changing policies of the Organization of Petroleum Exporting Countries (OPEC) as well as the major consuming nations can shape the energy sector's overall investment attractiveness.

2. Always remember the business is cyclical .

While there are longer-term secular trends in terms of demand growth and supply additions, the industry's overall importance to broad measures of economic performance periodically results in pronounced cyclicality.

3. The best cure for low oil and gas prices is low prices and vice versa.

History shows that $10.00 /bbl oil begets $25.00/bbl oil and, conversely, sharp upward moves to $30.00+/bbl oil are usually unsustainable. Low prices tighten supply versus demand; high prices do the opposite.

4. Contrarians are periodically highly rewarded.

When consensus is clearly negative about energy commodities the stocks are often excellent buys (i.e. 1986 and 1998); when consensus is uniformly positive watch out (i.e., 1979-1980)

5. Good exploratory well news travels fast; bad news often seeps out slowly.

When assessing the impact of high potential exploratory drilling, it seems that slowly developing announcements of results seldom match positive expectations. Remember the adage "buy on expectation potential; sell on actual announcement."

6. High financial leverage with typically high energy commodity price volatility can be a deadly combination.

Most energy company bankruptcies result from ill-timed uses of debt to acquire or develop production in anticipation of a commodity upswing that fails to materialize on schedule. Accordingly, corporate strategies emphasizing financial leverage are often a risky bet.

7. Quality of management does matter.

Significant capital destruction is not an uncommon occurrence among energy companies; accordingly, managements that exhibit consistent financial discipline in the capital allocation process often merit a premium.

8. Technology counts.

Many companies in the energy sector are often viewed as 'old economy' stocks. Nevertheless, the role of 'new' technologies in unlocking energy resources more efficiently and at lower costs is critical to corporate success.

9. Stock repurchases deserve attention.

In the 1950s and 1960s J. Paul Getty validated the idea that recapturing the barrels of oil equivalent behind outstanding common shares could be financially preferable to drilling new discoveries. In the 1970s and early 1980s Boone Pickens developed a variation on this idea. Thus, an astutely executed corporate stock repurchase program can provide a useful clue to a company's investment attractiveness.

10. Beware of popularized alternative energy concepts.

While diversification away from conventional hydrocarbon sources is undoubtedly both desirable and inevitable, the path to uncovering profitable and viable alternative energy enterprises is likely to be as tortuous and risky as many other sectors involved in pursuing technological innovation have also demonstrated.

www.ppcenergychannel.com

John Piper

John Piper is the founder and editor of *The Technical Trader,* a leading newsletter in the UK for traders.

John writes for a number of trading web sites, and speaks frequently at trading conferences and seminars in Europe and the USA, placing a particular emphasis on the psychological challenges of successful trading.

Books

The Way to Trade, Harriman House, 2006
The Fortune Strategy, Zena Press, 2006

Trading and the second marshmallow

Inroduction

One of the difficulties with trading is that the rules change as you progress. The novice must learn to cut losses and not much else matters at this stage. Once that rule is ingrained, it is down to running profits. But if you try and run profits at the 'cut losses' stage you will have a lot of problems.

Another of the difficulties is that many traders break the rules and win! But this can be disastrous, because the market is bound to catch you out if you follow the wrong rules. Trading has a logic of its own. If you allow losses to run, the logic is you will be wiped out. Over many different trades the market will exploit any weaknesses in either the trader or his/her system. Statistically a few 'bad' traders will do well for a while - but not in the long run.

1. Reduce position size to the point where you are comfortable.

It may seem odd that reducing position size is my number one idea for making more money, but it is so. Many traders put themselves under excess pressure, by doing so they are prone to make bad decisions and they lose money. So reduce position size and make more money!

2. Consider using option strategies - don't limit your options!

Options have a lot of plus points, and have a part to play in your strategy.

3. Find a trading mentor.

Trading is a very difficult business. Not least because it is a zero sum game. NO, cancel that - it is a negative sum game, because every time you enter the game you pay commission, not to mention all the other expenses involved, price feeds, computers, software, etc, etc. With futures, the amount every winner wins is paid for by all the losers, but *all* participants pay commissions and the other costs. So in aggregate it's a negative pot. It's no surprise so many lose.

If you need help with your trading, find someone who has experience to help you. Ideally a local trader - many are prepared to help because trading is a fairly dry business with little meaningful human contact. Otherwise you may need to find a professional who is willing to help but he may well expect to charge a fee. I do this myself, but your best bet is to try and find someone who is local to you.

4. Use stops which have some meaning.

Not all traders use stops and by not using stops everything becomes a lot simpler because you get wiped out fairly quickly. Actually that is not totally true but it is true for some, if not many. But if you are using an approach which does utilize stops then try and ensure your stops have some significance, otherwise you tend to be throwing money away.

5. Understand the logic of your trading approach.

Every approach to the market involves risk. As a trader, you must control risk, just as a tightrope walker learns to live with imbalance. Understand the logic of your approach and the risks you are taking, because that risk will come home to roost. In one sense the market is a generator of random sequences, especially if you follow a precise algorithm. If you or your approach has a weakness the market will find it in one of those random sequences.

6. Let profits run - wait for the second marshmallow!

Unless you let your profits run you will never cover your losses, let alone come out on top. You must also cut your losses. Most traders learn to cut losses quite easily but have trouble learning to run profits. This is not surprising. Cutting losses is an active function requiring careful monitoring of what is happening - it requires action. Running profits, in contrast, requires inaction, and doing nothing can be tough. In modern society we are used to quick gratification. We want our goodies and we want them now. The same goes for trading profits: once you see them, you want them - but you cannot have them if you want to let profits run.

The book *Emotional Intelligence* describes an experiment in which a child is left in a room with a marshmallow and told that if he does not eat it, he will receive a second marhshmallow. Apparently this simple test is a far better guide to success than any number of intelligence tests. It is also exactly what traders must do if they want to let profits run, so don't eat that marshmallow and you will get two!

7. Be selective

There are so many keys to success but I feel this is the one that separates those who make lots of money from those who just get by.

8. Don't predict.

Market action is not predictable. A trader does not predict action - he takes calculated risks. He risks a little to make a lot.

9. Don't panic.

This is critical. Panic is mother to losses. Part of this is not putting yourself under undue pressure. The more relaxed you are, the less likely you are to panic.

10. Be humble - big egos cost a lot to run!

A person who is full of himself has no room for anything else: he will not listen, or learn. A trader who is not humble may not listen to the market and will get wiped out. I suspect we have all heard stories of macho traders who take on the market and get turned into mincemeat. I believe humility is an essential for trading success.

---

john@ttttt.freeserve.co.uk

'Know your sectors. Often investors are not in the wrong stocks, but in the wrong sectors. Scroll through all the sector charts at least once a month and establish which ones are going up and which are not.'

David Linton

Mitchell Posner

Mitchell Posner is President of Kirkwood Financial, Inc., an advisory firm to financial institutions around the world, providing equity research on emerging market companies and industries in South America, Africa, Europe and Asia.

Selecting emerging market stocks

Introduction

Any investor with experience in picking U.S. or European stocks can, in theory, pick emerging market stocks, because stock screening and selection methods should work anywhere. In practice, fundamental techniques of securities analysis require adjustment for the special conditions in emerging markets.

1. Choose performance and valuation measures according to the market you are studying.

Unless there is a specific reason to screen for price-earnings ratios, price-book value, price-sales and price-cash flow, you needn't track each one. They will usually list the same types of stocks. Favor the most reliable data for the particular market. For example, in countries where book values are suspect, you might be better served by price-sales. In countries such as India and Malaysia, where strict American-style accounting practices apply, financial statement analysis is more worthwhile for screening. Market share is often a good benchmark. Well-managed companies tend to consolidate and increase market share when the economy expands.

2. Recognise the limitations of some traditional screening criteria.

Screen for both high-growth and high-dividend payout, and you won't have many stocks to choose from. It's like demanding fuel economy from a high-performance sports car: they just don't go together. Many fast-growing emerging market companies have limited access to financing and reinvest their profits rather than pay dividends.

Similarly, while P/E ratios enable you to make a rough approximation of a projected return on investment, they work best in situations that are slow and steady. And emerging market companies are anything but. So emerging market investors tend to pay less attention to P/Es as a measure of overpriced shares.

Local factors affect the P/E ratio. For example, accelerated depreciation can depress earnings, making the P/Es appear high relative to a similar company, because the local market adjusts for that depreciation.

3. Pay attention to company size.

Consider the size of a company from several perspectives: its ranking in the local stock market; in its sector; on the global scene. Some emerging market stocks, such as Argentina's YPF and Russia's Lukoil, are among the world's largest companies. Picking one of the 'ten largest' in a market is a mixed blessing. You gain liquidity, and usually greater disclosure, and the benefit of available institutional research. Such stocks are usually at the high end of the valuation scale, however. There aren't likely to be any bargains here. So there had better be significant growth in the company's future to justify the high price.

4. Treat liquidity as a primary consideration.

Emerging market share prices are often determined not by rigid financial measures, but simply by how much investors are willing to pay and how much money is available. You can pay very little for a stock, or you can pay a great deal, but you can't ignore market sentiment. That sentiment is best measured by how much capital is flowing in and flowing out, and who is buying or not buying. Local savings rates, the availability of pension fund investments, and the lifting of restrictions on foreign ownership also play a role in a foreign stock's liquidity.

5. Check financial strength, but make allowances.

Size counts, but financial strength counts more. Examine the standard financial ratios and pay close attention to a deteriorating balance sheet or potential bankruptcies. While there are many excellent managers in emerging market nations, there is less depth, and it is easy for a once-healthy company to go into a tailspin.

Nevertheless, don't set the bar too high. As financially-weakened emerging market companies tend to be heavily discounted by the market, you might find some bargains in potential turnarounds or acquisition targets.

6. Be careful not to pick low volatility and end up with low liquidity.

An emerging market stock with lower volatility than the overall market might seem like a more conservative buy. However, its lack of fluctuation could be a sign that the stock is quiet and liquidity is very low.

7. Don't rely solely on brokerage reports.

There are often conflicts of interest between research and investment banking departments. Aggressive investment bankers seeking new business and the chance to manage privatizations sometimes put pressure on research departments to avoid critical reports. Much of the available research is in the 'top ten' stocks. Don't expect the same depth and insight you are accustomed to finding in U.S. and European markets.

Stocks followed by fewer than eight analysts are called 'underfollowed stocks' and they offer the greatest opportunities. Fewer institutions are likely to participate. While this may add to volatility and lower valuations it also creates opportunity.

8. Get your portfolio balance right.

A common mistake in emerging markets investing is getting the stock picks right but the portfolio wrong. If strict application of your stock screens generates a list that is 75 percent Mexican, adjust your criteria to allow more diversification. A single-country bet is generally unwise over the long term.

9. Don't place too much reliance on technical analysis.

Certain technical indicators, such as relative strength, may be useful in emerging markets, but for the most part there is not enough reliable historical data for proper technical analysis. Technical analysis may have its day in emerging markets, but that day has not yet arrived.

10. Do not act impulsively on rumors.

Emerging markets move on rumors such as the pending resignation of a finance minister, a corruption scandal, local resistance to privatization, and so forth. If you are interested in emerging markets and have money in them, you won't be able to ignore these rumors. They will find you. However, do not be impulsive. Acting on rumors is often expensive.

'Don't pay active management fees for passive management by buying closet index funds.'

Joe Mansueto

Henriëtte M. Prast

Henriëtte Prast is a Senior Economist at the Nederlandsche Bank (Dutch Central Bank) and Associate Professor in Money, Credit and Banking at the University of Amsterdam. She has published on various subjects, including central banking, inflation and unemployment, regulation, and the role of psychology in financial markets. Currently she is specialising in Emotionomics, a term she has coined to describe research into the role of emotions in economics. She writes a weekly column on Emotionomics in Dutch financial newspaper *Het Financieele Dagblad*.

The emotional investor

---

1. Take control of your own investments.

Keep in mind that fund managers and investment analysts aim to maximise not your return, but their own future income, which depends on their reputation for being smart. Keynes observed that: "It is better for reputation to fail conventionally than to succeed unconventionally." By disappearing in the crowd, professionals make sure that their mistakes will be forgiven, as others made the same faults. This mediocrity preserves their reputation, but does not enhance your return.

2. Don't be conventional.

A corollary of the first rule - since you should be more concerned with returns than reputation - is to avoid convention. Keynes' observation may have been right for financial industry participants, but only for those with mediocre talents - and not for readers of this book!

3. Blame your faults on yourself, not others.

'Heads I win, tails it's chance.' Blaming someone else for your mistakes, and claiming the honour for your successes, may seem pleasant, but it does not make you either good company or a good investor. Moreover, you won't learn from past investment mistakes. Cognitive psychologists have labelled this behaviour 'biased self-attribution'. It leads to another empirically verified phenomenon: individuals are, on average, overconfident. If you are overconfident, you trade too much, as you think you are smart enough to see valuable information in what is actually irrelevant news. The excessive trading lowers your return, as transaction costs exceed the return from trading.

4. Dare to be a loser.

Do not expect all your investments to be successful. Even the best investors are not right all the time. In a success-oriented culture this is a difficult lesson for many investors to learn. But the success of each individual trade is not as important as the profitability of the whole portfolio. Sometimes it is necessary to sell the losers, for the sake of the wider portfolio. In military terms, some battles have to be lost to win the war.

5. Watch out for starry nights.

Experimental studies find strong evidence that investors chase trends once they think they see them. This is because, as psychological research shows, we have a tendency to see patterns in random events. For example, in a random pattern of stars we are determined to see the Great Bear. Due to this phenomenon, which is called the 'representativeness heuristic', we overestimate the news value of one element in a series of similar messages. As a result we over-react to information that is part of a string of similar, but unconnected, events.

6. Hip is out: stay away from cascades when you see one.

As our private information is never perfect, we infer much from the behaviour of others. The cascade model of investment predicts that we tend to follow others, perhaps neglecting our own valuable information. Try to think of investments as places to eat. When you see a queue outside a restaurant, you might conclude that it is a great place to eat. However, that queue might be there precisely because the person last in line followed your reasoning, and the one before him did too etc. Rely on your own information unless you are sure that others know more. The cascade may change direction quickly and in that case it is unlikely that you will survive.

7. Beware the gambler's addiction.

Addicted gamblers want to lose, not win. That is why they are easy prey when it comes to beating 'the market'. According to Freudian psychoanalysis, the addicted gambler is motivated by his repressed Oedipal conflicts. The male child's wish to become his mother's object of desire creates an ambiguous relationship (love/hate) with the father. Destiny is an avenging father substitute, and gambling challenges it. By losing, the gambler pays off his moral debt to his father. Important: before entering a casino you should see a psychiatrist to make sure you do not suffer from this neurosis!

8. Crisis, what crisis?

We tend to be 'disaster myopic'. If a long time has elapsed since the latest crash, we believe it will never happen again. Stay awake and look out for signs indicating that a crisis is looming around the corner.

9. Don't fall in love with your portfolio - or it will betray you.

According to cognitive psychologist Leon Festinger, we filter information to make it correspond to our fundamental opinion. Think of wishful thinking by a person who is in love and does not see the nasty habits of the objects of his desire. Investors, similarly, tend to turn a blind eye to information that does not suit them, and actively search for information that confirms that they have made the right investment decision. Be aware of this, and don't turn away from bad news about your portfolio.

10. *Carpe diem.*

Sit back and reflect before even thinking about investing. Remember that the purpose of investing is future consumption. Reconsider whether you really want three pairs of Jimmy Choo shoes by the time you are 65 rather than one pair of them now.

---

www.dnb.nl

'If the Price-Research Ratio (share price divided by R&D per share) is 5 or less it is nearly always worth buying the shares. This applies particularly to recovery situations.'

Conor McCarthy

Robert Prechter

Robert Prechter is President of Elliott Wave International. EWI serves institutional clients in analysing all major global stock, bond, interest rate and currency markets, as well as metals and energy markets.

Books

Conquer the Crash: You Can Survive and Prosper in a Deflationary Depression, John Wiley and Sons Ltd, 2002
The Wave Principle of Human Social Behavior, 2000, New Classics Library
The Elliott Wave Principle, John Wiley, 1978-2000
At the Crest of the Tidal Wave, New Classics Library, 1995

Requirements for successful trading

Introduction

Like most rewards life offers, market profits are not as easy to come by as the novice believes. Making money requires a good deal of education, like any craft or business. If you've got the time, the drive, and the right psychological makeup, you can enter the elite realm of the successful trader.

Most lists of 'trading rules' contain little more than contradictory homilies. The following is not a list of rules but a list of requirements you need for successful trading.

1. A method.

You need an objectively definable method of financial market analysis. It must be thought out in its entirety to the extent that if someone asks you how you make your decisions, you can explain it to him, and if he asks you again in six months, he will receive the same answer. This is not to say that a method cannot be altered or improved; it must, however, be developed as a totality before it is implemented.

A prerequisite for obtaining a method is acceptance of the fact that perfection is not achievable. People who demand it are wasting their time searching for the Holy Grail, and they will never get beyond this first step of obtaining a method. I chose to use an approach called the Wave Principle, which I think reveals the true pattern of market behavior. But there are a hundred other methods that will work if successful trading is your only goal.

2. The discipline to follow your method.

This requirement is so widely understood by true professionals that among them, it almost sounds like a cliché. Nevertheless, it is so crucial to success that it cannot be ignored. Without discipline, you really have no method in the first place. It struck me one day that among a handful of consistently successful professional options and futures traders of my acquaintance, three of them are former Marines. The pressures from trading are enormous, and they get to everyone. If you are not disciplined, forget the markets.

3. Experience.

Paper trading is useful for the testing of methodology, but it is of no value in learning about trading. In fact, it can be detrimental in imbuing the novice with a false sense of security. A novice may have successfully paper traded over the past six months and thus believe that the next six months with real money will be no different. In fact, nothing could be further from the truth. Why? Because the markets are not merely an intellectual exercise. They are an emotional challenge as well.

When trading, you must conquer a host of problems, most of them related to your own inner strength in battling powerful human emotions. The School of Hard Knocks is the only school that will teach it to you, and the tuition is expensive. There is only one shortcut to obtaining experience, and that is to find a mentor. Locate and learn from someone who has proved himself over the years to be a successful trader or investor - but they are hard to find.

4. The mental strength to accept the fact that losses are part of the game.

There are many denials of reality that automatically disqualify millions of people from joining the ranks of successful speculators. For instance, to moan that 'manipulators', 'insiders', 'program trading' or anything else is to blame for one's losses is a common fault. Anyone who utters such a conviction is doomed before he starts. The biggest obstacle to successful speculation is the failure to accept the simple fact that losses are part of the game, and that they must be accommodated.

Practically speaking, you must employ an objective money management system when formulating your trading method. There are many ways to do it. Some methods use stops. I think a better approach is to commit only a small percentage of your available capital on each trade and let your analytical method dictate your action. After all is said and done, learning to handle losses will be your greatest triumph.

5. The mental strength to accept huge gains.

This comment usually gets a hearty laugh, which merely goes to show how little people realise it to be a problem. How many times have you had this experience: You exit a trade to grab a profit, then day after day for the next six months you watch the market continue to go in the direction of your original position. You try to find another entry point and continue to miss. At the end of six months, your method finally, calmly says, "Get out." You check the figures and realise that your initial entry, if held, would have netted a huge profit.

So what was your problem? Simply that you had allowed yourself unconsciously to define your 'normal' range of profit and loss. When the big trade finally came, you lacked the esteem for your method required to take all it promised. So you abandoned both method and discipline. To win the game, make sure that you understand why you're in it. The big moves in markets only come once or twice a year. Those are the ones which will pay you for all the work, fear, sweat and frustration of the previous eleven months or even eleven years. Don't miss them for reasons other than those required by your objectively defined method.

www.elliottwave.com

'Don't buy more software than you need. Many traders load up on expensive software that is so difficult to use, they don't even get any benefit from it. Option traders sometimes spend thousands on fancy software and then wind up using only the Black-Scholes model portion of it.'

Lawrence McMillan

George Putnam III

George Putnam, III is the editor and publisher of *The Turnaround Letter* and several other bankruptcy publications, including *Bankruptcy Week*, *The Bankruptcy DataSource* and *The Bankruptcy Yearbook and Almanac*.

His material can be found on the Internet at www.bankruptcydata.com and www.turnarounds.com. He is also a Trustee of the Putnam Group of Mutual Funds.

Turnaround stocks

---

1. Be willing to go against the crowd.

By their nature, turnaround stocks are unpopular. That's why they have so much profit potential. If you wait until they are popular again, you will miss most of the gains. For example, back in 1993 when IBM dropped down to about 10 (adjusted for splits) most analysts called it a dinosaur. Then, when the stock got back up to 100 a few years later, everyone loved it again.

2. Previous stock prices are irrelevant.

Too often investors fall into the trap of saying "This stock used to trade at 50, and now it is at 5 - it must be a bargain." A stock is only a bargain if it is currently undervalued, and that depends solely on what the stock is actually worth today - not what investors thought it was worth last month or last year.

3. You can lose just as much money in a $1 stock as in a $50 stock.

This is a corollary to Rule #2. Many investors also say "The stock has dropped to $1 per share; how much lower can it go?" The answer, of course, is "to zero." Stocks do become worthless. And if the stock goes to zero, you will have lost just as much, on a percentage basis, if you bought it at 1 as you would have if you'd bought it at 50: 100% of your money.

4. Look for a solid core business.

A company can only rebuild if it has a solid foundation on which to base its recovery. If the business was based on a fad or an obsolete technology, the stock is not likely to rebound. But if the company's basic business remains sound, there is a better chance the stock will bounce back.

5. Evaluate management's ability to turn things around.

Evaluating management is important for any stock, but it is particularly important in a turnaround situation. In many cases, the management that got the company into trouble isn't likely to be able to get it out of trouble again. Therefore, a change in top management can be a good sign.

6. Look for someone else to do the heavy lifting.

The presence of a big investor who is willing to get involved and shake up the company can be a good thing. But make sure that the big investor owns the same security that you do. Sometimes the big investors own bonds or preferred stock, in which case they may not care what happens to the holders of the common stock.

7. Check the debt.

A heavy debt burden is often part of the reason that the company is in trouble in the first place. And a high level of debt significantly reduces the company's flexibility in making necessary changes to its business. Finally, if the company must restructure, the debt has to be taken care of before stockholders get any value.

8. Avoid stocks of companies in Chapter 11.

This is related to Rule #7. If a company goes into Chapter 11, the basic rule of bankruptcy is that senior creditors must get paid off before junior creditors get anything. Stockholders have the most junior claims of all in a bankruptcy, and very rarely is there enough value in a bankrupt company for the stockholders to receive anything. This is also related to Rule #2 and Rule #3 because Chapter 11 stocks are often temptingly low in price, but they almost always end up being virtually worthless.

9. Be patient.

Turnarounds take time. Moreover, even if the company has turned around, it may take still longer for investors to recognize the turnaround and to get comfortable with the stock again. (After all, many investors were burned by the stock on the way down.)

10. Diversify.

Diversification is important in any type of investing, but it is particularly important in turnaround investing. Turnaround situations always are affected by a large number of variables, and no matter how much research you do, you will always have some situations that don't work out the way you expect them to. The best way to minimize your risk in turnarounds is to spread your money over a large number of different stocks. That increases your chances of having some big winners to offset your inevitable losers.

www.turnarounds.com

'Rising inflation is toxic for both bonds and stocks because it points to tighter monetary policy and rising interest rates. Falling inflation is extremely bullish for the opposite reasons.

Most bear markets have occurred in response to rising inflation pressures, while falling inflation was the single most important force behind the powerful bull markets during the 1980s and 1990s.'

Martin Barnes

Alfred Rappaport

Al Rappaport is the Leonard Spacek Professor Emeritus at J. L. Kellogg Graduate School of Management, Northwestern University. He also directs shareholder value research for L.E.K. Consulting. He originated the Shareholder Scoreboard for *The Wall Street Journal*.

Books

Expectations Investing, HBS, 2001 (with Michael Mauboussin)
Creating Shareholder Value: A Guide for Managers and Investors, The Free Press 1998

Michael Mauboussin

Michael Mauboussin is a Managing Director and Chief U.S. Investment Strategist at Credit Suisse First Boston in New York. He is an acknowledged leader in the application of value-based tools in security analysis, and has lectured and published widely on the subject. He is an adjunct professor Columbia Graduate School of Business

Books

Expectations Investing, HBS, 2001 (with Alfred Rappaport)

Expectations investing

Introduction

'Expectations investing' represents a fundamental shift from the way professional money managers and individual investors select stocks today. It recognizes that the key to achieving superior results is to begin by estimating the performance expectations embedded in the current stock price and then to correctly anticipate revisions in those expectations.

Conventional wisdom suggests that investors need a host of approaches to value different businesses. Expectations investors recognize that while various businesses have different characteristics, it is important to value all companies using the same economic approach. Here are 10 expectations investing rules to increase your odds of generating superior returns.

1. Follow the cash.

Investor returns come from two sources of cash - dividends and changes in share prices. But a company cannot pay dividends unless it is able to produce positive cash flows. So without the prospect of future cash flows, a company commands no value. Stock prices therefore reflect transactions between investors willing to sell the present value of a company's expected cash flows and buyers who are betting on higher cash flows in the future. Cash flow is how the market values stocks.

2. Forget earnings and price-earnings multiples.

Savvy investors don't rely on short-term metrics such as earnings and price-earnings multiples because they fail to capture the long-term cash-flow expectations implied by the stock price. Indeed, the most widely used valuation metric in the investment community, the price-earnings multiple, does not determine value but rather is a consequence of value. The price-earnings multiple is not an analytic shortcut. It is an economic cul-de-sac.

3. Read market expectations implied by stock price.

Rather than forecast cash flows, expectations investing starts by reading the collective expectations that a company's stock price implies. By reversing the conventional process, you not only bypass the difficult job of independently forecasting cash flows but you can also benchmark your own expectations against those of the market. You need to know what the market's expectations are today before you begin to assess where they are likely to move in the future.

4. Look for potential causes of revisions in market expectations.

The only way for an investor to achieve superior returns is to correctly anticipate meaningful differences between current and future expectations. Investors do not earn superior returns on stocks that are priced to fully reflect future performance. Where do you look for revisions? Changes in volume, selling prices, and sales mix trigger revisions in sales growth expectations. Revisions in operating profit margin expectations originate from changes in selling prices, sales mix, economies of scale, and cost efficiencies.

5. Concentrate analysis on the value trigger (sales, costs or investment) that has the greatest impact on the stock.

Identifying the so-called turbo trigger enables investors to simplify their analysis and channel their analytical focus toward the changes with the highest payoffs.

6. Use competitive strategy analysis to help anticipate revisions in expectations.

The surest way for investors to anticipate expectations revisions is to foresee shifts in a company's competitive dynamics. For investors, competitive strategy analysis integrated with financial analysis is an essential tool in the expectations game.

7. Buy stocks trading at sufficient discounts from expected value.

The greater the discount from expected value, the higher the prospective excess return - and hence the more attractive a stock is for purchase. The sooner the stock price converges toward the higher expected value, the greater the excess return. The longer it takes, the lower the excess return.

8. Sell stocks that trade at sufficient premiums over expected value after accounting for taxes and transactions costs.

The higher a stock price's premium to its expected value, the more compelling the selling opportunity. Investors should sell a stock for three reasons: It has reached its expected value, better investment opportunities exist, or the investor revises expectations downward. But even these reasons may not be decisive after incorporating taxes and transactions costs into the analysis.

9. Don't overlook other significant value determinates that don't appear in the financial statements.

For example, ignoring employee stock options can lead to a significant underestimation of costs and liabilities. Past grants are a genuine economic liability and future option grants are an indisputable cost of doing business. In contrast, real options, the right but not the obligation to make potentially value-creating investments, are often a meaningful source of value for start-ups and companies in fast-changing sectors.

10. Heed the signals sent when companies issue or purchase their own stock.

An acquiring company's choice of cash or stock often sends a powerful signal to investors. Under the right circumstances, buybacks provide expectations investors a signal to revise their expectations about a company's prospects. Correctly reading these signals provides investors with an analytical edge.

---

www.expectationsinvesting.com, www.hbsp.harvard.edu

'Confidence factors are the primary influences on price levels in the U.S. market, not fundamental factors like growth and real interest rates.'

Jeremy Grantham

Jay Ritter

Jay Ritter is Cordell Professor of Finance at the Warrington College of Business Administration, University of Florida. He writes extensively for *The Journal of Finance* and other financial journals, and has contributed chapters on IPOs to several books, most recently, The Handbook of the Economics of Finance, published by North Holland.

IPOs

Buying at the IPO

1. 'Increase the price, double my order. Decrease the price, cancel my order.'

When an initial public offering (IPO) is being sold, a price range is listed in the preliminary prospectus, such as $12-$14 per share. The day before trading starts, a final offer price is set. Sometimes, before the final price is set, the price range will be revised up or down. If the price is lowered, it indicates that the underwriter is having trouble finding buyers, and the stock is unlikely to jump at the opening. If the price is increased, this indicates that it is a hot issue, and the price is likely to jump at the opening. During 1990-1998, if the offer price was lowered, the average first-day return (from offer price to close) was 4%. If the price was increased, the average first-day return was 32%. With short-term profits in mind, you should ask for more shares the more the price has been increased. The reason that wanting to buy more, the higher the price, doesn't violate the laws of economics is that the price change is telling you about the state of demand.

2. IPOs are a marketing tool.

In recent years, IPOs have become a marketing tool. That is, with many IPOs jumping up to far above the offer price on the first day of trading, receiving shares has become a source of profits for investors. Brokerage firms reward their most profitable customers with IPOs. If you are a profitable customer, due to having a large account or being an active trader, don't be bashful about asking for IPOs. Brokerage firms know that they risk losing customers if they don't give their best customers hot IPOs. If you don't ask, you won't get the hot IPOs.

3. If a broker asks you to buy, stay away from the issue.

Unless you are a very profitable customer for a broker, if the broker offers shares in an IPO to you, it probably indicates that the broker is having trouble selling the issue. This is a bad sign.

4. Check out what the web sites are saying.

There are a number of web sites that cover IPOs, and give updated information on whether a given issue is hot or cold. These differ from chat rooms, where anyone can say anything that they want. Some of the web sites include www.ipohome.com (Renaissance Capital) and www.ipomonitor.com. Links to other websites can be found at my homepage (bear.cba.ufl.edu/ritter), at www.iporesources.org, and on Yahoo's IPO page.

Buying and Holding

5. Pay attention to valuation.

A great company doesn't necessarily make a great investment. In recent years many technology companies have gone public and subsequently grown rapidly. But if the stock price already reflects huge future profits, the upside potential is limited.

As an example, on October 22, 1999 a young company, Sycamore Networks, went public. Sycamore had $11 million in sales during the prior year, and at the end of the first day of trading had a market capitalization of $14 billion. The chance that Sycamore's sales and profits would grow to numbers that could justify this valuation is miniscule.

When Microsoft went public in March 1986, it already was profitable, it had $162 million in annual sales, and its market cap was only $700 million. At a valuation of $700 million, Microsoft had a lot of upside potential. At a valuation of $14 billion, Sycamore did not have a lot of upside potential, even if things went right. In mid-2001, the market cap of Sycamore was less than $2 billion.

6. The IPO market is never in equilibrium. It's either too hot or too cold. Buy in the cold periods.

Since 1990, the U.S. has averaged 35 IPOs per month. But this average masks considerable variation. There have been 44 months with at least 50 IPOs, and 15 months with fewer than 20 IPOs. Periods of low volume include the six months after Iraq invaded Kuwait in 1990, the six months after Long-Term Capital Management ran into trouble in 1998, and the six months after the collapse of internet stocks in late 2000. During these periods, the IPO market virtually shut down.

In general, the best time to buy IPOs for the long run is when the IPO market is in one of its cold periods, with low volume. One of the great all-time investments in a company going public was that of Cisco Systems, which went public in February 1990, a month when only 12 other firms went public in the U.S.

Research that I have conducted with Tim Loughran of the University of Notre Dame shows that since 1970, firms going public during low-volume periods have outperformed firms going public during high-volume periods, where the performance is measured from the close of trading on the first day of issue to five years later. Of the internet IPOs from 1999 and 2000, by April of 2001 97% were trading below their offer price, and 99% were trading below their first-day closing price.

7. Avoid young companies in hot industries.

Historically, in the five years after issuing, IPOs have underperformed the market. Measured from the closing market price on the first day of trading, IPOs have underperformed the broader market by about 4% per year during the five years after issuing. This underperformance starts six months after the IPO, and is most pronounced for young companies going public during hot IPO markets.

A contrarian strategy works best with IPOs: older, more established, firms in industries that aren't hot have historically produced the best long-run returns, especially if the offering is from a period when valuation levels are relatively conservative and few companies are going public.

8. Beware of the lockup period expiration.

When a firm goes public, the pre-issue shareholders commit to hold their shares for a set period of time, during which selling is prohibited without the express written consent of the lead underwriter. This period is typically 180 days. Around the time of the lockup period expiration, the stock price drops several percent, on average. The drop is even bigger for tech stocks.

Laura Field and Gordon Hanka, in an article published in the 2001 *Journal of Finance*, show that this drop occurs during the period from a week before to a week after the lockup expiration. If you are thinking of buying a stock which went public five months ago, it is best to wait for a little over six months before buying. But beware, because starting six months after the IPO is when the long-run underperformance starts.

9. Don't confuse growth with profitable growth.

A firm or industry can grow rapidly, but this doesn't necessarily mean that the profits will grow rapidly. If there are no barriers to entry, stockholders won't benefit from growth. As an example, the airline industry has grown from almost nothing to one of the biggest industries in the country, as measured by sales and employment. But the airline industry has never been very profitable. Competition from new entrants (almost all of whom have gone bankrupt) and higher labor costs from unionized pilots have kept profits down.

Even with rapid technological progress, a firm won't make large profits unless its competition doesn't have access to the technology. If all of the firms in an industry gain from new technology, competition drives down prices. Consumers benefit, but stockholders don't necessarily benefit. Managers sometimes lose sight of this and overinvest.

10. Evaluate the prospectus, focusing particularly on the management.

As explained in *IPOs for Everyone* by Linda Killian, Kathleen Smith, and William Smith of Renaissance Capital, evaluating management quality and incentives, and the company's fundamentals, helps to pick the good IPOs and avoid the bad ones. Checking management is especially important with IPOs where there is no venture capitalist involved. If management compensation is set up to enrich management whether or not shareholders do well, it is a warning sign. A board of directors that is dominated by insiders is a warning sign. If management has granted large numbers of options to themselves, this is another warning sign. If the earnings numbers are boosted by aggressive accounting procedures, this is another warning sign.

But nothing is foolproof. A company might have entrenched management but still do well. For many years, America Online (now part of AOL-TimeWarner) boosted earnings by aggressively booking revenue from future monthly fees. AOL's stock climbed as their market share expanded and they crushed the competition, and after a few years they changed their accounting policies.

John Rothchild

John Rothchild is the bestselling author of the critically acclaimed A Fool And His Money, and Going For Broke. He co-wrote, with Peter Lynch, One Up On Wall Street, Beating The Street, and Learn To Earn.

A Former Editor of *Washington Monthly* and financial columnist for *Time* magazine and *Fortune*, Mr Rothchild has also written for *Harpers, Rolling Stone, Esquire,* and many other periodicals. He has appeared on The Nightly Business Report, the Today Show, and CNBC. His latest book about finance, The Davis Dynasty, is published in Fall, 2001.

Books

The Davis Dynasty: Fifty Years of Successful Investing on Wall Street, John Wiley & Sons Inc, 2001
Going for Broke: How Robert Campeau Bankrupted the Retail Industry, Jolted the Junk Bond Market, and Brought the Booming 80s to a Crashing Halt, Beard Books,U.S., 2000
The Bear Book, John Wiley, 1998
A Fool and His Money, John Wiley, 1998

with Peter Lynch
One Up on Wall Street, Simon & Schuster, 2000
Beating the Street, Simon & Schuster, 1993
Learn to Earn, Simon & Schuster, 1995

Surviving a severe bear market

1. Long-term may be longer than you think.

After severe bear markets, there are apparently endless stretches when little, if any, money is made from owning a typical portfolio of stocks. Judging by the Dow Jones Industrials, when stocks get ahead of themselves and falter, it can take many *years* - not many *months* - for them to regain lost ground.

The overused example is 1929, when the Dow topped out at 381 and took 25 years to go higher. Similarly, the Dow hit 685 in 1957 and traded lower than that in 1970. It hit 995 in 1966 and traded at 776 in 1981.

People who aren't prepared for a decade or more of mediocre to nonexistent returns, especially after an exciting run-up that often precedes these bearish intervals, tend to lose enthusiasm for buying and holding, and often quit the market at disadvantageous times.

2. After the bears ruin the party, don't keep dancing with the same old stocks.

Stocks that lead the rally to the top in late stages of bull markets - witness the so-called Nifty Fifty group in the early 1970s - aren't likely to lead the rally off the bottom in late stages of bear markets. Newer, smaller, and faster-growing companies rise to the top.

3. Don't be tempted by sucker rallies, unless you can love them and leave them.

Severe declines and lengthy recoveries (1929-1949; 1969-1981) are enlivened by exciting rallies that take stock prices to as much as a fourfold gain. These gains are lost just as readily, and the true recovery may lie years ahead.

4. When the last Chicken Little is debunked, the sky finally falls.

As stock prices rise into the thin air of overvaluation, leading to a big fall, all the bearish prognosticators are proven wrong.

In the mid-1990s, for instance, numerous high-profile Wall Street types turned publicly bearish, then lost credibility as prices continued to advance for five more years. At the market top in early 2,000, no high-profile bears were left to sound the alarm.

5. When bears rule the street, it pays to own things that pay you to own them.

This includes stocks that pay high dividends, preferred stocks, REITS, convertible bonds, and balanced mutual funds that own a mixture of the above assets. If it takes years for stock prices to rise, you might as well get some return while you wait.

6. 50 million Frenchmen can't be wrong, but a consensus of economists can.

Recessions are bad news for the stock market, and severe recessions can be terrible news, but don't rely on 'most economists' to give you the early warning. According to published reports, 'most economists' agreed the U.S. would avert recession in 1969-70, 1973-74, 1981-82, and 1990. They were wrong all four times.

7. Beware the New Era.

Every new generation or so, there's talk of a 'new era', a Camelot where the economic climate is forever balmy, and companies bask in a garden of prosperity. New era talk was popular in the late 1920s, the late 1960s and the late 1990s. In the first two instances, these new eras led into the worst two bear markets of the 20th century. The latest new era was followed by the great technology bust when investors in the tech-heavy NASDAQ market were down more than 50 per cent from NASDAQ's high.

8. Even bonds aren't bear proof.

Bond investors lose a lot of money in severe bear markets, such as the one that lasted 34 years from 1947 to 1981.

9. Your mutual fund won't save you.

Numerous big-name funds from the 1960s were gone by the end of the 1973-74 market wipe-out. Fund assets overall were down more than 30 per cent.

10. Ride with small stocks in post-bear rallies.

Small stocks tend to outperform off the bottom of bear markets, while larger-cap stocks tend to outperform near the tops of bull markets.

'Be leery of any company in which the analysts raise their target price while cutting earnings estimates. It simply doesn't make sense unless they're trying to hype it to issue stock.'

Herb Greenberg

Anthony Saliba

Anthony Saliba is founder and Chairman of International Trading Institute, a derivatives training company which has trained over 4,000 professionals in its 12 year history.

Mr Saliba started his trading career at Chicago Board Options Exchange in 1979 trading equity options as an independent. In the next 11 years, he expanded his trading horizons to include most CBOE products, currencies and the S&P 500 contracts on the CME, as well as agricultural and interest rate products traded on the CBOT. His trading skills were recognised by Jack Schwager in 'Market Wizards'.

Books

The Options Workbook: Proven Strategies from a Market Wizard, Dearborn Trade,U.S., 2001
The Options Workbook: Fundamental Spread Concepts and Strategies for Investors and Traders, Kaplan Business, 206

Trading listed options

Tony Saliba along with business partners Joe Corona and Chris Hausman share credit for these trading rules.

1. Speed is more important than accuracy when market-making.

Having a sophisticated pricing model, with a proprietary number of iterations is meaningless if you don't get in on the trade. Most differences in pricing can be made up with better hedging activities and less slippage.

2. Price is more important than speed when investing.

Customers who complain about commission levels will tell you that if they can get the trade done at a tick or two better in price, it's worth taking your time to do the trade right. Two years ago, even a minute for a turnaround was 'down-in-the-noise'; now investors can get speed and better pricing in options trades.

3. Don't worry about the put/call ratios, they're noisy bastards.

Institutional hedging, spread trading and overnight legs are among the culprits that render this daily indicator as valuable as a flip of the coin.

4. Volatility should be a thermometer for traders and a compass for investors.

Traders can take a constant reading of Implied Volatility, exploit it, and use it to maintain the financial health of their 'books', whereas investors making long-term investment decisions should make the journey using volatility as a co-pilot.

5. Options vernacular is inside out and upside down.

Spreads are considered 'risky, complex strategies that should only be used by advanced traders'. In reality, spreads reduce risk and are usually safer than an outright purchase or sale of a put or a call.

6. Implied volatility is meaningless in expiration week.

Option volatility on expiring options is not worth discussing because there is no vega. Too many traders get hung up looking at 'implieds' in expiration week - that game is over.

7. Another way to look at volatility is like a car zigzagging through a highway of news, avoiding/hitting bumps and potholes along its way.

In our age of technology, events drive volatility in a digital manner. Expect a changing landscape as news paints the path. Don't let volatility scare you away or upset your stomach. Enjoy the ride.

8. My favorite: 'A good spread at bad prices' .

Instead of blowing out of a loss immediately, look for a spread hedge and turn a bad trade into a good spread, but perhaps at a bad price. This is your 'repair' exit.

9. Getting out of a bad trade: 'The first cut is the cheapest.'

Too many options traders hang on to positions as they go against them, hoping that they will come back. This leads to massive hemorrhaging - repair immediately or cut and run.

10. When in doubt, get out!

When you put on a position that makes you feel uncomfortable, or that just doesn't inspire confidence, while hearing a little voice say: "get the hell out!" - trust your instincts.

www.salibaco.com

Thomas Schneeweis

Thomas Schneeweis is Professor of Finance at the School of Management at the University of Massachusetts, and Director of the Center for International Securities and Derivatives Markets (CISDM/SOM).

He is President of Schneeweis Partners, LLC, which specializes in analytical support in the areas of multi-advisor fund creation, asset allocation, and risk management services. He also edits *The Journal of Alternative Investments*, is head of the educational committee of the Alternative Investment Management Association and is a frequent speaker at academic and industry events dealing with alternative investments.

Hedge funds and managed futures investing

1. 'Beware of the unknown, beware of hedge funds.'

In fact, most hedge funds have lower risk than individual stocks or even stock indices. Individual stocks have an annual volatility (i.e. standard deviation) of about 30%. The S&P500's annual volatility is about 15%. Most hedge funds (with the exception of some long bias or global macro hedge funds) have an annual volatility below 15% and even commodity trading advisors (futures and option traders) have annual volatilities close to that of the S&P500.

2. 'Stocks for the long run.'

In fact, hedge funds do add benefits to established traditional stock and bond portfolios. Most stocks move up together and down together. As a result, in order to diversify, investors need to invest in investment vehicles such as hedge funds which are constructed to be less sensitive to stock market movements.

3. 'To know the future look at the past.'

The past foretells the future in many areas but not in stock and bond investment or in hedge funds. Each strategy makes money in unique markets. Only if the market conditions remain constant will the immediate past reflect the future.

4. Just look at the tracks if you want to know the animal.

Some hedge funds maintain that they are not correlated with the stock market when in fact they are merely an equity fund in hedge fund format. Test the actual performance of the hedge fund with indices which reflect traditional stock and bond investment, as well as hedge funds which reflect hedge fund performance. Stock and bond indices exist which reflect the performance of equity and fixed income portfolios

Similarly, there are a number of hedge fund indices (e.g., Zurich Hedge Fund Indices) which offer similar performance tracking for hedge funds.

5. Beware the man behind the curtain.

Some hedge fund managers maintain that their system is so secret that they cannot tell you how it works or why it works. When you meet these managers simply walk away. Never trust a man who will not tell you what is behind the curtain.

6. When all else fails, manipulate the data.

Many hedge fund managers will promote ideas that have no historical record of performance. At times this may be okay, but never rely solely on the data. Place your trust in the foundations of the trading idea not in the performance data.

7. 'Clothes maketh the man.'

In fact, as for any investment, one must look behind the size of the firm, the office space and so on, and concentrate on the actual source of the return. If the manager cannot tell you why the strategy makes money in less than five sentences, move on.

8. 'The Government will protect you.'

Some investors believe that there is greater government oversight and protection in traditional stocks and bonds than in hedge funds. In fact, most hedge funds have to meet regulatory requirements subject to the markets they trade (e.g., register as a CTA if trading in futures and option markets). However, in both traditional and alternative investment, no amount of government oversight can protect you from an incompetent manager or one who wishes to defraud you.

Caveat Emptor.

9. 'One always knows the value of one's stock portfolio but not one's hedge fund.'

Unfortunately, many stock and bond funds' net asset value does not reflect its true market value. For instance, emerging market prices are often outdated. By contrast, many hedge funds trade in the most liquid markets, such as futures and option markets, or in highly liquid equity markets. In addition, for most large investments daily pricing and evaluation is normal.

10. 'Only the wealthy should invest in hedge funds.'

Traditional Assets Forms of Investment (e.g. mutual funds, structured notes) exist for hedge funds. Moreover, new forms of investment are being created which let individuals invest in hedge funds with less than a $10,000 investment.

www.som.umass.edu

'Be aware of the economic cycle. While spending on eating out, health, fitness and other leisure pursuits is undoubtedly in long-term secular increase, it is also highly discretionary and one of the first to go in economic downturns.'

Simon Johnson

Steven Schoenfeld

Steven Schoenfeld is a Managing Director of Barclays Global Investors, and the chief investment strategist and team leader of its International Equity Management Group, which manages over $65 billion in developed international and emerging market index investments. He is the editor of *Active Index Investing* to be published in late 2002.

Effective international equity investing

1. An international/non-domestic equity allocation always provides diversification to an investor's portfolio.

International investing has come under fire in the US for two main reasons: tighter correlations between global markets, and the huge U.S. bull market of the late 1990s. Both these reasons are clear examples of short term performance and 'rear-view mirror investing'. Looking at long term performance, in the 336 months between 1973 and 2000, international equities (proxied by MSCI EAFE) and US equities (S&P 500) moved in opposite directions 115 times or 34% of the time. However, in the 132 months in which the S&P 500 went down, EAFE posted a positive return in 55 of those months - 42% of the time.

So, even though the common argument is that international doesn't provide diversification in the times when it's most needed (when the domestic market is falling), in reality, international markets have posted positive returns more often in those periods than over all periods. Higher correlations in recent times were driven by the increased dominance of tech stocks in all global markets, and as their weight has dropped the correlations are dropping as well.

In fact, the truly risky portfolio is the one that does not include some foreign equities. Even in the 90s, investing 20% of a portfolio in international equities (EAFE), would have reduced volatility from 13.4% to 12.9%. More impressively, over the last three years (ending Dec 2000) when the argument for international not being a good diversifier has been most popular, an equity portfolio with a 30% allocation to EAFE would have been less volatile than a portfolio fully invested in the S&P 500 - 16.4% vs. 17.7%.

2. Don't define international/foreign too narrowly - you'll often miss the best action.

Many investors define 'international' in a constrained way, for example: US investors just investing in EAFE/developed markets, thus missing out on opportunities in Canada and emerging markets. Similarly, many European investors focus too much on their home region, and outside the continent.

A broad, international portfolio that includes emerging markets and Canada in the proportion of their market capitalization (ACWI ex-US), has delivered better risk and return characteristics than one invested solely in the developed international markets (EAFE). The more complete portfolio would have returned 7.2% with an annualized standard deviation of 16.5% as opposed to a return of 6.9% with an annualized standard deviation of 16.9% for EAFE (Jan 1988 - Dec 2000).

3. Even as globalization accelerates, national factors/country allocation still matters - a lot!

As the world has become more integrated, the influence of sectors has increased. However, countries are still the key drivers of return differentials. This is because, even in an area as closely linked as the EMU, there are significant differences in government economic and fiscal policies.

More importantly, the level of human capital differs substantially across countries. This translates into either different industry compositions or, at the very least, different levels of value added processes in the same industry. For equity markets, this means divergent market returns and therefore far from perfect correlation. Some sectors have always been global in nature (oil, technology etc.) while others are clearly driven by local factors (retail etc.).

4. All emerging markets are not created equal - and those with a potential to 'graduate' are the long-term winners.

It is important to distinguish between 'top-tier' emerging markets which are on the path toward convergence with developed market standards (and often into developed-market trading blocs such as the EU and NAFTA). Portugal and Greece have both successfully graduated, and those investors who were there early benefited.

Future 'top-tier' emerging markets would include Mexico, Brazil, Israel, South Africa, Poland, Taiwan and Korea. It is countries such as these which have the potential for the most rapid economic growth and market returns.

5. Domestic multinationals - or even global multinationals - are no substitute for broad international equity exposure.

As attractive as the concept might sound - generally something like "buy global winners to capture the benefit of international markets without the risk" - the reality is that one does not get the diversification advantage of foreign stocks with multinationals.

Domestic MNCs tend to have a beta close to 1.0 with their home market, and large-cap global MNCs are usually the most highly correlated both with each other and with large developed markets. To truly reduce risk and potentially enhance return, one needs stocks with a high degree of local content, and adequate exposure to at least the top 15-18 emerging markets.

6. Concerns about the currency exposure of international equity investment tend to be overblown - for allocations of less than 15%, the appropriate attitude should be "don't worry, be happy"

The currency risk you take with foreign stocks is not always a bad thing. In fact, if international stocks are less than 15% of your total equity portfolio, the currency exposure actually adds diversification with minimal risk. That doesn't mean it will always help absolute returns, but it is not a cause for major concern.

7. Always/only using traditional active management isn't optimal for international equity exposure.

Despite the conventional wisdom that the inefficiency of international markets requires active management, it is important to remember that costs are typically higher outside the home country. And the more the manager trades, the higher these costs can be.

Traditional active funds have higher costs and fees due to higher turnover, a disadvantage of approximately 100 bps, resulting in a performance hurdle of approximately 150 bps relative to the index. Exploiting inefficiency is easier imagined than done: while many active managers beat benchmarks like EAFE in the 90s by systematically underweighting Japan, this is a much harder exercise today.

Furthermore, the move by MSCI and other benchmark providers to float-adjustment and broader coverage will provide fewer outperformance opportunities in non-index stocks. The most important benefit of international diversification comes from simply getting the exposure - international/global index funds let investors own the market and thus efficiently capture the primary benefit of foreign equities.

8. Global index investment is anything but passive.

Investment styles are often broadly divided into active and passive. The term passive is used to indicate the lack of a mandate to produce an excess return over the benchmark. However, in practice, a well run index fund is anything but passive. The first decision is the choice of benchmarks - this depends on the client's preferences for factors such as comprehensiveness, investability and degree of acceptance. The next step is to decide how to weight the component countries if the choice is a regional/global benchmark. The default is of course market capitalization weights. But, several other weighting methodologies exist - equal weights, minimum variance weights, GDP weights etc. For any set of weights except market capitalization weights, the rebalancing schedule also needs to be decided. That could again be based on either a calendar cycle or on a target percentage deviation from the initial weights.

Replicating the performance of the index within countries is not just a matter of buying the initial set of assets and letting them run. There is a litany of events that need to be addressed on a regular basis. These include reinvesting dividends, ensuring the optimal decision is made during all types corporate actions and managing the level of cash efficiently. A key area that differentiates a good index manager is how they respond to large index changes. Each index change requires a specific trading strategy that takes into account the magnitude of changes, the period between announcement and implementation, the amount to be traded and the presence of other parties on the same and opposite sides of the trade.

9. If you invest internationally 'a-la-carte' make sure you use the appropriate vehicles.

ADRs can be an effective tool to buy foreign stocks, but can give lumpy exposure. Single country closed-end funds tend to have erratic discounts and very high expenses. Regional mutual funds (and closed-end funds) provide uncertain asset allocation within the region - it's hard to know exactly what exposure you're putting in your portfolio.

International/global Exchange-Traded Funds (both country/regional and global sectors) are appropriate and efficient for both short-term and long-term investors - and for both passive and active approaches . You know what's in the fund, you can get in and out efficiently and at close to NAV, and you can use their modular structure to create virtually any variety of customized portfolios.

www.barclaysglobal.com

Lueder Schumacher

Lueder Schumacher is Co-Head of the European utilities team at Deutsche Bank, with a particular focus on German and Austrian utilities.

He joined NatWest Markets in 1996 having previously worked with Kleinwort Benson. Following the takeover of Bankers Trust, the utilities team, which has consistently ranked in the top three of all major investor polls over the past several years, has now become part of Deutsche Bank.

The utilities sector

Introduction

Utilities are generally valued just like other stocks, that is multiples such as EV/EBITDA, P/CF or a DCF provide a fair value range which can be broken on either side by certain overruling investment themes For example during the TMT bubble the global utilities sector showed almost a perfect negative correlation to NASDAQ as funds were withdrawn from defensive funds. However, utilities have a few distinguishing characteristics that make the valuation a bit more complicated.

1. Watch the use of cash.

Because utilities operate in a mature industry, they often have more money available than they can reasonably expect to invest in their core business. This leads to either diversification or re-investment risk, as utilities start to acquire other companies to put their cash to use.

2. Discounted cash flow valuations can give inflated numbers.

Further problems could arise from political or regulatory pressures, as utilities try to avoid showing an 'embarrassing richness', which could draw attention to their cash piles. The need to invest their cash flow irrespective of the availability of attractive opportunities means that utilities often struggle to invest their free cash flow at a NPV (net present value) larger than zero. In turn this means that a DCF (discounted cash flow) valuation can give inflated results. A DDM model (dividend discount model) therefore provides a more conservative approach.

3. Utilities require a higher equity risk premium.

The uncertainties of regulation also mean that utilities usually require a bigger equity risk premium to allow for the added uncertainty - a fact that contradicts the supposed predictability and associated safety of the cash flows.

4. Utilities can behave like bonds.

If regulation is very tight, utilities can become bond proxies, with a safe and predictable dividend flow, but little incentive to create extra value.

5. Watch out for the conglomerate discount.

Sometimes the urge to invest the free cash flow creates conglomerate structures, which result in a conglomerate discount being applied to the sum-of-the-parts of the Group. The reversal of this process, the focus on the core business and disposal of, usually non-profitable, non-core activities, then leads to additional performance as the conglomerate discount disappears.

6. Invest in companies that are restructuring.

• First, invest in utilities that are restructuring (for example E.ON and RWE in Germany).

• Second, invest in utilities that can re-invest their free cash flow in their core business (e.g. Edison in Italy).

• Third, invest in utilities that have accepted the difficulty of re-investing their free cash flow and opt instead to return cash to shareholders via special dividends and/or share buy backs (e.g. UK utilities in the past).

Charles Schwab

Charles R. Schwab is founder, Chairman of the Board and Co-Chief Executive Officer of The Charles Schwab Corporation. Mr. Schwab started his San Francisco based firm in 1971 as a traditional brokerage company and in 1974 became a pioneer in the discount brokerage business. Today, the firm is one of the nation's largest financial services firms, serving 7.7 million active investors with $858 billion in client assets.

Books

Charles Schwab's New Guide to Financial Independence, Random House USA Children's Books, 2004
Make Money Work for You Instead of You Working for It: Lessons from a Portfolio Manager, John Wiley & Sons Inc, 2004
It Pays to Talk, Random House USA Children's Books, 2002
Succeeding with What You Have (1920), R A Kessinger Publishing Co, 2003
You're Fifty-Now What? Investing for the Second Half of Your Life, Crown Business, 2001
Charles Schwab's Guide to Financial Independence, Crown Business, 1998
How to Be Your Own Stockbroker, MacMillan, 1985

Schwab principles for long-term investing

1. Start with the basics for long-term investing.

Begin by setting aside in cash at least two to six months' living expenses - an emergency fund that will be available in the event of illness or a period of unemployment. Then take advantage of employer-sponsored retirement plans and IRAs by contributing the maximum amount allowed. Finally, commit yourself to regular investing now so that you and your family will have enough later.

2. Get started now.

Every year you put off investing makes accomplishing your ultimate retirement goals even more difficult. As a rule of thumb, for every five years you wait, you may need to double your monthly investing amount to achieve the same retirement income. Social Security and pension plans alone are not enough for a comfortable retirement.

3. Know yourself.

Understand yourself as an investor: your emotions, your fears, and your tolerance for risk. Make sure you choose investments that you're comfortable with and that are appropriate for your long term goals. For some investors, particularly those with large or complex portfolios who want ongoing investment management, the services of a fee-compensated financial advisor may be appropriate.

4. Invest for growth.

Invest in stocks, either individually or in mutual funds, for long-term growth. In any given year, stocks can be more volatile than other investments, but over time, stocks have typically outperformed all other types of investments while staying ahead of inflation. Stocks should be the core of a long-term investing strategy.

5. Take a long-term view.

Patience is a virtue. Maintain the discipline to hold onto or add to appropriate investments through down markets as well as up markets.

6. Build a diversified portfolio.

In deciding how to allocate your assets, be sure to diversify, both among asset classes (stocks, bonds, and cash equivalents), and within each class. Choose an appropriate asset allocation model. Doing so can spread risk over a variety of investments and may provide more consistent and reliable outcomes.

For many investors, broad-based index funds are an excellent investment strategy. Index funds are a sound, low-cost choice for a core holding designed to track the market's performance.

7. Consider bonds and cash for diversification and income.

Bonds and cash can play an important role in an investor's portfolio, providing solutions for income and diversification needs. But to achieve your long-term growth objectives, look to stocks and stock mutual funds.

8. Minimize your expenses.

Over the long run, sales charges, loads, and high expenses can drag down the performance of even a well-diversified portfolio. Reduce your investment expenses by using no-load funds, low-cost stock and bond trading services, and tax-efficient mutual funds. For many investors, a buy-and-hold strategy can minimize the impact of capital gains taxes.

9. Stay on track.

Review your portfolio at least once a year, and certainly whenever personal circumstances change. You'll need to evaluate the performance of your investments against relevant risk-adjusted benchmarks, and, when necessary, to rebalance your portfolio to stay on track with your long-term financial goals.

10. Become a lifelong investor.

Investing for growth shouldn't stop when you retire. To make your money work for you throughout your retirement years, keep investing a portion of your portfolio for growth. Don't automatically shift all of your money into fixed-income and money market investments too early.

---

www.schwab.com

'Most of the time the market rises. Unless it is a real bear market, all attempts at market timing backfire and become very costly. But when you actually encounter a real bear market, recognizing it and taking corrective actions is near life saving.'

Ken Fisher

Gary Shilling

Dr. Gary Shilling is President of A. Gary Shilling & Co., Inc., an economic consulting firm. He has written a column for Forbes since 1983 and has become known as 'Doctor Disinflation'.

Books

How to Survive and Thrive in the Coming Wave of Deflation, McGraw-Hill, 1999

Investment strategies for a deflationary era

Introduction

Long-term, I forecast chronic deflation of 1% to 2% per year. Not the demand-deficient 'bad' deflation of the 1930s, but the 'good' deflation of excess supply - typical of peacetime when excess government spending is absent and especially during periods like the late 1800s, the 1920s and again today when bursts of new tech accelerate productivity. As spelled out in my recent book, *Deflation,* a successful investment strategy in this environment will be quite different than what worked during the now-ending age of inflation. Here are 11 elements in a winning strategy.

1. Treasury bonds are beautiful in deflation.

Long Treasury yields will fall to 3%. With deflation of 1% to 2%, real returns will run 4% to 5%, about twice the postwar average, but not especially high by long-term historical standards. Treasurys will also benefit from shrinking supply as federal surpluses lead to debt retirement. Further, Treasurys have three sterling features. They are the world's best credits, have little problem with being called well before maturity and have gigantic liquidity.

2. Avoid junk bonds.

In your zeal for yield, remember that junk bonds are really low-quality stocks that trade more on the issuing company's earnings prospects or on developing countries' financial plight than in relation to interest rates. Many junk bonds have been disasters in recent years, and the world of deflation may not be any kinder to them.

3. Don't expect great returns from stocks.

In mild deflation, stocks in general will be attractive, but a far cry from the tulip bulb-quality speculation of the late 1990s. Profits will grow in line with corporate sales, or about 4% to 4.5% per year in real terms. P/Es, governed primarily by interest rates in the long run, will stabilize along with bond yields. So, stocks will rise in line with profits, or 4% to 4.5% annually in real terms and in line with historical experience. With dividend yields returning to around 3%, total returns will average 7% to 7.5% in real terms, or 5.5% without deflation - very disappointing to those who think that the norm is the 1994-1999 era when the S&P 500 rose over 20% per year consecutively.

4. Risk-adjusted, Treasury bonds will be at least as attractive as stocks.

In the earlier postwar era, stocks way outperformed bonds, with the S&P 500 returning 13% per year in the 1948-2000 years while Treasury bonds returned 6%. But inflation reigned and real interest rates were low in that era. In mild deflation, the inherent riskiness and volatility of stocks will at least erase the difference between their nominal return of 5.5% and the 3% yield we foresee for long Treasurys.

5. Forget global diversification to reduce portfolio volatility.

Major country government bond markets move together, especially after adjusting for currency movements, as well they should. Quality differences are similar and any price gaps are arbitraged away quickly. As for stocks, in this age of 24-hour trading in a global economy dominated by multinational companies, markets often move in parallel, especially in times of U.S.-generated trouble. Furthermore, the dollar should remain strong in the forthcoming deflationary era, so many foreign investment gains for U.S. investors will be at least wiped out as foreign currencies fall against the buck.

6. New tech winners will be tough to find.

The productivity and excess supply spawned by new tech will be great for consumers, but investors will find few consistent long-term winners. As in past bursts of new tech, computers, semiconductors, the internet, telecommunications and biotech will continue to kill themselves with over-investment and excess capacity. Further, new tech is always superseded by newer tech. Product cycles continue to shorten, and competition will remain excruciating while, as in the past, today's new tech gizmos become tomorrow's profitless commodities.

7. Avoid old tech companies that produce big ticket consumer goods and services.

In deflation, consumers wait for lower prices before buying, which creates excess capacity and unwanted inventories. Price cuts to stimulate sales only confirm buyers' expectations, leading to further waiting for still-lower prices, etc. in a self-feeding cycle. In addition, American consumers should soon end their two decade borrowing and spending binge and embark on a saving spree. Expensive, postponeable purchases will be delayed. These two forces will damage autos, appliances, conventionally-built housing and airline travel. But don't forget that big ticket new tech gear like PCs are also vulnerable as consumers wait for lower prices and concentrate on saving.

8. Firms that aid savers and investors will thrive in mild deflation.

The likely saving spree by American consumers and disillusionment with do-it-yourself investing after the collapse in the late 1990s stock bubble will be good news for financial planners, asset managers, savings institutions, life insurance companies, mutual funds, and trust banks and others oriented toward high net worth customers. At the same time, credit card issuers, sub-par lenders and many real estate lenders will be hurt.

9. Real estate will suffer.

Low real interest rates and inflation spurred real estate in the earlier postwar era. With 20% down on a property with a 10% mortgage and 15% annual appreciation, you made a cool 35% return each year.

Nevertheless, as in the past, real estate prices will fall in the upcoming deflationary era and real interest rates will be much higher. So, with about 4% nominal mortgage rates and the same 20% downpayment, you'll lose 26% each year if the property price falls 2% per annum.

Further, real estate will suffer since the postwar babies are all housed, thrifty consumers will visit malls less and buy less, businesses will put more people in a given office space and encourage more teleconferences and fewer hotel-utilizing business trips, consumers will reduce travel and hotel and motel use and will postpone new houses while more efficiently utilizing already-ample space. In addition, new commercial buildings will be cheaper than old ones so, in reverse of earlier postwar practice, landlords will want long leases while tenants will demand shorter ones so they can threaten to move in a year or two if the rent isn't cut.

Real estate investment won't disappear in deflation, but rents will need to be high enough to cover ongoing costs, falling property values and high real interest rates while still providing an acceptable profit. Note that other tangible assets, including antiques, may also be trying investments in deflation.

10. Manufactured housing and rental apartments will succeed.

With real estate a difficult investment in deflation, many Americans will no longer combine their investments with their abodes - owner-occupied houses or apartments. This will help manufactured houses, which, due to factory efficiencies, cost about half as much per square foot as site-built structures and often have the same or higher quality. Also, multiwide units, where the sections are attached on site, are often indistinguishable from site-built houses.

In addition, factory-built housing tends to be smaller, which will appeal to thrifty consumers, young families, empty nesters, retirement home buyers and anyone else seeking cost-effective shelter. Similarly, rental apartments will be attractive as people separate their homes from their investments. Young families will rent apartments longer until they really need single-family housing, and older people who don't enjoy cutting the lawn may sell their money pits sooner and move into rental units.

Direct real estate ownership will be difficult in deflation (see #9) so REITs that concentrate on rental apartments may be better for investors than direct ownership.

11. Commodities will be weak.

Global deflation means an excess supply world with chronically-weak prices for commodities ranging from copper to sugar to crude oil to gold. Furthermore, the world's output will more and more be in products with high intellectual content - goods like semiconductor chips and services such as medical care - not commodities like steel and cement.

---

www.agaryshilling.com

Jeremy Siegel

Professor Jeremy Siegel has been a Professor of Finance at The Wharton School of the University of Pennsylvania since 1976. Professor Siegel received his Ph.D. from MIT and taught for four years at the Graduate School of Business of the University of Chicago before joining the Wharton faculty.

His book, Stocks for the Long Run, was named by *Business Week* as one of the top ten business books of the year in 1994. An expanded version was published in 1998 and was named one of the ten-best investment books of all time by *The Washington Post*.

Books

The Future for Investors: Why the Tried and the True Triumph Over the Bold and the New, Crown Business, 2005
The Strategy of Core Investing: Profiting from Stocks That Will Stand the Test of Time, Free Press, 2004
Stocks for the Long Run, McGraw-Hill, 1998 - expanded edition, 3rd 2002

Stocks for the long run, and diversification

1. Stocks should constitute the overwhelming proportion of all long-term financial portfolios.

Stocks are unquestionably riskier than bonds in the short run, but for longer periods of time, their risk falls below that on bonds. For 20 year holding periods, they have never fallen behind inflation, while bonds and bills have fallen 3 per cent per year behind inflation over the same time period. So although it might appear to be riskier to hold stocks than bonds, precisely the opposite is true if you take a long-term view.

2. Investors worried about equity exposure should consider government inflation-indexed bonds as an alternative.

Inflation-indexed bonds offer after-inflation returns that are competitive with standard bonds, and much safer in terms of purchasing power because the rate they pay is linked to inflation. Although they currently offer only half the long term yield of stocks, history suggest that over ten year periods they will outperform equities about one-quarter of the time. For investors who do not have a long-term time horizon, they are a safe alternative to stocks.

3. Invest the largest percentage - the core holdings of your stock portfolio - in highly diversified mutual funds with very low expense ratios.

Unless you can consistently choose stocks with superior returns, a goal very few investors have reached, your best balance of risk and reward will be achieved by investing in index funds or other highly diversified funds with very low expense ratios. Index funds do not attempt to beat the market, but by holding a large number of stocks in proportion to their market capitalization, they match the performance of the market as a whole at very low cost. From your point of view, matching the market is good enough to obtain the superior returns that have been achieved in stocks over time.

4. Place up to one-quarter of your stocks in mid- and small-cap stock funds.

Small stocks sometimes outperform large stocks, and sometimes underperform them. Since it is not possible to predict the times of relative performance, and since it is impractical to invest in all small caps individually, the best strategy is to invest in a small-stock index fund and leave your money there. If you ignore small caps entirely, your long-term returns are likely to be lower.

5. Allocate about one quarter of your stock portfolio to international equities, divided equally among Europe, the Far East, and emerging markets.

Since almost two-third's of the world's capital is now located outside the United States, international equities must be the basis of any well-diversified portfolio. Japanese stocks, despite their long bear market, should not be excluded because they have a low correlation with the rest of the world's markets, making them good portfolio diversifiers.

6. Do not overweight the emerging markets. High growth is already factored into the prices of many of the stocks of these countries.

There is a tendency for many investors to overinvest in emerging markets where promises of capital appreciation are high. But the markets of developing countries are extremely risky. It is important to spread your investing globally between Latin America, the Far East, and Central and Eastern Europe. As investors witnessed in 1997, problems can strike whole geographical areas quickly, such as the currency crises that began in Thailand

and spread to other Asian markets. Again, diversification is the key to reducing your risk exposure.

7. Large 'growth' stocks perform as well as large 'value' stocks over the long run.

Tech stocks on the whole have not been good long-term performers and investors should avoid or underweight stocks with P/E ratios over 50. Historically, large growth stocks with low dividend yield and high P/E ratios, have performed just as well over the long run as large value stocks with higher dividend yields and lower P/E ratios. But when the P/E ratio becomes excessive, as it did in 2000 for tech stocks, it is mandatory to cut down on one's exposure.

8. The 'Dow 10' strategy of buying the 10 highest-yielding Dow Industrial stocks has outperformed the market consistently over long periods of time.

This outperformance is mostly due to the fact that all of the Dow Industrials have been superior companies in their respective industries. These stocks are very responsive to a contrarian strategy that accumulates the stocks when they have fallen over a period of several years. A high dividend yield by itself is not a very important criterion in performance.

9. Small value stocks appear to significantly outperform small growth stocks.

In contrast to the big capitalization stocks, value does appear to outperform growth among the mid- and small-cap stocks. The very small growth stocks do worst of any class of stocks examined. Dreams of buying another Microsoft or Intel often compel investors to overpay for these stocks.

10. Avoid initial public offerings (IPOs) unless you buy at the offering price.

If you can buy new issues at their offering price, it is usually wise to do so. But don't hold on. IPOs, which often include small growth stocks, are extremely poor performers for long-term investors.

www.jeremysiegel.com

'Making an investment in a supposed beneficiary of a government decision is highly dangerous, because helping private sector companies make money is bottom of any government's list of priorities, while getting them to spend money on the government's behalf for no return is pretty high up.'

Max King

Howard L. Simons

Howard L. Simons directs the Trading and Energy tracks at the Illinois Institute of Technology's Center for Law & Financial Markets.

In addition to his CLFM duties, Mr. Simons is the Technical Editor of *Futures* magazine, for which he has written more than seventy articles since 1994. He also writes the weekly Futures Shock column for TheStreet.com.

Books
The Dynamic Option Selection System, John Wiley, 1999

Market interrelationships

1. Do you want to be long (short), or don't you?

Unless you were engaging in an arbitrage strategy, the position you have in a market is more important than the price at which you entered.

2. Are you hedging the dimes, or hedging the dollars?

Perfection is not the objective of a hedge strategy. Avoiding 80% of a major disaster is more important than worrying about the remaining 20%.

3. Own the decision points.

Never structure a position so that someone else can force your exit. Every time you've written an option, either directly or embedded, you've surrendered control of your trade to someone without your best interests at heart.

4. Smart generals run to the head of the troops.

The first objective of any trader is to find the path of least resistance, so follow the people who've found it. What good is a posthumous award for bravery? If you stay in the game, there's always tomorrow.

5. Markets move further and faster than we ever believe.

Traders protect themselves against small setbacks, and bet the large ones won't happen. That's why they do.

6. Being wrong is one thing, staying wrong is another.

Good traders take losses quickly.

7. The price is the news.

Understanding why a move is happening has no effect on your equity.

8. 'Can't go there' and 'can't stay there' are two different things.

Markets can reach unsustainable valuations and remain there for some time before returning to rationality.

9. The time to buy is when there's blood in the streets.

Someone else's, not yours. You can't buy the bottom if you've already lost all of your money.

10. When you trade a sympathetic market, all you get is sympathy.

If you're in a bad Lucent trade, don't start messing with Nortel. You'll only make a simple problem worse.

11. When you age bad wine, you get old bad wine.

Waiting for a position to reverse in your favor is a bad use of both mental and financial capital.

12. Take care of the downside, and the upside will take care of itself.

If you know the worst that can befall you and are willing to accept it, time and volatility will work in your favor.

Brian Skiba

Brian Skiba is a co-founder and Managing Director of Transformation Capital Partners, a private merchant bank in London.

He was Head of Software & IT Services research for Lehman Brothers in Europe until May 2001, and was a ranked analyst by Institutional Investor in both Europe and the US as well as Reuters and Extel. Before moving to Europe, Mr. Skiba was in charge of covering Enterprise Software companies for Lehman Brothers from their San Francisco office.

The enterprise software sector

1. Operating leverage is excessive in a software company.

An enterprise software business model is almost all fixed costs (people, facilities, marketing) and extremely low cost of production. Consequently after all fixed costs are met in the quarter, the money flows directly from the top line to the pretax level with often less than 5% cost of goods. When the industry is accelerating, software companies tend to 'crush' their numbers through this extreme operating leverage. This is why investors are willing to pay high price-earnings valuations in good times. The earnings estimates are likely to be dramatically revised upwards.

2. Operating leverage works against the company in tough times.

Unfortunately, operating leverage works in the opposite way too; and with impunity. When a company falls short on the top-line revenue number by maybe 5%, earnings can be short by 50%. Consequently, a shortfall in revenue is treated as a disaster in a software company, as these companies cannot quickly or easily change their cost structure - implying that forward earnings estimates are likely to plummet. A 50% correction on a software company is the norm when they miss earnings.

3. Buy 'real' software companies when they gap down.

Software companies are severely punished for missing numbers. And in *most* cases, a miss of a quarter spells trouble for the next few quarters or perhaps years. Rarely are these problems ironed out in the following quarter. But, for those investors with a 12-month investment horizon, buying an established software company, with a degree of size and maturity following a 50% gap-down can often be a winning strategy. The key is the company *must* be 'real' with size, scale, brand, product and proven execution skills. Patience will often pay off, but the time horizon must be at least 12 months.

4. People remain the key. Good product is necessary but second.

Software companies are nothing but a collection of people. The management, R&D talent, sales force, professional service and support organization all determine the execution level of the company. In most software markets, it is execution, not demand that remains the challenge. People must be honest, loyal and motivated to work for the company. Human talent is highly fluid, and once it begins to move from a company, it is like an unstoppable cancer.

5. If the software and the story sound too good - be cautious.

The world of software investing is littered with companies that had promising ideas, 'cool' technology and staggering industry forecasts as to the growth prospects, but somehow they often don't materialize. One reason is that people want to believe that software can solve world hunger, so they begin to dream about the unrealistic prospects. In some cases, like Lernout & Hauspie, the company made remarkable claims about its speech recognition capability, and the market was not really there yet. To make up for it, it 'created' some $200 million worth of fake sales, defrauded the investors, bankrupted the company and the founders are in a Belgium jail today.

6. News flow in normal times moves prices.

Valuations for software companies, in the short term, are highly impacted by movements in Nasdaq and in news flow. This is particularly so in a raging bull market. Software companies tend to put out a large number of press releases, the bulk of which are not material to the company's earnings prospects. Nonetheless, it puts the company back on the radar screen for technology investors, and a movement of 5-15% in a day from a press release is not atypical in a hot market.

7. Valuing a software company is all about forward growth expectations.

Ultimately, the value of a software company is determined by the free cash flow likely to be thrown off over the next 20+ years. Determining that cash flow is near impossible, but an educated guess begins with a model extrapolating forward revenue and earnings growth. Since the software model is an extremely leveraged one, rapid growth is usually combined with margin expansion, thus driving cash flow in the model. A modest drop in growth expectations can dramatically drop the forward expectations for cash flow as the impact works its way through the next 20 years in the model.

8. Software valuation movements tend to be highly correlated with the tech sector.

Most software companies tend to move in step with the Nasdaq and other technology indicators. In Europe, the TMT (telecom, media and technology) sector tends to move together, though European technology valuation tends to follow the US lead. In most cases, 80%+ of the movement of a software company stock is usually correlated with the technology-heavy indices like Nasdaq.

'Few competitive advantages are as difficult to fight as a brand name. An economic advantage can be overtaken eventually, a patent may be lifted, but a great brand can be sustained for years.'

Mike Kwatinetz

Jim Slater

Jim Slater was Chairman of the legendary financial conglomerate, Slater Walker Securities. He is the author of several investment books, and devised Really Essential Financial Statistics (REFS), the comprehensive monthly digest of financial data for stocks quoted on the London Stock Exchange. He is a popular public speaker and has lectured to both private investor and institutonal audiences on his method of investment.

Books

How to Become a Millionaire, Texere, 2000
Beyond the Zulu Principle, Orion, 1996
Investment Made Easy, Orion, 1994
The Zulu Principle, Orion, 1992

Building a margin of safety

1. Develop a method that suits you.

Carefully select a method of investment and then, based on personal experience and the performance of your portfolio, hone, temper and refine it until you are satisfied beyond doubt that it works for you. As you become more expert you can use several different methods at the same time according to market conditions.

2. Establish a margin of safety.

Any method, whether it be growth or value, should be based on establishing a margin of safety - a cushion between the amount you pay for a company's shares and the amount you believe they are worth. The attraction of building a margin of safety is that it helps to protect against downside risk and at the same time provides the scope for an upwards re-rating.

3. Adjust the margin of safety to your approach.

For growth stocks, a typical method embracing a margin of safety would be to seek out shares with strong earnings growth records and a relatively low price-earnings ratio in relation to their future growth rates. Ideally the growth rate should be at least one third more than the price-earnings ratio. To increase the safety factor, it is also highly desirable for the company to have a record of strong cash flow in relation to earnings per share and a strong balance sheet.

For value stocks, the margin of safety can be established by a low price-to-sales ratio, low price-to-book value and strong cash flow. Also with many undervalued asset situations it pays to look for recent relative strength and recent directors' buying which can be signals that a company is about to turn around.

4. Keep an eye on significant share dealings by directors.

Directors' buying is frequently linked to a change in a company's fortunes especially if the directors are buying a significant number of shares in a cluster of three or more. Equally, directors selling large tranches of shares is often a warning signal and should put you on red alert.

5. Judge management by their numbers, not by their manners.

The ability of management is very hard to quantify. If you go to see them or meet them at a presentation, they naturally put their best foot forward. Management can best be judged by several years of good results with brokers' forecasts confirming that they are likely to continue. The financial results are the best judge of management, not the people going to see them.

6. Look for positive relative strength to corroborate your view of a share.

Shares that perform well in the market are often winners in the making. With growth stocks, relative strength in the previous twelve months should be positive and certainly greater than the one month figure. O'Shaugnessy found in *What Works on Wall Street* that relative strength was in most years the best single investment criterion.

7. Run profits and cut losses.

This is much easier said than done but it is far better practice to add to winners and pare down holdings that are not performing well. This way your losses will always be small and your gains can be gigantic. Remember that the power of compounding is the eighth wonder of the world.

8. Never stop learning.

There is always a faster gun, so keep reading books on investment by well-known and established experts, attend investment conferences and consider joining an investment club. Also make sure that you have a regular source of sound statistical stockmarket data. In the UK, Company REFS does, of course, come to mind!

9. Be tax efficient.

Use annual capital gains tax allowances, PEPs, ISAs and a personal pension scheme to the maximum possible extent.

10. Don't kid yourself.

Do not be fooled by your own excuses. Measure your investment performance honestly and regularly and if, over a year or so, you find that you are not consistently beating the market, delegate to an expert manager or invest in a unit trust or tracker fund and use your surplus time and energy elsewhere.

---

www.global-investor.com/slater

'Be wary of companies with large convertible issues. This often indicates that a company cannot issue further equity, possibly because its shares are below the price of the last issue, or does not have a satisfactory bond rating.'

Colin McLean

Andrew Smithers

Andrew Smithers founded Smithers & Co. Ltd which provides economics-based asset allocation advice to 80 of the world's largest fund management companies. He is a columnist for London's *Evening Standard* and Tokyo's Nikkei Kinnyu Shimbon's *Market Eye*.

Books

Valuing Wall Street, (with Stephen Wright), McGraw-Hill, 2000
Japan's Key Challenges for the 21st Century (with David Asher), published in Japanese by Diamond

---

Protecting wealth and valuing the stock market

1. Never delegate asset selection.

Your interests, as the investor, are different from those of your broker or fund manager. It's not their fault; it's a fact of life. In the case of the broker this is obvious. You both want to make money. The more you deal, the more money he makes and, as a general rule, the less you do. But your fund manager also has different interests from you. As I write [July 2001], Wall Street is over-valued by about twice. The risks of the stock market falling over the next 12 months are around 70%. No one who understands this would put his money into shares. But for a fund manager the risks are different. If he goes liquid with his client's money, he has a 30% chance of damaging his business and possibly losing his job.

2. Learn how to value the stock market.

Remember that price matters. Anyone who tells you that it's always sensible to buy stocks is dotty. It's a sign of the times. No one said this in 1932, which was a wonderful time to buy stocks, but lots said it in 2000 which was a lousy year. Remember it can take you up to 20 years to get your money back even from a badly timed purchase of an indexed fund, and individual companies go bust. It's quite easy to know when share prices have gone too high. In a competitive economy, everything from toothbrushes to computers sells for what it costs to produce. The same is true for companies, though their prices can be above or below cost for several years. This is the problem. Sensible investors can have a bad time at cocktail parties for several years.

They will get out of the market too soon in the bubble years. There is no answer to this. If there were, the stock market would never get over-priced. Sensible investors can't be greedy or boast at parties. (This doesn't just apply to bull markets. Humility is valued in those rare bear market parties).

3. Know your aims.

Think carefully about what you want. If you are saving for a comfortable retirement, remember that when you invest. Don't forget to diversify - concentrated portfolios have huge risks. It's different if you think you are rich enough to retire and have made some money. Then you can have fun trying to pick winners. Unless the market is generally over priced (remember Rule 2), this is rather like playing the tables at Monte Carlo, but with odds in your favour. Instead of being certain to lose if you play long enough, you should win and you could win a lot. It's not very sensible, but if you want to have an outside chance of riches it's better than anything else on offer.

4. Remember your age.

If you are aged 30, stocks will normally be the right asset class for you. Even then remember Rule 2. If you are 70 it won't. Concentrate on TIPS (Treasury Inflation-Protection Securities) or cash. For ages between 30 and 70, the proportion of TIPS and cash should rise steadily. Over 10 years the real return on 10 year TIPS is virtually certain, but stocks can give big losses. At 70, 10 years is a lifetime.

5. Understand risk.

Stocks are highly volatile and therefore very risky. They are less risky over the long term than over shorter periods. In addition to the normal way that risks even out over time, there is an added reason for this. It is because their long-term returns tend to 'revert to a mean'. After periods of low returns, the next period has an above average chance of being a good time to hold stocks. Equally after a good period - and the last 20 years have been phenomenal - it is a bad time to hold stocks.

6. Costs are important.

Investors nearly always underestimate the importance of costs. The longer term your investment horizon, the more important this is. Over the long term, the real return on stocks, before tax or expenses, has been around 6.5% p.a. So if inflation runs at 2.5%, the nominal return that an investor can reasonably expect is around 9%. If you get this over 30 years, and start with $200,000 you will have $2.6 million at the end. If your costs come to 2% p.a., which they easily can, you will only have $1.5 million.

7. So is tax.

This is even truer of tax. There are ways in the US and UK for investors to save tax-free for their retirement. If you paid tax at 30% every year the investor who would have got $2.6 million will only receive $1.25 million. If he paid 2% costs he would only get $700,000.

8. Get interested and enjoy it.

This is a hard world where professional investors' interests are in conflict with yours. Understanding investment pays better than trust. Those who enjoy learning are those who do it best. If you can, get interested; if you can't, get out.

www.smithersandco.co.uk

'Many investors try to place buys with limit orders just below the ask, and wind up missing the purchase. If you really want a stock, particularly a big position, place a limit order at the ask, or even slightly higher. You will at least get the order. Don't miss the train to shave a dime.'

Robert V. Green

Joel Stern

Joel Stern is managing partner of Stern Stewart & Co., the New York corporate finance firm which devised the concept of EVA. He has advised companies of all sizes and on all continents on the implementation of EVA processes, and has lectured widely at business schools in the USA and Europe.

Books

Against the Grain: How to Succeed in Business by Peddling Heresy, John Wiley & Sons Inc, 2003
The EVA Challenge, John Wiley, 2001
Revolution in Corporate Finance, Blackwell, 1998

EVA as an enhancer of shareholder value

Introduction

Each day, millions of managers systematically destroy shareholder value. Why? It is not because they are incompetent, nor is it because they are dishonest and are diverting corporate assets to their own use. No, it is because they are responding rationally to the compensation systems used by the vast majority of corporations which actually reward them for over-investing in mature industries, over-spending on labor-saving automation, and over-paying for acquisitions.

EVA is the system developed by Stern Stewart to bring the interests of managers back into line with the interests of shareholders. The rules below explain why their interests are often misaligned, and how the implementation of an EVA system encourages management to make decisions that enhance rather than destroy shareholder value.

1. Rewards based on growth in EPS lead to over-investment.

In most companies, the measure of success is accounting earnings (or earnings per share). This measure includes a deduction for interest paid on debt, but no charge for the cost of equity capital. The result is that earnings often go up even though economic performance declines, a fact that can propel over-investment. Consider a company that borrows at 8% interest and pays a tax rate of 40%. The company's after-tax borrowing cost is 4.8%. But if it finances new investments with a target ratio of 70% equity and 30% debt, its after-tax interest cost on added capacity is only 1.44% (30% of 4.8%). Any investment that returns more than 1.44%, even if it is far below the company's weighted average cost of capital, will cause earnings and EPS to rise. Managers who are rewarded for growing earnings are sure to over-invest in expansion that causes earnings to rise but returns less than the full cost of capital. They also will over-invest in labor-saving automation even when the full cost of capital on the new equipment exceeds the savings in labor costs, because the reduction in labor costs boosts earnings, while the greater cost of capital on additional equity goes uncounted.

2. Rewards based on size encourage empire-building.

A second reason that conventional compensation systems encourage managers to destroy wealth is that most of them are based in one way or another on size. Under the Hay system that has become virtually universal, an executive's fixed compensation is a function of the number of people reporting to him or her, the size of the budget or the amount of revenues. This carries down from the chief executive to virtually every manager in the company, so every manager profits by empire building and pursuing growth for its own sake, regardless of whether the new business earns enough to cover the cost of additional capital.

3. Capped incentive compensation plans backfire on shareholders.

Most managers have incentive compensation plans that are capped, often at 150% or so of the target bonus level. No matter how much wealth they create for shareholders, their compensation tops out at the bonus cap. Yet managers do have a way of working around the cap. If they can make the business bigger, their Hay points go up, and since the target bonus is a percentage of fixed pay, their potential bonuses go up as well. It's a formula for growth at any cost, no matter how much it hurts the shareholders. It's not that these managers want to diminish shareholder wealth. Quite the contrary. All things being equal, they would much rather increase shareholder wealth. But all things are not equal. Because non-EVA systems use the wrong performance measure and poorly designed incentive structures, they make it perfectly rational for managers to do things that owners never would do. The managers, like the shareholders, are victims of perverse rewards.

4. The present value of expected future free cash flows is mathematically identical to a firm's economic book value plus the present value of expected future EVA.

The theory of modern finance and the associated empirical evidence tie changes in value to changes in the expected growth in EVA. Modern finance says that a firm's value is the present value of the free cash flows it will generate in the future. While it is not obvious to everyone at first glance, the present value of expected future free cash flows is mathematically identical to a firm's economic book value plus the present value of expected future EVA. Thus, if management drives the firm to increase EVA, this is consistent with increasing shareholder value.

5. To provide a superior return, management must bring about increases in EVA which exceed market expectations.

Since the current share price of a stock already incorporates current expectations about future EVA, increasing EVA at the rate already expected will simply earn shareholders a rate of return equal to the cost of equity capital, which is the required return for equity risk. To provide a *superior* return, management must bring about increases in EVA greater than the figure expected by the market.

To do this, management should focus on measuring economic book value and the components of EVA very carefully, and then use supportive management tools that are reinforced by an incentive system based on sustainable improvements in EVA. If CEOs and their management teams are paid significant rewards for achieving sustainable improvements in EVA, that is what they will strive to do. And those who succeed will produce significant improvements in shareholder value.

6. EVA makes a charge for equity capital.

In the accountant's version of residual income, management gets to use ordinary equity free of charge. This encourages the use of too much capital in the business because not enough is charged for the use of capital. EVA is Stern Stewart's special version of residual income

First, we levy a charge for equity capital at the minimum rate of return that shareholders demand.

Second, we make modest adjustments to both income and capital in measuring the return on capital employed. As an example, we capitalize investments in intangible assets such as research and development and brand value. This removes the charges for those investments from the income statement and puts them on the balance sheet. The reason accountants expense these items is that accounting originally evolved as a framework to help lenders determine if borrowers could repay indebtedness. If a firm fails, intangible assets clearly will have little or no value. EVA, in contrast, focuses on going-concern value - the measure that matters most to shareholders - instead of the lender's liquidation value.

7. EVA discourages excessive off-balance sheet borrowing.

When management borrows off the balance sheet, the borrowings are not recorded as capital employed under the normal accounting framework. The effect is to overstate the return on capital employed. EVA requires adjustments for off-balance-sheet borrowing - for instance, for operating leases - so that the borrowings are capitalized and the return on capital accurately reflected. If managers know that they cannot inflate ROCE through off-balance-sheet borrowing, they will be less inclined to do it.

8. EVA discourages expensive acquisitions.

EVA requires that goodwill on acquisitions remain on the balance sheet as part of the price paid. Only by including the full price paid as part of capital employed - and charging for the use of capital - will management be discouraged from overpaying. At the same time, we do not want to discourage genuinely profitable acquisitions or other investments simply because they do not have an immediate payoff. So we record strategic investments with delayed payoffs in off-balance-sheet 'suspense accounts', and move them onto the balance sheet (and into the calculation of EVA) when the investments are expected to produce income. In the interim, however, the suspense account grows by the cost of capital it has yet to produce. Some adjustments to accounting are industry specific. In natural-resource companies, for example, each year's gains or losses on reserves in the ground should be included in EVA.

9. EVA works best when it is used at all levels of an organization.

Once management decides to use EVA, it must ensure that EVA tools for decision-making are carried down through the organization. With the reinforcement of a strong incentive plan tied to changes in EVA, companies will not consider capital outlays that are value destroying. Investments earning less than the cost of capital will be rejected, both because they destroy shareholder value and because they reduce bonus payments. At the same time, managers will rush to make investments that increase shareholder value and bonuses. Most firms implement incentives down through middle management, but the very best performers carry it right down to the shop floor, so that all employees can earn significant variable pay and more closely align their own interests with those of shareholders.

www.sternstewart.com

Thomas Stridsman

Thomas Stridsman is a senior editor for *Active Trader,* a magazine devoted to helping the short-term trader on the American stock market.

Between 1997 and 1999 he was associate editor of *Futures* magazine, specializing in technical analysis, rule-based trading, and advanced money management techniques. While at *Futures* he also appeared as a speaker at industry seminars and conferences.

Before moving to Chicago in 1997, Stridsman operated his own web-based trading advisory service in Sweden and was chair of the Swedish Technical Analysts Federation.

Books

Trading Systems that Work, Irwin, 2000
Trading Systems and Money Management: A Guide to Trading and Profiting in Any Market (Irwin Trader's Edge S.) McGraw-Hill Education, 2003

Building and trading a rule-based strategy

1. It's not the goal that's important, it's how you get there.

Take your time, do your research, and make sure you feel good about yourself while doing it. Analyzing and trading the markets should be fun, and if you don't have fun, you're likely to become sloppy and make mistakes. Also, if you don't have the means to take certain risks, stay away from them, as taking too much risk will make you feel bad and act in panic, resulting in bad decisions and losses you couldn't afford in the first place.

2. Garbage in, garbage out.

When working on a trading strategy, make sure you have good data to work with that are suitable for your purposes and goals. If your strategy is for the stock market, make sure it's correctly adjusted for splits, dividends, etc. If it is for the futures market, make sure your time series are put together correctly depending on what type of calculations you would like to perform. Comparisons between different markets and time frames always require percentage-based calculations.

The Book of Investing Rules

3. One tool, one purpose.

Just as you wouldn't try to build a house with just a screwdriver, don't expect your strategy to work in every market condition or trade. If you're trying to ride the trend, use analysis tools suitable for that purpose. If you're trying to pick tops and bottoms within the trend, use tools suitable for that. Because each trading tool won't work equally as well all the time, you need to have an arsenal of tools working for you simultaneously.

4. Learn from the past, don't dwell in it.

When putting together a trading strategy using historical data, avoid indulging in too much *"woulda, coulda, shoulda"*. How much you could have made in the past is not interesting. What you need to do is to use the data to build robust strategies on sound principles and statistically significant results. To do this you need to do all your analysis work based on percentages instead of dollars or points.

5. A well-working strategy is better than a profitable strategy.

A well-working strategy is a strategy that works equally well on several different markets over several periods, measured in percentage terms. However, just because a strategy works well on a specific market it doesn't have to be profitable as long as the costs associated with trading it are not too high. Therefore, first make sure each strategy is well working, then make it profitable by only using it on suitable markets.

6. Compare the apples with the oranges.

Because a well-working trading model should work equally well - on average and over time - on several different markets, you have to assume that there are no significant differences in market behavior between any markets. Whether this is a fact or not is open to argument, but this is what you have to assume to build a robust trading strategy and trade it with sophisticated money management. And again, to achieve this you need to work with percentages.

7. Strive for mediocrity.

Know what your average trade looks like and strive to repeat it. Each time you deviate from it you, put yourself in unfamiliar territory that might result in bad decisions. If you don't know why your strategy is producing results that are better than expected, that very reason, or its inverse, might be what ruins you in the end, as you have no way to prepare for a market condition that you could see coming but foolishly ignored.

8. Diversify away the risks, not the profits.

When using a fixed fractional money management strategy, the fraction of your capital that you risk per trade equals your worst expected outcome. Therefore, risking more does not necessarily increase the growth rate of your capital, but will increase your risk. Furthermore, proper money management will speed up equity growth, provided that the markets traded are as low correlated with each other as possible. This means that even a losing market can add to the bottom line.

9. Your worst drawdown doesn't have to be in front of you.

For a portfolio traded with proper money management, the whole will be greater than its parts. Just because two markets are likely to be profitable when traded by themselves they don't have to be profitable when traded together. Therefore, the markets need to be picked so that when one market zigs the other market zags. Not to know which markets to trade and the optimal amount to risk, is to trade with a blindfold, balancing the drawdown precipice.

10. Optisize instead of optimize.

Every trading strategy has a constant optimal amount to risk relative to your equity. For a correctly built strategy, there is no way to predict the outcome of the next trade. The only amount you can predict is how much to risk. Therefore, you're much better off optisizing that amount, rather than optimizing the exact entry point. Optisizing means to make the most out of each trade in relation to your available equity, your overall strategy and other trading alternatives.

www.activetradermag.com

'Silver is the world's money of last resort. Should a severe economic collapse occur, leaving paper assets worthless, silver will be primary currency for purchase of goods and services. Thus, every investor should own some physical silver.'

David Morgan

Alan Sugden

Alan Sugden is a graduate of the Royal Naval Staff College, Greenwich, and a Sloan Fellow of the London Business School. He spent 20 years in the City as an analyst and fund manager, running the then £100m (now £850m) Schroder Recovery Fund for several years. He is a former director of Schroder Investment Management Ltd.

Alan Sugden's successful collaboration with Geoffrey Holmes produced nine editions of the definitive book on financial statement analysis for investors - *Interpreting Company Reports and Accounts*.

Books

Interpreting Company Reports and Accounts, FT Prentice Hall

Key questions for stock pickers

1. Do you like the sector? If you don't like the sector, don't invest in it, no matter how good the management may be.

Backing first class management in a declining sector is usually unrewarding. For example John Corrin led a management buy-out from ICI, paying £400,000 for a subsidiary that was losing £900,000 a year and was due for closure. Less than 5 years later they were taken over by Allied Textile for £10 million, and John Corrin became chief executive of Allied Textile.

John is head and shoulders above most management but, in the following years, although Allied Textile outperformed the Textile sector easily, it lost ground against the FT - All share index.

2. Is the company under the control of one person or one group of people? If so, other shareholders can be on a hiding to nothing.

For example, there is a ship repairing and leisure company listed on the London Stock Exchange whose chairman has taken full advantage of his controlling position by paying himself over £1.4 million in the last 10 years. His shareholders have had only two dividends in the same period.

What are the non-executive directors doing about it? You may well ask. Suffice to say that in 2000 there were two of them, each with a salary of

£6,000 per annum, compared with the Chairman/Chief Executive's £140,000 plus perks.

3. Is the post of Chairman and Chief Executive held by one and the same person? If so take care.

Research in the early 1980s on 'Company Pathology' showed that companies in which the posts were combined had more than a 50% higher chance of going bust than other listed companies. Maxwell (who had his two sons as Joint Managing Directors) and Asil Nadir at Polly Peck are two classics, but there are plenty of others.

Even if the company doesn't go bust, there's a danger of one man or woman having too much power. A recent example is Marks & Spencer which, in its unswerving loyalty to UK manufacturers, became strategically vulnerable in the rag trade. Most other retailers were increasingly sourcing from low cost countries. Marks & Spencer's Chairman was also its Chief Executive.

Remember that the most important duty of a Chairman is to replace the Chief Executive if he is not up to snuff. This can be difficult if they are one and the same person.

4. Are there any 'prestigious' names amongst the Non-Executive Directors? If so, don't rely on them to keep the company out of trouble.

Well known non-executive directors of companies that failed included: Lord Seiff (Sock Shop), Peter Walker and Lord Rippon (Maxwell), Prince Michael of Kent (London United), Professor Roland Smith (Pavion), Larry Tindale, much respected deputy chairman of 3i (Polly Peck) and Lord Stokes (Reliant). As a very able 'company doctor' put it, when asked what he thought of having 'august' names on the Board replied: "Augustness has got nothing to do with it; it's about paying attention."

5. Do you go to AGMs? Do so whenever you can; they can be very informative.

At the AGM of a company that had a good long standing reputation but didn't seem to be doing too well, a retired director of a subsidiary, when asked what he thought of the Group, replied: "There are too many people wandering around with wishbones, and not enough with backbones."

They can also be hilarious. One chairman, embarrassed by revelations of his extramarital affairs in a Sunday tabloid, shrewdly pre-empted criticism as he opened the meeting by saying how grateful he was to his family and his fellow directors for their loyal support "at this difficult time". The subject was then dropped. Or so we thought, until a little man in a raincoat got up and said that, on behalf of himself and other small shareholders, he would like to thank the Chairman for what he had done for the company (the share price had been doing well). Fair enough we thought. And then the little man added: "and if you want a little bit on the side, good luck to you, Sir, I say."

6. If the results of a company seem too good to be true, do you believe them? You shouldn't.

Some years ago the ebullient Chairman of a kitchen and bathroom manufacturer trumpeted record profits, up 25% on last year. In the same year, the chief executive of a listed house-builder was describing market conditions in the industry as "certainly the worst post-war years". A few months later the first company issued a profits warning. At least one subsidiary had been falsifying sales to meet unrealistic targets. The price tumbled. The Chairman resigned, and the company moved into 'intensive care'.

7. Is the annual report designed to inform, or to impress? The latter can be a sign of trouble brewing.

Look out for larger than A4 formats (Maxwell), glitzy photos with no captions, text printed on expensive glossy paper, too shiny to take a felt marker, (Parkfield, and many others). Mission statements should not impress you either. For example in 2000 RAILTRACK plastered the front cover of its annual report:

> "Our vision is the delivery of a safe, reliable, efficient modern railway for our customers and the nation . . We are making constant progress . . ."

8. Do you keep your eyes and ears open for good investment ideas? It's well worth doing so.

An elderly and rather 'County' widow we knew was out shopping one day. Noticing an attractive window display of white goods, she went in to buy a refrigerator. Inside, the shop was clean and smart, and the staff were very courteous in helping her buy a suitable fridge. When she got home, she looked at the receipt: British Home Stores. "Oh dear", she said to herself, "I never shop in places like that." Then she thought again, phoned her broker and bought some BHS shares. It proved a rewarding investment, as more and more people came to realize that BHS had improved hugely under new management.

9. Do you look carefully at the price-earnings ratio (prospective as well as historic) before buying, and do you avoid astronomical PEs?

Some years ago Polaroid's P/E ratio touched 80. You must be joking? No, I'm not. A more recent example was when Japan privatized NTT (Nippon Telecomm), on a P/E of 80. Not only was it done at the highest price NTT ever reached, it was also the signal for the top of the Japanese market.

10. Do you sometimes get the feeling that the management of a company is a bit 'iffey'. If so, avoid.

A pair of elderly and very traditional City stockbrokers (pinstripe trousers, stiff wing collars and bowler hats) recalled the case of a prominent City figure. And very well heeled that City figure was too: house in Eaton Square, sizeable dairy farm on his estate in Hampshire.

For years he prospered, but one day he was caught 'with his fingers in the till'. The precise details of his dishonesty escape me, but I do remember the comment made by one of the brokers: "We always knew he was bent; he was fined during the war for watering the milk."

Catherine Tan

Catherine Tan manages a number of Lloyd George Management's Asian specialist accounts including LG SLI Japan Fund, an Asian Internet Fund and an Islamic Fund.

Before joining Lloyd George Management in Hong Kong in 1998, she was a portfolio manager with DBS Asset Management in Singapore for 4 years. She was voted one of Asia's top ten fund managers in *Asiamoney* in 1997.

Investing lessons from the Asian markets

1. The only no-brainer is the person who believes in a no brainer. Challenge the consensus.

Stay clear of stocks labelled no-brainers. There is no such thing. The best investors are those who work the hardest. It is a knowledge game and superior knowledge leads to superior returns. Read widely, think laterally and remember that history has a tendency to repeat itself.

At the top of a cycle, excess capex (capital expenditure) is always disguised as productivity increase. Think USA today, and remember the Japanese and then later the East Asian miracle, where there was a clamour to explain why productivity (later exposed as a myth) was substantially higher. Special mention goes to Singapore's Senior Minister who claimed it was because of East Asia's Confucian values.

2. The only constant is change.

When a practice is continued because it has worked very well in the past, warning bells should ring. That is the worst reason to do something and is a sign of inertia or, worse, mismanagement. What is good today is easily bad tomorrow.

A case in point was the Thai dollar peg. In 1995, when asked if they would relax it, Bank of Thailand happily and adamantly rejected the idea saying it had worked so well in the past. In the process it built up pressure for the subsequent implosion. For everything, there is a time and season.

3. Earnings are well and good but cashflow rules.

Earnings can be 'manufactured' more easily than cashflow. If it's such a great business, it will show in the cashflow. Likewise when things seem bleakest - at the height of the Asian crisis, for example - you can make a lot of money buying stocks trading at huge discounts to their cashflows. Buy strong cashflows. Caveat below.

4. Cashflow return on investment (CFROI) matters.

Even with a cash cow business, be careful of majority shareholders or management whose interests may well be different from those of minority shareholders. Often cash-generative listed businesses are used to bail out failed or failing private enterprises through dilutive injections. If they cannot generate a decent return, the money should be returned to you.

5. Balance sheets, accounts and prospectuses are a good source of information.

They are underutilised and should be scrutinised. There is a lot hidden in them which tells you more than any analyst could. Look for inter-company loans, bank guarantees, receivables etc., and read the risks.

6. Macro matters.

No market is an island. Sector investing has taken roots and affects stocks everywhere. When America catches a cold, the rest of the world is still susceptible to pneumonia. In a liquidity rally, turkeys fly highest.

7. Know why you are in the stock.

This will help you know why and when you should get out of it. Revisit the reasons why you bought a stock often. Ask if anything's changed. Be very honest. If you are in it for the ride, don't try and cloak the decision. That way, you are more likely to get off before the ride ends.

8. Take profits. Take losses. Protect NAV (net asset values).

A bird in the hand is worth ten in the bush. If the stock has reached your target price, realise your profits. Revisit the fundamentals. If the only things that have changed are price and sentiment, sell. On the other side of the coin, don't be afraid to realise losses. If you wouldn't buy it today, don't hold on to it.

9. Follow the insider.

Monitor insider actions, management transactions and company buybacks. If the people on the inside are selling shares to you, it's a strong signal that the market's overheated.

A particularly savvy insider is Li Ka Shing whose cash raising has generally coincided with the top of the markets and whose buybacks have coincided with its bottoms. His IPO of Tom.com, for instance, was right at the height of the internet mania.

Research unusual stock actions, whether surging volumes or unusual price movements. They are often the first indicators that something's happening, for good or bad.

10. Asia is no different to the rest of the world, and the same global rules apply.

Don't make an exception. Don't be fooled into making exceptions.

www.lloydgeorge.com

'Study long-term charts. Once the long-term has been established, consult daily and intra-day charts. A short-term view alone can often be deceptive. Even if you only trade the very short term, you will do better if you're trading in the same direction as the intermediate and longer term trends.'

John Murphy

Paul Temperton

Paul Temperton runs The Independent Economic Research Company (TIER) and is spokesman for the European Commission on issues relating to the euro. He has previously worked as an economist for the Bank of England. Former roles also include being a director of Merrill Lynch's European Economic and Fixed Income Research Department.

Books
The UK and the Euro, John Wiley, 2001
The Euro, John Wiley, 1998

Investing in Euroland

1. The trend is your friend.
Economists, such as me, are not supposed to believe in such a rule: markets are supposed to be efficient and stock prices and currencies are supposed to be an unpredictable, random walk. But time and again that has not worked in the currency, stock and bond markets.

2. Big is best.
Consolidation will be the big theme in the coming years. Companies that have served local, fragmented markets will merge to become more efficient and take advantage of the larger pan-European euro-denominated market.

3. The Americans will shake Europe up.
The catalyst for that consolidation in the euro area will be American companies. American investment banks already dominate the financial markets across Europe. The same will happen in other industrial sectors.

4. Value investing will provide the best rewards.
The environment is one in which many companies offer good value on straightforward valuation criteria. Mr. Buffett openly admits he has yet to discover Europe. There are plenty of opportunities.

5. Technology-related growth stocks will still be a great area for long-term investors.

Nokia is Europe's pre-eminent technology company. Despite its recent setback the company will be the leader in the mobile telecommunications industry on a five to ten year view.

6. Privatization will continue and the rewards from investing should be good.

Privatization has made a great impact in the UK. The impact is only starting to be felt in much of the euro area. As inefficient state enterprises are moved to the private sector look for efficiency gains to generate attractive returns to stockholders.

7. The euro will be a success and will last.

Despite widespread skepticism, the euro will be a success and will last. It will bring widespread benefits, in the form of lower transactions costs and greater efficiency, for millions of consumers and companies across the euro area.

8. Don't bet on the UK joining the euro soon.

Whether or not the UK will join the euro will be in the balance for the next year or so. Prime Minister Blair clearly wants the UK to join. But a referendum is promised and there is no way that a convincing 'yes' vote in such a referendum seems achievable.

9. Don't understimate political determination.

However, politicians in Europe can be pretty insistent on getting their own way. Remember how France and Germany resurrected the idea of the single currency shortly after the 1992-1993 currency crises and eventually forced it through? If Blair really is determined for the UK to join he may find a way of getting the UK 'in' despite the referendum.

10. Europe's decade.

In terms of economic and stockmarket performance, Japan was the star of the eighties; America was the star of the nineties. We might just now be entering Europe's decade.

www.tier.co.uk

Richard H. Thaler

Richard Thaler is the Robert P. Gwinn Professor of Economics and Behavioral Science at the University of Chicago's Graduate School of Business as well as a principal at Fuller and Thaler Asset Management. He has been working on incorporating good psychology into economics for over 20 years, and is considered a pioneer in the field of behavioral economics.

Books
The Winner's Curse, Princetown University Press, 1992

Russell Fuller

Russ Fuller is President and Chief Investment Officer of Fuller & Thaler Asset Management, based in San Mateo, CA.

He sits on the editorial boards of the *Journal of Portfolio Management* and the *Financial Analysts Journal*.

Common mistakes investors make

Introduction

For amateur investors whose goal is to 'beat the market', we first suggest that the following facts should be accepted as truth.

• Few investors, including professionals, beat the market. You are unlikely to be one of the lucky ones.

• Most strategies to beat the market involve having either better information or making better use of that information. Neither approach is likely to work for an amateur. Why should your information be better than the information available to mutual fund managers who may have hundreds of analysts at their disposal?

These facts do not imply that it is impossible to beat the market, just that it is unlikely. At Fuller and Thaler we attempt to beat the market by exploiting the biases exhibited by other investors, and so far, we have been successful. However, our strategies would also be difficult for a home investor to implement. So, we suggest the following rules to make personal investing more successful.

1. Avoid overconfidence.

Most people are overconfident. Surveys reveal that over 90 percent of drivers think they are above average! This natural tendency toward overconfidence can be reinforced by sloppy bookkeeping. Few individual investors make a serious attempt at keeping track of their investment performance, and those who try often make mistakes, most famously illustrated by the Beardstown Ladies, who miscalculated their historical rate of return. If you really think you have beaten the market, we suggest checking your math.

2. Avoid 'hindsight bias'.

Most of us have 20-20 hindsight. We all now remember being sure that the internet bubble would burst, and may even delude ourselves into thinking that we thought that it would end in early 2000. Of course, none of us have this kind of omniscience in real time. Hindsight bias helps produce overconfidence by clouding our memory of how we have really done over time. If you want to really see how your predictions have held up over time, keep track - and get ready to be depressed!

3. Avoid compounding your past mistakes via regret.

One of the real benefits of managing one's own portfolio is the ability to sell losers for tax write-offs, and hold on to winners long enough to pay a lower capital gains tax. Many investors tend to do the opposite: they sell their winners to lock in a gain and hold on to their losers in the hope that they will be able to break even. Smart investors are willing to take their lumps.

4. Diversify, diversify, diversify.

The biggest mistake individual investors make is concentrating their portfolios, and the greatest sin of all is holding an excessive portion of your wealth in the stock of the company you work for. Many employees have more than half their 401(k) investments in their own company stock. This is a disaster waiting to happen.

5. Don't take yourself too seriously.

Relax, buy no-load index funds and spend the money you save on fine wine. (We particularly recommend good Australian Shiraz.) You will enjoy life more and even live longer!

www.fullerthaler.com

Van K. Tharp

Dr. Van K. Tharp is founder and President of the International Institute of Trading Mastery, Inc. He coaches on system development, peak performance trading, self-sabotage, position sizing, and how to trade the stock market. His articles appear frequently in industry publications and he speaks regularly at trading workshops and conferences.

Books

Safe Strategies for Financial Freedom, McGraw-Hill Publishing Co., 2004
Financial Freedom through Electronic Day Trading, McGraw-Hill, 2000
Trade Your Way to Financial Freedom [publisher], 1998

Trading and Position Sizing™

1. Whenever you enter into a position, always have a predetermined exit point at which you will concede you were wrong about the position.

This is your risk (R), and if you lose this amount, you have a 1R loss. Even if you are a buy-and-hold investor, you should have some point at which you will bail out of an investment because it is going against you (e.g. a drop of 25%). This rule essentially sets up all position sizing rules.

2. The golden rule of trading is to cut your losses short (1R or less) and let your profits run (more than 1R, i.e. a multiple of R).

Let's say you buy a stock at $50 expecting the price to go up $10, a 20% gain. You decide in advance to exit if the price falls by $1. Now assume that you have four failed breakouts (i.e. 4 x 1R losses) before you have your $10 gain (in this case a 10R gain). You were right only 20% of the time, but your losses totaled minus 4R and your profits totaled plus 10R. Your total gain was thus 6R, six times your initial risk.

3. When the total sum of your R-multiples for all of your trades is positive, you have a 'positive expectancy' system. You must have a positive expectancy system to make money in the market.

Expectancy is the sum of your R-multiples divided by the total number of trades. Thus, if you have 50 trades which give you a total R-multiple of 20, then from your 50-trade sample, you would estimate your expectancy to be

0.4. In other words, over many trades, on average, you will make 0.4 times your initial risk on every trade.

4. A low risk idea is an idea with a positive expectancy that is traded at a low enough risk level to allow for the worst possible contingency in the short term so that you can survive to achieve the expectancy over the long term.

This basically means that 'how much' you risk on any trade is critical. 'How much' is what we call position sizing. In my opinion, aside from personal discipline, it is the most important factor in your trading.

5. Anti-Martingale position sizing strategies work.

Martingale strategies do not work. Martingale strategies are strategies that have you risking more after you lose, such as doubling your risk after a loss. Because people tend to have long streaks against them, they do not work. Eventually you will go broke. In contrast, anti-Martingale strategies, which cause you to increase your position as you win, tend to be very successful. In general, strategies which are based on increasing your bet size as your equity goes up are anti-martingale strategies and they work well.

6. A simple strategy that will work for everyone is to risk a small percentage of your equity on every trade, such as 1% or less.

If you have an account that is worth $100,000, then risking one percent would mean risking $1000. If your stop (i.e. 1R risk) is $5, then you would buy 200 shares (i.e. 1000 divided by 5 = 200 shares). Furthermore, if you applied a 1% risk to the example given in Rule 2, after 5 trades you would be up about 6% since you would be gaining 1% per each R-value. You would be up exactly 6%, since you would only be risking 1% of your remaining equity on each trade.

7. You need to know the R-multiple distribution of your trading system to determine your position sizing strategy.

We frequently play trading simulation games in our workshops in which the R-multiple distribution of the potential trades are known but the value of each individual trade is unknown because the trades are selected randomly from the sample (i.e. a bag of marbles) and replaced. People can become very good at determining their objectives and achieving them in this sort of game.

8. Strategies that are designed to achieve only the maximum return (such as optimal f; the Kelly criteria, etc) are foolish and usually result in huge drawdowns.

For example, if you trade a system that is 55% 1R winners, 5% 10R winners, 35% 1R losers, and 5% 5R losers, then the percentage risk that will achieve the highest average return is 19.9%. With this percentage, you could achieve a huge return if the right sample occurs (i.e. all 10R winners), and this would also give you a very high average return, but you would generally lose a large amount of money on most samples. In other words, you might get one sample in which you make a total of a billion dollars, and many samples in which you lose money. If this were the case, you would have a high average ending equity (because of the huge return in one sample) even though most samples lost money.

9. Position sizing is the part of your trading system that will help you achieve your objectives.

Most people don't think about position sizing because they are too concerned over what stocks they should buy. However, as long as you have a positive expectancy system, position sizing is what will help you achieve your objectives.

10. Rather than place big bets, scale into positions that go in your favor.

Many long-term traders will only have one or two really successful trades each year that will account for most of their profits. You need to capitalize on those trades. And one way to do that is to add another position each time you can raise your initial stop to breakeven. For example, if you bought JDSU in Feb 99 and kept a 25% trailing stop, you would have made a 32R gain by the time you sold it on April 5th, 2000. If you had added another 1% position each time you raised your stock to breakeven, up to a maximum of 4 times, your exposure on JDSU would have been $5,700. In fact, the maximum exposure to your equity would have been about $1,430 on the 4th scale in. However, your total profit would have been $112,476.

---

www.iitm.com

'If a company shows consistent rapid growth in both earnings and revenues, has attractive P/E and P/S ratios, strong recent trends, and a product or service which offers excellent future growth prospects, *yet its stock is underperforming the market,* don't buy it. If everything looks strong fundamentally, but it has a low relative strength, something may be wrong.'

James W. Oberweis

David W. Tice

David W. Tice is President of David W. Tice & Associates, Inc., based in Dallas. The firm employs 11 full-time analysts to search for companies which are likely to fail to meet Wall Street expectations. The research is used to publish 'quality of earnings' warnings, and 'sell' recommendations to more than 200 money managers who collectively manage more than $2 trillion. His firm's work has gained recognition through several Barron's articles and from his appearances on CNBC and other financial cable programs.

Overvalued stocks and Ponzi schemes

---

1. Study stock market history - recognize where you are in the long-term secular cycle.

Most investors remember and learn from what has occurred in the recent past. Investors must realize that they must learn from periods that might extend beyond their own memory. Market cycles can last a long time, and people have too much at stake to make all the mistakes themselves, so they must learn from market history.

Most of the money in the stock market over the last 104 years has been made in secular bull markets. However, being invested at the tail end of secular bear markets can result in very poor investment performance for a very long period of time. Recognize that the greatest contributor to stock market performance is the P/E multiple afforded to earnings, and that in bull markets, the P/E multiple expansion is what drives stock prices.

2. Uniform opinion among analysts about an individual stock is dangerous.

When many Wall Street analysts are unanimously positive on a company, the stock price tends to be too high and reflects very favorable expectations. The key to making money in stocks is selecting companies where your analysis of fundamentals shows better prospects than the current Wall Street expectations. However when all analysts have very high expectations for a company, then it becomes very difficult to beat lofty expectations.

3. There are elements of Ponzi schemes in many areas of investment.

Always keep your eyes open for investments that require a bigger fool to continue to pay a higher price to have the investment make sense. These investments are dangerous, as eventually you run out of buyers willing to continue to pay a higher price. Determine that there are underlying economic fundamentals that justify the investment based on future cash flows, not just that someone is willing to pay a higher price.

These ponzi-like situations can be found both in the investment markets as well as in the fundamentals of real businesses. For example, the recent telecom boom was founded not on the ability of companies to make money, but on their ability to sell the bandwidth they developed on to a bigger company. This was a classic Ponzi scheme. When it was realised that the bigger telecom companies couldn't buy all the bandwidth that was being developed, stock prices crashed because the business models were not viable on their own merit without the benefit of a bigger fool buying them out.

4. Buy low, sell high - don't buy high, sell higher.

This advice seems straight forward, but is always difficult to follow. Attractive sounding growth stories have the most intrinsic appeal, but are always the highest priced in the market. These companies have the highest expectations, and it normally requires a bigger fool to keep paying a higher price to keep the stock price rising. Also, there usually exists very little downside asset value support in those cases where the growth story does not come through.

5. Consider selling short to reduce exposure and to create outperformance.

There are always many stocks which reach outrageous price levels and can be sold short. One great attribute of selling short is that it reduces overall equity allocation which reduces portfolio risk and equity exposure. Short exposure of 15% offsets long exposure of 75%, thereby resulting in net long equity exposure of 60%. Reduced equity exposure means lower risk, thereby helping investors generate improved risk-adjusted returns if stock selection is done well.

6. Be a contrarian and independent thinker

Always attempt to challenge the conventional wisdom which is normally wrong. Following the crowd is not normally the way to get rich. Great riches are typically earned by people who identify an opportunity before anyone else and who exploit those opportunities successfully. You should invest in the same manner.

7. Have a long time horizon - it's the key to riches.

Look for companies that are experiencing short term disappointment. Most investors attempt to chase short term performance which is very difficult to achieve. Earning a 50% performance return over three years, is equivalent to a 15% annual return. The chance of earning that 50% return is higher if all the other investors ignore a stock because they see the performance being too far in the future.

8. Look at micro-cap companies. The market is more inefficient, and the profits can be huge.

Companies with smaller market values are followed less by Wall Street and therefore generally carry lower expectations. If you can identify companies with great prospects before others do, your chances of generating outstanding returns are much greater.

9. Always think about risk vs. return.

Always seek the optimal trade-off between the two functions. Stocks that most people already know about generally possess lesser return potential. Companies that sell at significant multiples of revenue, possess the highest risk in case of disappointment or in a bear market. In a mania bull market, stocks with the highest risk can earn the highest returns for a while, but if market conditions change, they will decline the most.

10. Follow the smartest analysts who are indepedent thinkers.

Read and follow the advice of the most insightful analysts you can find. Sometimes those analysts with the best short term track record have been the ones taking the most risk. This should always be assessed. Look for analysts who make sense and who consider downside support as an important element of the investment strategy.

www.tice.com

'Many investors concentrate on picking winning stocks. For the most part they can't. I've found that, on average, the stocks investors sell subsequently outperform the stocks they buy, even before subtracting transactions costs. Most investors would be better off forgetting about picking winners and paying attention to doing the things they can actually do - controlling trading costs, managing taxes, and diversifying.'

Terrance Odean

Andrew Tobias

Andrew Tobias's 'The Only Investment Guide You'll Ever Need' (Harcourt) has sold more than a million copies. A graduate of Harvard College and Harvard Business School, he has written extensively for such publications as *Time, Worth,* and *Parade.*

Books

My Vast Fortune: An Investor's Fiscal Triumphs and Money Misadventures, Harvest Books, 1998
Investment Gurus: A Road Map to Wealth from the World's Best Money Managers, NYIF, 1998
The Only Investment Guide You'll Ever Need: Expanded and Updated Throughout, Harvest Books, 2005

Personal finance tips

1. A luxury once sampled becomes a necessity. PACE yourself.

2. Pay off your credit cards!

Not having to pay 18% on a credit card is as good as *earning* 18% -- tax-free, risk-free.

3. Buy in bulk when things are on sale.

You can easily stretch $1,000 to buy $1,400 of the very same items you'd have bought in the course of the year anyway. That's a 40% tax-free, risk-free return on your investment. Avoid doing this with alcohol, caviar or candy.

4. Buy low-expense, no-load fund mutual funds.

In the investment race, over the long run, the horse with the lightest jockey - the lowest expense ratio - usually wins.

5. People who buy stocks when they get a bonus and sell when they need a new roof are entrusting their investment strategy to their roofs.

6. If you buy individual stocks, use a deep-discount broker.

7. Don't buy things that are fairly valued. Buy things that are UNDERvalued.

8. People who try to get rich quick generally get what's coming to them.

9. If it looks too good to be true, it probably is.

Aesop probably said that, and maybe his great-great grandfather, too. But when I first wrote it, it seemed original.

10. As Jerry Goodman (Adam Smith) so aptly advised - 'Don't fall in love with your stock. It doesn't know you own it.'

11. Beware the permanent trend. Nothing lasts forever.

12. Beware spreads.

Always check to see how much you would lose if the item you bought today you immediately sold tomorrow.

13. Heed the words of Billy Rose, the old vaudevillian: 'Never invest in anything that eats or needs repairing.'

14. Be a buyer, not a sellee - figure out what you need, and then shop around for the best deal.

Don't invest in something because your old college chum, let alone a stranger, is pitching it to you.

15. Diversify - over asset classes, specific stocks, and over time.

For most people, the best strategy is a lifelong program of steady monthly investing in low-expense, no-load index funds.

16. And then the most obvious, and least original: Buy things when nobody wants them; sell when everybody does.

Or as Bernard Baruch famously put it: "Buy straw hats in the winter. Summer will surely come."

---

www.andrewtobias.com

Brian Tora

Brian Tora is Investment Director of Gerrard Limited, part of the Old Mutual Group. He has chaired the firm's Asset Allocation Committee for the past nine years.

He is a regular columnist for *The Independent*, *Fund Strategy*, *Money Marketing* and the *Investor Magazine*.

General principles and the dangers of looking back

1. Define your objectives.

It is all very well trying to be clever in the world of investment management, but unless you know what you are trying to achieve, you may just be barking up the wrong tree.

2. Take good advice.

Nobody knows everything. You are sure to be able to benefit from other people's experience and knowledge.

3. Don't marry your stocks.

I have seen too many professional investors fall in love with their holdings and fail to realise that they should get out at some stage.

4. Be prepared to take difficult decisions.

This would include selling something at a loss or buying back a share higher than the price at which you last sold it. All you are doing is recognising you have made an error.

The Book of Investing Rules

5. Never forget that the price and valuation of a share is a reflection of what other people believe, not just a result of your own opinion.

If the rest of the world does not agree with you, you may find the shares fail to meet your expectations.

6. Good businesses are dynamic.

Good investors should recognise that companies and markets are changing all the time.

7. Following fashion is fine . . .

. . . as long as you remember that a trend is only a trend until it stops.

8. Don't job backwards!

The worst investment managers are those that enjoy 20:20 hindsight. Revisit your mistakes by all means, but do not live in an 'if only' world.

www.gerrard.com

Romesh Vaitilingam

Romesh Vaitilingam is a specialist in translating economic and financial concepts into everyday language. He advises the Centre for Economic Policy Research and the Royal Economic Society, as well as investment managers and government agencies.

Books

The FT Guide to Reading the Financial Pages, FT Prentice Hall, 2001
The Ultimate Book of Investment Quotations, Capstone, 1999
The Ultimate Investor, Capstone, 1999
Financial Times Guide to Using the Financial Pages, Financial Times Prentice Hall, 2005

How the economy influences markets

1. The economy is an important driver of the stock market.

The central economic force of interest rates - plus the assorted effects of exchange rates, inflation, public spending and taxation - will eventually have a powerful influence on overall valuations, whatever the temporary investment craze.

2. In the short term, it can be hard to discern a clear relationship between the economy and the markets.

The markets clearly react to economic news - the latest figures on production, sales, consumer & producer prices, unemployment, and so on - but the reaction can often seem perverse, with share prices rising on bad news and falling on good news. This is because the markets anticipate the economic news, and securities prices reflect those expectations before the figures are announced. When they are announced, the reaction has less to do with the numbers per se than to whether they are worse or better than the expectations.

3. Over the longer term, the relationship becomes clearer.

At base, investors are looking for the likely impact of any economic indicator on the future course of interest rates. This is because interest rates are one of the two key variables that affect investment results. They act on share valuations like gravity: the higher the rate, the greater the downward pull. First, an increase in interest rates makes the return on shares vis-a-vis bonds less attractive, typically pushing down their valuations. Second, it means that future corporate cash flows should be discounted at a higher rate, which, unless expectations are revised, will reduce current share values. And third, the higher cost of borrowing generally has a damaging impact on corporate profitability.

4. National output, inflation and expectations of inflation are the key determinants of movements in interest rates.

If inflation is rising or expected to rise, it probably means the national monetary authorities - central banks like the Bank of England or the US Federal Reserve Board - will raise rates, with typically negative consequences for the stock market. If output - or at least the rate of growth of output - is falling, rates will probably be brought down.

5. The exchange rate is a further important influence on interest rates and share prices.

A significant decline in the national currency's value against other leading currencies is equivalent to a reduction in interest rates, potentially raising inflationary pressures through higher import prices. But depreciation is also of considerable benefit to companies selling extensively to overseas markets, making their products more competitive and their export divisions more profitable. The possibility of future depreciation also suggests a potential currency benefit from investing in promising shares in foreign companies.

6. Markets tend to react adversely to falling unemployment, at least when the economy is doing well.

Shorter dole queues hint at a tighter labour market - and the potential consequences of rising inflation and higher interest rates. Increased demand for goods and services raises the demand for labour to produce them. If there are unemployed and appropriately skilled workers available, they will be employed. But if manpower and skills are in short supply, there will be upward pressure on earnings, raising company wage bills and encouraging nervous central banks to take action on interest rates.

7. Rising oil prices are generally good for oil shares but not for inflation.

The OECD rule-of-thumb warns that a $10 increase sustained for a year adds half a percentage point to inflation and knocks quarter of a percentage point off growth. A sustained boom in crude oil prices inevitably feeds through to higher prices for heating oil and petrol and could add at least half a percentage point to the rate of inflation. High priced oil also has a direct 'micro' effect on profits since it is a significant input in many industries. Airlines are the most obvious victims as the cost of jet fuel increases, but chemical producers that rely on oil as a raw material also suffer. And even service sector companies make some use of energy, whether for travel or simply running their offices.

8. The government's budgetary policy can have a major impact on the markets.

Ideally, fiscal policy should support the aim of monetary policy to keep growth at around its trend rate without fuelling inflation. In particular, this means that any tax cuts or spending increases should not boost consumer demand when the economy is doing well. By cutting taxes and/or increasing government spending on health, education, transport, law and order, etc., the government can loosen fiscal policy, hence boosting domestic demand. Conversely, raising taxes and/or reducing spending - a fiscal tightening - depresses demand.

9. Many economic indicators provide valuable information for analysing particular sectors of the economy and companies operating within them.

Statistics for industrial output, for example, offer precise data on the performance of the various sectors that constitute the production industries. These include manufacturing - durable goods such as cars; non-durables like clothing and footwear, and food, drink and tobacco; investment goods such as electrical equipment; and intermediate goods like fuels and materials - plus mining and quarrying, which includes oil and gas extraction; and electricity, gas and water.

10. Trade figures also offer valuable insights into the relative performance of different parts of the economy.

More broadly, the trade balance - whether the country is importing more than it exports or vice versa - can have a significant impact on the sustainability of growth, the exchange rate and the level of inflation. A large and widening trade deficit is generally bad news both for the economy and the stock market.

romesh@compuserve.com

'Be sceptical of macro-economic forecasts. Forecasters have a very bad track record in predicting genuine booms and slumps. They sometimes fail to forecast a recession even when it has actually started.'

Paul Ormerod

Timothy P. Vick

Timothy Vick is the senior investment analyst for Arbor Capital Management, and a partner and co-portfolio manager of The Power Fund, a partnership that invests in emerging companies in the alternative power industry. He writes about economic trends, business strategy and valuation, corporate performance, and portfolio management.

Books

How to Pick Stocks Like Warren Buffett, McGraw-Hill, 2000
Wall Street on Sale, McGraw-Hill, 1999

Finding value in the market

1. Picture yourself as the owner.

When I see a stock priced at $50, my first instinct is to multiply the price by the shares outstanding - let's say 10 million - and ask myself whether the whole company is worth $500 million. My second question evolves from the first: If I had $500 million to invest in the company and could be the sole owner, would I buy it? Starting from this premise, your mind naturally will focus on basic business issues such as payback (how fast can the company generate $500 million in profits to return your investment), cash flow, debt levels, taxes, sales prospects, capital expenditure needs, and profit margins. Price fluctuations, moving averages, and chart patterns have no place in this exercise.

Generally, the longer it takes a company to return my investment, the more I am inclined to walk away, whether I'm looking at public or private entities. If I wouldn't want to own the entire company, I won't buy even 100 shares of it.

2. You win in investing by not losing.

Investing is, by virtue of its competitive nature, a 'Loser's Game' - winners are those who make the fewest mistakes. The most revered investors in history, those sitting atop the largest pile of assets, did not make a killing on one or two stocks, but sat tight with their money, deployed it slowly and prudently, and exploited opportunities that negated their chances of losses.

Experience has taught me that if you minimize your chances of losing money each time you buy a stock your overall returns will greatly exceed the average investor's. In contrast, short-term traders and institutional money managers are naturally prone to mistakes and underperformance. By doggedly chasing short-term returns to beat their peers and to keep pace with market indexes, they unwittingly force themselves to make dozens of poor investing decisions each year, which tends to limit and commoditize their returns.

3. Keep your eyes off the market - but be prepared to exploit it.

Confident investors don't look at stock quotes once a day, once a week, or even once a month. If you purchase an investment at a good price and are sure of the company, pricing will take care of itself. Daily fluctuations become just noise. I am always amazed by investors who claim to buy a stock for the 'long-term' yet continually monitor every price change, press release, and earnings revision. Eventually, their penchant to absorb useless news evolves into a psychological obsession to act - more often than not they will buy or sell prematurely for the wrong reason. Financial markets exist solely to execute your buy and sell orders: nothing more. Focus first on the performance of companies and use the market solely as a reference point to see if other investors are pricing the company properly. When you see a wide discrepancy between price and value, be ready to exploit the situation.

4. If you cannot understand it, don't buy it.

One of the chief ways I minimize mistakes is to invest only within my circle of competence. That should be an easy rule to apply, but humans have a tendency to beat their chests and feign unlimited knowledge when money is at stake. Every company or industry possesses, at most, two or three 'critical factors' that you need to analyze to determine your chances of making money. If you can understand the critical factors that make an airline, a hotel chain, a bank, or a maker of programmable logic chips, profitable, you will invest more confidently. If you cannot identify these factors, avoid the investment altogether. Likewise, if you cannot understand the company's earnings releases or its annual report, take your money elsewhere.

5. Rely on yourself, not on the opinions of others.

Ten days before the 1929 market crash, *The Wall Street Journal* jokingly questioned why "any ignoramus" can get away with talking about investments. Indeed, a man with an opinion is as common in finance as mosquitoes in summer - and is just as much of a nuisance. Because investing is as much an art as science, it invites anyone to pass judgment with little fear of reprisal. Great investors rely on facts (never on opinions) and their own ability to decipher facts. They rarely get good ideas talking to others and will never buy and sell solely on others' counsel. Think back to your worst investments over the years - likely they were bought on the recommendation of someone else. That's because every investor has unique risk and reward profiles - what's good for your neighbor, physician, golf partner, or brother-in-law will rarely work for you too.

6. Forecasts are useless, especially those about the future.

Aristotle once said that man has an innate desire to know the future, and that no desire is exploited more by his fellow man. The entire financial industry exists to sell product. If you don't understand this basic maxim, you'll be misled time after time.

The brokerage industry figured out long ago how to play to your hopes and fantasies, to conjure up forecasts and spurious mathematical reasons why an investment will sell for more in the future than it does today. Yet, in all my years of studying in business school, observing the conduct of managers, and practicing portfolio management, I've never come across anyone who has consistently been able to predict the direction of the market, the economy, interest rates, or a company's sales and earnings. As long as markets are emotional and fickle, and as long as business managers and investors are prone to react irrationally to fickleness, this poor track record will continue unabated. Invest in what *is*; not what could be.

7. Time is your natural friend.

In finance, time corrects all short-term anomalies. It exposes poor businesses masquerading as great entities, and gives truly great entities sufficient chance to maximize the reward to investors. Choosing good companies at fair prices seldom has produced losses for patient investors.

A company that increases earnings by 12% a year over 20 years will experience a roughly 12% yearly increase in stock price. However, if you bought and held the stock for just one of those 20 years, any return is possible. Great investors always stay mindful of their opportunity costs. Every poor investment has two costs - the near-term loss you generated and the long-term money you gave up by choosing poorly. A $10,000 loss early in your investing career costs you more than $2 million at retirement if you could have compounded the money at 20% annual rates. An investment sold too early can have the same effect. Most investments you sell today will one day trade for much higher than the price at which you sold. Think about that before you sell.

8. Don't diversify - it breeds sloth and mediocrity.

If you want to be simply 'average', behave like the averages. Nothing breeds middling returns more than collecting stocks as if they were postage stamps or vases. Pension and mutual fund managers have to diversify portfolios to protect their jobs and to counter the effects of huge money inflows. You don't. Having to watch 40 or more companies poses the same burden on an investor as owning 40 apartment buildings, or 40 restaurant franchises. Why diversify, if you're not up to the task? At some point, your portfolio of assets becomes impossible to monitor and you're left hoping that nothing extraordinary happens to any of the 40. Worse, you guarantee yourself middle-of-the-road returns - that has been proven mathematically. The great money is made holding a small collection of assets that you understand intimately.

9. Know the difference between 'investing' and 'gambling'.

If you buy any asset without first valuing it, you should admit to gambling. Indeed, any stock-picking method that isn't premised on a sober appraisal of intrinsic worth is useless, and ultimately degenerates into trial-and-error forecasting. If you cannot reasonably calculate what the asset is worth before you buy it (or what it could be worth) you cannot determine whether you will make money. More often than not, you will have to gamble on the actions of others to make a profit. True investing entails reducing the probabilities of error, which is accomplished only through objective analysis. When gambling, you lose all control over the outcome. Before you buy a stock, ask yourself what you really are relying on to make money - is it the growth in the value of the company, or are you simply hoping for a magical increase in price after you buy it?

10. Calculate what you can take out of the company.

Since most investors fail to appraise a company before buying it, they usually have no preconceived idea of what they can earn over time. That's a fatal mistake. You should be able to estimate the annualized rate-of-return you expect from every investment and be able to quantify how you derived that figure. If your criteria for investing are nebulous, you're more likely to make back-end mistakes about selling. Are you looking for a 50% price increase in one year? If so, what factors can cause that to occur, and how likely are those factors to occur? Are you looking for 15% a year for 10 years? If so, calculate what the stock must trade for in 10 years and determine the earnings that will be needed to support the price. Then ask yourself whether those earnings can be attained. In this business, price and return are inextricably linked. The lower the price you pay, the greater your potential return. It's that simple.

www.arborcapital.net

Pieter Vorster

Pieter Vorster currently covers the European Tobacco sector for CSFB in London. He has been with the company since it acquired Donaldson, Lufkin & Jenrette in 2000 where he was responsible for covering European Tobacco as well the South African Diversified Industrial sectors.

Prior to that he was an analyst at UBS Warburg and ABN Amro in South Africa.

The tobacco sector

---

1. Tobacco is a controversial industry.

Over the last 20 years, tobacco has become an increasingly controversial industry as the health risks associated with smoking lead to governments applying increased levels regulation and taxation. At the same time a strong anti-smoking lobby has developed and litigation against the industry has increased. As such, investors in the tobacco sector have had to become accustomed to dealing with a substantially higher level of extraneous factors when compared with other consumer staple industries.

2. Cash flows and earnings are fairly predictable.

One of the main characteristics of the tobacco industry is its strong and predictable cash flow. This means that tobacco companies are not reliant on share issues to grow and reduces the impact of share price fluctuations on the longer-term prospects of the industry.

3. Litigation and regulatory newsflow are not predictable.

As predictable as tobacco cash flows are, as unpredictable are newsflow relating to litigation and new regulations. Often, rational expectations of the outcome of a court case, particularly in the US, are met with sometimes unreasonable rulings in regional courts. Although most of these rulings are normally overturned in higher courts, they cause substantial uncertainty among investors in the sector.

4. Valuations are sensitive to news flow.

Over the last ten years virtually all the major share price movements in this sector have been related to litigation events. These events have introduced a large degree of volatility into the sector, which under normal circumstances would have been regarded as a stable low growth industry. As such, investors in tobacco stocks need to constantly monitor potential litigation and regulatory events, as these invariably have a substantial impact on stock price performance, as irrational as it may seem.

5. Traditional DCF valuations can be misleading.

Because of the combination of strong and predictable cash flows and unpredictable newsflow, traditional discounted cash flow models will almost always suggest that tobacco stocks are undervalued. However, investors need to adjust these DCF values with a litigation discount, depending on the specific litigation exposure of the stock. In doing so investors can identify when the implied litigation discount becomes excessive. In the past this has provided attractive buying opportunities.

Conversely, when virtually no litigation discount is implied in a share price, the stock would be vulnerable to adverse litigation and regulatory newsflow.

6. Be wary of earnings disappointments.

Profit warnings and earnings disappointments are rare among tobacco companies due to the predictable nature of the business. When they occur, they are often a sign of underlying problems in the company and should be investigated thoroughly. Stocks with repeated earnings disappointments are best avoided, even if they trade at a discount to their peers.

7. High levels of regulation are not necessarily negative.

Countries with high levels of regulation do not necessarily have low levels of cigarette consumption. Often the regulation acts as a barrier to entry and protects producers with already strong positions in these markets. However, markets that experience rapid *increases* in regulation and excise taxes will more than likely experience volume declines for a number of years. Following this period of initial decline, volumes generally stabilise.

Markets most at risk are those which have low levels of current regulation, but in which pressure for increased regulation is building. The EU accession countries are a good example of this.

8. International brands are growing faster.

Whereas global cigarette volumes are recording only marginal growth if at all, international brands are growing at an underlying rate of some 4-5% p.a.. This is an important source of growth for the industry and a trend that generally favours multi-national producers with strong brands.

9. Demographic factors are important.

Just like in any other consumer sector, demographics play an important role in the growth or lack of growth in the tobacco industry. On a country-by-country basis, population is the most important determinant of cigarette volumes. Those markets that are expected to experience growth in their young population are potentially attractive growth markets for cigarette manufacturers, whereas those with aging populations can generally be regarded as having unattractive volume growth potential.

10. Don't forget about pricing.

Whilst volume growth is important when evaluating the performance and potential of a cigarette producer, price growth is a more important determinant of profitability. This is because demand for tobacco products is relatively price inelastic. The most important determinant of global cigarette prices is per capita income and markets where this is expected to grow are those with potential price growth potential. In addition, producers who are able to command premium prices for their products in these markets stand to benefit more.

www.csfb.com

'The most valuable price sensitive information is to be found where you least expect. Look out for apparently dull comments on business issues from politicians or regulators. These could presage price sensitive changes in the regulatory environment. Or scour the apparently tedious industry supplements of newspapers like the FT. Frequently these contain fresh information on a company's trading performance or sector trends. The good stuff is *really dull*.

Robert Peston

Ralph Wanger

Ralph Wanger is Founding Partner of Chicago's Liberty Wanger Asset Management. Wanger is responsible for $8 billion in five mutual funds: Liberty Acorn, Liberty Acorn International, Liberty Acorn USA, Liberty Acorn Twenty and Liberty Acorn Foreign Forty. A graduate of the Massachusetts Institute of Technology with a Masters degree from the same university, Ralph Wanger lives in Chicago.

Books

A Zebra in Lion Country, Touchstone, 1999

Reasons to invest beyond the USA

1. Bet on good companies, regardless of what country they're in.

In about 1985, I realized that many of the U.S. companies I owned were getting their asses kicked. I started hearing all kinds of stories from my companies: "We had to close down our factory in Kentucky because somebody's bringing up stuff from Guatemala that we can't compete with." I figured we had better start looking at some of these foreign companies. I told my staff that we would find winners wherever domiciled, and bet on them. In investment, if you want the best returns, you have to ignore patriotism and sentiment.

2. Locals always have the edge.

Some investors insist that it is best to stick to U.S. companies where you can count on full disclosure, protective regulation, and plenty of Wall Street research. By owning multinational companies, they argue, you can still reap the harvest of growing economies abroad. In answer I would say that where U.S. companies do business abroad they are always going to be treated as outsiders. U.S. money is welcome, but there is a common tendency to take care of your own and freeze out foreigners, whether by legal or illegal means.

3. Don't keep all your assets in one currency.

You wouldn't put all your money in one stock or in one industry, and you shouldn't keep it all in one currency either. Owning foreign stocks and diversifying away from the U.S. dollar is probably valuable in itself, given the U.S.'s massive federal deficit and balance-of-trade deficit, both of which work against the dollar. With such a prospect, I want to own foreign as well as U.S. securities.

4. Look for industries where the U.S. has no equivalent.

Another reason why sticking to American multinationals isn't the same as directly investing abroad is that some foreign industries don't have counterparts in the United States. For instance, in Singapore you can invest in shipyard stocks. There aren't any shipyard stocks in the U.S. In Britain, you can buy an airport management company. There's no such thing in the U.S. Many of these stocks are very good investments.

5. Take advantage of less efficient markets.

Investing overseas nowadays is like investing in the U.S. twenty-five years ago. It's tough to find small companies in the U.S. that aren't followed by at least a regional firm of brokers, and the companies themselves are accustomed to media releases and conference calls. Everyone hears the news within seconds, so it is extremely difficult to gain an information edge. Overseas markets, in contrast, are far less efficient. You can still find businesses that others know little about - businesses growing at very fast rates. For several years at least, I see enormous potential.

6. Invest for the long term.

In many foreign markets, the dominant mentality is a trading one. Insider trading is permissible and rife, turnover is very high, stories abound, and the locals are mainly interested in running a stock up 25 percent and dumping it. There's no way you can outtrade the locals, so the secret is to become a long-term investor, to adopt a different time scale. Then, their edge washes out over time. If you can be in for the long haul - sometimes buying the stocks the nationals are dumping - and just sit with those stocks, you can realize the high growth available without being nailed by the short-term stories.

7. Consider mutual funds.

It's getting easier to be a direct investor overseas, but there are still difficulties in tracking companies, assessing economies, worrying about currencies, and dealing with local regulations, accounting differences and indifference to stock manipulation. For all these reasons, consider getting exposure to overseas stocks thrugh a mutual fund. But the chief argument for going the mutual route is that professional fund managers traversing the globe to develop corporate and analyst relationships are able to dig up investments that a private investor by himself could not hope to find.

8. Spread your bets.

At Acorn our emphasis is on picking companies rather than countries, but it's important to make top-down judgements as well. You don't want too much exposure in unstable countries. Too many people assume that their money will be safe in places where they wouldn't drink the water. In assessing how comfortable we feel about investing in a country, we consider the usual factors of political risk, inflation and interest rates, balance of payments, and the like. We want to feel the country is on the right track. And because it's impossible to eliminate all risk, we diversify.

9. Remember why you're there.

Sometimes you will get fed up with the smaller, developing markets - their illiquidity and volatility, the insiders' edge, the struggle to find out what's really going on. You have to remind yourself that with countries growing at 6 to 10 percent and companies growing at 25 to 30 percent, it's worth putting up with such inconveniences. A recent study conducted by Morgan Stanley Capital International for the years 1985-1993 showed that a combination of U.S. and non-U.S. stocks produced a higher return with less risk than a 100 percent U.S. portfolio. The allocation that promised the highest return with least risk was 60 percent U.S. and 40 percent non-U.S. combination. If you went to 80 percent non-U.S. stocks, your risk would rise to about the same level as if you had a 100 percent U.S. portfolio - but your return would also rise, by a couple of percentage points.

10. Final word.

The issue really isn't whether or not you should invest in non-U.S. stocks. The issue is whether or not you should be in stocks altogether. If you are in pain when a stock or stock mutual fund drops 5 percent, the answer is negative. But if you are a stock investor, you should be country-blind.

www.wanger.com

'The presence of a big investor who is willing to get involved and shake up a company can be a good thing. But make sure that the big investor owns the same security that you do. Sometimes the big investors own bonds or preferred stock, in which case they may not care what happens to the holders of the common stock.'

George Putnam III

Edmond Warner

Edmond Warner was chief executive of Old Mutual Securities. Previously he was Head of Pan European Equities for BT Alex Brown and Head of Global Research for Dresdner Kleinwort Benson. He has ranked highly in all the leading surveys of investment managers.

Investing in a bear market

1. Flick the switch.

You'll never make rational investment decisions if you're mesmerised by the gyrating prices on your screen. Steel yourself not to look at prices, read market reports or talk to stockbrokers during trading hours. Markets are not going to turn for the better just because you will them to. And, as prices have fallen so far, it matters little if you miss the first inch of their eventual recovery.

2. Pound the streets.

You don't just need a sense of perspective; you need the widest possible perspective. The best investment opportunities are those you discover by observation of the workings of the economy in the aftermath of the stock market collapse. If you can bear it, take the taxi driver litmus test.

3. Read a good book.

History never repeats itself exactly, but you owe it to yourself to be acquainted with the bear markets of yesteryear. At least if history does then repeat itself you can't say that you weren't warned. I'd recommend JK Galbraith's *The Great Crash*, a brief but insightful analysis of 1929 and all that went before and aft.

4. Avoid collateral damage.

In 1987 the real economy emerged from the crash virtually unscathed. This time the world may not be so lucky. It will take time for share price damage to have its full effect elsewhere. Use this opportunity to pull out of that house move, sell your granny's Gauguin and ask your boss for an extended contract.

5. Dust off the abacus.

Down and dirty financial analysis has been out of vogue for a couple of years. As share prices fall, so value emerges. But you'll only spot it if you are looking for it. And this means poring over the numbers, not chasing dreams. You can afford to keep it simple. Thoroughness will pay greater dividends than sloppy sophistication.

6. Beware false prophets.

Nobody knows where markets are going - not me, not you, not Abby Cohen at Goldman Sachs or the anonymous authors of Lex in the Financial Times. Your view has as much or as little validity as anyone else's. Keep this in mind and, when your analysis tells you it's time to buy, you'll find you have the requisite bravery.

7. Don't shoot the analysts.

The backlash against investment bank analysts is in full swing. Don't be diverted by the spectacle, however enjoyable it might appear. Use the research available dispassionately. As in all human life, you'll find there's good and bad there. Just be sure, once you've digested, to formulate your own conclusions.

8. Rebase to zero.

Ignore charts of historic share price performance. How a company was valued at its peak is no guide to its value today. Those shares that have fallen furthest may yet have furthest to fall. Start with a blank sheet of paper - no prejudices or preconceptions - and build an investment argument that reflects today's reality as you perceive it.

9. Yield to temptation.

Equities are but one tidbit on the investment smorgasbord. One way of comparing them with other asset classes is through their dividend yield. Seek out shares whose yields are approaching those on government bonds. Although unfashionable, this could prove the way back into the market with the least risk. Just be sure those dividends can be met out of the companies' profits.

10. Look for leverage.

Courage mon brave! When you decide the time has come to invest, be sure to do so with conviction. Use leverage to your advantage - be prepared to borrow; consider the use of derivative instruments. You could be a hero of the next bull market, if only in your granny's eyes.

www.oldmutual.com

Ben Warwick

Ben Warwick is Chief Investment Officer at
Sovereign Wealth Management. He is the
Market View columnist for
worldyinvestor.com, a contributor to
numerous industry publications, and the
publisher of a free monthly newsletter at
http://www.SearchingForAlpha.com).

Books

The Worldly Investor's Guide to Beating the Market, John Wiley, 2001
Searching for Alpha, John Wiley, 2000
The Futures Game, McGraw-Hill, 1999
The Handbook of Managed Futures, Dow Jones Irwin, 1997
Event Trading, Dow Jones Irwin, 1996

Searching for 'alpha'

Introduction

Alpha: investment return above a market index.

Considering the small number of mutual funds that produce market-beating
returns, the task may seem nearly impossible. Even so, there remains an elite
group of investment professionals who manage to produce market-beating
returns, year after year. What is their edge?

1. Embrace diversification.

The real trick to beating the market is not portfolio concentration - it's
holding a little bit of everything, and overweighing the sectors that have the
best chance to outperform. Although famous investors like John Maynard
Keynes and Warren Buffet have produced fabulous returns through a small
number of large positions, they are the exception rather than the rule.

2. Index the hard stuff.

Market sectors vary in how quickly they respond to information. Large cap
U.S. stocks, for example, are followed by so many analysts and reflect
company fundamentals so quickly that it is nearly impossible to add value
through active strategies. I recommend indexing such sectors.

3. Use active strategies in inefficient market sectors.

Although some parts of the market are tenaciously efficient, there are certain sectors - small cap stocks and high yield bonds are two examples - where active management can really pay off. For these sectors, use active managers that have a unique and scalable methodology to produce alpha (i.e. return over a market index).

4. Use the credit spread to 'tilt' your portfolio toward growth or value stocks.

The stock market is not one coherent group of equities. Different types of stocks react to changes in the economic environment in unique ways. Small cap stocks, for example, do better during recessions or when equities are in a downtrend. Large cap stocks tend to lead the market higher during the good times. Look at the credit spread (the difference between the yield of government and corporate bonds) to determine whether the economy is expanding or contracting (a growing economy is associated with a narrowing of the spread), and tilt your portfolio to the market sector that is poised to benefit the most.

5. Consider the yield curve when buying fixed-income investments.

An 'inverted yield curve' - a scenario when Treasury bills yield more than ten-year U.S. government notes - boasts a 30-year record of flawlessly predicting recessions. If this occurs, the long end of the yield curve will generate the best performance over the intermediate term. In a normal yield curve scenario, the middle part of the curve will usually deliver the best risk-adjusted return.

6. Utilize momentum strategies only during periods of economic growth.

Momentum traders buy stocks that have increased the most in the belief that they will continue to do so in the future. Although there is a plethora of evidence showing that market sectors exhibit trend-following behavior during periods of expansion, a weak economic environment usually prevents such momentum players from generating a market-beating return.

7. Consider alternative investments.

With the increased integration of the world economy, stock and bond markets have become globally linked. Prudent investors should consider skill-based investments in the futures markets and through market- neutral hedge funds (unregulated investment pools that generate profits through an arbitrage approach) to add value diversification to their portfolios. The steady returns of these investments go a long way in producing market-beating returns.

8. Think about taxes.

Taxes are frequently the largest expense investors face, surpassing both commissions and investment management fees. Tax gains are largely the result of the efforts of money managers who attempt to add value to the investment process by buying and selling of securities. Taxes can be minimized by indexing the hard stuff and by keeping all actively managed funds in a tax-deferred account.

9. Don't pick an investment manager based solely on past performance.

When considering a fund investment, there are more important things to look at than the manager's past return stream. Consider transaction costs, fees, and the fund's research budget. These three criteria are much better indicators of what may occur in the future.

10. Rebalance your portfolio on a regular basis.

Over the long-term, markets exhibit mean-reverting behavior; in other words, winners become losers and losers become winners. For this reason, it is important to periodically rebalance your portfolio by taking money away from those investments that have performed well in the past few months and reallocating it to those that have suffered losses. By doing this, investors can both increase their returns and reduce their dependence on a few bets that have appreciated significantly.

---

www.SearchingForAlpha.com,   www.worldlyinvestor.com

'Profits are higher in fast growing industries. Myth! They're not, because everyone else knows they are fast growing. Returns are often higher in unfashionable activities, like tobacco. Best are industries that grow faster than expected - whether expectations are high or low.'

John Kay

Henry Weingarten

Henry Weingarten, has been a professional astrologer for over thirty-four years. Since May 2, 1988, he has been the Managing Director of the Astrologers Fund, Inc., which employs astrology as the primary analysis tool to manage investment funds and advise institutional investors and money managers worldwide.

Books

Investing by the Stars, McGraw-Hill, 1996, 2nd ed. Traders Press, 2000
The Study of Astrology, ASI Publishers, 1969, 5th edition 1988

Ten guidelines for a stellar performance

1. Ubung macht den meister (Practice makes perfect).

Practice first, before using/losing real money.

2. Think global.

Most of a stock's price movement can be attributed to the broad market and sector participation. Plan top-down: First select countries/bourses/currencies, then sectors, then individual stocks. Bottom-up investing should be reserved primarily for special situations.

3. Timing is everything.

It is not what you know, but when you know it! I use astrology to 'be there first'.

4. Two out of three ain't bad.

When investing, I use fundamentals and astrology; when trading I use technicals and astrology. The best results i.e. most profitable, occur when several investing criteria, gurus or screens agree.

5. When in doubt, don't.

Even when I am 'sure', I am not always right (and I am a Leo!). If you are not sure, do not act unless necessary.

6. Make mistakes.

Nothing ventured, nothing gained. If you are never wrong, you are a newbie, a liar or a con artist. Learn to take losses quickly - the moment you recognize that the market is telling you that you are wrong.

7. Dance when the markets are wrong.

Trading and hedging can be used to hold long core positions without giving up too much.

8. Live on the edge.

Find your own edge or personal knowledge that is not priced into the market. Often, it is from your life experience. For me, astrology is my edge. Similarly, wear your portfolio like comfortable clothing - buy stocks that are you are comfortable owning.

9. Know when to hold them, know when to fold them.

Decide your exit strategies in advance. Most investors know how to buy, but few have learned how and when to sell. I believe that when a stock is more expensive than you are currently willing to pay for it, it is time to place a trailing stop or sell it.

10. Make a profit - don't be a prophet.

Use prudent money management and capital preservation. Never let one or two bad investments destroy your portfolio; diversify it sufficiently to manage risk and reward appropriately.

---

www.afund.com

Neal Weintraub

Neal Weintraub is a futures trader with over 10 years of experience and is a member of the Mid-America Commodity Exchange. He is the author of the Weintraub Day Trader (Windsor, 1991) and operates a daily market hotline. Weintraub also teaches at the Chicago Mercantile Exchange on fundamental analysis, computer trading, and trading with spreads.

Books

Tricks of the Floor Trader, Dow Jones Irwin, 1996
Trading Chicago Style, McGraw-Hill, 1999

Trading

---

1. You will run out of money before financial gurus run out of trading ideas.

2. Never trust an economic boom fueled by consumer debt.

3. Trading without an exit strategy leads to disasters.

4. Never deal with a broker that won't give selling ideas.

5. Money Honeys are pleasing to the eye but not your portfolio.

6. You can't eat a computer. Have some 'basic' stocks in your portfolio.

7. Day trading is like grabbing coins in front of a steam roller. You will get rolled over.

8. Know the difference between investing, trading and speculating.

9. You do not have to be in the market all the time. Remember, after the crash of 1929 the market did not see those highs until 1954.

10. By the time you hear news, the market has reacted and digested it over a dozen times.

11. News you hear or read about was manufactured by a public relations firm...it is not news, it is market propaganda.

'Software companies are severely punished for missing numbers. In most cases, a miss of a quarter spells trouble for the next few quarters or perhaps years. But, for investors with a 12-month investment horizon, buying an established software company, with a degree of size and maturity, following a 50% gap-down can often be a winning strategy.'

Brian Skiba

Martin J. Whitman

Martin J. Whitman is Chairman of the Third Avenue Value Fund. The investing principle of the Fund is to acquire common stocks of well-financed companies at a substantial discount to their private market value or takeover value. The Fund also seeks to acquire senior securities, such as preferred stocks and debt instruments, that have strong covenant protection and above-average current yields, yields to events, or yields to maturity.

Books

The Aggressive Conservative Investor, John Wiley & Sons Inc, 2005
Value Investing - a Balanced Approach, John Wiley, 1999
Active Investing, John Wiley, 1998

A fresh look at the Efficient Market Hypothesis

Introduction

Since the 1960's the theories embodied in Academic Finance have taken over security analysis almost completely. At its core is the Efficient Market Hypothesis which assumes that the market is efficient in its pricing. Put another way - security prices quickly and accurately reflect all the relevant information that might affect them, and it is pointless for ordinary investors to try to outperform the market consistently.

At TAVF we have a markedly different view of market efficiency than the academics. The difference is partly explained by the tale of the finance professor and the student who came upon a $100 bill lying on the ground. The student stooped to pick up the bill. "Don't bother," says the professor, "if it really were a $100 bill, it wouldn't be there."

The observations below explain how our view departs from that of the academics and why it is possible, in certain markets and using certain techniques, for investors to consistently beat the market.

1. While markets tend towards efficiency, very few ever achieve instantaneous efficiency.

The Efficient Market Hypothesis (EMH) argues that the market is efficient, or achieves instant efficiency, and that 'Outside, Passive, Minority, Investors'(OPMIs) should acknowledge this by using indexed portfolios, top-down market strategies and valuation methods based strictly on forecasts of discounted cash flow. While there are some 'special cases', in most markets the tendency towards efficiency is quite weak, especially where efficiency is defined as appraising a business or a security at a price that approximates to underlying value.

2. There exist myriad markets, not one.

One of the failings of the Efficient Market Hypothesis is that it fails to recognise that there are many different markets, not one. There are OPMI markets, hostile takeover markets, leveraged buy-out markets, strategic buyer markets, m&a markets based on 'paper' not cash, and so on. And - critically - each market has its own pricing parameters.

3. An efficient price in one market is often an inefficient price in another market.

The efficient price of a security depends on your perspective: for example an activist operating in an LBO market knows that in the vast majority of cases a buy-out will not be a do-able transaction unless the price offered in the takeover process represents a meaningful premium over the OPMI market prices. The OPMI market price may be 'efficient' within its own parameters, but it is an inefficient price as far as the LBO operator is concerned.

4. If you are an OPMI you should not generally participate in the markets that tend towards efficiency.

As noted, there are many different markets and some tend towards efficiency more than others. The markets that are most efficient are characterized by short term trading, and the securities being traded can be analyzed by reference to only a limited number of computer variables. Examples are the markets for credit instruments without credit risk (e.g. U.S. Treasuries), derivatives (e.g. options, convertibles, warrants, swaps) and risk arbitrage. Except in rare cases, the OPMI should steer clear.

5. The path to earning excess returns for OPMIs is not to obtain superior information, but rather to use the available information in a superior manner.

One of the tenets of the efficient market hypothesis is that OPMIs cannot consistently outperform the market, or relevant benchmarks, unless they have access to superior information. For 'activists' - the promoters, investment bankers, lawyers, and management who drive market actions - having this superior information can be the route to outperformance, but for

OPMIs it is difficult to access the information. That does not mean outperformance is impossible. It just means that the route is to use available information better, rather than to obtain superior information.

6. The main item of underused information is the balance sheet.

Most analysts, most of the time, ignore the corporate balance sheet in their analyses, focusing instead on earnings growth. If you are an OPMI, and you are looking to buy $100 bills for $50, it is much easier to do so using a balance sheet, rather than an income account or cash flow statement.

7. The market's long term tendency towards efficiency will reward purchases at a discount.

The main problem for fundamental investors is not in identifying $100 bills that can be bought for less, but rather in getting enough efficiency back into the price such that you can sell your $100 for its 'true' value - or at least, for more than the $50 you paid for it. Some funds try to force a market revaluation by identifying catalysts or becoming catalysts themselves (e.g. Gabelli in encouraging a bidding process at Paramount) but at TAVF, we spend little time identifying or seeking catalysts. We rely instead on a long-term tendency towards efficiency. Our view is that while it is difficult to time when individual situations will work out, enough situations in the Fund's portfolio are likely to work out on a lumpy, rather than consistent, basis, so that overall the portfolio ought to perform okay.

8. Fundamentals matter.

I started my observations about EMH with a story about a finance professor and a student picking a $100 off the sidewalk. The story highlights one weakness of EMH, but it misses the main point: Neither by training nor background would the finance professor have been able to identify what the piece of paper lying on the ground was - a $100 bill or a scrap of worthless paper. You have to be literate about fundamentals if you are to have any hope of distinguishing between $100 bills and garbage in the field of security analysis.

www.mjwhitman.com

'Consider selling short to reduce exposure and to create outperformance. There are always many stocks that reach outrageous price levels, that can be sold short. One great attribute of selling short is that it reduces overall equity allocation, which reduces portfolio risk and equity exposure.'

David Tice

Larry Williams

Larry Williams astounded the commodity world in 1987 when he parlayed $10,000 into over $1,100,000 in the 12 month Robbins World Cup Trading Championship. No one has come close to this record since and only the W.D. Gann may have done it before.

Larry received *Futures Magazine's* first Doctrine of Future Award in 1998 and Omega Research's Lifetime Achievement award in 1999.

Books

Trade Stocks and Commodities with the Insiders: Secrets of the COT Report, John Wiley & Sons Inc, 2005
The Right Stock at the Right Time: Prospering in the Coming Good Years, John Wiley & Sons Inc, 2003
Day Trade Futures Online, John Wiley, 2000
Long-Term Secrets to Short-Term Trading, John Wiley, 1999
The Definitive Guide to Futures Trading I and II, Windsor Books, 1989
How I Made $1 Million Trading Commodities, Windsor Books, 1979

Short-term trading and survival

1. It's all about survival.

No platitudes here, speculating is very dangerous business. It is not about winning or losing, it is about surviving the lows and the highs. If you don't survive, you can't win.

The first requirement of survival is that you must have a premise to speculate upon. Rumors, tips, full moons and feelings are not a premise. A premise suggests there is an underlying truth to what you are taking action upon. A short-term trader's premise may be different from a long-term player's but they both need to have proven logic and tools. Most investors and traders spend more time figuring out which laptop to buy than they do before plunking down tens of thousands of dollars on a snap decision, or one based upon totally fallacious reasoning.

There is some rhyme and reason to how, why and when markets move - not enough - but it is there. The problem is that there are more techniques that don't work, than there are techniques that do. I suggest you spend an immense and inordinate amount of time and effort learning these critical elements before entering the foray of financial frolics.

So, you have money management under control, have a valid system, approach or premise to act upon - you still need control of yourself.

2. Ultimately this is an emotional game - always has been, always will be.

Anytime money is involved - your money - blood boils, sweaty hands prevail, and mental processes are shortcircuited by illogical emotions. Just when most traders buy, they should have sold! Or, fear, a major emotion, scares them away from a great trade/investment. Or, their bet is way too big. The money management decision becomes an emotional one, not one of logic.

3. Greed prevails - proving you are more motivated by greed than fear and understanding the difference.

The mere fact you are a speculator means you have less fear than a 'normal' person does. You are more motivated by making money. Other people are more motivated by not losing.

Greed is the trader's Achilles' heel. Greed will keep hopes alive, encourage you to hold on to losing trades and nail down winners too soon. Hope is your worst enemy because it causes you to dream of great profits, to enter an unreal world. Trust me, the world of speculating is very real, people lose all they have, marriages are broken up, families tossed asunder by *either* enormous gains or losses.

My approach to this is to not take any of it very seriously; the winnings may be fleeting, always pursued by the taxman, lawyers and nefarious investment schemes.

How you handle greed is different than I do, so I cannot give an absolute maxim here, but I can tell you this, you must get it in control or you will not survive.

4. Fear inhibits risk taking - just when you should take risk.

Fear causes you to *not* do what you should do. You frighten yourself out of trades that are winners in deference to trades that lose or go nowhere. Succinctly stated, greed causes you to do what we should not do, fear causes us to not do what we should do.

Fear, psychologists say, causes you to freeze up. Speculators act like a deer caught in the headlights of a car. They can see the car - a losing trade, coming at them - at 120 miles per hour - but they fail to take the action they should.

Worse yet, they take a pass on the winning trades. Why, I do not know. But I do know this: the more frightened I am of taking a trade the greater the probabilities are it will be a winning trade. Most investors scare themselves out of greatness.

5. Money management is the creation of wealth.

Sure, you can make money as a trader or investor, have a good time, and get some great stories to tell. But, the extrapolation of profits will not come as much from your trading and investing skills as how you manage your money.

I'm probably best known for winning the Robbins World Cup Trading Championship, turning $10,000 into $1,100,000.00 in 12 months. That was real money, real trades, and real time performance. For years people have asked for my trades to figure out how I did it. I gladly oblige them, they will learn little there - what created the gargantuan gain was not great trading ability nearly as much as the very aggressive form of money management I used. The approach was to buy more contracts when I had more equity in my account, cut back when I had less. That's what made the cool million smackers - not some great trading skill.

Ten years later my 16-year-old daughter won the same trading contest taking $10,000 to $110,000.00 (The second best performance in the 20-year history of the championship). Did she have any trading secret, any magical chart, line, and formula? No. She simply followed a decent system of trading, backed with a superior form of money management.

6. Big money does not make big bets.

You have probably read the stories of what I call the swashbuckler traders, like Jesse Livermore, John 'bet a millions' Gates, Niederhoffer, Frankie Joe and the like. They all ultimately made big bets and lost big time.

Smart money never bets big. Why should it? You can win big on small bets, see #5 above, but eventually if you bet big you will lose - and you will lose big.

It's like Russian Roulette. You may well spin the chamber holding the bullet many times and never lose. But spin it often enough and there can be only one result: death. If you make big bets you are destined to be a big loser. Plunging is a loser's game; it can only set you up for failure. I never bet big (I used to - been there and done that and trust me, it is no way to live). I bet a small per cent of my account, bankroll if you will. That way I have *controlled* loss. There can be no survival without damage control.

7. God may delay but God does not deny.

I never know when during a year I will make my money. It may be on the first trade of the year, or the last (though I hope not). Victory is there to be grasped, but you must be prepared to do battle for a long period of time.

Additionally, while far from a religious person, I think the belief in a much higher power, God, is critical to success as a trader. It helps puts wins and losses into perspective, enables you to persevere through lots of pain and punishment when you know that ultimately all will be right or rewarded in some fashion.

God and the markets is not a fashionable concept - I would never abuse what little connection I have with God to pray for profits. Yet that connection is what keeps people going in times of strife, in fox holes and commodity pits.

8. I believe the trade I'm in right now will be a loser.

This is my most powerful belief and asset as a trader. Most would be wannabes are certain they will make a killing on their next trade. These folks have been to some 'Pump 'em up, plastic coat their lives' motivational meeting where they were told to think positive thoughts. They took lessons in affirming their future would be great. They believe their next trade will be a winner.

Not me! I believe at the bottom of my core it will be a loser. I ask you this question - who will have their stops in and take right action, me or the fellow pumped up on an irrational belief he's figured out the market? Who will plunge, the positive affirmer or me?

If you have not figured that one out - I'll tell you; I will succeed simply because I am under no delusion that I will win. Accordingly, my action will be that of an impeccable warrior. I will protect myself in all fashion, at all times - I will not become run away with hope and unreality.

9. Your fortune will come from your focus - focus on one market or one technique.

A jack of all trades will never become a winning tradee. Why? Because a trader must zero in on the markets, paying attention to the details of trading without allowing his emotions to intervene.

A moment of distraction is costly in this business. Lack of attention may mean you don't take the trade you should, or neglect a trade that leads to great cost.

Focus, to me, means not only focusing on the task at hand but also narrowing your scope of trading to either one or two markets or to the specific approach of a trading technique.

Have you ever tried juggling? It's pretty hard to learn to keep three balls in the area at one time. Most people can learn to watch those 'details' after about 3 hours or practice. Add one ball, one more detail to the mess, and few, very few, people can make it as a juggler. It's precisely that difficult to keep your eyes on just one more 'chunk' of data.

Looks at the great athletes - they focus on one sport. Artists work on one primary business, musicians don't sing country western and Opera and become stars. The better your focus, in whatever you do, the greater your success will become.

10. When in doubt, or all else fails - go back to Rule One.

'It is tempting, when valuing fast growing companies with strong technical advantages over their rivals, to assume that these conditions will continue forever. They will not. As the saying goes, *In the end everything is a toaster.*'

Nick Antill

Paul Wilmott

Paul Wilmott was described by the
Financial Times as 'the cult derivatives
lecturer'. He was an academic before
moving over to independent financial
research, training and consultancy. He is a
leading authority on quantitative finance
and derivatives. He has written a number
of bestselling books and ground-breaking
technical articles.

Books

Frequently Asked Questions in Quantitative Finance, John Wiley and Sons
Ltd, 2006
S. Bossu, P. Henrotte, and P. Wilmott, Finance and Derivatives: Theory and
Practice, John Wiley and Sons Ltd, 2005
Wim Schoutens, Andreas Kyprianou, and Paul Wilmott, Exotic Option
Pricing and Advanced Levy Models, John Wiley and Sons Ltd, 2005
Paul Wilmott and Henrik Rasmussen, New Directions in Mathematical
Finance (Wiley Finance S.)John Wiley and Sons Ltd, 2002
Paul Wilmott Introduces Quantitative Finance, John Wiley, 2001
Paul Wilmott on Quantitative Finance, John Wiley, 2000

Money management

---

1. Get into the habit of looking at stock price history, not just at today's value.

You've probably got a PC, maybe even Microsoft Excel or other spreadsheet
package. Use them to plot prices. There are lots of simple things you can do
on a spreadsheet that will help you make better trading decisions. And
learning about these can be fun as well as profitable. (But please don't use
any of that Technical Analysis nonsense!)

2. Think in terms of risk and return. Return is good.

How has your stock behaved lately? Has it performed well. If so, will this
continue? Can you quantify 'performed well'? It's not hard on a
spreadsheet. Try ranking stocks by their performance over some period, the
previous year, say. At the top of your list should go stocks with the greatest
growth.

3. Think in terms of risk and return. Risk is bad.

A risky stock is one that is highly volatile, one that bounces around a lot. Its price history will be very jagged, showing lots of peaks and troughs. Even if a stock rises a great deal it may be a poor investment if it has taken a bit of a roller-coaster ride to get there.

With volatile stocks timing is everything. The difference between getting out triumphantly at the top and getting out reluctantly at the bottom may be measured in weeks or even days, rather than years. Try ranking stocks by how volatile/jagged their price history looks. The more jagged, the higher up the list they go.

4. The 'better' you think a stock is the more you should invest in it.

This is the key. 'Better' means having a good return i.e. growth, with little risk i.e. volatility. If you followed my suggestions above and rank stocks according to recent growth and 'jaggedness' then you want a stock that's near the top of the growth list but also near the bottom of the risk list.

5. Diversify.

You cannot be right all the time. The best you can hope for is to be right most of the time. And to take advantage of this you must spread your risk. If one stock loses maybe another will win. Spread your money across investments that are unrelated - in technical jargon they are 'uncorrelated'. An industrial sector stock and a leisure stock may behave completely independently. Having said that, during stock market crashes they're both gonna tank together. And I can't help you there.

6. Be aware of transaction costs.

If you trade frequently you're going to quickly lose your money thanks to transaction costs, bid-offer spreads etc. If you are investing in a market with large transaction costs you should think extremely carefully before changing your position from buy to sell or vice versa. This takes us back to our old friend volatility. A stock price fall that makes you want to close your position could be a new trend or just an unfortunate downward blip in a particularly volatile stock.

7. Don't take this business too seriously, it's only money.

This speaks for itself. Also, don't invest money you can't afford to lose. If you find yourself forging your spouse's signature on their car ownership papers or dipping into your children's college fund, you've probably gone too far and should seek immediate help.

8. If a rich friend gives you financial advice, take it.

He got rich somehow, maybe picking stocks. And if his choices plummet then you could always touch him for a bob or two.

9. Put your stock certificates in a safe place.

Many's the time I've bought some stock and then lost the certificate. Have I lost the money? Will the stock be traced back to me on my death? I've no idea. But on the other hand – many's the time I've bought some stock and then lost the certificate. Have I lost the money? Will the stock be traced back to me on my death? And then years later I find the certificate. Whoopee! I'm rich!

10. Get out there and create some wealth.

To end on a serious note, what's the future for mankind if we all spend our time logged on to our online brokers? What would the world be like if everyone was a public sector employee, an accountant, lawyer or fund manager? I'm sure these are all important jobs (except, maybe, for lawyer) but *in proportion*. Somewhere at the bottom (or the top, depends on your point of view) of all this there is a small number of people actually 'making stuff'. Be one of them. Take your play money, and invest in yourself. Turn your hobby into your own speculative investment. Again this is a risk/return thing, but at least you have control.

---

www.paulwilmott.com

'Avoid companies that announce buybacks, but never follow through. Some companies are habitual offenders. They make buyback announcements to signal that they believe their shares are undervalued, but never follow through with their announced plans.'

David Fried

Tom Winnifrith

Tom Winnifrith is the founder and editor of www.t1ps.com, a web site which specialises in undervalued growth stocks. As a financial journalist he worked at *Investors Chronicle*, the *Evening Standard*, and AFX News. He also presented the award-winning Channel 4 series 'Show Me the Money' and is a contributing editor at *Shares* Magazine.

Long-term investing and backing good management

1. If you don't want to own a share for ten years don't buy it for ten minutes.

In other words there is no such thing as a 'trading buy' of what is fundamentally a bad investment - who says that you can call the bottom any better than the next man?

2. Remember that investing is a marathon not a sprint.

90% of day traders lose all their capital. If you buy a share you should be prepared to own it for 5 years.

3. Never back bad management.

If a manager has failed once - or is unproven - why trust him with your money? Only back those with a proven record of creating and adding to shareholder value.

4. Don't confuse investment with gambling.

Putting your money into biotech or unproven technology is not investment, it is punting. There is no need to gamble when you can invest in companies with sound fundamentals.

5. If you do not understand what a company does, or how it constructs its accounts or generates revenue, don't invest in it.

The company is being opaque for a reason.

6. Let the trend be your friend.

If a share price is moving steadily against you, do not view this as an automatic trigger to sell. But find out why it is moving - shares do not move for no reason. And be prepared to admit that circumstances have changed and that you would be making an error to hang on, even if it means booking a loss.

7. Do not confuse a low price with a cheap price.

It is often better to buy a stock on a year high than on a year low. And if you are sitting on a large paper loss but no longer believe in that company, book that loss and move your remaining funds onto a faster moving train.

8. Cash is king.

If a company is loss-making and you cannot see a clear path to it becoming self-funding, steer well clear. If it is profitable but fails to convert a decent portion of those profits into cash, you can do better.

9. If it sounds to good to be true, it *is* too good to be true.

If a share yields 15%, that means that the dividend will be cut. If a £20 million company tells you that it is sitting on a billion dollar product, it is lying. The market is rarely THAT wrong.

10. If you are wondering when to bank a profit, wait until all the brokers say buy and the stock is tipped in the Sunday Newspapers.

It can be promoted no more and it is time to get out.

---

www.t1ps.com

Ed Yardeni

Dr. Ed Yardeni is the Chief Investment Strategist, and a Managing Director of Deutsche Banc Alex. Brown in New York City. He writes Global Portfolio Strategy, which explores issues and trends in the economy and financial markets that are vital to a broad spectrum of decision-makers.

Dr. Yardeni has published articles in *The Wall Street Journal, The New York Times,* and *Barron's.* He writes a monthly column, The View From Wall Street, for *Capital* (Germany), *Nikkei Financial Daily* (Japan), *Milano Finance* (Italy), *FET* (Belgium), *Business Times* (Malaysia),and *Jornal Valor* (Brazil). He has appeared on numerous television and radio shows, including Wall Street Week, CNBC and CNN's Moneyline. He is a member of *Time Magazine's* Board of Economists.

Global economic trends

---

1. The New Globally Competitive Economy: invest in companies that can sustain above average earnings growth in highly competitive markets.

The end of the Cold War ended the greatest trade barrier of all times. Freer global trade and the globalization of markets will continue. So will the pressure to deregulate national economies and restructure businesses. Global markets will become increasingly competitive.

2. The Innovation Revolution: invest in companies with leading edge innovations and relatively little competition, particularly in high-tech and biotech.

In competitive markets, business must cut costs, increase productivity, innovate, and sell globally in an ongoing effort to offset deflationary pricing pressure on profits. Most of the benefits of these efforts will go to consumers' pocketbooks, not corporate earnings. However, companies that innovate regularly can be very profitable. But even innovators face competition and risk that high R&D costs will not be recovered.

3. Tech II - Wireless and Wired: invest in companies that provide the infrastructure hardware and software for wireless, internet, and optical fiber networks.

In the 1990s, during Tech I - the first stage of the High-Tech Revolution - the internet was the 'killer application' that powered the PC boom. During the current decade, wireless technologies are likely to lead Tech II. With wireless communications, companies will be managed on a truly real-time basis. This means that resources will be allocated even more efficiently than now possible, allowing for both dramatic cost reductions and productivity gains.

4. Productivity for the Masses: invest in low-tech companies that are using technology to cut costs, to increase productivity, and to innovate.

The secular rebound in the growth of productivity during the second half of the 1990s was concentrated in the technology sector, but it should continue and become more democratic during the current decade. Now many low-tech businesses are likely to use technology tools - including wireless, internet, internet, and ecommerce systems - more effectively.

5. The Outsourcing Imperative: invest in companies that build B2B systems, and also in outsource vendors.

Outsourcing is the modern-day equivalent of the division of labor, which is one of the main sources of productivity gains. B2B is likely to boost the outsourcing trend as companies focus on their most profitable core businesses.

6. The China Challenge: invest in capital goods companies, especially technology and telecom equipment manufacturers.

The 'China Challenge' should stimulate greater economic integration and prosperity within and among the three major regional economic blocs:

1. North Asia - including China, HK, Taiwan, Japan, and Korea
2. Euroland - including many new members from Eastern Europe
3. North America.

Direct investments into China are likely to grow dramatically. A more open China market should also benefit global consumer product and services companies.

7. Sweet & Sour Deflation: invest in Treasury bonds and interest-rate sensitive stocks, with low exposure to credit risk if possible.

Inflation will probably remain near zero over the rest of the decade. The risk is deflation, not reflation. Peace, free trade, competition, deregulation, technology, and China are all powerful sources of deflation. Productivity-led deflation can be profitable. Unprofitable deflation can cause a prolonged recession. In either case, Treasury bond yields could fall as low as 4%.

8. Demography is Destiny: invest in outsource manufacturing in emerging markets and also in consumer electronics suppliers.

Populations will age significantly in Japan, Germany, and the United States over the next two decades. Expect more pressure on politicians in aging nations to cut tax rates, to boost savings incentives, and to encourage equity investments. Invest in asset management companies and, of course, health care providers. Populations remain relatively young in most of Asia, Latin America, and the Middle East.

9. Jurassic Park: invest in companies that are likely to be acquired, and also in the investment banks that will collect the M&A fees.

Competitive pressures will force many companies to acquire or merge with competitors globally. Eventually, this may revive inflation. But, over the next several years, that's not likely. Consolidation means more rounds of restructuring, and job insecurity. Capital markets will continue to expand and become more integrated globally.

10. The Meaning of Life: Shopping!

In competitive markets, the only sure winners are consumers. If productivity continues to grow rapidly, then so will real income. The trend in purchasing power will set the pace for consumer spending. The key to global prosperity is Asia, especially China and Japan. If both nations transfer power to consumers with more open markets and tax cuts, then the outlook for global growth and equity investors will be a sweet one. If not, a sour deflationary future would be a real threat. In the sweet scenario, stock prices could double, even triple by 2010. In the sour version, a long-term bear market would result.

www.yardeni.com

'High money supply growth is associated with high bond yields. The crucial investment messages are: if money supply growth is high and rising, sell bonds, and conversely, if money supply growth is low and falling, buy bonds.'

Tim Congdon

Andy Yates

Andy Yates is Director of Operations at Digital Look, the leading UK and international company research and news alerts service. He was formerly a senior financial journalist with the *Investors Chronicle*, *The Independent* and the BBC.

Digital Look's market-leading e-mail service offers the latest customised information about share portfolios. Its service currently covers six countries including the major European and US markets, and is expanding to create a global share research service.

Getting the most out of bulletin boards

Introduction

Online bulletin boards allow investors to swap ideas, information and share tips. They have expanded hugely in recent years to become a major force in the internet investment world. Tens of thousands of bulletin board messages are posted every day about companies. As well as investors, they are beginning to attract close scrutiny from market regulators.

Although it's easy to dismiss the chat in online forums as uninformed gossip, a study commissioned by Bloomberg found that while on average earnings forecasts on amateur online forums were out by 21 percent from the actual figures, those from Wall Street professionals were out on average by 44 percent.

1. Lurk and learn.

Bulletin boards can be a daunting prospect for the uninitiated. Before jumping in at the deep end, get familiar with the contributors and the style of the bulletin board. Sit back and watch before you start posting on the boards, or 'lurk' as the online lingo goes. You will soon be able to distinguish between the popular posters and those unscrupulous posters determined to make a quick buck out of you.

Use bulletin board search engines to build up an historical track record of regular contributors so that you know who has proved to be reliable in the past.

2. No exaggeration.

You need to see bulletin boards for what they are - a useful and interactive way to gauge the latest sentiment about your portfolio or prospective investments. They are a hotbed of useful ideas and opinions, but also a great way for you to confirm the suspicions or opinions you have about the next potential hot shot in your portfolio.

So long as you take spurious comments with a healthy pinch of salt you can make money from the boards. As a general rule most comments are useful in some form or another but exuberant investors always tend to exaggerate the good and bad points about a company and often put two and two together to make five.

3. Watch out for 'wise men' bearing gifts.

Beware of contributors who claim to be top executives with inside information. At the height of the internet boom a poster claimed to be the chief executive of UK internet tiddler Pacific Media and unveiled plans for a major deal. The comments were even picked up by a national newspaper before the hoax become apparent. Companies announce things to the Stock Exchange - not to stock pickers on bulletin boards.

4. Don't believe in fairy tales.

Extracts of news reports or official Stock Exchange announcements are always posted on the boards. But it only takes a second to change a few vital facts and create a very different story.

A falsified article on US quoted group Emulex created havoc for the share price and led to the prosecution of a share-manipulating hoaxer. If in doubt, check it out. If a story appears just too good to be true, check the original source or the company's official web site.

5. Try not to get hooked.

For the regular investor, bulletin boards can be dangerously addictive and those that are hooked cannot miss their fix of daily gossip and innuendo. Apart from a pasty, bleary-eyed look, a bulletin board addict will also display the potential wealth-worrying symptoms of believing everything they read and a sheep-like ability to follow the herd. If you find that you are already displaying these symptoms - just say no and take a bulletin board break.

6. Bulletin boards can seriously damage your wealth.

Bulletin boards are full of the next 'hot' buy tip - the company whose shares are bound to rocket into the stratosphere. Ask yourself why contributors are so keen to give away their top secrets to the world. 'Pumping and dumping' is all too common. Make sure you are not the one dumped upon.

7. Go for quality not quantity.

Many of the top boards have rooted out the online *hoi palloi* by charging a subscription or policing their boards to ban online hooligans. While this can never be an exact science, it does give the board a mark of quality. You only have to compare the quality of posts on Yahoo! - which attracts the good, the bad and the very ugly - to, say, Motley Fool which doesn't suffer bulletin board fools gladly.

8. Open your eyes to the risks.

Digital Look's research has shown that the companies investors just cannot stop talking about tend to be more volatile in term of share price performance. On the one hand, bulletin board contributors tend to rabbit on about the more speculative and technology-focused stocks on the market - in other words, companies whose shares could double or halve in value, which makes them a great talking point. On the other hand bulletin board sentiment can itself have a big effect on these small to medium size firms, wreaking havoc on the market valuations. Whatever the reason - look before you leap into stocks that may not be the best investment for widows or orphans.

9. Keep yourself posted.

Whether you think bulletin boards are a force of good or the devil's spawn they do have an impact in today's helter-skelter online investment world. A seemingly inexplicable price movement can be explained by a bulletin board. Corporates, too, need to keep a close eye on them. Mega-mergers such as that between Reckitt-Benkiser and Glaxo Smithkline were revealed on the bulletin boards, suggesting that those in the know could not resist letting others know. And damaging and sensitive documents have a habit of popping up where you least expect them - a problem suffered by online directories group Scoot which was forced to hire private detectives to try and hunt down the culprits.

10. Don't get carried away with the hype and hope.

Buy tips far outweigh sell tips on bulletin boards - a trait that has remained even throughout the prolonged market slump we have had to endure recently. That tells its own story - over optimism means you are unlikely to end up with the optimum portfolio.

www.digitallook.com

'Don't buy 'market leaders'. Find a #7 company in an industry headed for the # 3 spot because its recognition increases and its P/E expands. There's more money to be made in finding tomorrow's winners than in chasing yesterday's.'

Foster Friess

Leonard Yates

Len Yates is the founder and President of OptionVue Systems, which specializes in options modeling software.

He has been an active options trader for many years and has made important contributions in the field of options pricing models - the most notable being the 'Yates adjustment' to the popular Black/Scholes model as applied to American style puts.

Books

High Performance Options Trading: Option Volatility and Pricing Strategies, John Wiley & Sons Inc, 2003

Options myths and mistakes

1. Myth 1: 'Options are too risky.'

Although options can be used to speculate on short term moves, they can also be used to lower the risk of a stock portfolio, and in place of stocks to invest in long term (up to 3 years) moves. There are many different ways of using options, some of them risky, some of them not.

2. Myth 2: 'Options are too complex.'

Options are kind of like the game of chess. You can learn the rules and be ready to play in just 20 minutes! Of course, then there's a few strategies you need to become familiar with. However, while chess variations are practically infinite, in options there are just a handful of different strategies, and it's not necessary to know them all before you get started.

3. Myth 3: 'Options are too expensive.'

On the contrary, options can be bought for as little as a few hundred dollars each.

4. Mistake 1: Thinking of an option like a stock.

An option can go to zero much faster than a stock! You have to act quickly if it starts to go the wrong way.

5. Mistake 2: Buying out-of-the-money options because they're cheaper.

Yes, they're cheaper, but they're less likely to reward you with a gain because you're asking the underlying to jump through a smaller hoop. Buy a smaller quantity of in-the-money options and you'll be more satisfied with the behavior of your option as the stock jiggles and chops its way in your direction.

6. Mistake 3: Buying options without regard for the current volatility level.

Recent volatility makes options more expensive. If you buy expensive options, you may be hurt when the market settles back down.

7. Mistake 4: Thinking that covered writing both lowers your risk and increases expected return.

Covered writing (selling calls against shares of stock) is often presented using numbers like 'return if stock unchanged' and 'return if stock is called away' - both very favorable outcomes. When the whole picture is considered (including the stock going way down or way up), covered writing lowers risk and lowers expected returns.

8. Mistake 5: Believing that there is a certain option strategy (e.g. covered writing, vertical spreads, horizontal spreads, etc.) that has positive expected returns in the long run.

There is no magic options strategy that makes money. Traders must pick a strategy to apply in each situation that sets up the desired risk/reward profile.

9. Mistake 6: Believing that selling options (naked or covered) has positive expected returns in the long run. (Ext. of Mistake 5)

Don't get too concerned with the time decay nature of options. An option's time decay is offset by potential movement in the underlying. The result: a fairly valued option conveys no edge to a seller or a buyer.

10. Mistake 7: Lack of preparation and education.

Read a book or two, attend a seminar, select good trading software, and do some 'paper' trading before diving into the real thing. When ready, select an options-friendly brokerage, and start trading with small, easily manageable positions.

---

www.optionvue.com

William T. Ziemba

Professor Ziemba is Alumni Professor of Financial Modeling and Stochastic Optimization at the University of British Columbia. He has written and co-written many books on financial theory and practice, of which the four below are the most recent.

Books

W.T. Ziemba and Raymond G. Vickson, Stochastic Optimization Models in Finance, World Scientific Publishing, 2006
Security Market Imperfections in World Wide Equity Markets, CUP, 2000
Worldwide Asset and Liability Modeling, CUP, 1998
Stochastic Programming: State of the Art, Baltzer Science, 1998
Finance, North Holland Handbook Series, 1995
The Efficiency of Racetrack Betting Markets, Academic Press, 1994

Lessons from the theory of gambling

1. Only bet when you have an edge.
You can never win betting situations with no advantage. Doubling up, or martingale systems, while highly touted, are flawed and will not work. You will have many small wins then a large loss that will wipe out all your gains and more.

2. Those who win on every trade are losers or liars.
No strategy will provide profits in all scenarios except true arbitrages, which are hard to find. The aim is to generate consistent profits over time and that will involve taking some losses. Successful traders take small losses on losing trades and make large profits on successful trades.

3. Know what you expect to gain from a trade before you enter.
Predetermine your exit point before you get into a trade - and revise this as new information unfolds. Discipline and organization is the key to successful implementation of successful trading strategies.

4. Do your research.
Fully research your strategy both in theory and with data, and update this constantly. Financial markets are partially predictable. Models that attempt to predict future asset prices need updated data constantly and model refinements periodically.

5. Truly diversify.

Correlation matrices are scenario dependent. Simulations around historical situations do not measure the true correlations. For example, bonds and stocks are generally positively correlated, but in crash situations they are negatively correlated.

6. Do not over bet.

Determine in advance the bad scenarios that could occur and how much you will lose in each case. Remember that the true size of the current bet, which is constantly changing, depends on the hedge ratio, namely, the change in portfolio value that occurs because of a change in the underlying index. What was a small futures derivatives position and fully risk controlled can turn quickly into a large position that amounts to overbetting. Hence the risk position of the portfolio is constantly changing and must be controlled carefully.

7. Evaluate the impact of all scenarios.

Evaluate all scenarios that could possibly occur, even those that have not occurred yet. Use similar situations to determine reasonable scenarios. Know in advance what to do if a particular scenario does occur.

8. Have deep pockets.

Have enough capital to withstand crises and use that capital to avoid these crises and profit from such crises. During crises, cash is in short supply and those who have it both avoid disasters themselves and profit from being able to buy/sell securities at advantageous prices. Calculate how much capital is needed to avoid disasters in extreme scenarios given your current level of investment bets. Since the latter is changing, the size of the bets must also be constantly monitored and changed.

9. Accept small losses.

Try to avoid large losses. Exit markets with small losses and preserve your capital.

10. Follow a risk control system.

Focus on not losing; it's more important. Focusing on winning can lead to massive losses as many traders and hedge fund managers have found out.

---

www.interchange.ubc.ca/ziemba/

Index